Outside
MAGAZINE'S

Urban Adventure

Chicago

Outside
MAGAZINE'S

Urban Adventure

Chicago

Lynn Schnaiberg

Outside BOOKS W. W. Norton & Company New York • London

Copyright © 2003 by Mariah Media Inc.

All rights reserved
Printed in the United States of America
First Edition

For information about permission to reproduce selections from this book, write to Permissions, W. W. Norton & Company, Inc., 500 Fifth Avenue, New York, NY 10110.

Manufacturing by The Haddon Craftsmen, Inc.
Book design by Chris Welch
Production manager: Diane O'Connor

LIBRARY OF CONGRESS CATALOGING-IN-PUBLICATION DATA

Schnaiberg, Lynn.
Outside magazine's urban adventure, Chicago / Lynn Schnaiberg.—1st ed.
p. cm.
Includes bibliographical references and index.
ISBN 0-393-32348-X
1. Outdoor recreation—Illinois—Chicago—Guidebooks. 2. Chicago (Ill.)—
Guidebooks. I. Outside (Chicago, Ill.) II. Title
GV191.42.I3S35   2003
796'.09773'11—dc21

2003003868

W. W. Norton & Company, Inc.
500 Fifth Avenue, New York, N.Y. 10110
www.wwnorton.com

W. W. Norton & Company Ltd.
Castle House, 75/76 Wells Street, London W1T 3QT

2 3 4 5 6 7 8 9 0

Contents

Acknowledgments

MANY INDIVIDUALS GENEROUSLY shared their time, wisdom, and passion to make this book possible. I apologize in advance if I've inadvertently missed this chance to thank any of them here. But here goes. Thanks to Vic Hurtowy and Ralph Frese of Chicagoland Canoe Base; incurable paddler Gary Mechanic; Chris Parson of Friends of the Chicago River; Ryan Chew of Chicago River Canoe & Kayak; Charlie Portis of Wateriders; the folks at Northwest Passage; Randy Warren and Randy Neufeld at the Chicagoland Bicycle Federation; gonzo cyclist Eric Anderson; Crowley's Yacht Yard; sailor Tom Keegan; John Fournier at Northwestern University Sailing Center; die-hard windsurfers and surfers Marc Stadler and Ed Coyne; surf leader Lester Priday; fat-tire explorer, surfer, and author Peter Strazzabosco; Jackie Butzen of Windward Sports; scuba master and author Cris Kohl; Captain Bob Schak; Erik Sprenne and Sandi Weindling of the Chicago White-water Association; whitewater encyclopedia Dag Grada; Jon Uhlenhop of Chicago Fly Fishing Outfitters; The Fishing Guy, Bob Long, Jr.; Nikki Seger of Orvis; Ed Bartunek of Chicago Area Mountain Bikers; expert birders and authors Sheryl DeVore and Lynne Carpenter; Doug Anderson; climber Tony Berlier of The Shop; Eric Ulner of the Access Fund and Vertical Heartland; Paul Kuenn of Dairyland Expeditions; Chris and Pam Schmick of Upper Limits; Chicago Urban Exploration; Gary Gibula of Sub-Urban Chicago Grotto; Bob Richards of Northern Illinois Nordic; runner and author Brenda Barrera; Brad Kushner of Raven Sky Sports; pilot Angelo Mantas; Peter Birren of the Reel Hang Glider Pilot Association; John O'Dell of the Illinois Hiking Society; the Sierra Club; and Debra Shore of Chicago Wilderness.

Thanks also to the Cook County Forest Preserve District and the Chicago Park District for fielding umpteen questions. Special thanks to Kristin Weber, map goddess, and to my editor, John Barstow, for his guidance and skill. And finally, to Geoff Bolan, my husband, proofreader-researcher, and enthusiastic companion on countless miles of Chicago-area exploration—I do not exaggerate in saying that this book would not have been possible without his unflagging support.

To Geoff Bolan, my husband, with whom I'm lucky enough to share the ultimate adventure: Life

Introduction

I **RECALL A CONVERSATION** with Tim Herlihey, the owner of Urban Bikes in Uptown, about the idea of urban wilderness. Herlihey moved back to Chicago from Boulder several years back. He misses the mountains sometimes, but he loves the urban rivers here, the Chicago, the Calumet. He adheres to a daily ritual in summer and fall, pedaling down to the lake and swimming after work with the darting gulls and fleet-footed sandpipers along the beach. "To me, Lake Michigan is like the Front Range, it's my mountain here. In some ways I think you can gain as much, if not more, here in the city because you have a different relationship with the outdoors. There's a detachment that sometimes goes on with wilderness experiences. We need a tie-in to the outdoors on a daily basis. It frustrates me that people think you can only have a wilderness experience if you hop a plane and fly out to the mountains. There's so much right here. And there's something about it that just feels, well, more real."

This is a book about playing. It is a guide to help you discover the surprisingly rich options for outdoor adventure in the city and beyond. And it offers up both a means of connecting with and detaching from the city.

Yes, Chicago is a sprawling thicket of concrete, brick, steel, and glass, its landscape utterly transformed from the city's humble origins as a swampy expanse lined with wild onions at the confluence of the Chicago River and Lake Michigan. But Chicago is also the gateway to a freshwater ocean, a grid dotted with wetlands and sloughs, rivers, trees, and snatches of prairie. After all, the city's founding motto from 1837 is *Urbs in Horto*, "City in a Garden." My hope is that this book will help you peel back the layers of urban topsoil so you can exploit the pockets of wildness that remain. Or find ways to turn that man-made topsoil into a playground.

But attitude is a big part of adventure. Throughout the process of researching this book, I ran across people who had already figured out ways of looking at the city through a different lens, who were willing to re-examine areas other city dwellers might have written off as devoid of possibility. Sometimes it just takes a simple shift in perspective to convert even seemingly familiar urban landscapes into uncharted territory for exploration. And once you start, that way of thinking becomes addictive.

Take Walter Marcisz's bird walks to spot threatened and endangered species breeding in remnant wetlands tucked amid the slag heaps and steel plants of the Lake Calumet area on the city's far southeast side. Or Eric Anderson and a corps of hard-core mountain bikers who explore the city fringes on nocturnal Urban Assault rides, wringing challenging terrain from the lakefront boulders, hammering through brownfields and scrap-metal yards. Or the guy I watched bouldering one fine spring day on the stone face of the bridge at Irving Park and Lake Shore at rush hour, dipping his fingertips into a purple chalk bag dangling from his shorts while cars whizzed past, oblivious to this devotee in their midst.

Ignoring the naysayers who still see the Chicago River as a mere glorified sewer, people like Charlie Portis are busy kayaking around Goose Island and gliding through downtown along the Main Stem, snagging stellar views of Chicago's architectural masterpieces in a Chicago Experience that ranks right up there with late-night cheddar fries at Wiener Circle. A group of intrepid urban explorers likes to descend 40 feet below City Hall and the rest of the Loop to wander a warren of old railway tunnels in a game of urban spelunking.

OK, Chicago may be better known for deep-dish pizza, one of the last great city ballparks, and Second City improv than stellar outdoor activities, but stop for a minute and think about it. For starters, we have a vast, watery wilderness right in our front yard. You can surf freshwater waves on a longboard minutes from downtown, hug the city shoreline from the cockpit of a sea kayak, fly-fish smallmouth bass from a pier, sail 10 miles offshore, scuba dive for pristinely preserved wrecks. The Cook County Forest Preserves alone have nearly 68,000 acres of open space with a 200-plus-mile trail network for horseback riding, hiking, running, and cross country skiing.

You can adventure before or after work, at lunch. Sure, there are limitations. Chicago isn't a pristine wilderness. It isn't always easy to adventure here. Only recently did the city make it possible to legally launch a kayak from any of its beaches. Access along the Chicago River is still fairly limited. Mountain bikers continue to fight to hold onto the metro-area miles they have worked so hard to get. To partake in some activities, like white water and caving, you'll have to travel farther outside the city limits than for others. But happily, this guide includes plenty of places to adventure for a day, a weekend, or more. And if you want to pick up a new outdoor addiction, there are listings of clubs, specialty shops, and instructional and guiding services to help you hook up.

A few final thoughts. Chicago is often referred to as a City of Neighborhoods. And that's a justifiable point of pride. But on the flip side, it can lead to boundaries both real and imagined. North Side, South Side. Cubs, White Sox. In many ways, Chicago remains a city divided. I hope this book helps break some of those barriers and gets you into territory you're not used to exploring. You have a much bigger playground if you take advantage of the entire city, not just one quadrant or another. Just keep an open mind and use common sense.

While we're on the topic of common sense, a word about basic water safety. Lake Michigan, like all the Great Lakes, is big water that demands respect and preparation. Lake conditions are notoriously schizophrenic: a sudden squall can quickly turn vinyl-smooth water into nasty big-wind-and-wave territory and get less-experienced paddlers and other water-bound explorers into serious trouble. Look no farther than the "Scuba Diving" chapter for evidence of the lake's temper tantrums—the lake floor is littered with boats doomed by storms. Though they may seem obvious to seasoned lake lovers, following are some fundamentals worth restating.

Check the marine forecast before venturing out. Watch for rip currents, especially around seawalls and anti-erosion structures. Dress for the water, not the air, temperature. The lake usually ranges from the 30s in winter to the 70s in summer. Hypothermia is not a hypothetical, even in early summer when the air temps can hit the 80s but the water close to shore can still be a chilly 50°. Be visible—use white lights at night. Play defensively; summer boat traffic can get intense along the city shoreline. The Coast Guard strongly recommends that paddlers wear a PFD and carry a marine radio, cell phone, flares, whistle, knife, first-aid kit, drinking water, spare paddle, paddle float, bilge pump, extra line, and sea anchor. A compass is never a bad idea. Nor is letting someone on land know details of where you're headed and when, no matter what water sport you're doing. For more safety info, check out www.uscqboating.org and www.boatsmart .net.

A book like this, covering such a wide range of activities, can only be highly selective and subjective. It includes some classic destinations and trails as well as less well known, unsung gems for Urban, Ex-Urban, and Definitively Un-Urban Adventure, culled from the minds of many, many dedicated outdoor zealots. It doesn't pretend to be a comprehensive or definitive guide. Ultimately, the idea is to get you thinking about the city in a different way, to get you excited about launching your own exploration and making your own secret discoveries. So get off the grid. And go play.

How to Use This Book

First off, use this guide with a spirit of adventure. Mileage is approximate. Route descriptions are brief, and odds are they won't include every landmark and every turn. The idea is to steer you toward some of the area's best places and to try to keep you from getting lost. Bringing your own good judgment, sense of direction, and perhaps most important, sense of humor to the enterprise is heartily encouraged. This is, after all, a book about having fun.

For the most part, route descriptions here, paired with the recommended map or maps, should be enough to get you there and back. Exceptions include the more technical pursuits, such as rock climbing or sailing, where you really need a detailed comprehensive guide or charts. Each chapter includes great guides that can give you far more route options, advice, detail, and background on history and safety than is possible in this book. By all means, if you get jazzed up about a particular activity, seek out those books. All are written by people passionate about their pursuit; this book would not have been possible without their advice and wisdom.

You'll want to pick up a few invaluable resources to help you navigate the urban and ex-urban environs. I like Rand McNally's *Chicago 6-County StreetFinder*, covering Cook, DuPage, Kane, Lake, McHenry, and Will Counties. DeLorme's *Illinois Atlas & Gazetteer* is a good overview, covering the state in 1:150,000 topo maps with all types of roads and many trails. But this book crosses plenty of state lines, given Chicago's geographic position and the fact that city dwellers recreate in a decidedly multistate fashion. So you might well find yourself wanting the Wisconsin, Michigan, and Indiana versions, too.

Look for *Exploration Extra* sidebars on a few sports like in-line skating, orienteering, and downhill skiing and snowboarding that didn't merit their own chapters; they include good info on relevant spots and the best ways to hook up with like-minded folks who share those passions. Also see the occasional sidebar *Pitching Tent* for especially sweet or surprisingly close-to-the-city camping options.

Now, some explanation on how the chapters are organized. Most spots are divided into *City Limits*, *Backyard*, *Short Hops*, and *Meccas*. *City Limits* means just that, within the limits of the city proper. *Backyard* means within 40 miles of downtown. *Short Hops* are, loosely, spots within a 3-hour drive of the city. *Meccas* are superlative spots, usually farther afield than a *Short Hop*, that take longer to get to but are well worth the drive. Given their distance from the city, most *Meccas* are intended for exploration over a weekend, a long weekend, or more. *Where to Connect* information at the end of each chapter is just that—a primer for hooking up with instruction, clubs, shops, outfitters, events, and guidebooks. Who knows, you might even meet a few new friends, a climbing partner, or someone else who digs those Sunday morning classics at The Music Box Theatre.

If you're new to Chicago, a quick explanation of the city layout will help you better navigate the terrain and this book. The vast majority of Chicago streets fall into a tidy, no-nonsense grid system that starts from State and Madison Sts. downtown. Street indexes identify streets by their distance north or south of Madison or east or west of State. Roughly 8 city blocks equal 1 mile. So Chicago Ave., 1 mile (or 8 blocks) north of Madison St., is 800 North. Ashland Ave., 16 blocks west of State St., is 1600 West. And remember, in the city the lake is always east.

Each destination or route has some stats. Here's a decoding of those you'll encounter most often:

Location: How far the destination is from downtown, measured from the intersection of Madison and State Sts.

Length: The approximate length of a trail, route, or paddle. Assume it's one way unless it's designated as a loop or out-and-back trip. In chapters like "Mountain Biking," for areas with a relatively limited number of miles where you'll likely cover multiple (or maybe all) trails, total available trail mileage is listed. Total trail miles are also listed in chapters like "Winter Sports," to give maximum options in places where there isn't just one standout trail.

Difficulty: Easy, moderate, or difficult. Sometimes beginner, intermediate, or advanced. These are very general ratings, which tend to be highly subjective anyway. Besides, part of the adventure in exploring new territory is not knowing exactly what to expect ahead of time.

Maps and books: Usually just the map that was easiest to use and most helpful in charting a route. And a phone number for how to get it. Particularly helpful books, too.

Dogs: Listed as yes (allowed) or no (not allowed). Virtually all places require that a dog be on leash; check for more specific regulations at trailheads or visitors centers.

Heads up: Things to look out for or hazards worth underscoring. And sometimes fuel, as in places to chow.

Description: A general description of the place, the terrain, and the route to give you a feel for what's in store.

Route: On-trail or on-water route directions. When distances are given, for turnoffs or trail junctions and such, they are usually rounded off to the nearest mile, so stay alert. Be aware that Cook County Forest Preserve trail maps are woefully lame and outdated (you'll laugh when you see the vintage photos). Most of the county's trails are unmarked. Be patient, and if you wind up on an inadvertent side trip just consider it part of the adventure.

Directions: Driving directions to the destination, river put-in, or trailhead. Directions are given from downtown Chicago, at Madison and State Sts. But they presume you can make your way to major highways, like Lake Shore Dr. or I-94. One note about I-94 that can be confusing for the newly initiated: it is signed as east or west, but more often than not from the city you're actually driving north (west) or south (east). Public transit options from downtown are

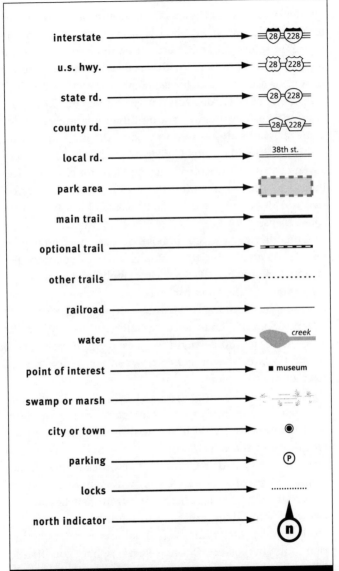

interstate	=28= =228=
u.s. hwy.	=28= =228=
state rd.	=28= =228=
county rd.	=28= =228=
local rd.	38th st.
park area	
main trail	
optional trail	
other trails	
railroad	
water	creek
point of interest	■ museum
swamp or marsh	
city or town	◉
parking	℗
locks	
north indicator	n

Legend

listed where practical. Although you'll find car directions for plenty of *City Limits* spots, you're almost always better off on public transit or a bike. For city and suburban bus and train schedules and fare information you can call the RTA (836-7000, no area code needed for the six-county region, or see www.rtachicago.com). See *Have Bike, Will Travel* on page 217 for a full transportation contact lineup. And on the bike theme, biking directions are given for some spots. It's always best to refer to the most up-to-date "Chicago Bike Map" and Chicagoland Bicycle Federation's seven-county "Chicagoland Bicycle Map" for changes, new bike lanes, etc. You'll want those to navigate the city on two wheels anyway. See "Biking," page 211, for how to get those maps.

One other key concept to note. You can maximize your options by combining trails among different chapters. For example, "Hiking & Backpacking" includes 11 spots. But many trails in the book can make a good hike. Check out the trails in "Running," "Mountain Biking," "Biking," and "Winter Sports." And the same holds true for lots of the other activities. So don't think you have to limit yourself to the trails in any one chapter when you're looking for new terrain to explore.

Lastly, a word from a native and unabashed Chicago fan. Chicago is a big, beefy city. I can't resist this quote from British author Rudyard Kipling, writing a report of his travels abroad in the late 1880s: "I have struck a city—a real city. And they call it Chicago. The other places do not count." Chicago is not a Denver, with umpteen miles of backcountry wilderness beckoning from just beyond the freeway. Sometimes you have to work hard here to find outdoor adventure, inklings of wilderness. But in my mind, that only makes it all the sweeter when you finally, inevitably do. Be safe. Have fun. Play hard.

outsidepix.com

Sea Kayaking & Canoeing

L **UCKY FOR YOU,** the Chicago area is blessed
with water, from the smallest capillary creeks
to the powerful inland sea of Lake Michigan.
The lake is the city's front yard, the Chicago River
a meandering backyard of sorts.

Where Chicago gets low marks for varied topography on land, Lake Michigan serves up an ever-
changing terrain. And the Chicago River boasts
links to the city's very origins. Paddling past—and
under—some of Chicago's 40-odd movable bridges
(more than any city in the world) is just plain cool.
Dodging beefy barges and contending with lake-
borne winds whipping mightily through the city is
part of the game.

Chicago has a healthy community of paddlers

and clubs to tap into, but kayaking here is young enough that the trailblazing luster hasn't worn off. A few years ago, Cory Nagel of Kayak Chicago knew everybody with a kayak strapped to the car. "I can't say that now," Nagel says. "But it's still very much a virgin market here."

The hardiest souls paddle year-round. But paddling outside the warmer months requires lots of preparation (not the least of which, a wet or dry suit) and skill. Still, winter paddling can be magical. Die-hard paddler Gary Mechanic describes cracking through thin ice like spun sugar over the lake, watching the waves roll underneath the glassy surface and exploring cavelike creations of ice along the shore visible only from the water. With shifting lake winds, the water can be iced up one day and clear the next.

Whenever or wherever you decide to dip paddle, a few housekeeping issues first. A river in flood or stormy weather, especially in fall and spring, can quickly turn a fairly easy trip into an advanced one. Know your skills and limitations before you set out. See *Where to Connect*, page 72, for details on getting instruction and hooking up with clubs—the best way to nab paddling partners and mentors.

There are waaaaay more waterways and routes to explore than can be listed here. Talk to Ralph Frese and Vic Hurtowy at Chicagoland Canoe Base. Many thanks to Mike Svob and his invaluable paddling guides for much of the good info below; you'll definitely want them for more detail and inspiration. Consider this a starting point to whet your appetite (see "White Water" and "Sailing" for other ideas). While Lake Michigan's waters are best suited to kayak exploration, the flatwater routes listed here for the most part can be done by sea kayak or canoe. If there's an exception to that—like a route with multiple portages where a canoe makes life infinitely easier—it's noted.

Put-in and takeout points are simply suggested ways to

get on the water. Call local outfitters before setting out—they're usually the ones with the best skinny on water levels and launches.

When there's an outfitter to rent you a boat on-site at a given waterway, it's listed. Otherwise, there are a few city outfitters that rent canoes and kayaks to strap on your car (see *Where to Connect*, page 74). If you're not paddling back to where you started, you can often shuttle by bike (or blade) rather than organize two cars. Just lock up a bike near your takeout; at the end of the trip, one person bikes back to the car and the others stay with the boat.

Now back to the reason why you're venturing forth in the first place: "When you get on the water, you feel like you're off the grid," Mechanic says.

So grab a paddle. And prepare to liberate yourself from the grind of urban life.

City Limits

River Renaissance

THE HISTORY OF the 156-mile-long Chicago River is essentially the history of Chicago. In turbo–*Readers' Digest* form, the history of the river that starts in Lake County and winds its way south through the city goes something like this: French explorers Marquette and Joliet in 1673 travel the Chicago portage, a low divide between the Chicago and Des Plaines Rivers that linked the Great Lakes with the Mississippi. The Illinois & Michigan Canal gets dug in 1848. Chicago booms. Shipping and industry boom. The river becomes an industrial alley with industrial-strength woes (cholera, anyone?).

Over the years, the manhandled river sees its waters polluted, dredged, dyed (eye-popping green for St. Patrick's Day), straightened, and reversed.

To stem widespread contamination, city leaders in 1900 reverse the river's flow in the main and south branches away from Lake Michigan (aka drinking-water supply) and toward the newly built Sanitary and Ship Canal. In the 1970s, the Metropolitan Water Reclamation District begins work on the Deep Tunnel—essentially a parallel river bored out of dolomite bedrock 300 feet below the Chicago River—designed to take in storm water and sewage overflow and carry it to the Stickney water treatment plant southwest of the city. The project is slated for completion somewhere around 2014.

The upshot? Better water quality.

"For many years, the river smelled awful on any number of days in the summer. It was fenced off. It was considered dangerous. It wasn't thought of as an amenity at all," says Chris Parson of Friends of the Chicago River. "That's all changing."

For the record, the Chicago River is still considered an "impaired" waterway, which is a nice way of saying you can paddle here but you don't want to dump and swim. (A former sewer department official was quoted in the newspaper in recent years saying of the Chicago: "It's a conveyance for the wastewater of the city of Chicago. It always has been. It always will be.")

But the river has come a long way. And it's undergoing something of a renaissance.

Today the river boasts 60-plus fish species (not including the "Chicago whitefish," code for used condoms that float to the surface after a heavy downpour). Wildlife abounds, from black-crowned night-herons and kingfishers to snapping turtles and muskrats. In the mid-90s, Parson says, the Merchandise Mart hired trappers to relocate a pair of cheeky beavers wreaking havoc at Wolf Point.

Luxury riverside condos and townhouses are popping up like bluebells in spring. Powerboats and others ply the down-

town waters in summer. And in 2000, the river got its first official canoe launch at Clark Park on the city's North Side, with
more in the works as part of the city's long-term Chicago River
plan. For its part, Friends of the Chicago River is working to create a continuous, multiuse riverside trail and has worked with
city neighborhoods to improve river habitat and expand access
to and use of the river.

The river's industrial pedigree is still very much intact; it
remains a working waterway with all the inherent traffic hazards paddlers are likely to encounter. In the minds of plenty of
Chicagoans, the Chicago River is a recreational underdog. But
in my mind, that's what makes it all the more compelling to
paddle. Hail to the underdog.

CHICAGO RIVER, DOWNTOWN URBAN CANYONS

Location: City central

Length: 8 miles out and back

Difficulty: Intermediate to advanced. For strong paddlers
with good self-rescue skills. Kayaks best. Check Lake
Michigan conditions; you paddle the lake for put-in and
takeout.

Put-in/takeout: 12th St. Beach

Outfitters: Wateriders (312-953-9287, www.wateriders
.com) runs architectural and other guided downtown kayak
trips. Chicago River Canoe & Kayak in Clark Park is the
closest rental, but it's a long round-trip (see *Where to Connect*, page 74).

Map and books: Chicago Architecture Foundation's river
cruise map for handy building ID. CAF is in the Santa Fe
Building at 224 S. Michigan Ave., (312) 922-3432, and the
John Hancock Center at 875 N. Michigan Ave., (312)
751-1380, *Guide to Sea Kayaking on Lakes Superior &
Michigan; The Chicago River: A Natural and Unnatural*

History; The Chicago River: An Illustrated History and Guide to the River and Its Waterways.

Heads up: Urban paddle par excellence. Strong winds, waves, and heavy traffic. High steel walls make most of the shore inaccessible and create reverb waves (powerboats often ignore no-wake zones and seem oblivious to kayaks). Paddle in fall after summer party boaters are in dry dock.

Description: Your perspective will be irrevocably altered. Lakefront postcard-perfect views. World-famous architecture. More than a dozen bridges. Setting out on the lake from 12th St. Beach, you pass the planetarium, the aquarium, Grant Park. As you approach Navy Pier, swing west into the Chicago River locks (wait for a green light to enter). After a short paddle under Lake Shore Dr., you're smack in the middle of downtown Chicago on the river's main stem.

From a kayak cockpit, traveling well below street level means traffic is virtually erased from view, leaving just the towering buildings imprinted against the sky. It feels slightly subversive, gliding on the downtown waters at rush hour, knowing your street-bound compatriots are sucking traffic fumes.

Paddle past the Beaux Arts neoclassic Wrigley Building, the modernist Mies Van der Rohe IBM Building, the Merchandise Mart. Catch the skyline reflected in the green-mirrored glass of 333 West Wacker, follow the bend and hang left (south). Once you hit River City around Polk St., turn around and paddle back. And prepare to be awed once again. FYI: a planned public launch at Weed St. off Goose Island will offer easy river access. See *Loop the Goose*, page 30.

Directions: Take Lake Shore Dr. south to the Museum Campus exit on McFetridge Dr. Head for the planetarium, follow the signs to the right (south) for 12th St. Beach, and park in the pay lot. Or try your luck at the metered spots on Solidarity Dr.

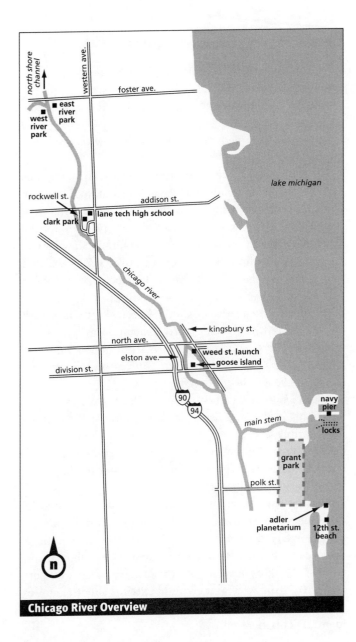

north shore channel

western ave.

foster ave.

west river park

east river park

lake michigan

rockwell st.

addison st.

clark park

lane tech high school

chicago river

kingsbury st.

north ave.

elston ave.

weed st. launch

goose island

division st.

90

94

main stem

navy pier

locks

grant park

polk st.

adler planetarium

12th st. beach

n

Chicago River Overview

CHICAGO RIVER, LOOP THE GOOSE

Location: Clark Park is around 3400 N; Goose Island is between 800 and 1600 N.

Length: 7 miles out and back (including the island loop) from Clark Park

Difficulty: Intermediate. Strong paddlers with good self-rescue skills.

Put-in/takeout: By the time you read this, the city plans to have finished a public launch on Weed St. just south of North Ave. on the island's east channel. Contact Friends of the Chicago River (see *Where to Connect*, page 73) for the latest. Otherwise, try riverside bar-restaurant Slow Down, Life's Too Short (otherwise known as LTS; 1177 N. Elston Ave., 773-384-1040). Clark Park is best bet if you need to rent a boat.

Outfitter: Chicago River Canoe & Kayak at Clark Park (773-32-KAYAK, www.chicagoriverpaddle.com)

Books: *The Chicago River: A Natural and Unnatural History; The Chicago River: An Illustrated History and Guide to the River and Its Waterways.*

Heads up: Industrial history lesson. Strong winds, waves, and heavy traffic. High steel walls make most of the shore inaccessible and create reverb waves. For fuel, Nicole's Café (1505 N. Kingsbury, 312-640-8883) serves great sandwiches, grinds its own flour, and has outdoor seating paralleling Goose Island's east side.

Description: Goose Island (besides being the namesake of a tasty hometown microbrewery) is an industrial pocket wedged incongruously among the Bed Bath & Beyond and Pottery Barns that make up the Clybourn corridor's cheek-by-jowl retail experience. The 160-acre island, 0.5 mile wide at its widest, extends about 1.5 miles from North to Chicago Aves. in the midst of rapid-fire residential gentrification.

Some historians say the island gets its name from the geese kept in the yards of Irish immigrants who lived on the island and worked in its factories, lumber yards, and tanneries in the mid-1800s (scrap metal and other industrial biz crisscrossed by RR lines occupy the island today). The island itself formed when workers dug clay to make bricks, simultaneously making way for more water traffic by creating the North Branch Canal on the island's east side.

Breathe in yeast-laden air from the Sara Lee bakery plant. Several cool bridges, frequent barges (give them wide berth), and downtown views round out the scene. Continue south for riverside warehouses-turned-condos and downtown (see *Downtown Urban Canyons*, page 27).

Directions: For Clark Park, see *Clark Park-River Park* below. Call first to launch from Slow Down, Life's Too Short. Exit I-94 west at Division St. Take Division east to Elston Ave. LTS is on the east side of the street. Show thanks by imbibing freely (post-paddle, of course).

CHICAGO RIVER, CLARK PARK-RIVER PARK

Location: Clark Park is around 3400 N.

Length: 5 miles out and back

Difficulty: Easy. Paddling north goes against the current.

Put-in/takeout: Paddle from Clark Park to River Park and back (or reverse: launch from River Park, 5100 N. Francisco Ave., between Argyle St. and Foster Ave. and a few blocks east of N. Kedzie Ave.).

Outfitter: Chicago River Canoe & Kayak at Clark Park (773-32-KAYAK, www.chicagoriverpaddle.com)

Map and books: Chicago River Canoe & Kayak has a basic map. *The Chicago River: A Natural and Unnatural History; The Chicago River: An Illustrated History and Guide to the River and Its Waterways.*

Night Journey

FROM SHORE, LAKE Michigan spreads before us like a glossy black blanket. Kayaking with lifelong paddler Gary Mechanic on a mid-August night, we launch from Diversey Harbor and head toward Navy Pier. It's humid, but a soft, cool breeze skims the lake.

White light from the top of the Hancock serves as an urban substitute for moon rays, throwing shimmer onto the water's surface. Powerboats speed past, kicking up wake swells. Mechanic plays in the surf, but I'm fixed on the skyline's constellation of electric city stars. It feels surreal seeing this from the vantage of a low-slung kayak. The small white lights clamped on the fronts of our boats look to me like feeble beacons, easily lost from view in a wave.

As we paddle in the dark, I can feel the lake's ever-changing terrain. Mechanic says he thinks of sections of the water as "neighborhoods." When we near Theater on the Lake around Fullerton, for example, the waves reverb off the protective shore wall, making for short and choppy water. Then suddenly, the water goes all smooth and rolling.

I realize I've shut out the sounds of cars speeding down Lake Shore Dr., shut out the sounds of powerboats making a beeline for home harbors, shut out all sounds but that of the lake itself.

"Being in a kayak out here, you're in such intimate touch with the lake, moving along low and slow," Mechanic says, a feeling amplified by riding the waters at night, senses sharp. "You feel its every move. It's very special."

Special? Definitely. And if this isn't urban adventure, I don't know what is.

Heads up: Great after-work route

Description: No muss, no fuss. Long-time kayaker Gary Mechanic likes this stretch because "it's one of the few places in the city where people treat the river as their front yard." Neighbors in Ravenswood Manor have lovingly tended the riverbanks with brown-eyed Susan, ferns, rock gardens, and a mostly hidden riverside path. Porches and docks jut onto the river.

Kayaking at rush hour on a Friday afternoon, traveling north against the river's mellow current, it's just me and a few mallards. Traffic is at a standstill on the Wilson Ave. Bridge, but I'm gliding on through, garnering a few excited shouts from bridge-bound kids on their bikes. At River Park, where the stick-straight North Shore Channel carries on due north, a fisherman is thigh-deep casting for bass. Chris Parson of Friends of the Chicago River likes paddling at night along the fairly deep man-made channel in spring or fall when roosting waterfowl are in abundance. It's like paddling through a tunnel. "And it feels a bit like a secret passage."

Directions: Clark Park is at 3400 N. Rockwell St. behind Lane Tech High School, just south of Addison St., west of Western Ave. By car, exit I-94 west at Addison. Follow Addison east, cross the river, and take the first turn south (right) onto N. Rockwell. Clark Park is on your right. By bike (if you're renting your boat at the park), pedal the Elston Ave. bike lane to California Ave. Turn right (north) on California. Turn right (east) on Addison. Cross the river and turn right (south) on Rockwell.

By transit, the Brown Line L Addison stop is about 1 mile east of Clark Park. 49 Western and 152 Addison buses stop nearby.

All About Access

OVER THE YEARS, local paddlers have confronted plenty of obstacles to get safe, public access to area waterways.

"A few years back I had to trespass, like a conscientious objector, to get onto the Chicago River," says Gary Mechanic, director of the Illinois Paddling Council's Access Project. And on Lake Michigan, the crown jewel of Chicago kayaking, lifeguards regularly blocked paddlers looking to launch from city beaches. "We have miles and miles of beach and we just wanted 10 feet. It was ridiculous."

No wonder Mechanic used to call himself an "urban guerilla kayaker."

Now, a coalition made up of the Illinois Paddling Council, Northeastern Illinois Planning Commission, Illinois Department of Natural Resources, and Openlands Project is working to bolster access.

For city paddlers, one of the most immediate fruits of the coalition's labor is the Lake Michigan Water Trail, about a dozen official access points (marked by buoys on water and signs on land) spread up and down Chicago's 29 miles of lakefront.

Of course, there's plenty more Lake Michigan shoreline north and south of the city limits. Efforts are underway to expand the water trail and ease city-dweller access to the North Shore lakefront (for now, it's complicated and costly to legally launch along the tony lakefront burbs since each has its own permit and fee structure for nonresidents).

But the coalition's sights are set well beyond Chicago and the lake. The hugely ambitious Northeastern Illinois Regional Water Trails Project aims eventually to create water trails covering nearly 500 miles along 10 waterways in the 6-county metro Chicago area (including the Chicago River, Des Plaines, Fox, and Calumet area waterways).

Water trails are essentially "the blueways in the green-ways," Mechanic says—a series of access points spaced a few miles apart, tied together by coordinated signs with logistical information (like mileage or dams and other hazards) and insight into area ecology or history.

"We don't want to turn these waterways into Disneyland. We don't want to take the adventure out of it. But there's a degree of ease that could be there that just isn't there yet," he says. There's no hard-and-fast timeline for finishing the regional water trail plan; it's a work in progress. And it's going on against a backdrop of fairly regressive state laws: less than 8% of Illinois' 33,000 miles of canoeable streams are considered legally open to public use. Still, Mechanic says, "there's no question that access today is way better than it was even 2 years ago."

The third-generation Chicagoan dreams of a day when stressed-out urbanites can hop on the Metra from downtown, walk a block or two to an outfitter, rent a boat on a quiet river, paddle, get out downstream, and grab a train back downtown. Sigh.

"We're definitely not anywhere near that in Chicago," he says. "Not yet."

LAKE MICHIGAN

Location: Go east until you hit the Big Blue (sometimes green or gray). Good North Side, Central, and South Side city launches.

Length: Varied. You can spend endless hours exploring.

Difficulty: Intermediate to advanced. Beginners with an outfitter or guide. Less experienced kayakers should stick close to shore, inside piers and breakwater.

Put-in/takeout: See Directions for some options.

Outfitters: As of this writing, the only spots for lakefront kayak rentals were through the Park District at Montrose Ave. and 63d St. Beaches, Memorial Day–Labor Day only: Montrose Ave. Beach (312) 742-0600; 63d St. Beach (312) 745-1905; Chicago Park District (312) 747-2474. Kayak Chicago (773-209-1800, www.kayakchicago.com) runs Wednesday night group paddles to Navy Pier in summer to watch the fireworks.

Maps and books: Chicago Park District's (312-747-2474) "Chicago's Lakefront" map has Lake Michigan Water Trail launch and land sites; NOAA chart 14927 for Chicago lakefront; NOAA 14926 small-craft book for Chicago and south shore of Lake Michigan. *Guide to Sea Kayaking on Lakes Superior & Michigan.*

Heads up: For experienced, well-equipped kayakers, especially outside summer. Fall is great; boat traffic drops, but winds pick up. Always check lake conditions and forecast first (http://205.156.54.206/om/marine/gtlakes.htm). Waves and weather can get nasty in a hurry.

Description: 22,300 square miles of water surface and 1,180 cubic miles full: they don't call this an inland sea for nothing. Lake Michigan is Chicago's wilderness, vast and untamed—a wilderness that demands respect (see *Cross-Lake Adventure*, page 39).

Lake Michigan offers open-water coastal kayaking right in our front yard. It's what keeps a lot of Chicago kayakers sane. Thankfully, lakefront launching and landing are a lot easier thanks to the recent creation of the Lake Michigan Water Trail, a series of official access points along the city's shoreline (see *All About Access*, page 34).

Most city paddlers pick a launch spot, determine their direction, and head off. Check out the Museum Campus peninsula. Circle pine-fringed Promontory Point around 55th St. Or just play in the surf. Determined to have an offshore destination? Strike out for one of the half-dozen or so cribs,

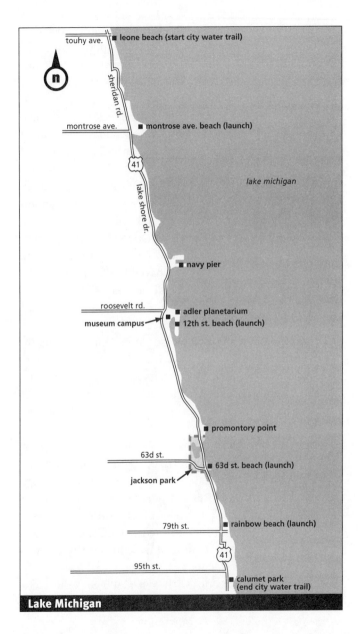

touhy ave.

■ leone beach (start city water trail)

n

sheridan rd.

montrose ave.

■ montrose ave. beach (launch)

41

lake shore dr.

lake michigan

■ navy pier

roosevelt rd.

■ adler planetarium

museum campus →

■ 12th st. beach (launch)

■ promontory point

63d st.

■ 63d st. beach (launch)

jackson park →

79th st.

■ rainbow beach (launch)

41

95th st.

■ calumet park
(end city water trail)

Lake Michigan

the islandlike water-intake structures a few miles out that carry water to filtration plants through 16-foot tunnels bored out of the limestone bedrock 110 feet below the surface. But don't try to land on the cribs. It's dangerous and illegal.

Lake Michigan offers plenty of possible urban escapes—see "Sailing" for ideas. Some who crave a less man-made landscape head southeast to Porter Beach and paddle along the Indiana Dunes (see "Hiking & Backpacking," page 333). Others head north to Illinois Beach State Park in Zion just below the Wisconsin border (see "Windsurfing & Surfing," page 117). But most city paddlers stick to the urban shoreline. The skyline views are tough to beat.

Directions: Everyone's got their own favorite launch. Below, a few suggestions, all of which are easily accessible by bike, blades, or foot from the paved Lakefront Trail:

- North Side: Montrose Ave. Beach is 4400 N. By car, take Lake Shore Dr. north. Exit Montrose Ave. Go east to the parking lot closest to the beach house (or continue north for the Wilson Ave. launch ramp). By transit, take the Red Line L to Wilson Ave. It's a 1-mile-plus walk: east on Wilson to N. Marine Dr., south to Montrose, east to the beach. Or take the 78 bus to Marine and Montrose. Walk east on Montrose to the beach.

- Downtown: 12th St. Beach (1200 S) is by the Museum Campus just south of the Loop. From Lake Shore Dr., take the Museum Campus exit (from the north it jogs around Roosevelt Rd. and puts you onto McFetridge Dr.). Follow signs to 12th St. Beach, south of the planetarium. Try your luck at the metered spots on Solidarity Dr. or suck it up and park in the pay lot (the last one before the planetarium).

- South Side: For 63d St. Beach (6300 S), take Lake Shore Dr. south to 63d St. Turn east at the light into the lot. By transit, take the Green Line L to E. 63d St. (Red Line stops at 63d farther west.) From there, take the 63 bus east to the beach.

Rainbow Beach is at 79th St. (7900 S). Take Lake Shore Dr. south until it turns into South Shore Dr. (it jogs behind the South Shore Cultural Center around 71st St.). Turn east on 79th. Follow the winding road past the filtration plant to beach parking.

Cross-Lake Adventure

CHARLIE PORTIS HAS paddled in Alaska's Kenai Fjords, Hawaii's Waipio Valley, Vietnam's Halong Bay. But mostly, the Chicago-area native and founder of Wateriders Adventure Agents has explored closer to home.

In 1996 he decided to take a page from Dr. Hannes Lindemann. Forty years earlier, Lindemann crossed the Atlantic, alone, in a 17-foot folding kayak with a sail—the smallest known craft ever to make a trans-Atlantic journey. He paddled and sailed 3,000 miles from the Canary Islands to St. Martin in 72 days, chronicling his mental and physical journey in the epic tale *Alone At Sea*.

Granted, Portis's Lake Michigan crossing would be a bit less ambitious, but an adventure nonetheless. He'd paddled from the city up the North Shore and back umpteen times in his folding kayak and sail rig. "I figured given the right conditions, why not go farther?"

He and a friend, both strong, experienced paddlers, set a course from 63d St. Beach to New Buffalo, MI. On test runs, Portis knew his sail-kayak could hit 4 knots. So he figured if they left at sunrise, they could make the crossing in 10 or 11 hours and not lose daylight.

"We also knew that if the shit hit the fan, we could dig in

and paddle like crazy for 5 hours," Portis says. "You can't be a lillydipper out there."

Tuesday, October 1, 1996. They picked a day smack dab in the middle of a 4-day forecast of fine weather and safe, south-westerly winds. They had wet suits. A GPS. Cell phones. They made sure the Coast Guard knew where they were headed. They launched.

The morning brought virtually zero wind, so "we paddled our butts off." Eventually, the winds picked up, so the sail kicked in. The Chicago skyline slipped behind them as they moved farther off shore.

"You feel like you're really in sync with the lake. You feel the vastness," Portis recalls. "I remember looking back over my shoulder at Chicago and it was that 'where the lake meets the prairie' feeling. And then it just got smaller and smaller and smaller." The term "inland sea" suddenly made a whole lot of sense.

A sailboat or two passed by over the hours. "Mostly they said 'What the hell are you guys doing out here?' We took every precaution, but at the end of the day, you're just out there. You're in the middle of the lake; you're 15 miles from any-where," Portis says. "That's when we started quoting Linde-mann." (Where Lindemann's mantra was "Never give up. Take no assistance. Keep moving west," Portis's was "Never give up. Take all assistance. Keep moving east.")

With the sun dipping lower and the prospect of a nocturnal paddle far from shore less than tempting, the duo decided to angle off course and land in Michigan City. They traveled 36 miles in 9 hours. "We definitely cherry-picked the day. All the stars were in alignment, with perfect wind and weather," Portis says.

He has paddled Lake Michigan enough to know that the stars can quickly un-align. "This lake can turn really scary in an instant. All it takes is a northeastern wind to whip through on a summer afternoon and you get into serious weather and waves." Case in point: when he and some friends crossed the Manitou Passage from Leland, MI, a few years back, they hit 6-foot swells and low clouds that wiped out views of land in all directions. It took the trio 4.5 harrowing hours to make an 8-mile crossing to South Manitou Island.

"Bottom line," Portis says, "you must respect the lake."

CALUMET RIVER AND O'BRIEN LOCKS

Location: Far Southeast Side

Length: 7–8 miles (more if you explore Lake Calumet)

Difficulty: Intermediate-advanced. Wakes, waves, and traffic. Kayaks best. Check Lake Michigan conditions; you paddle the lake to get to the takeout.

Put-in: Riverside Marina (136011 S. Calhoun Ave.) off 136th and Torrence Ave. (Lazy current means you can do this as a round-trip if you don't mind logging more miles.)

Takeout: Paddle about 0.5 mile south of the river's mouth along Lake Michigan to the Calumet Park boat ramp at E. 95th St.

Map: Calumet Ecological Park Association (773-374-8543, www.lincolnnet.net/cepa) for a general map (*not* a paddling guide) of the proposed Calumet National Heritage Area.

Heads up: Thanks to Gary Mechanic for a route inspired by fabled "Heavy Duty Industrial Urban Kayaking" trips into neighboring Hoosier waters by fearless paddler Erik Sprenne.

Double heads up: As of this writing, the Army Corps of Engineers was letting paddlers through the O'Brien Locks, but that could change. Call first (773-646-2183). Check out the locks from the observation area on the south side of

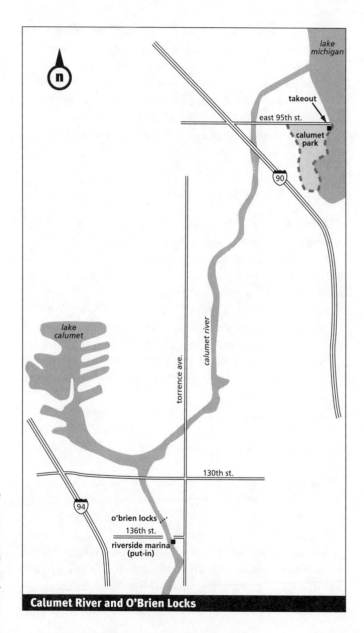

lake michigan

takeout

east 95th st.

calumet park

90

lake calumet

calumet river

torrence ave.

130th st.

94

o'brien locks

136th st.

riverside marina
(put-in)

Calumet River and O'Brien Locks

130th St. near the Ford plant. Bummer: you may have to pay $10 to launch at Riverside Marina, open year-round and until the wee hours of the morning for nearby shift workers. Bonus: free darts and cheap suds.

Description: Let's put it this way. When I talked to the manager at Riverside Marina about their policy for letting paddlers launch, she said, "You know, to be honest, we don't really get kayaks down here."

Precisely. This trip on the city's hardscrabble southeastern border is straight-up urban adventure—not for the faint of heart. Yes, it's best to avoid hot summer days that cook up a stench (fall is best). Yes, asthmatics should beware. Yes, the water is severely polluted. But this trip offers up hulking cranes, conveyor belts, and grain elevators in a part of the city that's rarely explored. And Mother Nature has proved remarkably resilient in finding ways to infiltrate the industrial environs.

That means incongruous views of egrets wading along marshy riverbanks against a backdrop of enormous storage tanks and other factory esoterica. Marshes, ponds, and wetlands, remnants of what was once a vast, wet prairie system, dot the landscape. Shortly after paddling under the 130th St. Bridge, turn left (west) to explore 540-acre Lake Calumet (it was once on the short list to be paved over as Chicago's third airport). Bird life abounds; state-endangered black-crowned night-herons are making a comeback here. Duck out of the lake to continue northeast on the Calumet until you reach its mouth at Lake Michigan.

Now tell your friends where you've just kayaked and see if they believe you.

Directions: Take I-94 east to the 130th St. exit east. Turn right (south) on Torrence Ave. Turn right (west) on 136th St.; it dead-ends at Riverside Marina.

Local Legend

R ALPH FRESE IS an original.

A fourth-generation blacksmith, Frese is also a canoe builder and restorer, lifelong paddler, environmentalist, historian, and founder of Chicagoland Canoe Base, audaciously dubbed "the most unusual canoe shop in the USA."

In 1994 he received the American Canoe Association's first national Legends of Paddling award for his lifetime contribution to paddlesport.

Frese and his deputy, Vic Hurtowy, are the go-to guys if you want to know something—virtually anything—about area waterways. Just be prepared to sit and listen for a while.

And don't be surprised if the 75-year-old Frese heads to his desk and pulls out, say, a 1941 copy of "Hunting and Fishing" (it has a photo of the type of boat Frese had as a kid). The office filing cabinets are mere preludes to his home library stocked with thousands of tomes with titles like *Location of the Chicago Portage Route of the 17th Century* and *Firearms, Traps & Tools of the Mountain Men*. One wall holds a half-century's worth of slides from local paddling trips.

For Frese, paddling is a way of life, a way to be in touch with nature and history in a most tangible way. He grew up in the same Portage Park neighborhood where his shop sits today (3 miles from the nearest river), on the city's northwest side. As a boy, Frese spent lots of time mucking about the neighborhood wetland prairie jumping with crayfish and frogs.

"I figured if it was this good on shore, it must be twice as good on the water," Frese says. He started building his own boats. Then he started helping other kids build boats. He was hooked. And he's still building boats today. (He eventually took over his father's blacksmith business, which gradually morphed into the paddle shop. Over time, he also amassed a collection of 90-odd native and antique watercraft.)

Frese can see the landscape stripped of the urban topsoil's asphalt and cars. He points across the street to the shopping mall parking lot. I see a shopping mall parking lot; he sees the southwestern edge of the St. Lawrence River watershed.

Talking to Frese, it's clear he intuitively understands that adventure is as much about the mind as the body. That a paddle down the lower Des Plaines is not just about what you see and hear, but what you know of its place in history. "Who's to say you're not paddling the very same water molecules Joliet did?" Frese asks as he launches into an explanation of how the river eventually drains into the Gulf of Mexico, evaporates, and recycles back to the Des Plaines as rainwater.

He sees the thrill of discovery imminently possible in urban environs. He's paddled for six decades, but just this year he found two types of wild orchids he'd never seen before.

Frese has zero patience for Chicagoans who drive huge distances to paddle far-flung waters when they've left unexplored a plethora of waterways in their own backyard. By way of reinforcement, he likes to remind people that "Chicago's reason for being is because it's on an ancient canoe trail."

The paddle shop itself is stuffed to the gills with boats and related gear. Frese's workshop, including the forge he built, is next door. Ask Frese to show you the realistic-looking birchbark canoes he's fashioned out of fiberglass; he made four of them for the 1978 TV miniseries "Centennial" with Richard Chamberlain and Robert Conrad.

The "most unusual canoe shop." Well, where else would you be able to pick up esoterica like the title *Skin Boats of Saint Lawrence Island, Alaska*? And where else would you find Ralph Frese.

Backyard

NORTH BRANCH OF THE CHICAGO RIVER

Location: About 20 miles N of Chicago

Length: 10 miles

Difficulty: Beginner to intermediate

Put-in: Carry your boat down the gravel path to the Willow Rd. dam. Put in at the wide concrete steps downstream on the east side of the river.

Takeout: After paddling under the bike bridge, take out in the small open patch on the right bank at Whealan Pool in Caldwell Woods off Devon Ave. Short path to the parking lot.

Maps and book: "The Unofficial Paddling Guide to the Chicago River" from Friends of the Chicago River highlights this route, also known as the "Unofficial Ralph Frese Canoe Trail," named for the owner/founder of Chicagoland Canoe Base (see *Local Legend*, page 44). *Paddling Illinois*.

Heads up: Easy urban escape. It's a pain to portage in a kayak—you've got three dams plus downed trees to dodge here—so you're better off in a canoe.

Description: This is the Chicago River in its most natural state, twisting a gradual eastward course through restored prairies, savannas, and forested public lands from the northern burbs to the takeout in the city. Though bikers cruising the North Branch Trail appear in flashes through the woods, you feel supremely solitary, gliding under almost total tree canopy in spots, creating enough hush to tune into the movements of hefty snapping turtles and bullfrogs.

The river is narrow and intimate, ranging from about 20

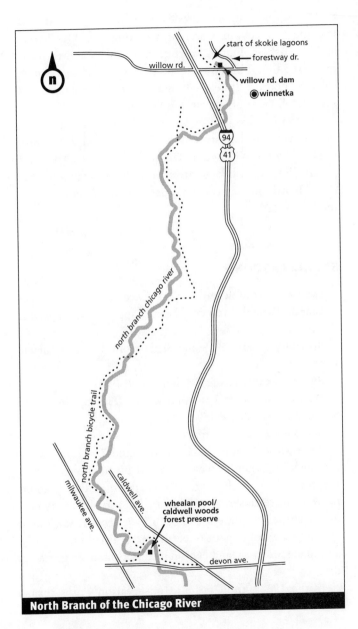

start of skokie lagoons

forestway dr.

willow rd.

willow rd. dam

⊙winnetka

94
41

north branch chicago river

north branch bicycle trail

caldwell ave.

milwaukee ave.

whealan pool/
caldwell woods
forest preserve

devon ave.

North Branch of the Chicago River

to 40 feet, offering decent odds of spotting deer, muskrat, fox, and even coyote. Watch for perching great blue herons and kingfishers. During migration, warblers and thrushes travel the liquid highway. If the river hasn't frozen, snowy sojourns here are "like paddling through a Christmas card," says Ralph Frese of Chicagoland Canoe Base.

Directions: Take I-94 west. Exit Willow Rd. east. Turn left (north) onto Forestway Dr. Park on Forestway or drop the boat by the Willow Rd. dam and park at the Tower Rd. parking lot. Great bike shuttle: pedal back north along the paved North Branch Trail that parallels the river (see "Biking," page 219).

SKOKIE LAGOONS

Location: About 20 miles N of Chicago

Length: Variable. You could easily spend hours exploring the 190 acres.

Difficulty: Beginner. Some dams to portage, but placid water.

Put-in/takeout: Tower Rd. launch off I-94

Map: Cook County Forest Preserve's "Fishing Guide" for rough map (312-261-8400).

Heads up: Full-moon magic

Description: It must have been around 7 P.M. one summer evening when I stealth-paddled up to the great blue heron perched on the edge of a small tree-filled island. I moved a little closer, acutely aware of every dip of my paddle. Eventually, I got close enough to see that it saw me. It let me get within about 6 feet before it lifted off, silently, and made for the island behind me. The moment made my day.

In the 1930s, the Civilian Conservation Corps turned what the Potawatomi Indians called the Chewab Skokie,

"big wet prairie," into the network of seven lagoons connected by quiet winding channels and dotted by wooded
islands. At the Willow Rd. dam, the lagoons feed into the
Skokie River, which eventually becomes the North Branch
of the Chicago.

Despite being hemmed in by suburban development—
not to mention the Edens Expressway immediately to the
west—bird and wildlife viewing here is consistently good.
Red fox, muskrat, deer, and even mink are known to make
appearances, as do plenty of fishermen angling for largemouth bass, walleye, or bluegill. Motorboats verboten. And
the more you explore smaller channels, the quieter it gets.

Directions: Take I-94 west to the Willow Rd. east exit.
Turn left (north) on Forestway Dr. Turn left (west) on
Tower Rd. After the bridge (often full of anglers), turn left
(south) into the Tower Rd. boat launch lot.

DES PLAINES RIVER CANOE MARATHON COURSE

Location: About 38 miles N of Chicago

Length: 19.5 miles

Difficulty: Easy but long

Put-in: Oak Spring Rd. in Libertyville

Takeout: Dam #2 Woods (Cook County Forest Preserve)
in Mount Prospect, between Euclid Ave. and Foundry Rd.
off Des Plaines River Rd./US 45.

Outfitter: Offshore (River Tree Court mall on southeast
corner of Milwaukee Ave. and Townline Rd./IL 60, 847-
362-4880, www.offshore-chicago.com) in Vernon Hills
rents canoes and single and tandem kayaks. Launch out
their back door.

Maps and book: Lake County Des Plaines River Trail map
shows bike trail and launches (847-367-6640, www.co.lake
.il.us); Des Plaines Canoe Marathon route (www.members

.dencity.com/g-jaros/desplaines/). *Paddling Illinois* for other Des Plaines routes.

Heads up: Put in at IL 60 to shorten up by about 5 miles. Two dams to portage. Downed trees, rocks, and random concrete obstacles to jockey around. Decent bike shuttle.

Description: Each May, hundreds dip paddles on this suburban section of river for the Des Plaines River Canoe Marathon, started more than four decades ago by paddling guru Ralph Frese (see *Local Legend*, page 44).

Sandwiched by forest preserve land, this tree-lined stretch grants some quality quiet for spotting great blue herons and snapping turtles. And even when you're paddling behind a Sam's Club, the sloping wooded banks serve as a decent buffer from civilization. Unfortunately, the area around Dam #1 is an eyesore, with a glass-strewn, street-level portage.

Expect a workout, especially in summer when low water means little current to help you along the muddy green water. You're near the finish line after you pass a pretty stone bridge and see the red warning sign around the bend for Dam #2. Take out is on the right (west) side up a steep bank.

Directions: Take I-94 west. Exit west on US 176/Park Ave. Turn right (north) on St. Mary's Rd. Turn left on Oak Spring Rd. Look for Lake County Forest Preserve launch sign on the left side of the road. Bike shuttle along the river on Cook County Des Plaines Division dirt trail (see "Mountain Biking," page 274, and "Biking," page 229). When the trail dead-ends at Lake-Cook Rd., ride 4 miles north along the Milwaukee Ave. shoulder—beware heavy traffic—until you can pick up Lake County's Des Plaines River Trail off Riverside Rd. (one-lane road east off Milwaukee Ave.).

For IL 60 access, take I-94 west. Exit west on Townline Rd./IL 60. Launch is on south side of IL 60.

City
Treasure

HE LINCOLN PARK Boat Club is like a paddling nerve center for Chicago.

If you live in the city and don't own your own boat but want to paddle, this is the place to go. And if you do have your own craft, joining here is one of the best ways to tap into the local scene. For $220 a year you get access to the club's roughly 100 paddling boats, from standard sea kayaks to sprint and whitewater kayaks, as well as standard and racing canoes. There's plenty of recreational and competitive rowing equipment, too, since about half the club's 500-plus members are rowers.

Founded in 1910, the club's boathouse on the Lincoln Park Lagoon near the zoo offers protected lagoon waters and quick access to Lake Michigan via Diversey Harbor. A new satellite site on the Chicago River was mostly dedicated to rowing in 2001, but kayaking resources are expected to grow there, too.

Members range from neophytes to folks who've done the Eco-Challenge and paddled in far-flung locales like Greenland. There's a steady diet of weekend paddling trips and social events, plus weekly evening and Friday sunrise group paddles. Monthly meetings start with a group paddle and end with a free instructional workshop (the club offers more formal instruction, too). The all-volunteer outfit keeps prices low by asking members to pitch in with club-sponsored races or other needs. Members get a shot at boat storage ($8 a foot per year).

LPBC (773-549-BOAT, www.lpbc.net) is on the west side of the Lincoln Park Lagoon, south of Fullerton Ave. Street access on the south side of Fullerton Ave. through the Lincoln Park Zoo parking gates. On foot or bike, follow the multiuse trail that winds through Lincoln Park to the zoo's main entrance. There's no sign for the boat club; just watch for where the path jogs east down to the lagoon edge.

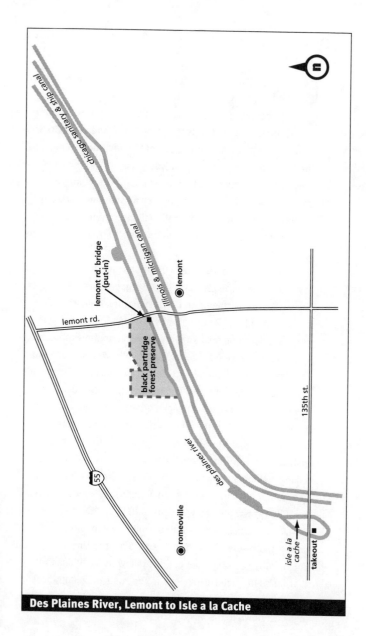

chicago sanitary & ship canal

illinois & michigan canal

lemont rd. bridge
(put-in)

○ lemont

lemont rd.

black partridge
forest preserve

des plaines river

55

○ romeoville

135th st.

isle a la
cache

■ takeout

Des Plaines River, Lemont to Isle a la Cache

DES PLAINES RIVER, LEMONT TO ISLE A LA CACHE

Location: About 30 miles SW of Chicago

Length: 5.5 miles

Difficulty: Easy. Strong winds in parts.

Put-in: Below Lemont Rd. Bridge in Lemont

Takeout: Gravel landing off Isle a la Cache museum parking lot; swing left after you paddle under the 135th St. Bridge in Romeoville.

Outfitter: Will-U-Canoe in Willow Springs (708-839-2311 or 877-937-4945) rents canoes and runs shuttles for this route and longer trips. Call for directions; they're planning a move downriver. If you get a big enough group, owner Wayne Hermansen (a chef in a former life) can whip up feasts like his signature pig roast.

Book: *Paddling Illinois.*

Heads up: Part of the Illinois & Michigan Canal National Heritage Corridor, perched on bluffs above the Lower Des Plaines, Lemont has an historic Main St. worth ambling.

Description: After Lemont's brief industrial stint, trees line the mostly straight-ahead river on either side. If the water's high enough, veer north off the main river the first chance you get (by a big stand of cattails) to explore a maze of back channels. Scan the treetops for enormous great blue heron nests; look down to see beaver-gnawed stumps.

Egrets and cormorants were actively fishing in the marshy river frontage of Black Partridge Forest Preserve when I paddled through here in early September. Nice color on the wooded bluffs in fall. The otherwise slack current picks up as you approach Isle a La Cache (you'll see a small red sign; take the right channel). Used by fur trappers and traders centuries back, the 80-acre island is one of the only ones left on the Des Plaines.

Directions: Take I-55 south. Exit Lemont Rd. south. Turn right (west) on Old Lemont Rd., *before* the big bridge over the Des Plaines, Sanitary and Ship Canal, and I&M Canal. Old Lemont loops around and under the bridge. At the dead-end, turn left and park under the bridge.

Short Hops

LOWER FOX RIVER

Location: About 94 miles SW of Chicago

Length: 10.5–11.5 miles

Difficulty: Rated P.G. paddling. Decent current, some easygoing riffles.

Put-in: Ramp behind the bar (Scooters Saloon, 815-496-9501) at the southwest corner of the Sheridan Rd. Bridge in Sheridan

Takeout: Ayers Landing off Somonauk Rd. on the right (west) side of the Fox, just below Indian Creek (small fee to park and land with your own boat). Or about 1 mile downstream (past the Wedron Bridge) at Chet's Fox River Tavern in Wedron.

Outfitters: In Wedron, Ayers Landing (800-540-2394 or 815-434-2233) and C&M Canoe Rental (815-434-6690 or 815-433-9798) offer canoe rental and shuttles to Sheridan as well as Yorkville and environs for overnight trips. Freeman's Sports in Yorkville (630-553-0515) offers shuttles to Wedron from Yorkville and rents kayaks as well as canoes.

Book: *Paddling Illinois.*

Heads up: Paddlers have long canoe-camped (discreetly) on islands on the Fox. You're within striking distance of Illini (815-795-2448) and Starved Rock (815-667-4726) State Parks if you're not hell-bent on river camping.

Description: A gem. Ancient 40-foot sandstone cliffs abound, topped by towering pines. Swallows dart in and out of their nests bored into the cliff faces. October is prime time here with peak hues on the cedar and yew hugging the river. Summer brings heavier canoe and tubing crowds, but this stretch gets a reprieve from motorboat traffic because it's usually too shallow. Profuse columbines bloom riverside in May.

A half-dozen or more tributary creeks radiate from the river along your way. Fishermen haul smallmouth bass, walleye, and bluegill from 15-foot holes. Check out the diminutive box canyon on the river's west bank shortly after the put-in, after a narrow island. And keep your eyes peeled for beaver, muskrat, deer, red-tailed hawks—and the dozen turkey vultures that tend to roost near the takeout at Ayers Landing.

Want an overnight? Paddle the 27-mile dam-free stretch from Yorkville to Wedron. The Yorkville to Sheridan stretch lacks the dramatic cliffs, but the densely packed maple and oak should be enticement enough if you're looking to escape the concrete jungle. In Yorkville, put in at the Yorkville public boat landing, just downstream from the IL 47 bridge.

Directions: Take I-55 south to exit 253/US 52. Go west on US 52. Turn right (north) onto Sheridan Rd. Follow Sheridan through town. Scooters Saloon is on the outskirts of Sheridan, on the left side of the road before the bridge. It charges a few bucks to park and launch.

KISHWAUKEE RIVER

Location: About 70 miles NW of Chicago

Length: 16 miles. Easily broken up into two shorter chunks: Belvidere to Cherry Valley (7-plus miles), Cherry Valley to New Milford (8.5 miles).

Difficulty: Beginner to intermediate. Riffly sections.

Need to maneuver curves and narrow channels. Deadfall and wire in spots.

Put-in: Landing at the Appleton Rd. Bridge (some refer to as Twin Bridges or Stone Quarry Rd. Bridge) just downstream of Belvidere Park off US 20. Check out the park's 1845 Baltic Mill.

Takeout: Atwood Park in New Milford, south side of the river just past pedestrian bridge. For the shorter trip, take out in Cherry Valley at the Baumann Park landing on the east side of the river after the State St. and RR bridges.

Book: *Paddling Illinois.*

Heads up: Paddling in Perrier

Description: Vic Hurtowy of Chicagoland Canoe Base has been paddling the Kish since 1977. It's one of his favorites. Why? "It's close and it's clean," he says. "From downtown, you're here in an hour and a half. And you can paddle this river every Sunday for six weeks and see something different every single time."

The Kishwaukee is a Class A stream, which is about as close as you get to a waterway free from human disturbance; it's one of the state's three highest-quality river systems. No surprise that anglers flock for smallmouth bass, northern pike, walleye, and bluegill.

The river draws 28 endangered, threatened, and watch-listed creatures, from the mulberry wing butterfly to the sandhill crane and the spiked mussel. Hurtowy has seen mink, coyote, bald eagles, and river otter here. You're practically guaranteed sightings of red-tailed hawks. Local communities have preserved a wooded landscape along much of the Kish, which never grows beyond 100 feet wide and narrows to 30 feet in parts. Belvidere to Cherry Valley is the more challenging paddle, riffly and more winding. Cherry Valley to New Milford has more gradual curves and the lovely bluff-lined Kishwaukee Gorge (don't worry: it's not steep).

Directions: For Belvidere, take I-90 west to the Genoa Rd. exit just outside Belvidere. Turn right (north) on Genoa. Go left (west) at the first light, onto the US 20 bypass. Turn right on Appleton Rd. The launch is on the west side of the bridge just downstream of Belvidere Park.

For Cherry Valley, take I-90 west. Use the same exit above. Take US 20 west past Appleton Rd. Cross the toll-way, turn left (south) on Elgin St. Take Elgin through downtown Cherry Valley. Turn left on Walnut St., which takes you into Baumann Park.

LOWER WISCONSIN RIVER, WISCONSIN

Location: About 190 miles NW of Chicago

Length: 21 miles

Difficulty: Nice and easy, but watch for undertows. High water can pose a problem for paddlers—not to mention campers on sandbars.

Put-in: Peck's Landing just upstream of WI 23 bridge in Spring Green

Takeout: Victora Riverside Park landing on the south bank before WI 80 bridge in Muscoda

Outfitters: Northwest Passage (847-256-4409 or 800-RECREATE, www.nwpassage.com) in Wilmette runs guided weekend-long kayaking trips on the Lower Wisconsin. A slew of outfitters rent canoes and run shuttles up and down the Lower Wisconsin. River veterans include Bob's Riverside Resort in Spring Green (608-588-2826 or 888-844-2206, www.bobsriverside.com) and Rent-a-Canoe in Boscobel (608-375-5130, www.mwt.net/~ysys/white.htm).

Book: *Paddling Southern Wisconsin.*

Heads up: Camping allowed on all state-owned land, basically anywhere below the high-water mark, which mostly means sandbars (pitch away from the water's edge to avoid washouts). If a private landowner insists you're on his land, play nice and move on. Call (800) 242-1077 for water levels from Prairie du Sac dam upstream; 10,000 cfs or less should mean sandbar camping aplenty. No glass on the river (strictly enforced). FYI: Wisconsin River Race uses this stretch in mid-July.

Description: OK, so technically it could take you a tad over 3 hours to get here from the city. It's not the shortest short hop. But you'll be amply rewarded for the extra 30 minutes or so you spend with your derriere snuggled against the vinyl.

Running dam-free for 92 miles through pristine landscape, the Lower Wisconsin is glorious. More than 45 species of mammals (otter, beaver, muskrat, and even the elusive bobcat or badger) and nearly 300 species of birds call the river corridor home. Oodles of public landings mean it's easy to patch together a trip from a few hours to a whole week.

The 25-mile section between Prairie du Sac and Spring Green sees the most traffic. The section highlighted here is less traveled but still well within striking distance of the city to make for a very sweet weekend canoe-camping journey, chock-a-block with sandbars and islands begging to play host to your tent.

Though the river is popular, it's not impossible to shake the maddening crowds. A friend recently paddled from Muscoda to Boscobel over a picture-perfect summer weekend. She saw exactly three people on the river. Let's just say that such solitude makes for some nice opportunities (like achieving an all-over body tan).

Directions: Take I-90 west. Take the west exit for US 12/US 18 to loop around Madison. Follow the US 12/US 14 west beltline to US 14. Take US 14 west to Spring Green. Turn left (south) onto WI 23. You'll see the put-in landing on the left (east) before you cross the bridge. If you hit the Frank Lloyd Wright visitors center, you've gone too far.

ROCK RIVER

Location: About 100 miles W of Chicago

Length: 22 miles. Easily split into two 11-mile trips: Oregon to Grand Detour, Grand Detour to Dixon.

Difficulty: Beginners OK. Watch for wind and tricky current in spots. Broad river (at least 500 feet), nice for kayaks.

Put-in: TJ's Bait, Tackle and Canoe Rentals off First St. south of IL 64 in Oregon

Takeout: For Dixon, boat ramp just upstream of the Dixon dam on the west side of river off Fellows St. For Grand Detour, gravel landing at Grand Detour wayside (west side of river) off IL 2, across the road from the John Deere Historic Site.

Outfitter: TJ's Bait, Tackle and Canoe Rentals (815-732-4516, www.inwave.com/~canoe/) in Oregon rents canoes and runs shuttles to Castle Rock State Park and Grand Detour (but not Dixon). Owners Tim and Jan let paddlers with their own boats put in for a few bucks.

Map and book: TJ's has a basic river map; *Paddling Illinois*.

Heads up: Primitive canoe camping in Castle Rock State Park (815-732-7329); bring your own water. Call first; TJ's sometimes takes big groups there. Regular camping at Lowden State Park (815-732-6828) or White Pines State Park (815-946-3717).

Description: Fat-cat Chicagoans in the late 1800s and early 1900s built summer estates up and down the Rock River valley for good reason. Rolling hills (subtle hills, but hills nonetheless). Rock cliffs looming 50 feet above the

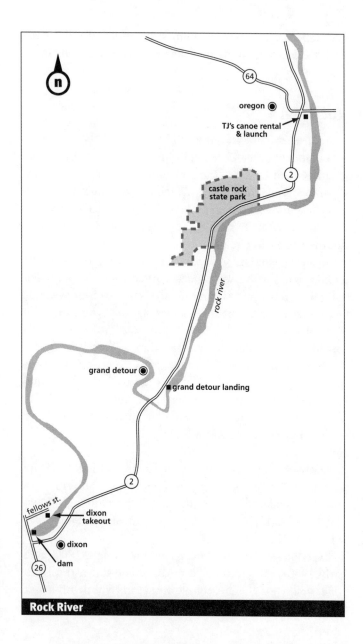

64

oregon ●

TJ's canoe rental
& launch

2

**castle rock
state park**

rock river

grand detour ●

■ grand detour landing

2

fellows st.

dixon
takeout ■

● dixon

dam

26

river, topped by white pines and oak. Oregon, Grand Detour (home to the John Deere Historic Site, paying homage to the blacksmith who revolutionized farming on the prairie—and brought us awesome lime green baseball caps), and Dixon are worth exploring. Nary a Starbucks in sight.

From Oregon to Grand Detour, the river is shallow enough in parts to keep motorboats at bay. About 6 miles downstream, pull onto the sloping bank on the right (north) at Castle Rock State Park and climb up the observation deck to take in valley views. Scan the cliffs for bald eagles. Cast for walleye, northern pike, white bass, or bullhead. Grand Detour's name becomes obvious as the river swings abruptly west and cups the town in a horseshoe bend. If you strike out for Dixon, bigger cliffs await.

Directions: Take I-290 west to I-88 west. Before Rochelle, take I-39 north. After about 7 miles, take IL 64 west into Oregon. Cross the bridge over the Rock. At the end of the bridge, turn left (south) onto First St. Go two blocks to TJ's at 305 S. First. (I-90 alternative: take I-90 west to Rockford. Pick up the US 20 bypass to I-39. Follow I-39 south to IL 64 west into Oregon. Follow directions above once in Oregon.)

MIDDLE FORK OF THE VERMILION RIVER

Location: About 165 miles S of Chicago

Length: 12 miles

Difficulty: Beginner to intermediate. Some tight turns and tree limbs to avoid. Nice and riffly, especially in spring (average gradient 5 feet per mile).

Put-in: Kinney's Ford canoe launch off County 2600 N in Middle Fork State Fish and Wildlife Area

Takeout: East side of river at Kickapoo State Park bridge off County 1880 N

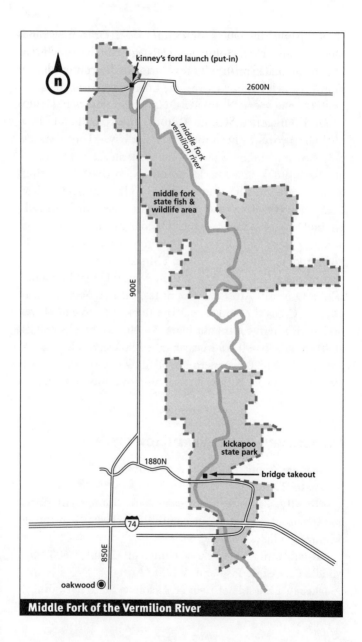

kinney's ford launch (put-in)

2600N

middle fork vermilion river

middle fork state fish & wildlife area

900E

1880N

kickapoo state park

bridge takeout

74

850E

oakwood

Middle Fork of the Vermilion River

Outfitter: Kickapoo Canoes (217-354-2060) rents canoes and kayaks and runs shuttles. Boat rentals are inside Kickapoo State Park, across the road from the takeout bridge off County 1880 N.

Maps and book: Not paddling guides, but general maps from Middle Fork State Fish and Wildlife Area (217-776-2614) and Kickapoo State Park (217-442-4915); *Paddling Illinois*.

Heads up: The only National Wild and Scenic River in Illinois.

Description: A river once threatened by strip mining and dams is now a place where the scarce river otter is being reintroduced, where the blue-breasted darter makes its only home in Illinois, and where several species of mussels attest to the river's health.

You've got boulders, bluffs, cliffs, and shale walls. Come in spring for orchids, jack-in-the-pulpit, nodding trilliums, and brisk emerald green water clear enough to see straight to the sand and gravel riverbed. Small hillside springs draw nesting swallows; hawks ride thermals overhead. Anglers casting for smallmouth, crappie, and bluegill dot the river's sand and gravel bars—nab one yourself for a nap or picnic. Heavily wooded banks lined by sugar maple, walnut, and ash are interrupted by only one building on this stretch. The hush is palpable.

Directions: Take I-57 south toward Champaign. Pick up I-74 east and follow it to Oakwood, exit 206. Turn left (north) on County 850 E, which turns into County 900 E. Follow County 900 E to County 2600 N. Turn left (west) on County 2600 N. Follow the gravel road to the launch.

middle fork of the vermilion river

DON'T LET THE 3-hour drive through nondescript flatland fields of corn and soybeans fool you. "Pondside" primitive backcountry campsites in the Middle Fork State Fish and Wildlife Area are tucked away in a thick forest of deciduous trees, a few sites banked on 100-foot cliffs. The half-dozen sites are mercifully spread out; no need to see—let alone get to know—your neighbor unless you want to.

One Labor Day weekend my husband and I showed up on a whim to camp, figuring we were likely to get shut out. Instead, we practically had the place to ourselves, snagging a site along the namesake pond. We watched a full moon rise over the hickory trees in an impossibly clear sky and fell asleep to the sounds of contented frogs and hooting great-horned owls.

Most action centers on the river (a 10-minute walk to the east), but there's also 35 miles of interconnected unnamed hiking, equestrian, cross-country skiing, and snowmobile trails radiating from the campsite. Mountain biking is prohibited in the Fish and Wildlife Area; to ride, head for the 10 miles of knobby track in Kickapoo State Park. There's a nice 8-mile out-and-back hiking/running trail there, too.

Details: Sites are first-come, first-served.

Take I-57 south toward Champaign. Pick up I-74 east and follow to Oakwood, exit 206. Turn left (north) on County 850 E, which turns into County 900 E. Follow County 900 E to County 2400 N. Check in at the park HQ and pick up your $6 camping permit. From there, it's a half-hour hike in to Pondside (ask the ranger where to park for the trailhead—some trails are closed in hunting season). If you get skunked at Pondside, head for Kickapoo State Park. Less inspired, but you can escape the RV crowd by heading for the wooded walk-in spots off the Sauk path (first-come, first-served). Middle Fork State Fish and Wildlife Area (217-776-2614) or Kickapoo State Park (217) 442-4915.

Meccas

BOUNDARY WATERS CANOE AREA WILDERNESS, MINNESOTA (CANOE)

Location: Ely, MN, is about 576 miles NW of Chicago.

Difficulty: Intermediate to advanced. More—and longer—portages mean a tougher trip. Less experienced canoeists should go with a guide.

Outfitters: A slew serve Boundary Waters and Ontario's adjoining Quetico Provincial Park, helping you with everything from ultra lightweight boats, permits, and provisions to mapping routes and organizing a fly-in to get you to remote lakes fast. Veterans include Canadian Border Outfitters (800-247-7530, www.canoecountry.com/cbo) and Canadian Waters, Inc. (800-255-2922, www.canadianwaters .com) in Ely and Gunflint Northwoods Outfitters (800-328-3325 or 218-388-2294, www.qunflintoutfitters.com) in Grand Marais.

Maps and books: Must-have bible comes in two hefty volumes, *Boundary Waters Canoe Area: The Western Region* and *The Eastern Region*; BWCAW maps—F series for overview, E series for more detail—from W. A. Fisher Company in Virginia, MN (218-741-9544, www.fishermapsmn .com).

Heads up: For permits, see www.bwcaw.org or call (800) 745-3399. Worth a visit to the Web site for Friends of the Boundary Waters Wilderness, www.friends-bwca.org.

Description: This is *the* mecca of flatwater canoeing. The stats speak for themselves: 1,500 miles of canoe routes, 1,000-plus lakes, hundreds of miles of creeks and rivers, and more than 2,000 campsites all within a 1-million-plus-acre wilderness that stretches along a 150-mile swath of boreal forest on the Minnesota-Ontario border.

Lucky for you, not much has changed in the Boundary Waters since the glaciers melted. This is where you come for real solitude, a commodity worth its weight in gold for over-stimulated urban souls. You earn that solitude by following the golden rule: the more portages you're willing to do, the fewer people you'll see. And the more likely you'll see (or hear) the moose, black bear, and timber wolf that live here.

Given the sheer magnitude of the place, making a pilgrimage here requires a good deal of planning. Permits to enter the wilderness area, part of the Superior National Forest, are highly sought after. Especially for a maiden voyage, working with an experienced outfitter can save lots of heartache and hassle.

Directions: Take I-94 west across Wisconsin to Eau Claire and US 53 north. Follow US 53 north past Duluth to MN 169. Take MN 169 north, then east, to Ely.

GARDEN PENINSULA, LAKE MICHIGAN, MICHIGAN (KAYAK)

Location: Garden Corners is about 350 miles NE of Chicago.

Difficulty: Intermediate to advanced. Less experienced kayakers should go with a guide. Fairly protected waters, several small bays and coves in Big Bay de Noc. Longer crossings for advanced, experienced paddlers only.

Outfitters: Great Northern Adventures (906-225-TOUR, www.greatnorthernadventures.com) in Marquette runs guided 2- and 3-day kayaking trips. Fred and Kelly Powers of Wilderness Trail Outfitters (906-474-6448, www .wildernesstrailoutfitters.com) in Rapid River run guided kayak trips.

Map and books: NOAA chart 14908, includes Little Summer and Summer Islands; *Guide to Sea Kayaking on Lakes Superior & Michigan; Paddling Michigan.*

Heads up: Onetime commercial fishing hotspot has Grade A perch, smallmouth, and northern pike. Great biking on the peninsula's paved rolling roads.

Description: This thin peninsula juts 20-plus miles into Lake Michigan from the U.P.'s southern shore, dubbed the "banana belt" for its temperate climes compared with the Superior shoreline a mere hour's drive north. Sparsely populated, Garden Peninsula is like a smaller, less visited, more rural cousin of Wisconsin's Door County to the south.

The peninsula's western shoreline along clear, green Big Bay de Noc sports chalky 150-foot limestone cliffs dotted with wind-carved tunnels; Burnt Bluffs by Sand Bay take on an orange hue at sunset. Kayakers pitch tents at Fayette State Park, tucked inside diminutive Snail Shell Harbor, home to a remarkably well-preserved iron-smelting town abandoned in 1891.

Other highlights include Snake Island, a gull and cormorant rookery, and secluded beach camping at Portage Bay on the peninsula's marshy pine-fringed eastern (exposed) shoreline. And more miles to log in Little Bay de Noc. . . .

Directions: Take I-94 west to I-43 north. Pick up US 41 in Green Bay and take it north through Escanaba. At Rapid River take MI 2 east to Garden Corners. From there, MI 183 runs south down the peninsula to Fayette.

APOSTLE ISLANDS NATIONAL LAKESHORE, LAKE SUPERIOR, WISCONSIN (KAYAK)

Location: Bayfield is about 460 miles N of Chicago.

Difficulty: Intermediate to advanced, depending on route and weather. Inner islands are more protected. Cold-water paddling demands wet or dry suit. Less experienced kayakers should go with a guide.

Outfitters: Trek & Trail (800-354-8735, www.trek-trail .com) and Adventures in Perspective (715-779-9503, www.livingadventure.com) in Bayfield rent kayaks to qualified kayakers, run guided trips, and offer instruction. Northwest Passage (847-256-4409 or 800-RECREATE, www.nwpassage.com) in Wilmette runs multiday guided trips.

Maps and book: Get Apostle Islands Lake Survey Charts 14973 or 14966 from the National Park Service's Apostle Islands HQ in Bayfield (715-779-3397, www.nps.gov/apis). *Guide to Sea Kayaking on Lakes Superior & Michigan.*

Heads up: Average summer winds blow 5 to 20 knots with 1- to 4-foot waves. But 40-knot winds and 6- to 12-foot seas are not uncommon.

Description: The Apostles, an archipelago of 22 (not 12) islands off Wisconsin's northernmost tip, are tailor-made for kayak exploration. Apostle Islands National Lakeshore encompasses 21 of the 22 islands (the 22d, Madeline, has some 200 residents), from tiny 3-acre Gull Island to 10,054-acre Stockton Island.

Most distances between islands are just a few miles, allowing for short crossings and reasonable shelter from nasty weather. Trips to the more exposed outer islands are more demanding. "People often underestimate what it takes to get out to some of these islands," says Mary Sweval of Trek & Trail outfitters. "This lake eats ships."

Highlights include paddling through mazes of sea caves, tubes, tunnels, and arches. Add to the mix pristine sand beaches, remnant old-growth forest, backwater lagoons, historic lightouses, abandoned fish camps, and shipwrecks—bald eagles and black bears, too. If you strike out for an outer island in non-peak season—September's a good bet—you might get your own island to call home for the night.

Directions: Follow I-94 west to I-39/US 51 north. At Iron-wood follow US 2 west past Ashland to WI 13, hugging the shoreline to Bayfield.

UPPER IOWA RIVER, IOWA

Location: Kendallville is about 300 miles NW of Chicago.

Difficulty: Intermediate. Normal conditions mean plenty of Class I riffles. Sharp turns and strainers.

Outfitter: Hruska's Canoe Livery in Kendallville (563-547-4566, www.bluffcountry.com/hruska's.htm) runs shuttles and rents single and tandem kayaks as well as canoes.

Map and book: Hruska's has a basic river map. *A Guide to the Upper Iowa River.*

Description: Granted, Iowa isn't the first state that comes to mind for paddling. But tucked into the state's northeastern corner is a gem. You get 110 canoeable miles on the Upper Iowa, from Lime Springs to the Mississippi.

Vic Hurtowy of Chicagoland Canoe Base swears that canoe-camping here made him think of a Colorado sojourn along the Poudre. "It was that good. I felt like I was out West but I was smack in Iowa."

From Lime Springs to Decorah, the river meanders 52 miles through a landscape that morphs from gently rolling prairie to vertical limestone palisades rising 100 feet up from the water's edge. Look for nesting eagles in the wooded bluffs jammed with fir, maple, walnut, and ash. Trout streams abound; the river is prime bass water. Canoe-camping on sandbars and riverbanks round out the idyll. For maximum peace, come before or after the Memorial Day-to- Labor Day throng. Fall waters are sometimes low.

Directions: Take I-90 west to Madison. Pick up US 18 and drive west across the Mississippi (it eventually becomes US 18/52). Follow US 52 west and north to Decorah. About 14 miles north of Decorah you'll hit County A18. Follow County A18 west about 7 miles to the Kendallville stop sign. For Hruska's, turn left, cross the river, and you'll hit the outfitter in a block or so.

PICTURED ROCKS NATIONAL LAKESHORE, LAKE SUPERIOR, MICHIGAN (KAYAK)

Location: Munising is about 390 miles N of Chicago.

Difficulty: Intermediate to advanced, depending on conditions. Less experienced kayakers should go with a guide. Cold-water paddling.

Outfitter: Carl Hansen of Northern Waters Adventures (906-387-2323, www.northernwaters.com) in Munising is a font of local knowledge. Kayak rental to qualified paddlers, paddling school, and guided day- to weeklong kayak trips in Pictured Rocks and Grand Island.

Map and book: Pick up "The Big Map," 46086-C5-PF-062, with topo lines and other good stuff from the National Park Service (Pictured Rocks National Lakeshore in Munising; 906-387-3700, www.nps.qov/piro). *Guide to Sea Kayaking on Lakes Superior & Michigan.*

Heads up: Momma Superior stays cold, even in late summer. Wind and waves. Grand Island offers some shelter in parts, but a north or northwest wind can trigger big seas in a hurry. Sheer cliff walls make for scarce landings.

Description: If you hate kayaking under stone arches, alongside 200-foot cliffs, and past waterfalls, don't come here. Established in 1966 as the first national lakeshore, Pictured Rocks gets its name from the amazing hues of ochre and green imbedded in the mineral-streaked cliffs that run along about half of the lakeshore's 40-mile length.

Cliffs dominate the west part of the lakeshore, dune bluffs and sand beaches the east section. Paddle from Beaver Lake—one of many inland lakes scattered throughout the park's 72,000 acres—through Beaver Creek and out onto Momma Superior.

A string of kayak-accessible campsites make multiday trips along the shore possible, but beware stiff competition with backpackers. July and August account for half the annual visitation to the park; reserve early or go on a guided trip. The town of Grand Marais, at the eastern end of the park, hosts the Great Lakes Sea Kayaking Symposium every summer.

Directions: Take I-94 west to I-43 north. Pick up US 41 in Green Bay and take it north through Escanaba. Around Trenary take MI 67 north to MI 94 in Chatham. Follow MI 94 east to the turnoff for Munising, north on MI 28.

Open-Pool Practice

O N THE CITY'S northwest side, Northeastern Illinois University at 5500 N. St. Louis Ave. holds open-pool sessions for paddlers to practice and play over the colder months. They've got a limited number of first-come, first-served boats for use, or bring your own (make sure it's clean.) Wednesdays 7–9 P.M., mid-November to mid-April, $7 a night. Talk to Bill Quinn for details (773-442-5565, www.neiu.edu). For pool time south of downtown, Kayak Chicago (773-209-1800, www.kayakchicago.com) runs sessions Wednesdays 7–9:30 P.M. for $10 a pop at University of Illinois-Chicago pool, 901 W. Roosevelt Rd. (just west of Halsted). Bring your own boat or call first to check boat and gear availability for rent.

Boat Storage

ONE MORE INCENTIVE to join Lincoln Park Boat Club (773-549-BOAT, www.lpbc.net), which offers members a shot at limited storage spots. Other options: Chicago Park District (312-742-5369) in 2001 charged $100 to store a canoe or kayak on outdoor racks at Montrose Ave. and 63d St. Beaches, Memorial Day to Labor Day only. Dave Olson at Kayak Chicago (773-209-1800, www.kayakchicago.com) hopes to offer year-round indoor storage soon at Montrose.

Where to Connect

The Basics

Rule of thumb: know your skills before you plan an excursion. If you're new to the sport, consider a guided paddle first. Friends of the Chicago River and Wateriders run guided trips on the Chicago River (see below). Plenty of paddling clubs offer members informal instruction through clinics and group trips. See below for more formal instructional options.

- Northwest Passage (847-256-4409 or 800-RECREATE, www.nwpassage.com) in Wilmette teaches kayak basics with evening paddles on Lake Michigan. Free 1-day sea kayak "extravaganza" with basic instruction once or twice a year. Instruction for all levels (in Wilmette and Chicago), including basic kayak navigation and rescue-and-roll pool clinics in fall and winter.

- Lincoln Park Boat Club (773-549-BOAT, www.lpbc.net) offers a full range of paddling classes, from a 4-hour introductory session to American Canoe Association instructor certification. Clinics include advanced rescue and cold-water paddling.

- Kayak Chicago (773-209-1800, www.kayakchicago.com) offers beginner to advanced instruction. Summer classes at Montrose Beach. Cold-weather pool classes at University of Illinois-Chicago pool. Private instruction and race training.

- Chicago Whitewater Association runs winter pool classes, mid-October to mid-March. Great way to get fundamentals like Eskimo roll, even if whitewater boating's not your gig. City classes usually at New City YMCA (1515 N. Halsted at North Ave., 312-266-1242). Suburban locations, too. See www.northstarnet.org/eakhome/cwa/ or call Sigrid Pilgrim at (847) 328-0145.

Clubs and Organizations

- Lincoln Park Boat Club (773-549-BOAT, www.lpbc.net) is on the west side of the Lincoln Park Lagoon, south of Fullerton Ave. (see *City Treasure*, page 51).

- Chicago River Rowing and Paddling Center (312-616-0056, www.chicagorowing.org) is focused on rowing but has a growing paddling community. Members get boat storage and access to the Chicago River from downtown boathouse (a former Coast Guard station) at the mouth of the river just south of Navy Pier.

- Chicago Area Sea Kayakers Association (www.caska.org) is a group of 200-plus sea kayak owners with regular Chicago lakefront paddles (full-moon trips in summer) and weekend overnights around the Midwest.

- Friends of the Chicago River (312-939-0490, www.chicagoriver.org) runs a host of Chicago River paddling, walking, and scouting trips. Sponsors annual river cleanup and recruits adults and teens for intensive 4-month training to become river guides. See Web site for a list of "unofficial" Chicago River access points.

- Illinois Paddling Council (www.illinoispaddling.org) works to conserve and restore the state's rivers and lakes and lobbies to improve paddlers' access. Promotes paddling safety and education and sanctions races. For $15 (let's see, that's maybe four lattes?) members help make paddlers' voices heard by Land o' Lincoln powers that be.

- Prairie State Canoeists (www.psc.ctsserver.com) is one of the state's largest canoe/kayak clubs, running 100-plus paddling trips a year, most of them within 100 miles of Chicago.

- Lake Michigan Federation (312-939-0838, www.lakemichigan .org) works to restore fish and wildlife habitat, conserve land and water, eliminate toxins in the lake's watershed, expand the Lake Michigan Water Trail, and minimize beach closures caused by microbial contamination.

- Badger State Boating Society (www.bsbs.org), otherwise known as BS-squared, runs flatwater and whitewater trips and clinics. Many members hail from southeastern Wisconsin.

- Hoosier Canoe Club (www.hoosiercanoeclub.org) for Indiana waters.

Shops and Outfitters
*For City Limits canoe or kayak rentals

- *Chicagoland Canoe Base (4019 N. Narragansett Ave., just north of Irving Park Rd., 773-777-1489, www .chicagolandcanoebase.com) is the city's most comprehensive one-stop-shop for canoes, kayaks, and related gear—including sail rigs and several models of folding kayaks. Wide selection of books and maps. Used boats on occasion. Owner Ralph Frese and manager Vic Hurtowy know a ton about local and regional waters. Canoe and kayak rental.

- *Chicago River Canoe & Kayak (773-32-KAYAK, www.chicagoriverpaddle.com) rents canoes and kayaks Thursdays through Sundays in the warm weather months at Clark Park, 3400 N. Rockwell St., behind Lane Tech

High School. Stay tuned: owner Ryan Chew plans to extend his season and hours and may open more riverside sites.

- *Eastern Mountain Sports (1000 W. North Ave., 312-337-7750, www.ems.com) rents and sells kayaks and gear. Look for expanded paddling outreach programs here.

- *Chicago Park District rents kayaks Memorial Day through Labor Day at Montrose Ave. (312-742-0600) and 63d Street (312-745-1905) Beaches.

- Wateriders (312-953-9287, www.wateriders.com) runs architectural and other guided downtown kayak trips on the Chicago River from AAA Boatyard at 1111 N. Elston Ave., just south of Division St.

- Great Lakes Outfitters at the Great Lakes Naval Training Center (847-688-6978 or 847-688-5417, www.Ntcmwr.com /recreation/greatlakeout/index.html) in North Chicago rents a slew of watercraft, including canoes and kayaks, at very reasonable rates with lake access from the marina. Security concerns in the aftermath of the 9/11/01 terrorist attacks made rentals off limits to civilians, but that policy could change.

- Moosejaw (1445 W. Webster Place at Clybourn Ave., 773-529-1111, www.moosejawonline.com) sells a full range of kayaks and related gear. Demos most weekends.

- Rutabaga Paddlesport Shop (800-I-PADDLE or 608-223-9300, www.paddlers.com) in Madison, WI, is billed as the Midwest's largest canoe and kayak shop and draws Chicago paddlers on pilgrimages. Passionate and knowledgeable staff (seek out Garrett Walters). Good selection of used boats. Store policy makes it easy to trade up. Check online schedule of free paddling-related talks and local paddles. Full slate of kayak instruction (weekend clinics) and skills certification.

- Offshore (River Tree Court mall on Milwaukee Ave./IL 60,

847-362-4880, www.offshore-chicago.com) in Vernon Hills rents and sells canoes, kayaks, and accessories.

- REI (8225 Golf Rd. in Niles, 847-470-9090, and 17 W. 160 22d St. in Oakbrook Terrace, 708-574-7700; www.rei.com) sells canoes, kayaks, and gear. Canoe rental at Oakbrook Terrace.

- Galyans (601 N. Martingale Rd. in Schaumburg, 847-995-0200, and 810 E. Butterfield Rd. in Lombard, 630-317-0200; www.qalyans.com) sells canoes, kayaks, and gear.

Events

- Paddling in the Park (www.paddlinginthepark.com) is a 2-day canoe and kayak festival in late July at the Twin Lakes Recreation Area in Palatine. Affordable clinics in solo and tandem canoe, river and coastal kayaking, canoe sailing, and whitewater paddling. Meet vendors, test-drive new boats, and network with other paddlers.

- Chicago River Flatwater Classic is a 7-mile race in late September for all skill levels down Chicago's namesake river from Clark Park to Ping Tom Memorial Park in Chinatown. Contact Friends of the Chicago River.

- The Des Plaines Canoe Marathon (www.members .dencity.com/q-jaros/desplaines/) celebrated its 45th year in 2002. The May canoe/kayak race runs 19.5 miles from Libertyville to Mount Prospect.

- Canoecopia is an enormous 3-day canoe and kayak expo in March in Madison, WI. Dizzying array of cutting-edge boats. Exhibitors include outfitters, outdoor adventure camps, nature centers, and other paddling-related folk. Speaker topics have ranged from history of wooden canoes to kayaking Aleutian islands. Contact Rutabaga Paddlesport Shop.

- Lincoln Park Boat Club in 2001 started what it hopes will

be an annual Lake Michigan kayak race and gear swap in August.

- New Year's Day paddle on North Branch of the Chicago River has been known to draw up to 200 snowproof souls, many in elaborately bedecked boats. Contact Vic Hurtowy at Chicagoland Canoe Base.

Books

- Beymer, Robert. *Boundary Waters Canoe Area: The Western Region* and *Boundary Waters Canoe Area: The Eastern Region*. Berkeley, CA: Wilderness Press, 2000.

- Hill, Libby. *The Chicago River: A Natural and Unnatural History*. Chicago, IL: Lake Claremont Press, 2000. Not a paddling guide but a highly readable history of Chicago's namesake river.

- Hillstrom, Kevin, and Laurie Collier Hillstrom. *Paddling Michigan*. Guilford, CT: Globe Pequot Press/Falcon Books, 2001.

- Knudson, George E. *A Guide to the Upper Iowa River*. Decorah, IA: Luther College Press, 1971.

- Newman, Bill, Sarah Ohmann, and Don Dimond. *Guide to Sea Kayaking on Lakes Superior & Michigan: The Best Day Trips and Tours*. Guilford, CT: Globe Pequot Press, 1999.

- Solzman, David M. *The Chicago River. An Illustrated History and Guide to the River and Its Waterways*. Chicago, IL: Wild Onion Books, an imprint of Loyola Press, 1998. A few routes, but mostly great history, maps, and photos.

- Svob, Mike. *Paddling Illinois*. Black Earth, WI: Trails Books, 2000.

  ———. *Paddling Southern Wisconsin*. Black Earth, WI: Trails Books, 2001.

- Vierling, Philip E. *Illinois Country Landings*. Series of self-published guides done by a local canoeist. Extremely detailed and heavy on geology. Some are out of date but worth checking out at Chicagoland Canoe Base. Vierling covers the DuPage, Kishwaukee, Des Plaines, Fox, Mazon, Vermilion, and Little Vermilion Rivers.

Link

http://pages.ripco.net/~jwn/ for Chicago area paddling/fishing guide.

Sailing

outsidepix.com

IN THE LATE 19th century, tall-ship traffic toting grain, iron ore, and lumber made Chicago one of the busiest sailing ports in the Western World, along with New York, London, and Hamburg. Today Chicago boasts the nation's largest recreational harbor system with some 5,000 boats at the southern end of Lake Michigan's 307-mile-long playground, 118 miles across at its widest point.

The good news is you don't need to be a yacht-owning, champagne-sipping Thurston Howell to sail here. There are plenty of places to learn how to sail or build on your skills, go on a group sail, race, or rent and captain a boat. See *Where to Connect*, page 97, for some affordable alternatives to having your own boat.

79

Sailing

Sailing Overview

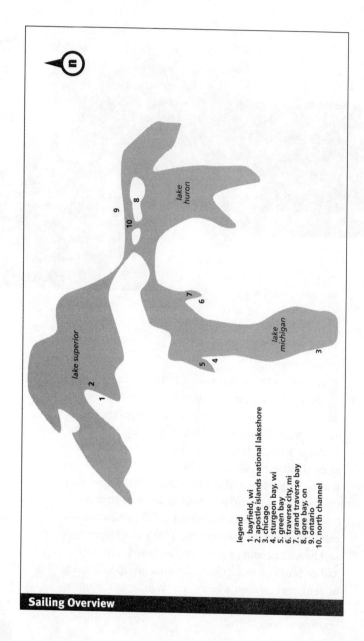

lake superior

lake huron

lake michigan

legend
1. bayfield, wi
2. apostle islands national lakeshore
3. chicago
4. sturgeon bay, wi
5. green bay
6. traverse city, mi
7. grand traverse bay
8. gore bay, on
9. ontario
10. north channel

A strong cadre of yacht clubs supports a robust racing scene, from Penguin dinghies skimming the Skokie Lagoons to high-performance 45-footers heeling along Lake Michigan's horizon. Summer sees several major regattas. Wednesday nights bring casual beer-can races, Saturdays more serious fare. And Chicago marks the start of the world's longest freshwater race, the storied Chicago-to-Mackinac, first run in 1898.

Summer sailing generally brings light winds, though Lake Michigan's notoriously unpredictable weather can always pose a challenge (see *Brats*, page 90). Most day-sailing takes place within the cityscape: remember, on average you're not going to cover more than 5 or 6 miles an hour. Don't expect to get to a secluded wilderness anchorage within a typical weekend sail from Chicago. Common weekend picks include the sand-dune-swept shorelines around Michigan City, IN, to the southeast, or north to Illinois Beach State Park in Zion.

As Grant Crowley of Crowley's Yacht Yard explains, "the water itself—and escaping the urban stress—is the destination here in Chicago."

But prime freshwater cruising grounds are yours if you expend the effort to move north up the lake, away from the urban edge. Charter a boat from Traverse City, MI, and explore wilderness areas like the Manitou Islands. Or make a pilgrimage to the place that turns sailors all dewy-eyed, Lake Huron's North Channel, reverently referred to as one of the top cruising grounds anywhere on the globe. For the record, all cruising hot spots in this chapter make for ideal sea kayaking territory, too, with local outfitters catering to both the sail and paddle crowd.

Beer-Can Racing

A T 5:15 ON a mid-August Wednesday evening, I've become part of a steady trickle of bodies bearing coolers moving ever east from Loop office towers to slips up and down the city harbors. From May to October, Wednesday night means beer-can-racing night. (The hump day leaves enough time for racers to recuperate from and prepare for more serious weekend regattas.)

On a good night, hundreds of sails—racers and cruisers alike—fill the horizon. I'm on Bob Tollefson's *Windancer* at Columbia Yacht Club. My job, as a racing newbie, is to serve as "rail meat," a mass of cells whose sole purpose is to ride the Mumm 30's rail and provide counterbalance. I also get to perfect the art of bucket-peeing; the guys just go over the rail.

Once a fast-moving summer lightning storm tumbles through, we're off on a 4-mile course. Wind direction dictates the start mark, a few miles offshore. After a slow start for the first buoy, we pin *Nightmare*, a 70-footer that looks to be carrying an entire neighborhood block party, but they manage to sneak by. Shouting, most of it good natured, commences on both boats; *Windancer*'s crew nimbly throws up the spinnaker to loop the 4-mile crib (named for pre-lakefront landfill times when the water intake structure was, in fact, 4 miles from where the shoreline used to be, at Michigan Ave.).

As the boat picks up speed and kicks onto a sharp heel,

we're bent over the rail reaching for the water, cool chop spray-
ing my Teva-clad feet. I feel like we're flying, carving a
southerly path through the water; it turns out we're only going
about 8 mph. (By way of comparison, *Windancer* has been
known to hit 19.7 knots, about 23 mph, without a spinnaker.)

About an hour and a half later, we hit the final mark and it's
over. Beers are ceremonially cracked. The sky has gone purple
and the city lights glow. We cruise around as the sonic booms
from Navy Pier's fireworks show bounce off the skyscraper fronts.
Glittering sediment hangs in the air, casting a pearl-like glow on
the sails making their way to the harbors for post-race partying.

"This is why I'm out here," says Tollefson, who's raced 35
years on the Great Lakes and as far away as Russia. "It's you,
the water, the wind, and the boat—that's all you think about. I
can't think of a better way to spend a summer night in the city.
It's pure escape."

I'll second that.

Heads up: if you don't know someone who knows someone
who knows someone who owns a boat that you can tag along
with for a beer-can race, you can race (and get some training)
on a J30 for $75 Wednesday nights with Chicago Sailing Club at
Belmont Harbor (773-871-SAIL, www.chicagosailingclub.com).
No prior racing experience required. Other racing options
through Chicago Park District, Sail Chicago, and Chicago Sailing Club (see *Where to Connect*).

If you're bold, head down to the lakefront harbors. Some
boat owners are kind enough to pick up eager would-be free-
lance racers—even neophytes can be of use as rail meat. Toting
a cold six-pack can't hurt your chances. If you're serious about
big-boat racing, see the Web sites for Crowley's Yacht Yard,
MORF (Midwest Offshore Racing Fleet), and many of the yacht
clubs for online bulletin boards listing crew seeking boats and
boats seeking crew. Details in *Where to Connect*.

CHICAGO LAKEFRONT

Location: Nine city harbors run from 4400 N to 9500 S (public rentals in summer from Belmont Harbor, 3200 N; Montrose Ave. Beach, 4400 N; and 63d St. Beach, 6300 S).

Outfitters: Chicago Sailing Club (773-871-SAIL, www .chicagosailingclub.com) at Belmont Harbor rents keelboats to qualified sailors and offers captained J22 or J30 charters by the hour, plus day and evening group sails and Wednesday and Saturday night cruises on J30s to Navy Pier fireworks in summer. From Memorial Day to Labor Day, Chicago Park District (312-747-2474) rents Barnett 14s, Hobie 16s, Hobie 18s, and trimarans at reasonable rates to qualified sailors at Montrose (312-742-0600) and 63d St. (312-745-1905) Beaches. See *The Basics*, page 97, for details on affordable access to a fleet through Sail Chicago, a nonprofit volunteer-run club.

Map and Book: NOAA chart 14927 for Chicago lakefront; NOAA 14926 small-craft book for Chicago and Lake Michigan southern shore.

Description: Lake Michigan's propensity for mood-disorder weather aside, Chicago boasts prime sailing grounds. Happily for greener sailors, other than a few shoal areas clearly marked on nautical charts, once you get a half mile or so offshore you generally don't have to sweat water depth, rocks, or other subterranean obstacles that make for tricky navigation elsewhere. Summer brings light winds and freshwater breezes (lightning storms, too); spring and fall more powerful winds prevail.

Rudder in hand, you can easily spend an entire day cruising past the city's 29 miles of virtually unbroken lakefront parkland and beach. Cast for summer smallmouth bass and perch. Watch small planes take off and land at Meigs Field just south of the Museum Campus. Sail to dockside sustenance at Jackson Harbor Grill (killer blackened salmon on sourdough). Cruise north to ogle lakefront mansions and the Bahai Temple in Wilmette. Or follow the advice of Dan Bochnovic, manager at Crowley's Yacht Yard, and head for "the playpen," the glassy protected water hemmed in by the breakwater between Oak St. Beach and the water filtration plant just north of Navy Pier. Drop anchor, or raft up with other boats, and swim while the gulls cry overhead.

For maximum quiet, head a few miles offshore, zone out as the cityscape recedes, and tune into the wind and open water.

Directions: For Belmont Harbor, exit Lake Shore Dr. at Irving Park Rd. Go east on Irving Park, under the bridge, and turn right onto the park road by the golf course. Follow the park road south past the totem pole to the harbor parking. Chicago Sailing Club is at B dock, just south of the harbormaster building. By transit, take the Red Line L to the Belmont Ave. stop. Take the 77 bus or walk about 1 mile east along Belmont, under Lake Shore Dr. onto the lakefront path, and to the harbor's north end.

For Montrose Ave. Beach, exit Lake Shore Dr. at Montrose Ave. Take Montrose east to the parking lot closest to the beach house. By transit, take the Red Line L to the Wilson Ave. stop. It's a 1-mile-plus walk: east on Wilson to N. Marine Dr., south to Montrose, east to the beach. Or take the 78 bus to Marine and Montrose.

For 63d St. Beach, take Lake Shore Dr. south to 63d St. Turn east at the light into the lot. By transit, take the Green Line L to E. 63d St. Take the 63 bus east to the beach (not recommended at night).

Of course, it's an easy bike ride along the Lakefront Trail to all harbors, too.

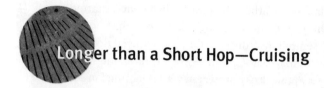

Longer than a Short Hop—Cruising

Summer's prime-time freshwater cruising, with temperatures in the 80s and light to moderate winds. Problem is, that's also when hoards of winter-ravaged Midwesterners emerge from hibernation and head for the water. Things tend to get lonelier after Labor Day. September can be a great sailing month, with thinner crowds, stronger winds, and warm waters heated by a summer's worth of sunny days (not to mention possible discounts on bareboat charters). The trade-off? A higher risk of storms or fog.

When considering a multiday sail, keep an open mind. Weather any time of year can play havoc with the best-laid plans. The spots that follow have enough options for everything from a day-sail to a weeklong journey or more. And each has outfitters for a bareboat or captained charter. As of this writing, a bareboat charter on a 27- to 46-foot boat ran from $1,100 to $3,900 a week. Add about $200 a day for a captain.

Sailing times are very rough estimates; how much ground you cover varies greatly depending on wind and weather conditions. That said, sail on. And partake of one of the world's oldest adventure sports.

Cruising Life

T HE GREAT LAKES Cruising Club log book is the cruising bible of the inland seas. Weighing in at 25 pounds, doled out in four thick-as-Yellow-Pages volumes, the guide covers every harbor (1,000-plus) in the Lakes' nearly 11,000 miles of shoreline.

The club's 2,400 members regularly update the book (particularly helpful given the Lakes' changing water levels), dishing out first hand navigational knowledge on ports, gunkholes, and other anchorages. The Chicago-based club was organized in 1934 because many areas of the Lakes—including the North Channel and Georgian Bay—were then uncharted by government agencies.

Since then, club members have explored all of the Lakes and their connecting tributaries, including the Mississippi, the Erie Canal, the Trent-Severn Waterway, the Rideau Canal, and the St. Lawrence River. Die-hard cruisers—many of whom spend entire summers on their boats—meet up with like-minded adventurers at the club's annual July rendezvous in metro-area spots such as Duluth, MN, or remote wilderness anchorages like Dead-End Bay in the North Channel. Nice life if you can get it. Great Lakes Cruising Club: (312) 372-2344 or www.glcclub.com.

The Mac and the Goats

CHICAGO MARKS THE starting point for the annual Race to Mackinac, the world's longest freshwater race. Every July some 300 boats leave Chicago Yacht Club's dock to haul 333 miles up the length of Lake Michigan to Michigan's Mackinac Island, a storybook 2,000-acre carless island flush with whitewashed inns and fudge shops just over the Straits of Mackinac on Lake Huron. (The 290-mile Port Huron-to-Mackinac race also finishes on the island, taking turns with Chicago to run either the second or third week in July.)

Run since 1898—minus a few years during World Wars I and II—the race was originally conceived as a sporting way to get Chicago yachts up north in a hurry to escape the city heat and hit much-loved summer cruising grounds like the North Channel (see page 94).

Most sailors finish after 2 or 3 days and nights of nonstop sailing. Chicago's *Pied Piper*, a Santa Cruz 70, designed to race in the biennial Los Angeles-to-Honolulu Transpac, set the record to date in 1987: 25 hours, 50 minutes, 44 seconds. (*Pied Piper*'s victory smashed a 76-year-old record set by a 100-foot schooner in 80-mph winds.)

Some ocean sailors view lake races like the Mac with skepticism—most famously Ted Turner, who apparently got a chuckle out of talk about Lake Michigan's temper tantrums the night before the 1970 race. That was the year 88 of 167 boats never made it to the finish line as winds of 50-plus knots gusted over the lake's 300-mile fetch for the better part of 12 hours, breaking masts, ripping sails, and whipping up 13-foot waves. Turner's *American Eagle* finished second. Chastened by the battering, Turner reportedly said "I hereby publicly retract anything and everything I have ever said about inland racing."

Saltwater snobbery aside, the storied race and its fickle weather have loyal fans. Members of the Island Goats Sailing Society are inducted after racing the Mac 25 times or more. Chicago Goat Deane Tank, Sr., 68, hasn't missed a Mac in 41 years. Tank, who penned a history of the race on its 100th anniversary, says the name was inspired by the way sailors smelled after 3 days on the water. Like plenty of Island Goats, Tank has done his fair share of ocean racing, but he relishes the challenges of the freshwater giant.

"It's really one of the world's great sailing traditions," Tank says. "And I'm afraid I'm afflicted for life."

LAKE MICHIGAN, MICHIGAN'S LOWER PENINSULA

Location: Traverse City, MI, is about 315 miles N of Chicago.

Outfitters: Bay Breeze Yacht Charters (616-941-0535 or 877-941-0535, www.bbyc.com) in Traverse City has bareboats from 27 to 44 feet. ASA-accredited sail school. Daysailing $375 and up depending on boat size. Half-day sails, with captain only, from $250. Modern Skate and Surf (231-933-7873), a few miles east of Bay Breeze, rents kayaks.

Events and festivals: Traverse City has several regattas throughout the summer, including the Hound Dog in late June. Charlevoix's Labor Day Red Fox Regatta is a biggie.

Book: *Lake Michigan: Ports O' Call.*

Heads up: Sailing weekdays avoids the tourist crush. Beware Traverse City cherry festival, when half a million visitors descend on a town of 15,000 for 2 weeks after the Fourth of July. Arrive on Mackinac Island early in the day for first-come, first-served mooring during July races that end there from Chicago and Port Huron.

Description: Strike out from Traverse City, nestled into the southernmost end of Grand Traverse Bay. If you're short on time, stick to cruising the nearly 40-mile-long maple-and-beech-fringed bay. Drop anchor at Old Mission Harbor on the 15-mile-long peninsula, dotted with vineyards and orchards, dividing the bay's lower section. Or head for quaint Charlevoix, an 8- or 9-hour sail from Traverse City; check out Mount McSauba Beach and the 8-mile network of woodland trails behind the dunes.

You'll want more than a long weekend to reach and explore the rugged Manitou Islands off Leland, a roughly 16-hour sail along a forested and sugary sand shoreline from Traverse City—including a crossing of shipwreck-strewn Manitou Passage. Part of Sleeping Bear Dunes National Lakeshore, the Manitou have miles of hiking trails, old-growth cedar stands, quiet beaches, lighthouses, and dune bluffs (see "Hiking & Backpacking," page 355).

Spend the night nestled in the harbor on lobster-claw-shaped South Manitou—the only natural deep-water harbor on the east side of Lake Michigan between Chicago and the Straits of Mackinac. Take in moonlit views of 400-foot-high dunes on the mainland's Pyramid Point. Longer trips can add Beaver Island, about 30 miles off Northport; if you're up to it, brave the shoals to bird on nearby High and Garden Islands. Or cruise to carless Mackinac Island (great bike riding, horseback riding, and fudge eating), straddling the state's upper and lower peninsulas. Maybe you'll make it for the Fourth of July stone-skipping contest.

Directions: Take I-94 east to Benton Harbor. Take I-196 north to Grand Rapids. At Grand Rapids, take US 131 north toward Cadillac. Take M 115 toward Frankfort to MI 37 N. MI 37 dead-ends at Grand Traverse Bay. Go left (west) on Grandview Parkway for about 1 mile to reach the Bay Breeze marina.

Brats

AILING BACK FROM the Chicago-to-Mackinac race in 1998, Eric Johnson was heading for Sheboygan, WI, to partake of the Rust Belt city's famed bratwurst. "We were within sight of Sheboygan in sunshine," Johnson says. "And 30 seconds later, that sun was gone."

The sky went black. The wind picked up and a huge gust socked the 32-foot racer, hurling it sideways into the water, taking the spinnaker along with it. Pelted by rain in 30-mph winds and 6-foot seas, Johnson and the rest of the crew managed eventually to right the boat and haul in the massive soaked sail.

"We were just trying to control the boat after we got it upright, trying to keep it pointed into the wind, but we were spinning in circles. Next thing we knew, the sky cleared, the sun came out. We saw port and went into it. We really didn't know where we were yet. We come up to the gas dock and ask the attendant, this high-school girl, 'So where do you go to get brats in this town?' She looks at us kind of funny and says, 'We go to Sheboygan.' "

Turns out the storm had blown them 45 miles off course down the shore to Port Washington. They never did get the brats.

GREEN BAY, WISCONSIN'S DOOR PENINSULA

Location: Sturgeon Bay, WI, is about 230 miles N of Chicago.

Outfitters: Sailboats Inc. (800-826-7010, www.sailboats-inc .com) has 30- to 36-foot bareboats, day-sailing $375 and up. Classic Yachts of Door County (920-746-1150, www .classicyachts.com) has 25- to 40-foot bareboats, one 27-footer for day-sailing, $175. Snug Harbor Inn and Boat Rental (920-743-2337 or 800-231-5767, www.snugharborinn .com) rents sailboats and pontoons. Bay Shore Outdoor Store (920-854-7598, www.kayakdoorcounty.com) in Sister Bay rents 15-foot sailboats from South Shore Pier through Ephraim Sailing Center in Ephraim (920-854-4336) and 14-footers at Nicolet Beach in Peninsula State Park (920-854-9220) near Fish Creek in 2-hour blocks. Rentals are about a half-hour drive north of Sturgeon Bay. Sailing lessons and kayak rental.

Events and festivals: Sturgeon Bay hosts the Door County Maritime Festival the first weekend of August with an antique boat show, regatta, and Venetian boat parade. Hook Race from Racine to Sturgeon Bay in late July.

Maps and book: NOAA chart 14902 for overview; 14909

for upper Green Bay; 14910 for lower bay including Sturgeon Bay. *Lake Michigan: Ports O' Call.*

Heads up: Door County's abuzz with festivals (and visitors) virtually year-round.

Description: Where Lake Michigan roils with fog and waves, Green Bay (truly emerald green) tends to stay sedate in the lee of the Door Peninsula's limestone windblock, making the bay side favored cruising grounds. But the bay's placid surface can be deceiving; Green Bay is littered with the corpses of boats confounded by rocky shoals and narrow passages. Be sure your chart-reading skills are up to snuff.

The peninsula's got 425 miles of shoreline to explore, with bays backed by rocky beaches, craggy bluffs, orchards, and bucolic meadows. This is serious fishing territory: smallmouth, walleye, and northern pike abound bayside. Chicagoans make the trip for long-weekend sails, poking in and out of village harbors along the bay shore. Chambers Island, about 5 miles from Fish Creek, and Horseshoe Island off the northern tip of Peninsula State Park offer rare sheltered anchorages.

Longer trips can be had to weather-beaten Washington Island, a onetime Icelandic settlement 70 miles north of Sturgeon Bay (great road biking). Dinghy over to 775-acre Rock Island State Park to hike and explore the massive limestone Viking Hall and boathouse (remote beach camping, too). Skilled sailors can take on tricky currents for a northern crossing to Michigan's Garden Peninsula (see "Sea Kayaking & Canoeing," page 66).

Directions: Take I-94 west to Milwaukee. Take I-43 north to Green Bay. From Green Bay, take WI 57 north to Sturgeon Bay. Once you hit town, take Business 42/57 about 1 mile to the waterfront and Quarter Deck Marina for Sailboats Inc. Go past Quarter Deck Marina for Classic Yachts in Harbor Club Marina, adjacent to the Michigan St. Bridge.

Meccas

APOSTLE ISLANDS NATIONAL LAKESHORE, LAKE SUPERIOR, WISCONSIN

Location: Bayfield is about 460 miles N of Chicago.

Outfitters: Sailboats Inc. (800-826-7010, www.sailboats -inc.com) has 30- to 36-foot bareboats, 2-day minimum. Superior Charters Inc. (800-772-5124 or 715-779-5124, www.superiorcharters.com) has 27- to 46-foot bareboats, 2-day minimum, and instruction. Captain Paul Bratti runs instructional half-day, full-day, and overnight sails on his 34-footer *Sarah's Joy* (888-272-4548 or 715-779-5468, www .animaashi.com). Check with Bayfield tourism office (800-447-4094) for a list of boats available for day-sailing. See "Sea Kayaking & Canoeing," page 68, for kayak out-fitters.

Events and festivals: Regatta-filled race week first week in July, kicked off by a 66-mile circumnavigation of the Apostles.

Maps and book: NOAA 14973 for Apostles only, 14966 for overview. *Superior Way: A Cruising Guide to Lake Superior.*

Heads up: Mega crowds in Bayfield for annual apple fes-tival the first weekend in October. Powerful nor'easter can wipe out boating for days at a stretch.

Description: Bayfield's home to the Great Lakes' largest bareboat charter fleet for good reason: the Apostles offer I-thought-I-saw-it-in-a-dream island hopping. Day-sailing to the closer-in of Apostle Islands National Lakeshore's 21 islands is eminently doable, but you'll want a week to explore the outer islands.

Though Lake Superior's not to be trifled with—it's dang cold, and fog's possible even in prime summer months—the water's deep even between most islands, making navigation more straightforward than in Green Bay. You've got 100 or so anchorages to choose from (including a couple dozen gems); Quarry Bay off Stockton Island offers good protection. The islands' exposed northern faces tend to be rock, the southern ends fine-sand beaches wrought from years of pounding on the native sandstone.

When it's calm, head for the north end of Devils Island; dinghy into sea caves and listen for the rhythmic booms of subterranean blowholes and chasms. Tour boats and hundreds of sailboats (and kayakers) in glorious summer. For solitude, come in late September for peak maple, hemlock, and birch colors after inland woods have already flamed out (just be prepared for greater fog risk and temps that may not climb past 50°).

Directions: Take I-90 west to Madison, where it becomes I-90/I-94. Take US 51 north through Wausau and on to the Michigan-Wisconsin border. Just before Ironwood, MI, take US 2 west through Ashland to WI 13 north. Take WI 13 along the lakeshore to Bayfield. Superior Charters is 2 miles south of Bayfield off WI 13 on Port Superior Rd. Sailboats Inc. is on Mannypenny St. off WI 13 in downtown Bayfield at Apostle Islands Marina.

NORTH CHANNEL, LAKE HURON, ONTARIO

Location: Gore Bay, Ontario, is about 650 miles NE of Chicago.

Outfitters: Canadian Yacht Charters (800-565-0022 or 705-282-0185, www.cycnorth.com) in Gore Bay has bareboats from 27 to 41 feet, day-sails (with or without captain) to Benjamin Islands, and instruction. Bay Breeze Yacht

Charters (877-941-0535, www.bbyc.com) in 2002 planned to build a base on Michigan's Drummond Island (about 60 miles and a 15-minute ferry away from the Mackinac Bridge). Manitoulin Wind and Wave in Kagawong (705-282-1999), a few miles east of Gore Bay, rents and sells sea kayaks.

Maps and books: Canadian hydrographic charts 2299, 2257, 2205. *Well-Favored Passage; The Ports Cruising Guide to Georgian Bay, the North Channel Ports, and Lake Huron.*

Heads up: Gunkholing nirvana. Tricky island anchorages demand keen navigation skills.

Description: "The North Channel is the mecca, the place every Chicago sailor wants to cruise," says Bonnie Barsky, chair of Chicago Yacht Club's cruising fleet. Little wonder Chicago boats were in such a hurry to get up here even a century ago (see *The Mac and the Goats*, page 87).

Here's why: hundreds of granite and quartz islands fill the 20-mile-wide channel along some 150 miles of protected waters from Sault Ste. Marie to Killarney, sandwiched by the Ontario mainland and the LaCloche mountain range to the north and by Drummond, Cockburn, and Manitoulin Islands to the south.

Among the oodles of secluded anchorages dotting the channel's coves, bays, inlets, and fiords, the Benjamin Islands are legendary; ancient pink granite topped by hardy pines growing from cracks in the rock. If your draft and skills allow, brave the rocks to snuggle into one of the smaller coves at sunset and wait for the northern lights.

Virtually all the islands are public government lands, which means you get to go ashore to hike, camp, swim, and fish for lake trout, coho salmon, and whitefish (keep your eyes peeled for the occasional moose and black bear). Some swear the trip from Chicago is worth it just for early summer wild blueberries.

Directions: Drummond Island is a shorter drive from Chicago than Gore Bay (about 165 miles less) but a 1- to 2-day sail away from the North Channel's favored islands. For Gore Bay, take I-94 east past Benton Harbor, MI, to pick up I-196 north to Grand Rapids. In Grand Rapids, take US 131 north to Reed City. At Reed City, take US 10 east to US 27 north. Follow US 27 north to I-75 north to Sault Ste. Marie. Cross the border into Ontario and follow Trans Canada 17 toward Espanola. At Espanola, head south on Provincial Highway 6. Cross to Manitoulin Island and take Highway 540 to Highway 542 to Gore Bay.

Polish Sailors

EYEBALL THE CONSONANT-JAMMED shop signs along Milwaukee Ave. between Addison and Diversey and you'll see evidence of Chicago's claim to the world's largest population of Poles outside Warsaw. (While you're at it, stop in at Czerwone Jubluszko—Red Apple—for pierogi a-go-go.)

After graduating from Poland's merchant marines and spending several years aboard a fishing vessel plying the North and Baltic Seas, Isidore Ryzak joined the throng and came to Chicago at 27. Frustrated by language barriers and steep membership fees of local yacht clubs, in 1969 Ryzak and two fellow new arrivals founded the Joseph Conrad Yacht Club, named for the Polish-born author and avid sailor.

"He was a seaman, and he had to leave Poland with pain, like many of us," Ryzak says.

The club is open to all, but most of its 120 members are relatively recent arrivals; meetings are held in Polish at the group's Montrose Ave. storefront headquarters.

"Many love sailing but just can't afford their own boats," says Ryzak, a successful businessman who years ago moved out of what he calls the city's "Polish ghetto" and into manse-filled Winnetka. A few club members have solo-sailed the globe or the Atlantic; several have raced the Mac.

Joseph Conrad and its umbrella group, the Polish Yachting Association of North America (which Ryzak directs), offer sailing instruction and certification exams in Polish, sponsor summer races, and in 2001 hosted an international sea chantey festival in Chicago, including the club's own group, "Mlynn." The chanteys, traditional sailors' work songs thick with allegory, have seen a resurgence of popularity in the homeland, especially Krakow, Ryzak explains. Spectators are welcome for club races and events. Joseph Conrad Yacht Club: (773) 334-2615, *www.jcyc.com*.

Ice

DRENALINE-MINDED SAILORS PRAY for ice in winter. Why? Depending on design and class, ice boats can reach speeds up to five times the speed of the wind. Ultra-modern class A Skeeters—known as the "Formula One" class of ice boating—reach speeds well over 100 mph. Area ice-boating meccas include Lakes Geneva and Como near Lake Geneva, WI, Lakes Pewaukee and Nagiwicka near Milwaukee, and Lakes Mendota and Monona in Madison. Want to know more? Get in touch with Melges Performance Sailboats (262-275-1110, www.melges.com) in Zenda, WI, just over the state line. The outfit's owned by sailing legend, and Zenda-area native, Buddy Melges.

Where to Connect

The Basics

If you don't know how to sail, Chicago has plenty of places to learn everything from the fundamentals to more advanced skills such as night sailing, meteorology, and racing technique. Certification by the American Sailing Association (ASA) or the U.S. Sailing Association lets you rent sloops anywhere in the country.

Fortunately, there are also a few ways to get regular access to a fleet that cost a fraction of what it would to own and maintain your own craft.

Sail Chicago (312-583-2220, www.sailchicago.org), an all-volunteer, member-run nonprofit community sailing club affiliated with Hostelling International, has been around since the 1950s and offers urban sailors the next-best thing to owning a boat. No sailing experience is required to join. Novices can crew for skippers, take part in daily lakefront cruises, and learn to sail through the club's classes (taught by members, some of whom are U.S. Sailing–certified instructors). More experienced members can rent boats, skipper group cruises or races, teach sailing, and take at-risk youth for free sails.

For as little as $10 to $60 for a 4-hour block (depending on day of week, time of day, and boat size), qualified members can rent through the club's fleet of 14 sailboats—principally 19-foot Rhodes with a few 30-footers—scattered among Monroe, Montrose, and Belmont Harbors. To rent, you need to earn a skipper card, which for the basic Rhodes 19s entails taking the club's dryland, basic skills, and skipper training courses (about $450 for some 50 hours of instruction in 2001), plus pass a swim test and on-the-water checkout. If you can demonstrate that you know how to confidently rig a boat, sail upwind and downwind, and tack and jibe, you may be able to skip the basic skills course.

Annual membership in Sail Chicago, which also offers racing and racing instruction, runs about $75. Members are required to volunteer 20 hours a year and pitch in with boat maintenance and repair in summer (first-year members exempt).

Former director Thomas Applegate sums up the club's scene. "Our mission is about providing affordable access to sailing. We don't have a lot of flashy boats, and if you want to drink martinis on the deck, you're better off at the yacht clubs."

Northwestern University Sailing Center in Evanston (847-491-4142, www.northwestern.edu/fitness-recreation/facilities/sailingcenter.html) offers qualified sailors use of its 15 Laser-class and dozen Club 420-class boats for about $300 a season (mid-May to mid-October). Monthly memberships run $129. (If you're a qualified windsurfer, pay just $25 extra and you get access to the center's windsurfing equipment, too.) Most qualify for a basic NU skipper rating after successfully completing an affordable 4-week beginner course; weather conditions dictate which rating is required to take out boats. The sailing center is about 15 miles north of the Loop and easily accessible by L or Metra.

Yacht clubs in the city usually offer associate, social, or crew memberships for those without boats (who then get to meet those who do have boats), but several require sponsorship by current members and tend to be pricier than either the Sail Chicago or NU option. But if big-boat crewing and racing are your gig, the yacht clubs are the place to network.

Schools and Clubs

- Chicago Park District runs affordable learn-to-sail classes from Burnham Harbor (1200 S, just south of the planetarium on the Museum Campus; 312-742-1700); $150 for 9 hours instruction on Colgate 26s. Students can join Wednesday night beer-can races. Saturday racing clinics. Boat rentals. Nationally recognized sailing program for the disabled; call (312) 747-7684 for the Judd Goldman Adaptive Sailing Program.

- Chicago Sailing Club (Belmont Harbor B dock 3200 N; 773-871-SAIL, www.chicagosailingclub.com) offers beginner–advanced instruction. Racing leagues, Wednesday night racing, regular group sails (with or without captain), captained charters, hourly rentals for qualified sailors.

- Sail Chicago/(312-583-2220, 312-409-6000 for lessons; www.sailchicago.org) sailing club offers affordable instruction (including racing) and access to a fleet at Monroe,

Montrose, and Belmont Harbors for qualified sailors. Beginner–intermediate instruction; classes fill fast. Registration starts February 1. Wednesday night and Saturday race leagues.

- Northwestern University Sailing Center in Evanston (1889 South Campus Dr., off Sheridan Rd. just north of Clark St. Beach, 847-491-4142, www.northwestern.edu/fitness -recreation/facilities/sailingcenter.html) offers affordable beginner–advanced instruction and access to a fleet.

- Great Lakes Marina at the Great Lakes Naval Training Center (847-688-6978 or 847-688-5417, www.Ntcmwr.com /recreation/greatlakeout/index.html) in North Chicago rents sailboats (and a slew of watercraft) to qualified skippers and offers instruction at very reasonable rates. Security concerns in the aftermath of the 9/11/01 terrorist attacks made rentals off limits to civilians, but that policy could change.

- Offshore Sailing School (Jackson Harbor 6400 S, 800-221-4326, www.offshore-sailing.com) offers all levels of instruction, including racing.

- Chicago Yacht Club (400 E. Monroe St., 312-861-7777, www.chicagoyachtclub.com) offers adult beginner instruction at Belmont Harbor. Crew and racing instruction. Associate memberships. Active racing fleets. Sponsors NOOD, Verve, and Mac races.

- Columbia Yacht Club (111 N. Lake Shore Dr., 312-938-3625, www.colyc.com) offers beginner–advanced instruction. Associate memberships. Active racing fleets. Tri-State Race sponsor.

- Jackson Park Yacht Club (6400 South Promontory Dr., 773-684-5522, www.jpyc.org) offers associate memberships. Members get access to fleet of Vanguard 14 FJs. Fall and spring frostbite races.

- Chicago Corinthian Yacht Club (601 W. Montrose Ave.,

773-334-9100, www.corinthian.org) offers social and crew memberships. Racing includes One Design.

- Burnham Park Yacht Club (1500 Linn White Dr., 312-427-4664, www.bpyc.com) has social memberships and may begin adult instruction. Racing.

- Midwest Offshore Racing Fleet (www.racemorf.org), known as MORF, sponsors 30-plus races a season. Active online crew pool for those seeking boats.

- Chicago Women's Sailing Network (www.torresen.com /cwsn/) helps women network to find crew spots or appropriate instruction. Sponsors spring race clinics, occasional seminars.

Shops
These shops carry nautical charts, cruising guides, and other sailing paraphernalia.

- Crowley's Yacht Yard (2500 S. Corbett St., one block west of Halsted St. on Archer Ave., 312-225-2170, www .crowleys.com) has been around a long, long time.

- West Marine (627 W. North Ave., 312-654-1818, www .westmarine.com)

- Boater's World Discount Marine (1661 N. Elston Ave., 773-227-7900, www.boatersworld.com).

Events
- Strictly Sail show (800-817-7245; www.sailamerica.com) end of January–beginning of February at Navy Pier. Seminars, demos, sailing schools.

- Chicago Venetian Night (www.ci.chi.il.us/SpecialEvents), usually end of July, is the city's longest-running annual lakefront event (45 years in 2002). Lighted boat parade, free Grant Park orchestra concert, fireworks, and mondo crowds.

- Heritage Boat Club Festival (888-613-8953, www.woodship .com) in August. Chance to check out some cool wooden boats.

- The Mac (312-861-7777, www.chicagoyachtclub.org), 333-mile Chicago-to-Mackinac race up Lake Michigan, draws more than 3,000 sailors from around the world. Runs second or third week in July, alternating dates with Port Huron-to-Mackinac race up Lake Huron.

- Chicago NOOD Regatta in June (usually starts Father's Day weekend) features 3 days of racing for some 300 boats. Part of nine-event national racing circuit. Same contact as Mac.

- Verve Cup Race Week has 3 days of racing, second or third weekend in August, featuring Verve Cup Offshore regatta, drawing sailors across nation. Same contact as Mac.

- Tri-State Race runs 3 days around Labor Day from Chicago to St. Joseph, MI; St. Joseph to Michigan City, IN; Michigan City to Chicago. Contact Columbia Yacht Club, which sponsors the first leg.

Books

- Brazer, Marjorie Cahn. *Well-Favored Passage: The Magic of Lake Huron's North Channel.* 4th ed. Chatham, MA: Sea Fever Gear Publications, 2001.

- Dahl, Bonnie. *Superior Way: A Cruising Guide to Lake Superior.* 3d ed. Duluth, MN: Lake Superior Port Cities, 2001.

- Manley, Steve, and Ann Vanderhoof. *The Ports Cruising Guide to Georgian Bay, the North Channel Ports, and Lake Huron.* Toronto, ON: Overleaf Design Ltd., 2001.

- Wright, Matthew. *Lake Michigan: Ports O'Call.* Evanston, IL: O'Meara Brown Publications Inc., 2001.

Sailing

WINDSURFING ON LAKE Michigan and a clutch of smaller inland lakes around Chicago? No problem. But surfing, as in on a surfboard? That usually requires a bit more proof.

Marc Stadler pops the video into his VCR and hits play. There he is at Dempster St. Beach in Evanston on a mid-October day, catching 30-second rides on nicely peeling waist- to chest-high waves on Lake Michigan. "It was so smooth, like melting butter," Stadler says, gazing longingly at the screen.

Stadler got into surfing here after heading umpteen times to area beaches to windsurf, only to have the wind abruptly (and characteristically) die out. But the waves, they were still rolling in. Which leads to this point: when the conditions are right, wind-surfing and surfing here on the Third Coast can be a blast.

No, Chicago is never going to rival the Gorge in the Pacific Northwest for sailboarding or Maui for surfing. Because both sports require wind (see *Swell: Ocean versus Lake*, page 107). And, Chicago's Windy City moniker aside, Stadler says: "Meteorologically speaking, Chicago is way down the list of windy cities."

Lake Michigan waves are generated entirely by wind and weather. And the lake is notorious for predictably unpre-dictable wind and weather. Prime season for big-wind sail-boarding and surfing here is spring and fall, which means the hard core trade in their tankinis and baggy shorts for hooded wet suits (or dry suits), gloves, and booties.

Still, the Chicago area has a dedicated corps for both sports. And as Aussie transplant Lester Priday, former co-director of the Eastern Surfing Association's Great Lakes Division, likes to point out, the Great Lakes have more coastline than the East and West Coasts of the continental U.S. combined. So there are tons of spots to explore.

This chapter focuses on spots within a reasonable drive of the city that have both windsurfing and surfing options (inland lakes excepted) so you have the best odds of hitting the water before the winds and/or waves wimp out. For wanderlust inspiration, pick up Chicago surfer Peter Straz-zabosco's quirky *Surfing the Great Lakes*.

Small inland lakes such as Silver Lake and Lake Andrea, within a 15-minute drive of each other just over the Wis-consin line, and *Backyard* favorite Wolf Lake in Indiana offer quality (mostly flatwater) windsurfing for all levels. They're ideal places to learn in summer's light wind or take refuge in strong offshore days when the wind can blow you into trouble in a hurry on Lake Michigan.

Sailing on Lake Michigan demands more skill. The lake can start out smooth as glass but quickly turn into a monster-wave ride suitable only for the most advanced sailors. For warm-weather surf and sail, Michigan *Meccas* Grand Haven and Muskegon are well-placed midway up the lake's eastern shore to maximize summer's prevailing southwesterlies.

Weather and wind prediction is not an exact science, but die-hards like Stadler come pretty close (see *Addiction*, page 110). Chicago hard cores keep an open mind, a full gas tank, and an excuse at the ready to ditch work when the wind and waves kick.

If this all seems like a lot of work—and actually, advances in windsurfing rigs have drastically reduced the learning curve—addicts say the rewards are huge.

"The focus you need is really mentally cleansing, the stoke is incredible" says Chicago windsurfer and surfer Ed Coyne. "It's a Zen-like state where it's just you and the elements. You can't control the elements, you can only click with them. And most of the time, you can wipe out without getting hurt—it's not like mountain biking, this is water. You can really go for it without having to pay that harshly."

OK. So go for it.

Know Before You Go

KNOW YOUR LIMITATIONS. Windsurfing guru and master instructor Jackie Butzen of Windward Sports breaks it down like this:

Beginners can sail independently in winds up to 10 knots.

Intermediates can use a harness and sail up to 20 knots easily.

Advanced can sail in 20-plus knots, use straps, know how

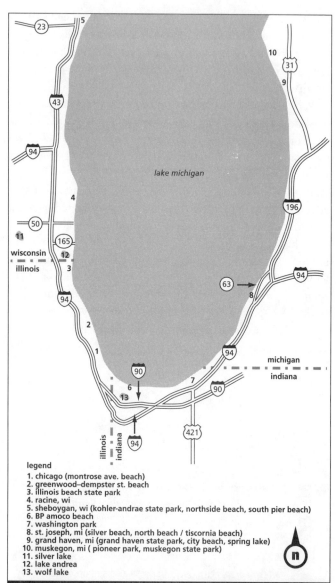

legend
1. chicago (montrose ave. beach)
2. greenwood–dempster st. beach
3. illinois beach state park
4. racine, wi
5. sheboygan, wi (kohler-andrae state park, northside beach, south pier beach)
6. BP amoco beach
7. washington park
8. st. joseph, mi (silver beach, north beach / tiscornia beach)
9. grand haven, mi (grand haven state park, city beach, spring lake)
10. muskegon, mi (pioneer park, muskegon state park)
11. silver lake
12. lake andrea
13. wolf lake

Windsurfing & Surfing Overview

to do a water start, and can do tricks (like a Spock, a 360-degree spin in the air).

- Protective footwear is always a good idea; launch areas are often rocky.
- A sideshore or side onshore wind (blowing from sea to land at an angle) is ideal for windsurfing. An offshore (blowing from land to sea) creates a "wind shadow," or "dirty" wind, near shore as city buildings block the wind, making it tougher to get out and back to shore.
- Try to get to the beach as the wind builds, not when it's closing out (or face struggling through big swell just trying to get off shore with your rig).
- Beware Lake Michigan rip current.
- Stick closer to shore when the wind gets fluky; it could stop at any moment. And trying to swim from way off shore with your rig is no fun.
- Always be aware of who's in the water around you. Though this chapter combines the sports, windsurfers and surfers should not try to share the same break (see *Vibe*, page 115). And, of course, stay out of swim areas.

Swell: Ocean versus Lake

WIND EQUALS WAVES. Where Lake Michigan has some 300 miles of fetch (the distance wind travels over water) and notoriously fickle winds, ocean swell benefits from more predictable trade winds and can draw from storms raging thousands of miles away from land.

To kick up decent swell on Lake Michigan, the wind has to blow steadily about 20 mph for at least 5 hours or so. Ideally, you want to surf after the wind has died; if it stays windy, the waves often stack on top of each other, making them tough to catch. The dawn after a night storm or just before dusk's "glass off" on an otherwise windy day tend to make for good surf.

Lake Michigan's man-made gifts are harbor-mouth piers and other breakwalls that focus and clean up waves; just beware submerged rocks and metal around the structures. Offshore sandbars help wave formation, too.

Understanding some basic differences between ocean salties and lake freshies before you hit the beach is key (thanks to Peter Strazzabosco for enlightenment). For more tips on technique, weather prediction, and surf spots, check out his *Surfing the Great Lakes*.

- Freshwater has shorter waves with a shorter period (the time between waves), so swells are tougher to catch and can be deceiving; a 5-footer may look like a 2-footer from shore.
- Freshwater is less buoyant, which makes paddling out tougher. The shorter period also means you may have to paddle through a slew of waves just to get to your takeoff.
- Lake waves tend to be smaller and "mushy" compared with steeper and cleaner—more hollow—coastal waves.

Especially if you're new to freshie waves, stick to a long board, 9 feet or longer. Longer, thicker boards offer more float and help maximize short waves. Of course, you can always ride the waves with a boogie board or skim board—they're easier to master and cheaper than a full-on surfboard.

"Every so often you get some hotshot from California or Hawaii just rip up the little waves with their short boards because they've got it together, but we ride big cruisers," says Larry Williams, a veteran freshwater surfer from Sheboygan, WI. "Longboard" Larry has surfed his share of salt water since he first got hooked in 1966. His analysis? "Surfing in the oceans is pretty dang easy compared to here," he says, with only the slightest hint of hyperbole. "You want bragging rights? Surf the Midwest freshwater."

Of course, there are some clear advantages to scrapping for waves on the freshwater coast. No coral. No sharks.

City Limits

MONTROSE AVENUE BEACH

Location: 4400 N

Special regulations: Let's just say this. Rules around windsurfing or surfing from city beaches are less than crystal clear. Regulars say there's some risk of being shut out by lifeguards or ticketed by cops. Problem is, best conditions usually pop when the beaches are officially closed, outside the Memorial Day–Labor Day beach season. "Surfing is sort of a guerilla sport in the city," says Chicago sailboarder and surfer Marc Stadler. Information from the beach house (312-742-0600) in season.

Heads up: When it's working, www.windmonitor.iit.edu, the wind site, can be helpful.

Description: Montrose is not necessarily the city's best windsurfing or surfing spot, but it's the most popular because it's the place historically deemed "friendly" to these sports. And Montrose is part of the Lake Michigan Water Trail, with an official launch-land site for "small, human-powered boats." Windsurfing's good on all but westerlies and southwesterlies, when you'll have to get about 3 miles offshore to catch uninterrupted air. Southerlies or rare southeasterlies make for nice flatwater sailing from the bay-like beach. But when the wind comes out of the north, surf's up (the pier by the beach house functions almost like a point break). Veteran Ed Coyne broke a rib wave-sailing here in a 30-mph nor'easter. "I turned to jump a wave and it just came up like a fist and knocked me off the board; I never saw it coming. It can get kind of gnarly here." On the South Side, Rainbow Beach off 79th St. has similar conditions.

Directions: Take Lake Shore Dr. to Montrose Ave. Drive east on Montrose to the parking lot closest to the beach house.

Addiction

THERE'S A CAVEAT when I call Marc Stadler to get together. He's checked the forecast and there might be good wind on this particular October Tuesday. "All my social plans are contingent on wind," the 48-year-old Merc trader says. "It's the only time I blow off family and friends. And they all understand; if the wind blows, I've got to get out."

Ed Coyne deliberately picked the office farthest from the window at the Park Ridge insurance company he owns so he wouldn't constantly scan for wind. "I'm worthless if it's windy out or there are waves to be had," he explains.

Coyne and Stadler, windsurfing and surfing partners, each have logged about two decades sailboarding (including racing) and a decade-plus surfing here. Their garages are hopelessly stuffed with about two dozen surfboards and windsurfing rigs designed for every wind condition.

These guys are hooked.

They've sailed year-round here, flying 30 mph across the water and disappearing between 15-foot swells on Lake Michigan. Stadler shows off two walnuts perched in a small plexiglass box; the "frozen nut" award from a local windsurfing club, bequeathed to those with the best show of year-round stamina. Stadler sailed 48 months straight; Coyne went 60.

"You get cleaner waves in winter," Stadler says. He and Coyne don polypro under 5-mil wet suits and surf when ice floes dot Lake Michigan's surface and the 32° water takes on a slightly gelatinous feel. They hit the beach with a cooler full of hot water, which they dump into their suits pre- and après-surf sessions to restore the feeling in their limbs. They've surfed at night, when sensation replaces sight and they know to start paddling when they feel their boards rising at the start of a swell.

Half the battle is figuring out when to hit the water. "You've got to hook up with people here or you'll just be missing good days and be down at the beach when there's nothing," Coyne says. And you've got to be on deck because it's so fleeting, Stadler says.

The Web and its bounty of raw meteorological data have meant urbanites with demanding professional jobs—the ranks of Chicago windsurfers and surfers include doctors, lawyers, stockbrokers—have the tools at hand to predict wind and waves, making the surfer-as-slacker an outdated stereotype here in the city.

Stadler makes sense of a flurry of online sources to come up with detailed local wind and weather predictions in his "skeg report" (a skeg is a surfboard fin), which he e-mails to a loyal following. He's often spot-on. (Recently, by Friday afternoon he had predicted the winds would hit Evanston's Greenwood St. Beach between 2 and 4 P.M. on Sunday. By 5 P.M. Sunday, he says, "it just hit like a freight train.")

Stadler and Coyne agree, the area's mercurial winds and waves throw up challenges to would-be windsurfers and surfers. So what if about half the annual surfing competitions held around the Great Lakes get canceled or rescheduled for no-show waves? When the stars align, the buzz is real.

"When I'm sailing a mile or so offshore, I'm thinking I've got the keys to the secret garden," Stadler says.

"Be prepared for the addiction," Coyne says. "It's just too much fun."

Backyard

WOLF LAKE, HAMMOND, INDIANA (WINDSURFING)

Location: About 18 miles SE of Chicago

Size: 385 acres on Indiana side

Special regulations: Maximum motorboat horsepower of 75 (mostly fishermen)

Fee: $10 nonresident day pass to windsurf and park, $55 season pass, Memorial Day–Labor Day. Information from Hammond Park District (219-853-6378).

Season: Year-round (but lake freezes)

Outfitter: Windward Sports (773-472-6868) runs lessons here in summer and rents rigs for $15 an hour; 10-rental card for $135.

Heads up: Local mecca. Wind report at (219) 659-5510.

Description: So what if a northerly wind can carry stench from neighboring steel mills. The Indiana side of this mercilessly subdivided lake (by the state line, the toll road, dikes, and railroad tracks) plunked in the midst of one of the area's heaviest industrial zones draws windsurfers from around the region. It's also the place plenty of Chicagoans come to learn and practice. Sailors flock for clear summer southerlies or southwesterlies; good on west and northwest winds, too. Beginner friendly, it's small and shallow enough to walk around the perimeter if you have to. Especially good in a westerly if you don't have the skills to be out on the big pond to the east (that'd be Lake Michigan). But don't be fooled; you'll see plenty of advanced sailors, especially on days when heading to the lake would be suicidal—like in a strong offshore wind that can blow you waaaaay out.

Windsurfing & Surfing

Look for restoration of Wolf Lake's natural habitat in the coming years; the lake's endangered wetland and prairie vegetation is drawing increased attention. Remarkably, 170 species of birds have been spotted here, including wintering swans.

Directions: Take the I-90 toll road south to just over the Indiana line. Exit at US 12/20/41 (Indianapolis Blvd). Take US 41 (Calumet Ave.) South to E. 121st St. Turn west into the Wolf Lake lot from 121st. Head to the concession building closest to the batting cage for instruction, rentals, and launch. Or launch from the south end of the lot and lake.

GREENWOOD-DEMPSTER STREET BEACH, EVANSTON

Location: About 15 miles N of Chicago

Special regulations: Against city ordinance to windsurf or surf outside mid-May–end of October (regulars say it's rarely enforced).

Fee: $25 nonresident day launch, $175 nonresident season launch, mid-May to end of October. Launch permit gives access to permit-only parking off Greenwood St.; spots fill fast. Information from Dempster St. Beach, (847) 866-4167, Memorial Day–Labor Day only.

Description: Facing slightly northeast, Dempster has good windsurfing in almost all wind directions. As Evanston Windsurfing Association's home beach (some call it Greenwood St. Beach since the two are contiguous), there's a strong community here. Northwesterlies can make for great surf but tricky sailing; west winds usually mean glassy water, but you'll have to spend a while tacking against the wind to get back to the beach. Epic wave sailing when the wind picks up out of the north, northeast, and southeast. Swirly current. Look out for particularly strong current and giant eddies at the north end of the pier.

Directions: Take Lake Shore Dr. north. Before Hollywood Ave., get in the right lanes to stay on Sheridan Rd. Take Sheridan through Evanston (it'll jog a few times; just stay right at South Blvd. and follow the green signs). Turn east onto Dempster St. and follow until it dead-ends.

"BP/AMOCO BEACH," WHITING, INDIANA

Location: About 17 miles SE of Chicago

Special regulations: You're technically on private property, so don't do anything to make BP/Amoco unhappy. Be prepared to be asked to leave.

Fee: Whiting Park charges nonresidents $15 to park, Memorial Day–Labor Day.

Season: Year-round

Heads up: Industrial-strength shred

Description: I laughed the first time I saw it. About 8 or 10 guys in head-to-toe wet suits at the end of October riding northwesterly fueled chest-high lake swells cleaning up nicely in the shadow of smoke-spewing steel mills and a British Petroleum/Amoco oil refinery lining the nearby peninsula. I talked to a few guys from Madison who'd driven down for a surf competition (originally scheduled for Michigan City, but characteristically, the waves didn't cooperate). They *loved* this place. Locals swear by the "Secret Site" for windsurfing and surfing, just east of Whihala Beach County Park. If the waves read big at the Kenosha NOAA buoy, diehards head here. Good on northerlies; a northwest wind can create a point break. Many hop to the other side of Whihala to surf and sail from Hammond's Lakefront Park just west of the Empress Casino.

Directions: Take the I-90 toll road south to Indianapolis Blvd. (US 12/20). Follow Indianapolis south to 119th St. Turn left (east) onto 119th to Front St. Turn left onto Front, cross the RR tracks. The beach is to your right after the tracks. Drop your gear and park on 119th St. or continue through Whiting Park to park in the pay lot.

Vibe

GREAT LAKES SURFERS say the territorialism, or "heavy local vibe," that shows up on the sodium-enriched breaks of the East and West Coasts is virtually absent here. Although some locals like to keep favorite breaks secret, newcomers to a beach are generally welcome.

Of course, it helps that only an estimated 300 regulars surf Lake Michigan (and fewer than 800 on the Great Lakes as a whole), making crowding a rare problem. Still, even on the Lakes, following surfing's strict etiquette is expected whenever there's more than one surfer at a given spot.

Key rules: don't "drop in" on a wave from another surfer (paddling into a wave they're about to surf). Don't cut into the lineup to catch waves; paddle beyond other surfers or defer to those who've waited longer. Talk to locals about the pecking order if you're new on a beach.

Chicagoan Ed Coyne, who's surfed on both coasts and Hawaii, recalls showing up to surf at Illinois Beach State Park in Zion on a killer fall day. "A beautiful peeling wave was rolling in and this local guy called out and said 'Let the new guy take this one.' You'd never hear that on the coast."

As veteran Sheboygan, WI, surfer Larry Williams likes to say about the Great Lakes surf scene, "the aloha spirit is more alive here than anywhere else on earth."

Short Hops

SILVER LAKE, SALEM, WISCONSIN (WINDSURFING)

Location: About 70 miles N of Chicago

Size: 464 acres

Special regulations: No boat trailers

Fee: $8 pass for noncounty residents Memorial Day–Labor Day

Season: Year-round (but lake freezes)

Map: Call Silver Lake County Park (262-857-1869) for an area map.

Heads up: Weed fin is a must from about mid-May on.

Description: Good for south, west, and southwesterly winds. Best in spring before the milfoil weeds grow obnoxious and summer's gonzo water-skiers and motorboats descend. Great for beginners; more advanced sailors can take advantage of early southerlies and westerlies before Lake Michigan warms up. Designated rig and launch next to the swim area. Popular year-round fishing spot.

Directions: Take I-94 west across the state line to WI 50. Take WI 50 west past Paddock Lake. Turn south onto County F and look for the county park entrance sign.

LAKE ANDREA, PLEASANT PRAIRIE, WISCONSIN (WINDSURFING)

Location: About 57 miles N of Chicago

Size: 110 acres

Special regulations: No motor boats. Information from Village of Pleasant Prairie (262-694-1400).

Season: Year-round (but lake freezes)

Heads up: Couldn't be easier; just minutes off I-94. And weed-free, deep water.

Description: Park along Terwall Terrace and launch just after you enter the park. Watch out for the rocks. Wide open and good on most wind directions (west, southwest, south, or northeast) but can get gusty. One of the last area lakes to freeze and first to melt (locals say they've sailed here as early as February and as late as December). Southport Rigging, 10 minutes away in Kenosha, gives lessons here (see *Where to Connect*, page 129).

Directions: Take I-94 west to WI 165 east. After a few quick miles, turn north onto Terwall Terrace, which wraps around the lake's east side. Park n' launch before you hit the Recplex.

ILLINOIS BEACH STATE PARK, ZION

Location: About 52 miles N of Chicago

Special regulations: You must carry your rig or surfboard; don't drag them along the beach.

Season: Year-round

Maps: Illinois Beach State Park (847-662-4828 or 847-662-4811) has park maps, or pick them up at the southern unit office off Wadsworth Rd. just past the resort.

Heads up: Friendly crew of regulars

Description: Head for the park's northern unit. Windsurfing's best on northeast wind. Surfers and sailors tend to congregate around the Camp Logan area north of 17th St.; sand break works well on strong northeasterly or northwesterly wind. Lake's recent low water level has hurt the waves here a bit. If the wind and waves quit on you, you can always hike one of the short trails (see "Hiking & Backpacking," page 341). Kayakers play here, with several launch and land sites as part of the Lake Michigan Water Trail (see "Sea Kayaking & Canoeing," page 36). Or try northerly breaks (like "Juicy Hole") at the north and south ends of North Point Marina a few miles north in Winthrop Harbor.

Directions: Take I-94 west to IL 173. Go east on IL 173 to IL 137. Turn left (north) onto IL 137 and take it about six blocks to 17th St. Turn east onto 17th and follow it into the park and toward the lake. Park in the southeastern-most lot. Carry your rig or board along the trail to the beach.

WASHINGTON PARK, MICHIGAN CITY, INDIANA

Location: About 60 miles SE of Chicago

Fee: $5 parking weekends and holidays, April–end of September; $2 weekdays Memorial Day–end of September. Information from Michigan City Parks and Recreation (219-873-1506).

Season: Year-round

Heads up: Pretty, popular beach backed by stands of dune marram grass. Plus a 1904 lighthouse.

Description: Windsurfers launch from Washington Park's long sandy beach with big waves and shorebreak on northerlies. Beware rip current. Sail *away* from the pier (check out the funky catwalk to the lighthouse) and watch for kayak surfers. Surf near the pier; look out for the rocks. Or head to favored surf on the other side of the pier along the narrow swath of beach unofficially dubbed "Billy Beach" by local fishermen (the beach is on NIPSCO, Northern Indiana Public Service Company, property). It's got a narrow range to go off, but if the stars align, you get coastal-like clean waves feeding through the breakwater channel by the marina.

Directions: Take I-94 east (or I-90 if you don't mind tolls) to US 421. Go north on US 421, which turns into Franklin St. in Michigan City. When Franklin dead-ends, turn right (east) onto Fourth St. and take your first left (north) onto Pine St. Follow Pine across US 12 and around City Hall. For Billy Beach, turn left (west) onto a service road after the RR tracks but before the bridge across Trail Creek (there are a few free parking spots at the end of the service road). For Washington Park, continue across the bridge on Pine St. Stay in the left lane and park in the main marina lot.

ST. JOSEPH, MICHIGAN

Location: About 90 miles NE of Chicago

Special regulations: No launching watercraft from Silver Beach. Windsurfers can launch from Silver Beach before Memorial Day and after Labor Day only (but can land at Silver Beach any time).

Fee: $6 nonresident parking or $25 season pass for Silver Beach, May 1–October 31; information from Silver Beach County Park (616-983-7111 ext. 8435). $5 nonresident parking or $35 season pass for Tiscornia Beach, Memorial Day–Labor Day; information from St. Joseph public works (616-983-6341). General information from St. Joseph tourism (616-982-0032).

Season: Silver and Tiscornia Beaches open year-round

Outfitter: Outpost Sports (616-983-2010 or 219-259-1000) rents boogie boards, kayaks, and skim boards near Silver Beach from late spring to fall. Call ahead for surfboard rental.

Heads up: Strong local surf scene (good summer surf n' sail). Surf-cam at www.qtm.net/sjwebcam/.

Description: Novices beware: St. Joe's can get big-wave

sailing, especially in any north wind. Sailing and surf are good on south to southwesterlies, too. Windsurfers frequent Silver Beach, south of the pier and the mouth of the town's namesake river, but are known to hop to the city beach north of the pier (often called North Beach, but its real name is Tiscornia Beach). Surfers use both beaches.

Directions: For Silver Beach, take I-94 east to St. Joseph. Exit M 63 east. Take M 63 east to downtown. Turn left (west) onto Port St. Turn right (north) onto State St.; it will wind south and then west (changing names several times), dead-ending as Broad St. at the entry to Silver Beach County Park.

For Tiscornia Beach, follow M 63 (Main St.) north, cross the river, and turn left (west) on Momany Dr. At Upton Dr. turn right. Turn left (south) on Marina Dr. Turn left on Ridgeway, heading toward North Pier. Turn right (west) on Tiscornia Park Rd. and park.

Meccas

Ice, Ice Baby

IT'S FEBRUARY. THE wind's kicking 15 knots and you're flying across the ice around 35 or 40 mph on a sail rigged on top of hockey skates. Why?

"It's a ton of fun. It's good practice for windsurfers and just another form of the same rush," says Ralph Ruffolo, ice-boating enthusiast and owner of Southport Rigging in Kenosha, WI. "And it's a long winter."

Windsurfing on ice, also known as freeskating or ice sailing, involves using a windsurfing sail and a (usually) homemade

Windsurfing & Surfing

board with skating blades (think skateboard with blades instead of wheels). You need solid, smooth ice—not to mention a helmet, lifejacket, elbow and kneepads, and a taste for the slightly insane. Though ice boating—as in racing in a sailboat on ice—is more prevalent in this area, you may see some freeskating at Wisconsin ice-boating meccas like Lake Geneva and Lake Como near Lake Geneva, Lakes Pewaukee and Nagiwicka near Milwaukee, and Lakes Mendota and Monona in Madison.

No ice? No problem. Chicago sailboarder Ed Coyne puts his windsurf sail on top of a double-runner sled and speeds down snow-covered streets.

SHEBOYGAN, WISCONSIN

Location: About 145 miles N of Chicago

Fee: $10 nonresident daily pass to Kohler-Andrae State Park, $30 annual fee. Information from Kohler-Andrae State Park (920-451-4080) and Sheboygan parks (920-459-3366).

Season: Open year-round (sorry, sail and surf best in fall and winter)

Maps: Use Sheboygan city and county map for overview (800-457-9497); contact Kohler-Andrae State Park for a park map.

Heads up: Quality four-season camping in Kohler-Andrae State Park (to reserve a spot, 888-947-2757, www .reserveamerica.com). Good area wind readings from NOAA buoy off Sheboygan (www.ndbc.noaa.gov/station_page .phtml?$station=sqnw3).

Description: Halfway up the west side of the lake, Sheboygan has enough fetch to get swell from both north and south. In the 1960s and '70s, this bratwurst-obsessed hamlet was home to a thriving surf club. Though the club is defunct, surfing is not. (Filmmakers from the 2002 surf flick *Liquid*, put together by the son of Bruce Brown, of *Endless Summer* fame, made a stop here to shoot.) "Longboard" Larry Williams, who's surfed in his hometown since 1966, says the area has 20-plus named breaks—far too many to detail here.

Larry's best advice: on a strong southerly try the "Elbow" at the bend in the North Pier. Move north up the shore along bay-shaped Northside Beach, home turf for the Dairyland Surf Classic every Labor Day weekend, and "The Reef," a break a mile or so off Michigan Ave. that Williams swears "on a south swell breaks into a hollow tube that'll hide a Volkswagen." Check out the jetties on your way north to North Point Park.

Windsurf or surf from the unofficial beach just south of the Sheboygan River and South Pier (check out the funky limestone columns left from a felled bank); amazing swell in a northerly. A few miles south, Kohler-Andrae State Park is a good—very pretty—windsurfing spot. OK surfing, too. Best on northeast, northwest, and southeast winds.

Directions: Take I-94 west into Wisconsin. At Milwaukee, take I-43 north toward Sheboygan. For Kohler-Andrae, take exit 120. Go east about 1 mile on County V to the park entrance.

For Northside Beach, take I-43 into Sheboygan, exit WI 23 east. Take WI 23 to 4th St. Turn left (north) onto 4th, turn right (east) onto Michigan Ave. to Broughton Dr.; pick your spot along Broughton, which hugs the shore from the marina and North Pier to North Point Park.

To get to the South Pier beach, take WI 23 to 8th St. Turn right (south) on 8th. Take E. Water St. at the roundabout, which turns into Illinois Ave./Fisherman's Rd. and dead-ends at the water.

GRAND HAVEN, MICHIGAN

Location: About 173 miles NE of Chicago

Special regulations: Red flag at state park warns of rip currents, especially common on southwest winds.

Fee: North Beach Park (616-738-4810) $5 daily parking late May–mid-September. Grand Haven State Park (616-847-1309) $4 daily/$20 annual vehicle permit April 1–October 31 (good for all Michigan state parks). Information for city beach (616)-842-3493, for Spring Lake's Lakeside Beach (616)-842-1393.

Season: All open year-round (Grand Haven State Park's main gate is locked outside April 1–October 31; park in the fisherman's lot by South Pier off Harbor Dr.).

Outfitter: Chapter 11 Sports (866-SURF-MICH or 616-842-9244) in Spring Lake, 0.5 mile inland from Grand Haven, rents 8-foot "Fun Shape" boards (long and thick for easy learning and small wave catching) and sells skim boards, surfboards, and boogie boards. Owner Ned Silverman will hook you up if you want some surf instruction or local wisdom.

Map: Get Grand Haven area map for overview (Grand Haven, Spring Lake, Ferrysburg): (616) 842-4910.

Heads up: As close as you'll get to *Endless Summer* from Chicago. Prime position for scooping up prevailing summer southwesterlies. Surf-cam at www.lakemichigancam.com.

Description: "It's a pretty mellow scene here; you get everyone from surgeons and lawyers to slackers living the surf lifestyle. It's growing but it's not obnoxious yet," says Ned Silverman, whose Chapter 11 Sports offers evidence of local love of surf. "You can go pretty much anywhere up and down the beachfront. There are breaks everywhere."

Though low lake levels have hurt some area breaks, this

resort town, like its Wisconsin cousin in Sheboygan, has a long surf history: the Great Lakes Surfing Association was founded here in 1966. South Pier's ground zero for the surf scene, with a break dubbed "Rockpile": big waves on southwest and strong northwest winds. Silverman says you might see 30 or 40 wave rats at the pier on a busy summer day (some just jump off the end into the swell).

Grand Haven State Park is good in any west wind for windsurfing; sand breaks to surf on southwest, northwest winds. Moving down the beachfront: city beach is best on north or northwest for windsurfing and generally produces more mellow surf than South Pier.

Sprawling, winding Spring Lake, chock full of wooded bayous and points, is a good windsurfing alternative to the Big Lake. Away from the fray (and motorboats), a little over 1 mile north of the north pier off North Shore Rd., North Beach Park in neighboring Ferrysburg gets sand breaks on northwesterlies and has decent windsurfing. North of there, there's always P.J. Hoffmaster State Park.

Directions: For Grand Haven State Park, take I-94 east into Michigan. After St. Joseph-Benton Harbor, take I-196 north to Holland. At Holland, take US 31 north into Grand Haven. Take Franklin St. exit west to Harbor Dr. Turn left onto Harbor as it follows the river and swings south along the lake. Follow signs to the park entrance. City beach entrance is farther south along Harbor.

For Spring Lake, take US 31 to the Spring Lake exit (M 104). Take M 104 (Savidge St.) east to Lake St. Turn left (north) on Lake and continue until it dead-ends. You're at Lakeside Beach. Launch.

grand haven, michigan

WILD, SECLUDED, AND private it's not. But camping at Grand Haven State Park is about as close as you'll get to sleeping on the beach (legally, anyway). You can roll out of your tent at sunrise, grab your rig or surfboard, and hit the wind and waves before your neighbor's Rice Krispies start popping.

Stretching from surf central South Pier at the mouth of the Grand River south to the city beach, the park covers a half-mile of beachfront. If you want a shot at a lake and lighthouse view, try for a spot between sites 161 and 123 or so on the outer loop. Other sites on the outer loop face the river boardwalk.

The blacktop, electric sites are obviously more geared to the RV bring-the-whole-family crowd. Bring extra-long stakes to pitch tent in the sand. If you want shade, bring your own; no trees here, all sand. Similarly DIY with campfires (no fire rings here). No booze.

Details: Camping season runs April 1–October 31. You may have to use a pit toilet (and forego showers) at either end of the season. All 174 sites have electric hookup and cost $20 a night, whether you tap electricity or not. All sites reservable, up to 6 months in advance, at (800) 44-PARKS or www.dnr.state .mi.us. See Grand Haven entry for directions.

MUSKEGON, MICHIGAN

Location: About 187 miles NE of Chicago

Fee: Pioneer County Park (231-744-3580) parking permit $4 daily, $24 seasonal, May 1–September 30. Muskegon State Park (231-744-3480) parking permit $4 daily, $20 annual, year-round. No fee for Muskegon city's Bronson Park (231-724-6704).

Season: All open year-round

Heads up: Some say recent summer waves are better here than Grand Haven; camping at Pioneer County Park and Muskegon State Park. Surf-cam at www.mlive.com /beachcam/muskegon.

Description: Just 15 miles north of Grand Haven, Muskegon gets its advantage from the same prevailing summer winds, but it's probably better known for its Winter Sports Complex in Muskegon State Park, home to one of the country's few luge runs (see "Winter Sports," page 433). Windsurfers and kayak surfers frequent Pioneer County Park, with sand breaks on southwest and northwest winds. Ditto for the city's Bronson Park, a short hop south. Waves build at the breakwall and along the beach on northwest, west, and southwest winds at Muskegon State Park (between Pioneer and Bronson). Great forested dunes along 2.5 miles of beach (12 miles of hiking trails through bogs and dunes, too, when the wind dies).

Directions: Take I-94 east into Michigan. After St. Joseph-Benton Harbor, take I-196 north to Holland. At Holland, take US 31 north into Muskegon. Exit left onto M 120. For Pioneer County Park, turn right (west) onto Giles Rd. and follow until it dead-ends. Turn right (north) onto Scenic Dr. and follow 0.25 mile to the park entrance.

For Muskegon State Park, follow M 120 about 8 miles to the park entrance. For Bronson Park, take US 31 to Sherman Blvd. Turn left (west) onto Sherman and follow until it hits the park.

Kiteboarding

 CHICAGO WINDSURFER FOR 15 years, Tim Grossnickle took a trip to Hawaii's Kailua Bay in 1999 and saw guys jumping waves with kite rigs.

"It looked crazy fun," he says. And he figured he could take advantage of Chicago's light summer winds—you can have fun with as little as 8 knots—feeding the kite 175 feet in the air to catch a clean north wind. "You get skunked less than with windsurfing. My best windsurfing year in the city was 40 days. I've gotten to kite 75 days this year."

Now Grossnickle is one of a handful of Chicagoans to pioneer the sport locally. Kiteboarders, or kitesurfers, ride a board while strapped into a harness connected by lines, which they manipulate, to an enormous kite (Grossnickle's got from 4 to 14 meters). Jumps are the thrill; you can get big ones off even small waves. Grossnickle describes it as "water-skiing behind a helicopter. It's pure lift."

I met Grossnickle and kiteboarding buddy Terry Kurzynski at Montrose Beach on a 60° November afternoon (love global warming). The wind had turned too gusty and shifty to get in the water, but I caught the drift just grabbing hold of Kurzynski's harness. It's pure power when the kite gets aloft; I'm throwing my full weight back to keep Kurzynski from taking a trip across the lake, digging my heels into the sand but still getting hauled across the beach on the verge of a face plant. Grossnickle isn't sure how far the sport will go in the Second City, but just to be sure he's snapped up the domain www.chicagokitesurfers.org.

Besides windsurfers, the sport also seems to attract wake boarders, snowboarders, pilots, and stunt kiters, says Mike Portman, a former windsurfing and snowboarding instructor who now teaches kiteboarding in Racine, WI. For lessons and gear, contact Portman at (262) 681-3367 or boardum@prodigy .net. Also see www.freshwatersurf.com. Mackinaw Kite Company in Grand Haven, MI, has gear, lessons, and events (800-622-4655 or 616-846-7501, www.mackinawkiteco.com).

Where to Connect

Clubs and Organizations

- Evanston Windsurfing Association, EWA (www.evanston windsurfing.org), is *the* sailboard club, with a smattering of surfers, too. Moonlight sails, Windless Wednesday BBQs, clinics, weekly Sunday 2 P.M. races at Evanston's Greenwood St. Beach.

- Eastern Surfing Association, Great Lakes Division (www .lakesurf.com), draws members from across the Great Lakes and sponsors a slew of U.S. Surfing Federation–sanctioned competitions. Snicker not: Great Lakes surfers have advanced to the ESA's championships at Cape Hatteras every year for the last decade. Co-director Jim Hoop is a Chicagoan (and former city lifeguard). Contact Hoop at (773) 582-3057.

- Great Lakes Surfing Association (www.kacm.com/GLSA .html), founded in 1966 in Grand Haven, MI, holds a steady stream of social events and competitions. Contact Rick Boss at (616) 494-0811 or rickboss_2000@yahoo.com.

- Surfrider Foundation (www.surfrider.org), a nonprofit organization dedicated to environmental protection and free access based in San Clemente, CA, has a fledgling Lake Michigan chapter.

Shops and Instruction

- Windward Sports (3317 N. Clark St., 773-472-6868, www.windwardsports.com) is the city's only sailboard shop, opened in 1982 by windsurfer Jackie Butzen. Boogie boards, wake boards, kiteboarding, plus limited surfboards and related gear; in-line skating, snowboarding, skateboarding, too. Special orders. Windsurfing rental to qualified sailors (about $45 a day). Beginner–advanced instruction. Two-day full certification course for beginners runs around $140.

- Membership at Northwestern University Sailing Center in Evanston (1889 S. Campus Dr., off Sheridan Rd. just north of Clark St. Beach, 847-491-4142, www.northwestern .edu/fitness-recreation/facilities/sailingcenter.html) gives you access to beginner–advanced windsurfing rigs. Monthly membership to the public runs around $129, seasonal membership $300 (May–October). Beginner–advanced instruction. $189 for 6-hour beginner course includes 1-month membership plus 10% discount if you sign up for the rest of the season. Also see "Sailing," page 100.

- Bob Bechstein, EWA member, offers private beginner–intermediate windsurfing lessons at Evanston's Greenwood St. Beach. Contact him at (847) 568-0605 or pctrainer@rcn .chicago.com.

- Southport Rigging (800-877-7025 or 262-652-5434, www.southport-rigging.com) in Kenosha, WI, sells windsurf and kiteboard rigs and surfing accessories. Regular demo days. Demo rig rental $65 a day. Free kids' clinic in summer. Beginner–advanced sailboard instruction.

- Isthmus Sailboards (800-473-1153 or 608-849-4991, www.isthmussailboards.com) in Waunakee, WI., just outside Madison, is all about windsurfing. Some kiteboard gear, too.

- Wind Power Windsurfing Center (920-922-2550, www .windpowerwindsurfing.com) in Fond du Lac, WI, offers instruction for all levels on Lake Winnebago.

- Chapter 11 Sports (866-SURF-MICH or 616-842-9244, www.Chapter11sports.com) in Spring Lake, MI, near Grand Haven, is one of the only shops in the region to keep surfboards in stock, new and used.

Events
- Windward Sports Crib Run, out-and-back race from Montrose to the crib, the weekend after Labor Day. Contact Windward Sports, above.

- Shred Fest Regatta in May (usually week before Memorial Day) at Silver Lake in Salem, WI, outside Kenosha. Contact Southport Rigging, above.

- Three-day board sailing swap meet, second weekend in April in Kenosha. Contact Southport Rigging.

- Swap meet at Evanston's Greenwood Beach in early May. See EWA Web site, above.

- Windfest Midwest in Governor Nelson State Park near Madison, WI, late June in 2002. Free learn-to-wind-surf/kitesurf clinics, cutting-edge gear, and windsurfing luminaries. Contact Isthmus Sailboards, above.

- MOWIND (Midwest Organizers of Windsurfing) organizes sailboarding races and events across the Midwest; (414-646-8299, www.amoka.com/mowind/html.

- Dairyland Surf Classic, Lake Michigan's biggest annual surfing event, draws about 100 surfers from as far as Toronto and Duluth to Sheboygan, WI, over Labor Day weekend. Kicks off the Great Lakes surf season with surf contest,paddle race, surfboard show. And brats. Contact Eastern Surfing Association's Great Lakes Division, above.

Book
- Strazz, P. L. (aka Peter Strazzabosco). *Surfing the Great Lakes: An Insider's Guide to Monster Waves along North America's Fresh Coast*. Chicago, IL: Big Lauter Tun Books, 2000.

Link
www.glerl.noaa.gov/metdata/chi/ for real-time wind and other sundry meteorological data from the crib off Oak St. Beach.

Scuba Diving

EXOTIC CORAL REEFS and rainbow-hued fish are not what draw divers deep into Lake Michigan. It's shipwrecks. As hard as they've been on ships, the Great Lakes are very good to their wrecks, an estimated 3,000 to 10,000 of which litter the lake bottoms—approximately 950 in Lake Michigan alone. Unlike ocean salt water, which eats wood and metal, cold freshwater puts whatever sinks in an almost permanent deep freeze.

With Chicago's historic role as a shipping pow-erhouse, you don't have to leave the city to visit some extraordinary sites. Captain Bob Schak, who's been guiding divers for two decades on Lake Michigan and tugs barges on the lake in the off-season, sums it up: "You're diving on history here. It's dark. It's cold. It's not for everybody." But plenty who descend wind up addicted to exploring the parallel offshore universe.

Visibility on the lake has vastly improved from decades past when Schak says "we were diving by braille." His first couple hundred dives on the *Prins Willem V* he never actually *saw* the wreck, he just explored it by feel (for the record, he's done about 500 dives there).

Schak likes winter diving, when visibility averages 80 feet (otherwise it gets to around 30–35 feet, though conditions vary from day to day and site to site). The primary area dive season runs from April through November, though some charters in Milwaukee go year-round. Early spring demands a dry suit; the rest of the season it's an 8-millimeter wet suit—that'd be a quarter-inch of rubber—along with gloves and hood. Schak dives up to 50 feet in swim trunks on calm summer days without the north winds that drive cold air through the city, but don't count on too much tankini or trunk time.

Of course, the lake is home to more than just wrecks. There are burbot (dubbed "lawyer fish"), coho salmon, brown and rainbow trout, carp, drum, sturgeon, longnose suckers, goby, white perch, smallmouth bass, crayfish, and the eel-like sea lamprey. There are even tennis-ball-size freshwater sponges. And the ubiquitous interloper, the zebra mussel (see *Aquatic Attack*, page 135). Watch out for fishing line and anchors on local dives.

Conditions are generally tougher here than you'd find, say, on a live-aboard in the Caribbean. Lake Michigan is decidedly moody. The upside is if you can handle the waters here, locals say you can dive anywhere. In addition to exploring the freshwater ocean in the city's front yard, there are several inland quarries within 3 hours of the city that draw student and veteran divers alike.

Many thanks to local scuba expert Cris Kohl, whose

excellent Great Lakes wreck guides greatly informed this chapter. By all means, get yourself a copy of *The Great Lakes Diving Guide* and *The 100 Best Great Lakes Shipwrecks*, vol. 2, *Lake Michigan and Lake Superior* (both have latitude and longitude coordinates to help locate wrecks with a GPS). You'll never look at the lake the same way again.

City Limits and Backyard

The city charters in *Where to Connect* can take you to any of the major dive sites (this chapter includes a sampling of the more than 25 wrecks favored by city divers). Weather conditions—and of course your skill level—often dictate which wrecks you can visit. For details and more wrecks, see Cris Kohl's invaluable guides. Lake Michigan's first shipwreck was the schooner *Hercules*, wrecked in 1818 by what is now 63d St. in Chicago, according to Kohl. Apparently, by the time the local Native Americans found human remains along the shoreline some days later, wolves and bears had mutilated the bodies beyond recognition. City wilds indeed.

DAVID DOWS

Difficulty: Intermediate

Description: The *Dows*, named for a prominent Chicago businessman, was built at a time when cargo sailing ships were fast being replaced by steam. The 365-foot-long schooner first launched into Lake Erie waters in 1881 and wound up on the bottom of Lake Michigan 8 years later, about 6 miles from the city near the shoals off Indiana. In her time, the *Dows* was the world's largest five-masted schooner. The *Dows* made some of the fastest crossing times of the day, once sailing the 254 miles from Toledo to Buffalo in 18 hours. After being converted to a towed barge, the *Dows* sank at anchor, carrying a load of coal to Chicago during a bitter November storm (no lives were lost). Today the wreck is buried in some 40 feet of water, the hull mostly intact as schools of carp circle and crayfish poke out from underneath rocks and timbers.

MATERIAL SERVICE BARGE

Difficulty: Beginner/intermediate

Description: In the 1930s, the *Material Service* supplied gravel and sand via the Chicago River for Chicago landmarks like the Merchandise Mart. Latticed by low bridges, the river demanded a special ship be built to avoid the cost and delay of having to raise the bridges for passage. With a maximum height of 14 feet, 6 inches from waterline to top, the 239-foot-long steel barge could haul 2,400 tons of cargo. On July 29, 1936, the barge was en route from Lockport to the Material Service yard at 92d and the Calumet River when she started to take on water in the holds, sinking a half-mile from Calumet Harbor, taking down with her the captain and most of the crew—trapped in their berths or pulled under by suction. (After several inquiries, the captain was found to be at fault.) The wreck, which lies just northeast of Calumet Harbor, sits upright in about 30 feet of water. Salvage efforts wreaked some damage, but much of it's intact. Divers often explore the holds; the openings are roughly the size of a garage door. Average visibility is usually pretty low, about 7 feet.

Aquatic
Attack

ITY DIVERS WEAR gloves not just to protect themselves
from the cold but from the razor-sharp shells of the zebra
mussel. Thanks to ocean-going freighters dumping their
ballast water in the Great Lakes, these dime-sized saltwater transplants started showing up in the mid-1980s and have
proven remarkably adept at adapting to their new freshwater
environs. Too adept, many divers would say.

Though some credit the mussels with helping to improve
visibility in the Lakes—a single mussel can filter about a liter of
water a day—the mussels have blanketed some shipwrecks,
practically obscuring entire sections of a ship. Aesthetics
aside, divers worry that the mussels will eventually damage the
wrecks. The weight of so many mussels piled on at once has
made Coast Guard buoys sink and parts of shipwrecks col-
lapse, according to wreck-diving author Cris Kohl.

WINGS OF THE WIND

Difficulty: Intermediate

Description: About 3.5 miles off the Wilson Ave. crib, the
two-masted schooner that sank in 1866 was only discovered by professional divers in the late 1980s. Built by ship-
makers in Buffalo, NY, the ship was bound to Chicago with
240 tons of coal on the night of May 12, 1866, clouds blot-
ting out any trace of moonlight. Around 3 A.M. the lookout
cried out a warning. A ship toting lumber bore down on
Wings out of the blackness, and the two collided. The other
ship, the H.P. *Baldwin*, was unharmed and took on the
Wings of the Wind crew as the ship slipped under the surface. A salvage operation later that year stripped the boat's

coal cargo, severely damaging the stern. Although the ship's been well stripped of hardware, the bow is intact with a large wooden windlass on deck. The 142-foot-long ship is about 40 feet underwater.

CAISSONS

Difficulty: Intermediate

Description: If you believe the legend, thank Mrs. O'Leary's cow for this dive site. In 1871, the city was sauna dry; just 6 inches of rain had fallen by October. Wooden houses, barns, fences, sidewalks, and factories made the city a tinderbox. On October 7, the story goes, Mrs. O'Leary's cow kicked over a kerosene lamp in the barn, starting the Great Chicago Fire. Fanned by 60-mph winds, the 3-day fire decimated the city, leaving nearly 100,000 people homeless. To get ready for reconstruction, clean-up crews loaded debris onto barges and dumped it into the lake a few miles off Grant Park in about 50 feet of water. The Caissons is the resulting underwater archaeological bonanza, filled with pottery, tools, charred bricks, bottles, and other artifacts. After 131 years of loot picking, you have to swim slowly over the lumpy sandy bottom to scan for strange shapes to unearth.

GEORGE W. MORLEY

Difficulty: Beginner

Description: You don't reach this wreck by boat; it's less than 100 yards offshore in roughly 10 to 16 feet of water off Evanston's Greenwood St. Beach. Intact from hull to keel, with the prop shaft visible, the wooden steamer caught fire and sank in 1897 with no lives lost. It's buoyed in summer.

Check in at the beach office for directions; you'll have to show your certification card and pay a beach entrance fee.

Directions: Take Lake Shore Dr. north. Before Hollywood, get in the right lanes to stay on Sheridan Rd. Take Sheridan through Evanston (it'll jog a few times; just stay right at South Blvd. and follow the green signs). Turn east onto Dempster St. and follow until it dead-ends. Parking can be tight.

WELLS BURT

Difficulty: Intermediate

Description: Resting 3 miles off Evanston in about 40 feet of water, the *Wells Burt* lay undisturbed for more than 100 years before divers discovered it in 1988. Built by the Detroit Dry Dock Co., the 201-foot-long wooden ship launched in 1873. In late May 1883, on a day when Chicagoans reported seeing monster waves crashing along the lakefront, the coal-carrying ship hit a brutal storm en route from Buffalo. With her mast ripped loose, she swamped and sank with all 11 crew members on board. Though the wreck was vandalized in the early 1990s, it's still in great shape, with two-thirds of the decking in place, deck equipment like the capstan and windlass, and a hold easily accessible through the hatches. The *Wells Burt* lists slightly to port.

Short Hops

To visit one of Milwaukee's star attractions (the city has more than 20 wrecks), get in touch with the folks at

Pirate's Cove dive shop in Milwaukee (see *Where to Connect*, page 147).

PRINS WILLEM V, MILWAUKEE, WISCONSIN

Difficulty: Advanced. Several divers have died exploring this multilevel wreck.

Description: The *Prins Willem V* holds the dubious distinction of having sunk twice. The first time, in 1940, the 258-foot Dutch freighter was deliberately sunk before she was fully built to block use of a Rotterdam waterway by invading Nazi troops. In 1949, after the war, she was raised, refitted, and put to work toting freight between the Great Lakes and a host of northern European ports. On the night of October 13, 1954, the *Prins Willem V* set out from Milwaukee Harbor, loaded with umpteen tons of hides, slabs of pork fat, car parts, film projectors, lawn mowers, and TV tubes, bound for the St. Lawrence and the Atlantic. About 2 miles from the Milwaukee lighthouse, the ship ran into the towline between a barge and a tug; the pressure on the line drove the barge into the ship's side, punching out a 20-by 8-foot hole. The ship staggered on the surface another few miles, giving the crew the chance to jump ship before it sank in 80 feet below. Most of the cargo was eventually removed, but the ship is in perfect condition (except for its fatal hole). The wreck is just under 4 miles east of Milwaukee in 48 to 90 feet of water. Penetration dives for only the most experienced. Visibility is usually 15–25 feet.

MILWAUKEE, MILWAUKEE, WISCONSIN

Difficulty: Advanced
Description: The *Milwaukee* is a 338-foot ferry steamer.

On October 22, 1929, she was loaded with freight cars, carrying everything from lumber and bathtubs to canned peas and—this being Wisconsin—cheese. Gale-force winds rocked the ship hard enough to make the railroad cars jump their tracks and smash into the seagate, allowing water to pour in and sink her and all 52 crew aboard. The railroad cars she was carrying are still aboard and can be explored. A small hole cut by divers permits exploration of the engine, but deep silt and poor visibility make it extremely dangerous. The wreck is about 3 miles offshore, 7.5 miles northeast of the Milwaukee Harbor light. She sits in 90–125 feet of water; visibility is often 15 feet or less.

Mud Puppies?

SALAMANDERS DON'T USUALLY hang out in the offshore waters of Lake Michigan, but Captain Bob Schak says they're there. "I've seen them in 30 feet of water, as deep as 45 feet. They live in the boiler tubes of old wrecks. We don't know how they survive in winter," the veteran diver says. True to the name of certain salamander species, mud puppies—or water dogs— "bark underwater," says Schak. "It sounds like a barking dog."

Joel Brammeier, habitat coordinator and science manager for the Lake Michigan Federation, says while there are native salamanders in the Great Lakes basin, they tend to hang out closer to shore, spending their underwater time in the protected shallows. "But I suppose anything's possible."

Most salamanders Schak has seen are 5 to 12 inches long, but he swears there's one 4-foot giant he visits on the wreck *Tacoma*. "I like to go at night. He's always hanging out in the same spot; I go down there and play with him. He knows me now and he's really friendly."

Quarry Dives

Following are a few tried and true local favorites for inland diving within 3 hours of the city. In general, these quarries serve as part classroom, part playground. Many city dive shops take students here to practice their skills and get certified in a highly controlled environment. But more experienced divers frequent them too because, well, they're fun. Most have sunken "wrecks" of their own to explore.

PEARL LAKE, SOUTH BELOIT, ILLINOIS

Location: About 95 miles NW of Chicago

Outfitter: Dive season at the privately owned resort (815-389-1479, www.pearllake.com) runs from April through October. Air fills and a site map are available at the restaurant building. Daily entrance fee.

Description: Popular training site, with maximum depth of 85 feet and a dozen training platforms at varying depths in water with average visibility 20 feet (it's typically best in August and September). The 30-acre lake has a sunken school bus, a two-man 33-foot yellow submarine, an alligator statue, and a Beechcraft twin-engine airplane among its underwater offerings. Turtles and thick schools of bluegill drift the shallows and pester divers for handouts. Every now and then, one of the 30-pound channel catfish makes an appearance. Three species of clams, several varieties of snails, and a prolific population of crayfish. Night dives by reservation.

Directions: Take I-90 west toward Rockford to the South Beloit exit/IL 75. Stay on IL 75 west. At the third stoplight turn left (south) on IL 251. Bear right on Chaney Rd., then left on Dearborn Rd. Follow the road to the sign for Pearl Lake Club. Register at the restaurant.

FRANCE PARK, LOGANSPORT, INDIANA

Location: About 130 miles SE of Chicago

Outfitter: Diving Den (765-452-1034, www.diving-den .com) in Kokomo has a divemster at France Park weekends from early April through late October; air fills and rentals on site. Daily entrance fee. Call for night dive schedule. Link to the park Web site from Diving Den's.

Description: Divers like to check out the resident spoonbill sturgeon population, also known as paddlefish (*Polyodon spathula*) because of its paddle-shaped snout. The "living fossil" first developed some 20–40 million years ago and can grow to 6 feet long and weigh in at 200 pounds. There are some whoppers here, and even better, they're fairly approachable. Stingless freshwater jellyfish are also in abundance. Plus a sunken 1940s school bus and pickup truck. Average depth is 20 feet, maximum is 28 feet. Avoid in the thick of summer; algae greatly obscure visibility. Near the park entrance, check out the big clay oven once used by Italian immigrant quarry workers to bake fresh bread.

Directions: Take I-90 east to Indiana to I-65 south. Follow I-65 south to US 24/exit 201. Go east on US 24. You'll hit the quarry about 2 miles before downtown Logansport.

HAIGH QUARRY, KANKAKEE, ILLINOIS

Location: About 60 miles S of Chicago

Outfitter: The privately owned quarry (815-939-7797,

www.haighquarry.com) charges a daily fee; rentals and air fills available.

Description: Its proximity to the city makes the 14-acre spring-fed quarry a major training site for Chicago divers. Maximum depth about 90 feet. Eight training platforms among the paddlefish, catfish, perch, crappie, three types of bass, and northern and red ear sunfish. Abandoned mining equipment and a 33-foot cabin cruiser fill out the underwater landscape.

Directions: Take I-94 east to I-57 south. Follow I-57 south to IL 50/exit 315. Stay right on the ramp and continue south on IL 50 to Armor Rd. Cross east back over I-57 and turn right (south) at the stoplight for Cardinal Dr. Continue south on Cardinal to the T-intersection. Turn left (east) on North Ave. Look for the dive sign off the gravel road on your right. Check in with Tina at the office.

QUARRY LAKE PARK, RACINE, WISCONSIN

Location: About 80 miles N of Chicago

Outfitter: Reef Point Diving (262-886 8501, www.reefpointdiving.com) in Racine is the closest shop. Daily entrance fee.

Description: Once you pass through the swim area, the bottom drops precipitously to a maximum depth of 100 feet. You can also wall dive here; you won't find Caribbean coral, but the sharp drops are pretty spectacular and require divers to maintain good buoyancy control. Underwater regulars include carp, trout, crayfish, snails, and zebra mussels (which means you should wear gloves to protect yourself from their nasty shells). While the surface water warms up quite a bit in summer, the water below 30 feet is still bitter and calls for a 6-mm wet suit and hood year-round. Gorgeous swimming. Anglers and playboaters on the Root River alongside the park (see "Fishing," page 198, and "White Water," page 162).

Directions: Take I-94 west. Exit at WI 20 east. Take WI 20 east about 6 miles to WI 31. Turn left (north) on WI 31. Take the right split (east) onto County MM. You'll see the Horlick Dam and a Days Inn. Turn right (east) on Northwestern Ave./WI 38. Cross the bridge over the Root and stay in the right lane. The park entrance is less than 0.25 mile on your right.

Meccas

ISLE ROYALE NATIONAL PARK, MICHIGAN

Location: From about 418 to 610 miles N of Chicago depending on what outfitter you use or what ferry you take. Ferries depart from Houghton and Copper Harbor in Michigan and Grand Portage, MN

Difficulty: Advanced. Managing additional cold-water gear and deeper depths makes for challenging diving. One veteran outfitter recommends a minimum experience level of 50 open-water dives with experience in shipwreck, deep, and cold-water diving.

Outfitters: Captain Ken Merryman at Superior Trips (651-635-6438 or 763-785-9516, www.superiortrips.com) in Fridley, MN, has run scuba trips on his classic live-aboard since 1976. Superior Divers (734-426-4276) in Grand Portage, MN. Isle Royale National Park (906-482-0984, www.nps.gov/isro) has a full list of approved outfitters and ferry details.

Map and books: NOAA chart 14976. *Shipwrecks of Isle*

Royale National Park and *SS America* are both available from the nonprofit Isle Royale Natural History Association (800-678-6925, www.irnha.org).

Description: The deep, icy waters around the 45-mile-long Lake Superior wilderness island, dotted by treacherous shoals, hold 10 wrecks; 3 have multiple decks and rooms for penetration dives. Definitely not a place for novices: diving depths range from 20 to 140 feet, and water temps can dip to 34° in a hurry. Early season (June) brings stellar visibility of 40 to 70 feet. On the 183-foot freighter *America*—which transported passengers, the fish catch, supplies, and mail on three trips a week from Duluth to the island around the turn of the century—divers, and even snorkelers, can see the bow under just 2 or so feet of water, but the stern digs into an 80-foot bottom. Descending on the 1928 wreck, which the nonprofit Great Lakes Shipwreck Preservation Society is actively restoring, divers can check out such artifacts as the remains of a piano in the ship's social hall and a Model T truck. Pieces of side-wheels from the island's oldest wreck, the *Cumberland*, a side-wheel steamer sunk in 1877, are still visible. Technically, the *Kamloops* is the toughest dive, impeccably entombed 175 to 260 frigid feet below since 1927.

Directions: Check with your outfitter since there are so many jumping-off points for trips to Isle Royale.

STRAITS OF MACKINAC UNDERWATER PRESERVE, MICHIGAN

Location: About 430 miles NE of Chicago
Difficulty: Intermediate–advanced
Outfitters: Straits Scuba Center (586-558-9922) in St. Ignace has two boats; owner Larry McElroy is president of

the Michigan Underwater Preserve Council. Scuba North (888-692-3483 or 616-947-2520, www.scubanorth.com) in Traverse City.

Book: *Shipwrecks of the Straits of Mackinac.*

Description: Michigan's nine underwater preserves protect roughly 2,000 square miles of Great Lakes bottom-land—about the size of Delaware. The Straits seem tailor-made for producing stellar shipwrecks. The vital shipping corridor connecting Lakes Michigan and Huron, straddled by a 5-mile-long bridge connecting the state's lower and upper peninsulas, narrows to as little as 3.5 miles in places. Throw in thick fog banks that often cut visibility to near zero, heavy traffic, dangerous shoals, icy conditions in winter, ice floes in late spring, and the occasional ripping gale and the deal is sealed. The 148-square-mile Straits preserve holds about 40–50 shipwrecks, roughly half of them intact. (Some estimate the entire Straits area holds 80-plus wrecks, most sunk before 1900, but many have yet to be discovered.) Water depth in the Straits reaches 300 feet in spots, but most dives are in the 80 to 100-foot range; currents can be an issue. A must-see: the two-masted, 110-foot *Sandusky*, which left Chicago on September 18, 1856 with a cargo of grain. Two days later, the ship foundered in a violent gale and sank with all hands lost. Perfectly intact, the wooden hulled ship sits upright in 65 to 90 feet of water. *Sandusky*'s rare hand-carved figurehead is an exact replica; the original was whisked away to a museum after vandals tried to strip it. The 1927 *Cedarville*, loaded down with limestone, was rammed by a Norwegian freighter in the night fog of May 7, 1965, and went down with 10 men. The ship lies upside down, tilted to port (very disorienting). The bow and stern are considered separate dives because of the ship's 588-foot length. There's also a great shore dive to an old breakwall with an unidentified shipwreck, along with scattered tools and pottery, from St. Ignace harbor in about 15 feet of protected water.

Directions: Take I-94 east through Indiana past Battle Creek, MI. Take I-69 north to Lansing, then pick up US 27 north. Stay on US 27 north to I-75 north. Take I-75 north to Mackinaw City and cross the bridge over the Straits into St. Ignace.

BONNE TERRE MINE, BRIDGETON, MISSOURI

Location: About 306 miles SW of Chicago

Difficulty: Beginner–advanced

Outfitter: West End Diving (314-731-5003, www.2dive .com) in Bridgeton, about 60 miles south of St. Louis, owns the mine and runs guided diving trips weekends year-round by reservation; beginner-advanced instruction, too.

Description: This might be as close as you get to the center of the Earth. For a century, Bonne Terre Mine wrested tons of lead from the ground. When the mine was abandoned in 1962, crystal-clear filtered groundwater slowly filled its lower three levels, engulfing miles of enormous caverns, tunnels, and shafts. Most dives average 40 to 60 feet; the "billion gallon lake" is consistently 58° with 100-foot visibility. Guides lead divers past old mining equipment, train tracks, ore carts, staircases, elevator shafts, rock pillars, calcium falls, and steam-powered jackhammers. Twenty-four dive trails lit by halogen lights run 7 miles, ranging from basic "open-water" caverns to cavelike tunnels. All the while, you're deep beneath the town's train station, pharmacy, funeral parlor, City Hall . . . . Freaky.

Directions: Take I-55 south through St. Louis. About 50 miles south of St. Louis, take exit 174b to US 67. Take US 67 south about 20 miles to the Bonne Terre exit. Turn right; the mine is 0.5 mile on the left.

Where to Connect

Charters

These are the guys to call if you want to head out wreck diving on Lake Michigan from the city. All city charters run out of Burnham Harbor, just south of the Museum Campus. The main season usually runs from April through November. Some scuba shops also arrange trips, but this is the most direct route.

- Dive Chicago-Great Lakes Explorer (312-922-5090, www .divechicago.com). Captain Bob Schak has been diving in Lake Michigan for 30 years and guiding divers for two decades.

- Odyssey (312-326-3330). Captain Butch Saldana has been guiding wreck dives for 20 years on Lake Michigan.

- Discovery Dive Charters (815-786-1337, www .discoverydivecharters.com)

- Chicago Dive Charter (312-842-1480, www .chicagodivecharter.com)

- Pirate's Cove dive shop in Milwaukee (414-482-1430, after hours 414-588-6764, www.nitroxplus.com/piratescover .htm) runs year-round dive charters in Wisconsin. Captain Jerry Guyer is probably the most experienced captain on the lake.

- Shipwreck Adventures (815-378-8152, www .shipwreckadventures.com) in Winthrop Harbor near the Illinois-Wisconsin border runs trips all over the Great Lakes.

- Enterprise Marine (847-520-4689, www.captaindales.com) in Waukegan Harbor focuses on wrecks from the northern suburbs into southern Wisconsin but does some city dives, too.

Clubs and Organizations

- Aquarium Divers Scuba Club (www.aquariumdivers.com) includes diving volunteers, staff, and friends of the Shedd Aquarium and meets at the Shedd. Dive travel includes regional sites as well as more far-flung destinations, as Fiji and Bonaire.

- Windy City HammerHeads (www.uwsafaris.com /page100.html), affiliated with Underwater Safaris, visits area dive sites.

- Illinois Council of Skin and Scuba Divers (www .illinoisscubacouncil.org) is an umbrella organization of skin and scuba diving clubs throughout the state.

- Underwater Archaeological Society of Chicago (708-636-5819, www.chicagosite.org/uasc.htm) is a volunteer, non-profit group that studies and preserves local shipwrecks and other underwater resources. The group often presents its findings with slide and video shows at the Shedd Aquarium, where it meets.

- Chicago Aquanauts Scuba Association (www.scubaclub .org) runs local, regional, and international dive trips and has a strong training program with PADI-certified instructors teaching specialties like wreck diving. Club meets in Mount Prospect.

Dive Shops

Many dive shops in the metro area offer Professional Association of Diving Instructors (PADI) and National Association of Underwater Instructors (NAUI) courses. Once you're certified, you're eligible to rent equipment at dive destinations pretty much anywhere.

- Underwater Safaris Scuba Center (2950 N. Lincoln Ave., Chicago, 773-348-3999, www.uwsafaris.com), a full-service shop, is also home to the Handicapped Scuba Association Training Center of Illinois. In 1992, co-owner Marianne

Preker helped start Project TIDE, which aims to teach teens with disabilities independence through scuba diving.

- Adventures in Scuba (Riverpoint Center, 1730 W. Fullerton Ave., Chicago, 773-935-3483, www.advscuba.com)

- Aquanauts Odyssey (9815 S. Commercial Ave., Chicago, 312-326-3330) dropped its retail business, but veteran diver and owner Butch Saldana still offers instruction and repair.

- Mike Parnell's Magnum Scuba (14 E. 11th St., Chicago, 312-341-3483, www.magnumscuba.com)

- Scuba Systems (3919 Oakton St., Skokie, 847-674-0222, www.scubasystems.com)

- Elmer's Water Sports (1310 Oakton St., Evanston, 847-475-7946, www.elmerswatersports.com)

- Underseas Scuba Center (611 N. Addison, Villa Park, 630-833-8383, www.underseas.com)

- Scuba Emporium (708-389-9410 in Alsip, 708-226-1615 in Orland Park; www.scubaemporium.com) has been around since 1974. Kayak diving courses among the offerings.

Event

- Our World Underwater (www.ourworldunderwater.com), in late April at the Donald E. Stephens Convention Center in Rosemont, is a consumer scuba and dive-travel show that draws crowds of 12,000-plus.

Books

- Daniel, Stephen, and Thom Holden. *SS America: A Diver's Vision of the Past.* St. Paul, MN: Great Lakes Shipwreck Preservation Society, 2001.

- Feltner, Charles E., and Jeri Baron Feltner. *Shipwrecks of the Straits of Mackinac.* Dearborn, MI: Seajay Publications, 1991.

- Harrington, Steve. *Divers Guide to Michigan*. St. Ignace, MI: Maritime Press, 1998.

- Johnson, Kathy, and Greg Lashbrook. *Diving and Snorkeling Guide to the Great Lakes*. Houston, TX: Pisces Books, 1991.

- Kohl, Cris. *The 100 Best Great Lakes Shipwrecks*, vol. 2, *Lake Michigan and Lake Superior*. West Chicago, IL: Seawolf Communications, 1998.

  ———. *The Great Lakes Diving Guide*. West Chicago, IL: Seawolf Communications, 2001.

- Lenihan, Daniel J. *Shipwrecks of Isle Royale National Park: The Archeological Survey*. Duluth, MN: Lake Superior Port Cities, 1994.

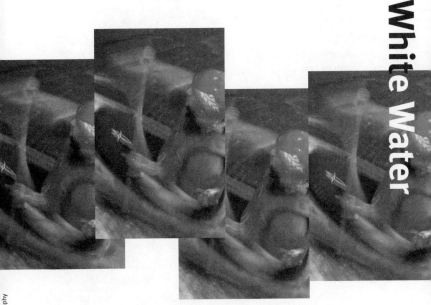

THAT THE CHICAGO Whitewater Association (CWA) exists speaks volumes about the dogged dedication metro-area paddlers bring to the sport. Chicago is about the farthest place from whitewater ground zero you can get (no hills = no rushing rivers).

The good news: you've got some options within a couple hours drive of the city—from the nation's first artificial whitewater course in South Bend, IN, to beginner-practice riffly rivers like the DuPage and bona fide homegrown Illinois white water on the Vermilion. And when the surf's up on Lake Michigan, you've got city-limits wave play.

Alas, local devotees say, the sport requires more than great paddling skills.

151

"There's no getting around it," says Erik Sprenne, a CWA officer and past president. "You've got to love long-distance driving to be a whitewater paddler in Chicago."

Regular Chicago paddlers can drive in their sleep to a clutch of well-loved northern Wisconsin rivers within a 5- or 6-hour drive of the city. The region's central river, the Wolf, is a top destination for instruction and, conveniently, lies just 40 minutes from the Peshtigo and a hair over an hour from the Menominee. All three rivers offer rafting trips, the best way to get a taste of white water if you're not an experienced paddler.

And for the hard core, rivers up and down the Appalachian range (Tennessee's Ocoee, West Virginia's Gauley, Pennsylvania's Youghiogheny, North Carolina's Nantahala) are fair game for a weekend trip. Ditto for creeks and rivers in the Midwest's northernmost reaches where fearless whitewater addicts make spring ice-out pilgrimages or gas up the car at a moment's notice if a warm-weather rainstorm brings water levels up. It's the Drive, Paddle, Sleep, Paddle, Drive routine: leave Friday after work, drive all night, paddle all day, pass out, wake up Sunday morning, paddle again, drive all night back home, muscles screaming.

"I've driven 12 hours to a river and found no real water, so you drive another 100 miles to find a river everyone is happy with," Sprenne says. "It's just part of the territory living here."

Spring is whitewater prime time, but this chapter includes summer and fall options, too. Online USGS gauges are listed where available (the U.S. Geological Survey gauges let you track real-time water flow for a given stream; see Links in *Where to Connect*, page 181). Descriptions and maps here can't list a river's every feature; for more details and great maps needed to safely run white water see Mike Svob's brilliant Illinois and Wisconsin paddling series and the classic *Whitewater, Quiet Water*.

For safety and logistical reasons—not to mention entertainment—paddling is really a group sport. No book can take the place of hitting the water with someone who knows it well. Luckily, there's no shortage of clubs for finding boating partners, or finding out about closely guarded "secret" streams, the ones in surprising places that come up only occasionally and require what boating guru Dag Grada calls "whitewater voodoo," mastery of the art and science of weather prediction and rainfall analysis.

Final words: always scout first. Portage when in doubt. And if the water looks too high, follow the inverse of the Nike maxim (Just Don't Do It). But mostly, frolic in the froth.

City Limits

LAKE MICHIGAN

Location: Chicago Central. Strong North and South Side picks, too.

Length: Whatever you're up for

Difficulty: Intermediate to advanced. Cold water and serious surf depending on conditions.

Map: Chicago Park District's "Chicago's Lakefront" map (312-747-2474) shows launch and land points at city beaches along the Lake Michigan Water Trail (just be aware that beaches are technically open Memorial Day–Labor Day only; most kayakers haven't faced problems launching outside that time).

Heads up: Closest-to-Loop whitewater practice; check weather at http://205.156.54.206/om/marine/gtlakes.htm.

Description: Wait until a nor'easter blows 20 mph or so for several hours, make up an excuse to leave work ("surf's up" doesn't usually cut it), and head to the lakefront to hit the waves. Peak winds in spring and fall (September's often tops). Kayak surfing is supremely fun and great training for whitewater boaters. Beware: Lake Michigan can dish it out. Rip current and above-your-head waves are brought to bear given the right conditions. Study the surf the way you'd scout a river before plunging ahead.

Good beach picks include Leone and Montrose on the North Side and Rainbow Beach on the South Side. Crescent-shaped 12th St. Beach abutting Meigs Field scores points for being closest to the Loop, but there's fierce parking competition with museum-goers on weekends. Go early or save this spot for the weekday grind. If you've got wanderlust for ex-urban surf, see the "Windsurfing & Surfing" chapter.

Directions: Leone Beach is roughly 7200 N. Take Lake Shore Dr. north until it turns into Sheridan Rd. Take Sheridan to Touhy Ave. Turn east on Touhy and follow to the beach parking lot.

Montrose Beach is 4400 N. Exit Lake Shore Dr. at Montrose Ave. Take Montrose east to the parking lot closest to the beach house.

12th St. Beach is just south of the Loop. From Lake Shore Dr., take the Museum Campus exit (from the north it jogs around Roosevelt Rd. and puts you onto McFetridge Dr.). Follow signs to 12th St. Beach, south of the planetarium. Try your luck at the metered spots on Solidarity Dr. or suck it up and park in the pay lot (the last one before the planetarium).

Rainbow Beach is at 79th St. Take Lake Shore Dr. south until it turns into S. Shore Dr. (it jogs behind the South Shore Cultural Center around 71st St.). Turn east on 79th St. Follow the winding road past the filtration plant to beach parking.

 Short Hops

DUPAGE RIVER

Location: About 45 miles SW of Chicago

Length: 5 miles

Difficulty: Class I–II (some features might hit Class II+ in higher water). Beginner.

Put-in: Hammel Woods Forest Preserve in Shorewood

Takeout: Shepley Rd. Bridge on west side of river

Gauge: USGS 05540500

Book: *Paddling Illinois.*

Description: The Chicago Whitewater Association takes beginners here in spring to get a taste of river after they've learned the basics in CWA's winter pool classes. This riffly stretch in Will County has decent current with rocks, eddies, waves, and ferry spots. Check out the surf wave that emerges when the water's right, about 0.25 mile above the I-80 Bridge. Most riffles are packed between I-80 and Shepley Rd.

Directions: Take I-55 south to US 52 (Jefferson St.) exit. Turn right (west) on US 52. At IL 59 (Brookforest Ave.) stoplight, turn right (north). Take IL 59 to the Hammel Woods entrance. Turn right (east) into the forest preserve and follow signs to the Grinton Grove picnic area. Carry your boat down a path and across a footbridge to the landing downstream of the dam.

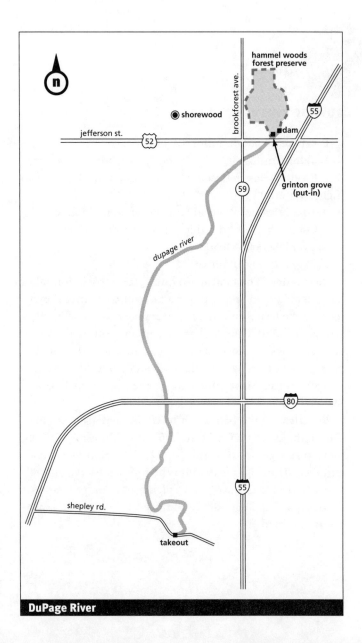

hammel woods
forest preserve

shorewood

brookforest ave.

jefferson st. 52

55

dam

59

grinton grove
(put-in)

dupage river

80

55

shepley rd.

takeout

DuPage River

EAST RACE WATERWAY, SOUTH BEND, INDIANA

Location: About 90 miles E of Chicago

Length: About 0.3 mile (1,900 feet)

Difficulty: Class II. Beginner friendly, but intermediates best able to maximize play.

Season: First Saturday in June to mid-August

Outfitter: East Race (574-233-6121 or 574-299-4765, www.ci.south-bend.in.us/PARKS/index.htm) rents rafts and related gear, plus one- or two-person funyaks.

Heads up: The more you play, the less you haul your boat. East Race regulars rig up a wheel device to fit in their boat for EZ rolling back to the top of the run.

Description: Fighting Irish be damned. Whitewater boaters flock to South Bend not to ogle the blue-and-gold gridiron powerhouse but to partake of the country's first artificial whitewater course, built in 1984.

The downtown course comes off the St. Joseph River and has hosted regional U.S. Olympic team trials. But it's beginner friendly, with rescue staff at the ready with throw ropes to get you out of trouble. It's short and fast, normally running around 450 cfs. Challenge yourself by trying to catch as many eddies as possible. Great practice for surfing, 180s, some enders and peel-outs. The very end of the course, where the run meets the river, serves up a tasty spot for practicing rolls in current.

Use the hose at the end of the run to rinse off (some boaters complain about poor water quality.) If you bring your own kayak, it costs $4 weekdays, $8 weekends. Come Saturdays at 11 A.M. when kayakers and canoeists get the place to themselves; at noon, the course opens to the raft and funyak rental crowd.

Directions: Follow I-90 south to Indiana (I-90 eventually merges with the I-80 toll road). Take South Bend exit 77. Follow Michigan St./US 33/IN 933 south. Turn left (east) at

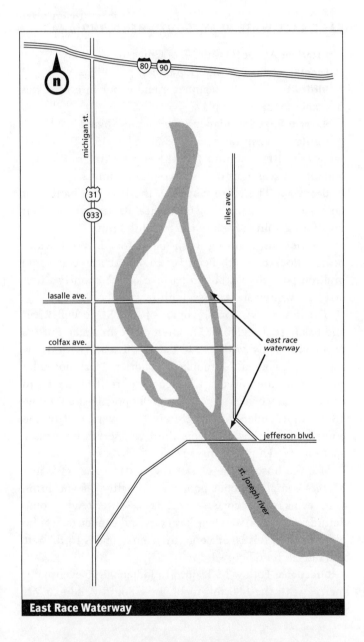

East Race Waterway

Colfax Ave., crossing the St. Joseph. Turn right (south) on Niles Ave. and park near the course start by Jefferson Blvd.

By transit, if you're not hauling a boat, you can take a South Shore train (800-356-2079, www.nictd.com) from downtown to the South Bend airport station. From there, hitch a cab to East Race or take the Transpo Lincolnway West bus (219-233-2131) downtown to the main bus terminal. From there, it's an eight-block walk to East Race. Walk north on Michigan St. to Colfax Ave., turn right (east) on Colfax, and cross the river.

VERMILION RIVER

Location: About 106 miles SW of Chicago

Length: 7.5 miles

Difficulty: Class II (III). Intermediate and up.

Put-in: County N2249, a gravel road west off IL 178 just north of Lowell Bridge. Look for Vermillion River Rafting sign at road's end (respect private property there).

Takeout: Oglesby Bridge, also known as Ed Hand Rd. Bridge. (Turnoff is poorly marked. Heading west on IL 71 past IL 178, turn left, or south, at the big green sign pointing south to Oglesby.) A parking ban is being considered. Help out by parking well away from the road on the shoulder; *do not* park or drive along the guard rail by the stairs to load your boat.

Gauge: USGS 05555300. 500 cfs minimum. Online gauge near Leonore is several miles upstream of the run. Rough rule of thumb: divide the Leonore reading in half for Lowell. If Leonore reads 6–8 feet, chances are it's good at Lowell. Check on-site gauge at Lowell Bridge. At 4 feet or above, the river gets pushy. At 7 feet or above, it's in flood.

Outfitters: Vermillion River Rafting (815-667-5242, www .vermillionriverrafting.com) in Lowell rents rafts and one-

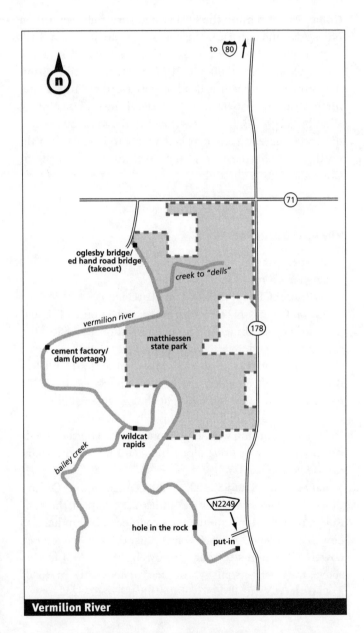

to (80)

(71)

oglesby bridge/
ed hand road bridge
(takeout)

creek to "dells"

vermilion river

(178)

matthiessen
state park

cement factory/
dam (portage)

bailey creek

wildcat
rapids

N2249

hole in the rock

put-in

Vermilion River

and two-man funyaks from May through mid-July. Canoe the Vermilion (815-673-3218, www.canoethevermilion .com) in Streator rents canoes for flatwater and whitewater sections and runs kayak shuttles; camping, too.

Maps and books: *Paddling Illinois.* Also see www.wpr .pair.com/vermilion.

Heads up: Homegrown mecca

Description: A rebuttal to those who think Illinois white water is a contradiction in terms. Rolling through Mathiessen State Park for a stretch, you're rewarded with plenty of play as well as 200-foot-high sandstone cliffs, white cedar, and waterfalls.

By July, the Vermilion is usually bony, but it can pick up again with fall downpours. Rapids are well spaced with forgiving pools. Popular play spot: Hole in the Rock, a cluster of chutes formed by several big rocks that comes up shortly after the put-in. Three or 4 miles into the trip, massive boulders on river-right mark the approach to Wildcat Rapids, the river's Class II–III drop. Scout first: the rapid can collect whole trees at higher water. After Wildcat, some boaters detour south onto Bailey Creek. **Caution:** the looming cement plant means you're heading for a deadly low-head dam (portage). Keep your eyes peeled for a creek to the east about 1 mile after the dam; if the water's high enough, paddle through the canyon to a 45-foot waterfall in Mathiessen.

Directions: Follow I-55 south to I-80 west. Take exit 81 for Starved Rock State Park. Turn south onto IL 178. Take IL 178 about 8 miles south until you hit County N2249. Turn west onto N2249 and follow to the landing at the end of the road. You should see the sign for Vermillion River Rafting (owner Bob Herbst lives right here). Check the Illinois Area Paddler message board (www.rivers-end.org/iap) for the latest on the takeout situation. There's talk of building an off-road parking/access site.

ROOT RIVER, RACINE, WISCONSIN

Location: About 80 miles N of Chicago

Length: 0.4 mile

Difficulty: Intermediate and above. Beginners will just get flushed through. Regular boaters say more than 1,000 cfs makes for Class III water.

Put-in: Below Horlick Dam and the bridge on the river's east side. Access from Quarry Lake Park.

Takeout: Quarry Lake Park. Exit after the last drop, before the golf course and bridge downstream.

Gauge: USGS 04087240. Minimum 250 cfs; 450–800 cfs optimal for intermediate play.

Heads up: Urban playspot gem. Gorgeous swimming in Quarry Lake. Stop for pizza at Wells Brothers (262-632-4408) in town.

Description: Short but sweet. The Root has sufficient flow many months of the year. And when it's up, usually in spring or after a decent downpour, "it's just downright fun," says Milwaukee boater and Root fan Mark Corsentino. You get about a half-dozen play spots, with ledges, wide and smooth surfing waves, and holes galore. Vertical moves at the run's end depending on levels (above 1,800 cfs or so, Corsentino says, and it's a dang fine rodeo hole).

Rock walls and tree-lined banks make for a surprisingly pretty urban run. But don't be fooled, the water is bona fide city stuff: keep nose plugs tightly affixed and don't forget the dry top. Happily, the deep, clean water of Quarry Lake beckons for a decontaminating dip (the lake is also a popular scuba spot: see "Scuba Diving," page 142).

Most boaters take out before the golf course. If you continue another riffly mile or so, you can check out the Root River steelhead facility. Which brings up a crucial point: the Root draws hoards of anglers for trout and salmon runs in spring and fall (see "Fishing," page 198). With playspots in short supply, local boaters are very protective of this under-the-radar favorite. Some asked that it not be included in this book, lest one wayward boater spoil the party for everyone. Prove them wrong. Tread gingerly. Don't tread on fishermen's lines. And play nice to keep the Root open to all.

Directions: Take I-94 west. Exit at WI 20 east. Take WI 20 east about 6 miles to WI 31. Turn left (north) on WI 31. Take the right split (east) onto County MM. You'll see the Horlick Dam and a Days Inn. Turn right (east) onto Northwestern Ave./WI 38. Cross the bridge over the Root; stay in the right lane. The entrance to Quarry Lake Park is less than 0.25 mile on your right. (It's 75 cents to enter during peak season, Memorial Day–Labor Day.) Go past the rest building and park in the lot closest to the river, west of Quarry Lake. Carry your boat north along an informal river path (it starts as a paved path from the parking lot) to the dam. Put in below the dam and bridge.

Longer than a Short Hop

WOLF RIVER, LANGLADE COUNTY, WISCONSIN

Location: About 250 miles N of Chicago

Length: 3.5 miles (the Wolf has about 30 miles of white water depending on conditions).

Difficulty: Section III is Class II–III intermediate run at normal levels. Fine for beginners in rafts. For kayakers, intermediate–advanced.

Put-in: Herb's County M launch

Takeout: Buettner's Wild Wolf Inn on the east side of river off WI 55 just south of County M

Gauge: USGS 04074950. Or call Bear Paw (see below) for

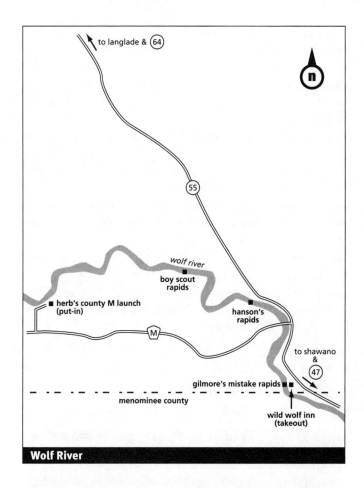

to langlade & 64

n

55

wolf river

boy scout
rapids

■ herb's county M launch
(put-in)

hanson's
rapids

M

to shawano
&
47

gilmore's mistake rapids ■ ■

menominee county

wild wolf inn
(takeout)

Wolf River

the latest reads. Local paddlers often refer to the gauge on the west side of WI 55 just north of the intersection with WI 64. Park by the historic marker and go down the steps. Minimum 6 inches or 300 cfs for Section III.

Outfitters: Expect to demonstrate your skills to rent a boat. Wolf River Guides (715-882-3002, www.wolfriverguides .com) rents canoes and whitewater kayaks to qualified boaters and runs guided paddling trips on the Wolf and area spring-run-only Class II and III rivers; instruction. Bear Paw Outdoor Adventure Resort (715-882-3502, www.bearpawinn .com) rents whitewater kayaks to qualified boaters, runs shuttles in summer, and rents canoes and kayaks for flat-water trips; lodging and camping, instruction. Herb's Rafts at Buettner's Wild Wolf Inn (715-882-8612 or 8611, www .wildwolfinn.com) rents rafts for self-guided trips of varying length along 25 miles of river from Hollister to the border with the Menominee reservation. Big Smoky Falls Rafting (715-799-3359) on the Menominee reservation sells kayak-ers permits for $25 including shuttle and rents rafts for 1- to 4-hour trips on Class III+/IV Section IV water (best to have prior rafting experience).

Map and books: Call any Langlade-area outfitter for a Wolf River map. *Paddling Northern Wisconsin; Whitewa-ter, Quiet Water.*

Heads up: Potential for year-round white water. Primo trout fishing.

Description: The Wolf is whitewater HQ for many Chicago paddlers. A popular teaching, racing, and rafting stream, the Wolf has enough sections to keep beginners and more advanced boaters busy. Locals divide the river into four sections that roughly reflect the maximum difficulty at normal levels (Section II from Hollister-Langlade is Class II and so on). The Wolf peaks in spring, but plenty save it for July or August when other options are sucked dry. Head out early morning or late afternoon to avoid heaviest raft traffic.

Section III runs about 11 miles from WI 64 to the Wild Wolf Inn; most boaters shorten it up and put in off County M. The short stretch crams in three major rapids: Boy Scout Rapids, Hanson's Rapids, and Gilmore's Mistake, a prime playspot at the takeout. The section's biggest drop, Gilmore's Mistake, offers up big wave-trains and surfing at a riverwide hole. It's bony at low levels—face plants not advisable. Take out after the boulder garden at the Wild Wolf Inn landing.

The inn's superlative location overlooking Gilmore's Mistake—and the owners' kindness in offering kayakers easy access to the rapids—has made it a popular kayaker hangout with good grub and an unfettered view of rodeo-boater stunts. You need a permit from the Menominee Nation to continue past Gilmore's Mistake and get to the river's most challenging Section IV (Class III+/IV). The Wolf is a National Wild and Scenic River (eagles and water-fowl abound), but the stream's under threat from a proposed zinc and copper mine at its headwaters in Crandon.

Directions: Take I-94 west to Milwaukee. Take the I-894 bypass to I-41 north. After Appleton, take WI 47 north toward Shawano. At Shawano, take WI 55 north. Wild Wolf Inn is about 30 miles north of Shawano on WI 55 (and about 6.5 miles south of the WI 55/64 intersection). To park and play at Gilmore's Mistake, head for the lot at the left of the Wild Wolf Inn (go down the hill to the designated parking area and carry your boat about 100 yards to the put-in; don't block or park at the turnaround). Check in at the Wild Wolf Inn before you head to the County M landing. From the inn, take WI 55 north and turn west onto County M. After about 2.5 miles on County M, turn north for Herb's landing.

wolf river, wisconsin

SAVVY BOATERS (to say nothing of anglers, hikers, and mountain bikers) bed down in Nicolet National Forest, 661, 000-plus acres of towering pine and hardwood forest, chock-a-block in summer with raspberries, blackberries, and blueberries prime for picking. With 580 miles of trout streams, 1,170 lakes, and more than 400 spring ponds—not to mention 800 miles of trails—you've got plenty to explore if you hit paddling burnout.

Head for Boulder Lake campground, closest to the Wolf's whitewater action. Cast a line for dinner on the 362-acre namesake lake; you may haul walleye, northern pike, bass, or panfish. Swim or bask on the sandy beach around dusk and wait for the loons, one of the Nicolet's 320 bird species.

Nicolet Nordic Ski Trails are within striking distance of Boulder Lake for 11 mellow miles of hiking and mountain biking (you've also got endless miles of logging roads, old railroad grades, and abandoned truck trails to explore on foot or mountain bike). A little farther afield from whitewater ground zero, Jones Spring Area, 2,000 acres with three placid lakes off limits to motors, has a few very sweet hike-in camping spots at Fanny Lake. Wood ducks and other wildlife abound; keep your eyes peeled for bald eagles, deer, black bear, and sables.

For maximum remoteness, head for a primitive tent site in one of the Lakewood ranger district's 14 dispersed camping areas, or just snag a backcountry site—you're allowed to pitch a tent virtually anywhere in the Nicolet. Insects are the only things that may interrupt your reverie: pesky black flies swarm until mid-June, deer flies are out in force in June and July if the weather's dry.

Details: Summer spots go fast at Boulder Lake, open May 1–October 31; reservations at (877) 444-6777. Regular sites $12 a night. Maps and skinny on dispersed sites or backcountry camping at Nicolet's Lakewood District Office (715-276-6333, www.fs.fed.us/r9/cnnf/index.html). To get to Boulder Lake, take I-94 west to Milwaukee. Take the I-894 bypass to I-41 north. After Appleton, take WI 47 north toward Shawano. At Shawano, take WI 55 north to County WW. Turn west on County WW. Turn north on Campground Rd. (FR 2166).

PESHTIGO RIVER, MARINETTE COUNTY, WISCONSIN

Location: About 275 miles N of Chicago

Length: 5 miles

Difficulty: Class III run can reach Class IV in spring with plenty of strainers. Fine for beginners in rafts. For kayakers, intermediate and up at normal levels.

Put-in: Mouth of Otter Creek on Farm Dam Lane off County C

Takeout: Public landing 12 on east side of river, 0.5 mile south of County C Bridge on Landing 12 Lane

Gauge: USGS 04067958. Minimum 220 cfs or 0 inches on paddlers gauge at County C Bridge near takeout. Pushy around 400 cfs; high water around 800 cfs.

Outfitters: Kosir's Rapid Rafts (715-757-3431, www.kosirs.com) rents one-man funyaks and runs guided rafting trips in spring high water; self-guided rafts after spring until mid-September. Kayak shuttles. Cabins and camping. Wildman Whitewater Ranch (715-757-2938, www.wildmanranch.com) runs guided high-water rafting trips, and rents thrill cats, funyaks, and rafts spring—fall, instruction. Owner Bill Wildman is a whitewater boater who plays blues harmonica; in summer you can catch quality blues bands (like Chicago regulars Devil in a Woodpile) in concert at the ranch. Cabins and camping, high ropes course. Wolf River Guides (715-882-3002, www.wolfriverguides.com) runs guided kayak trips, instruction.

Books: *Paddling Northern Wisconsin; Whitewater, Quiet Water.*

Heads up: Back-to-back rapids. Yee-haw.

Description: Dubbed the Roaring Rapids, this section offers up almost continuous rapids, half a dozen complex Class II–III drops with long boulder gardens as bookends. Spring is prime time on the Pesh (it's got a smaller water-

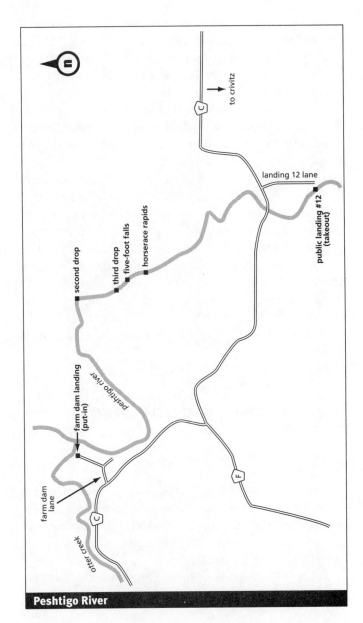

Peshtigo River

N

to crivitz

landing 12 lane

second drop

third drop

five-foot falls

horserace rapids

public landing #12 (takeout)

farm dam landing (put-in)

peshtigo river

farm dam lane

otter creek

C

F

shed than the Wolf and is more technical), but a summer
rain can push levels to 400 cfs of fun.

Huge backrollers at Second and Third Drops at high
water. At decent water levels, a straightforward chute
opens in the river's center for Five-Foot Falls, a riverwide
ledge—only skilled paddlers should take the east channel
(hit it just right or find yourself hugging the huge boulder
at the bottom). Breathe deep for Horserace Rapids, the section's toughest, with fast boulder gardens leading into a
steep gorge that narrows to about 20 feet. Scout or portage
west and beware Dragon's Teeth, or Diamond Splitter,
rocks at the bottom. When you get a minute to rest, take in
the old-growth hemlock and red pine flanking the river.

Directions: Take I-94 west to Milwaukee. Take I-43
north to Green Bay. At Green Bay, take US 141 north to
Crivitz. Turn west onto County A until you hit County C.
Turn west onto County C. Continue on County C, crossing the river. Keep right to stay on County C as it forks
with County F. Turn east onto Farm Dam Lane from
County C.

MENOMINEE RIVER, MARINETTE COUNTY, WISCONSIN

Location: About 300 miles N of Chicago

Length: 3 miles

Difficulty: Class III+ (IV). OK for beginners in guided
rafts. Advanced kayakers. Boaters who haven't paddled the
Menominee should strongly consider rafting first. Scout
from Piers Gorge foot trail before attempting run (good
spectator spots trailside, too).

Put-in: Downstream of Little Quinnesec Dam in Niagara, WI, off US 141. Alternate hike-in put-in off Piers Gorge Rd. from US 8.

Takeout: Landing after Terminal Surfer on Michigan side (north) off Piers Gorge Rd.

Gauge: USGS 04065106. Or call powerhouse at (715) 251-8230. All-season runs possible; discharge is dam controlled and rarely dips below 1,000 cfs. Great playboating at 2,000 cfs. Experts flock at 4,000 cfs.

Outfitters: Kosir's Rapid Rafts (715-757-3431, www.kosirs .com) and Wildman Whitewater Ranch (715-747-2938, www.wildmanranch.com) run guided rafting trips from late spring through fall. Wolf River Guides (715-882-3002, www .wolfriverguides.com) runs guided kayak trips for qualified paddlers.

Books: *Paddling Northern Wisconsin; Whitewater, Quiet Water.*

Heads up: Midwest's version of big-water Western rivers; some compare to the Colorado.

Description: The mighty Menominee crashes through 300-foot rock walls of Piers Gorge along the Wisconsin-Michigan border with enough playspots to spend an entire day working your way down the gorge. Lots of kayakers hike in along the trail from Piers Gorge Rd. (you can also do Piers Gorge as a carry-in park-and-play). But if you put in at Niagara, you're rewarded with Class II+ Sand Portage Falls, ideal for fast-water ferries and surfing.

Use the landing on the Michigan side (north) to scout or portage Missicot Falls, a 10-foot riverwide Class IV waterfall. Beware Volkswagen Rock downstream—higher water hides the beast. Great surfing and enders around the rocky island that leads into the Class II–III Sisters (or Twin Sisters). Some boaters come just to play in the Sisters, which serve up huge surfing holes at almost any water level. The river slows a bit before Terminal Surfer: doesn't look like much, but don't be fooled, it's a sticky hole.

Directions: Take I-94 west to Milwaukee. Take I-43 north to Green Bay. At Green Bay, take US 141 north to Niagara. From US 141 (River St.), turn right (east) onto Pine St. Turn left (north) onto Mill St. Put in on the Wisconsin side (south) downstream of Little Quinnesec Dam.

For an alternate put-in, from Green Bay take US 141 north to the split with US 8. Follow US 8 east and north, crossing the river onto the Michigan side. Turn left (west) onto Piers Gorge Rd. and park in the farthest lot. From there, hike your boat along the river's foot trail to the landing for Missicot Falls.

Wausau Whitewater Park

T'S NOT OFTEN open to recreational paddlers—four or five days a summer—but when it is, plenty make the pilgrimage to Wausau to play on this world-class course, which hosts a steady diet of slalom and rodeo competitions (including the World Cup Finals and U.S. Slalom National Championships in 2001). It's a favorite of the U.S. Canoe and Kayak Team. Depending on releases, the 535-meter slalom course running through downtown on the Wisconsin River can get up to Class IV; Big Drop rodeo hole to boot. Check http://home.dwave.net /~wkcc/ or call (715) 845-8200 for the skinny on rec releases and events. Wausau is about 282 miles north of Chicago. Take I-90 west past Madison. Take I-39/US 51 north to exit 192. Go east on Washington St. and cross the river. Entrance is across from the library.

Mecca

Endless Spring

P LENTY OF CHICAGO river jocks in search of thrills point their vehicles south for the Gauley or Ocoee. But the hardiest souls ditch the crowds and make spring pilgrimages north to paddle homegrown snowmelt runs in the frigid upper reaches of Michigan, Wisconsin, and Minnesota.

Why? Because they're beautiful. Many of these North Woods runs cut out of the bedrock along the Lake Superior shoreline offer deep canyons, waterfalls, and boreal forest aplenty. And "because they're ours," says Dag Grada, an encyclopedia of Midwestern white water from DeKalb, IL. "You basically get the chance to have high-grade white water in the Midwest without having to drive a ton."

Rivers on Minnesota's North Shore of Lake Superior (Duluth to the Canadian border) are generally within a 10- to 12-hour drive from Chicago. South Shore runs (roughly from Marquette in Michigan's Upper Peninsula to the Wisconsin-Minnesota border) can be had within 8 or 9 hours.

Although torrential downpours may give boaters a crack at running the Shores' creeks and rivers in summer or fall, with some exceptions these are spring waters. "It's a rite of spring. The flowers bloom and all the boaters head north to freeze their heinies off," Grada says. Most runs demand a high degree of boat control, strong river-reading skills, and "a healthy dose of respect," he says. Grada describes epic portages around unrunnable falls crashing through vertical rock walls as "effectively bouldering with boat."

Bigger, better-known whitewater rivers like the Presque Isle,

Montreal, and St. Louis are well documented on the printed page. But dozens of smaller—extremely challenging—creeks and rivers, like the Silver (see page 175), are mostly the stuff of "oral history," Grada says. All the more critical, then, for boaters to connect with experienced paddlers who know the ins and outs of these fickle waters. Highly skilled boaters from clubs like the Wisconsin Hoofers and Minnesota Cascaders (see *Mad City*, page 177, and *Where to Connect*, pages 179–80) take fairly regular spring journeys up north.

While some of these gems are roadside runs, just getting to the put-in on others is an adventure. Fred Young, an Illinoisan responsible for putting down first descents up and down the Shores in the '70s with the Hoofers, recalls the feel of utter remoteness on some early spring exploratory runs, turning a bend and running into moose and bear lumbering through the snow. Some rivers, like the Big Carp in the U.P., have been run only once because roadless access is so tough, Grada says. Some have yet to be run at all.

Grada, who's river-hopped up and down the Shores, has hiked in 3-foot pack snow to get to the Upper Yellow Dog, his dry suit tied off at the waist, kayak dragging like a sled from a sling around his trunk. He's spent several miles locked in low gear churning through axle-deep mud at 5 mph to get to an exploratory run on the Big Garlic around Marquette. (Spring paddling is sole reason this flatlander owns a four-wheel drive.) And he's sledded a quarter mile or so down a ski hill in his kayak (helmet on, of course) to the put-in on the North Shore's Poplar River.

"Yeah, we're desperate Midwestern paddlers," Grada says. But he clearly wouldn't have it any other way. Forget endless summer, he says. "We're hoping for endless spring."

SILVER RIVER, L'ANSE, MICHIGAN

Location: About 385 miles N of Chicago

Length: Lower Silver 4 miles, Upper Silver 2.5 miles

Difficulty: Upper Silver Class IV–V expert run, average gradient 150 feet per mile; Lower Silver Class IV+ expert run (or advanced boaters with experienced guidance), average gradient 62 fpm. Both highly technical; venture forth with a strong group that knows the Silver's dangers and charms.

Put-in: Dynamite Hill Rd. Bridge for Lower Silver (Dynamite Hill Rd. Bridge divides Upper and Lower sections), about 8 miles east of L'Anse.

Takeout: Silver Falls Park off Skanee Rd.

Gauge: USGS 04043150. Online gauge is new; correlations to runnable levels were still to be determined as of this writing. Until correlations are established, boaters should survey the river downstream of Dynamite Hill Rd. The river is relatively wide and rocky here. If rocks are showing and it looks like you can just make it through without scraping too much, Grada says, it's probably decent level (the river narrows away from the bridge). If rocks are covered, consider it too high to run safely without prior experience here.

Maps and books: DeLorme's *Michigan Atlas & Gazetteer*; www.americanwhitewater.org.

Heads up: Classic expert U.P. creek run. Stop at Hilltop Restaurant on US 41 in L'Anse for cinnamon rolls that weigh in at a full pound each (Grada describes them as "loaf-of-bread sized"). Quality carb and sugar high.

Description: Come spring, L'Anse, MI, a onetime logging and sawmill village curled around the lower tip of Lake Superior's Keweenaw Bay, draws hard-core kayakers to some of the Midwest's most challenging white water. The Silver—steep and technical—serves up gold-standard creek boating when it's up, often just a week or so in 35° late April–early May ice-out. It's a favorite of intrepid boater Dag Grada:

"The Silver was the first U.P. river I paddled, and that on a rare and precious '70s and sunny' spring day in 1994. The Silver may well be the epitome of the South Shore creek boating experience. Winding its way through the pines, this intimate 30- or 40-foot-wide stream crashes at a marked downhill pitch. The Upper offers a dazzling variety of challenging, technical drops that come rapid-fire while the Lower is similar, just with more space to rest and recover between drops. None of the drops, in and of themselves, are particularly difficult for an experienced, skilled paddler. It's just when they're stacked one atop the other, sometimes so close that there's barely room for a paddle stroke or two before you go flying into the next, that things become . . . ummm . . . 'interesting.' And there's something incredibly gratifying in turning upstream for a moment's rest into a pine-bowered shoreline eddy, looking back up at the cascading wall of water you've just worked and played your way through."

Most boaters run only the first part of Silver Falls, the Lower Silver's finale. The falls' main section has *muy* nasty hydraulics. Silver-lovers typically run the Upper and Lower in one shot. If you're new to the Silver, run the Lower a few times before attempting the relentless Upper. (On the Upper's hairier rapids, like the Cabin Section or Hail Mary, setting rope safety points is a must.) Warm-up or chaser? Grada and boating buddies often hit the Falls River, a 2-mile run of continuous Class III and IV ledges on the edge of town starting from Mead Rd.

Directions: Take I-94 west to I-43 north. After Green Bay, take US 141 north into Michigan until it hits US 41. Take US 41 north to L'Anse. Dynamite Hill Rd. is on the south side of town off US 41, just south of Hilltop Restaurant.

Turn east (right) onto Dynamite Hill Rd. and follow about 6–8 miles. The road eventually turns to gravel and hits an unmarked fork. (If you take the right fork, it takes you to Indian Rd. Bridge, put-in for the Upper Silver.) Continue straight to hit the put-in at Dynamite Hill Rd. Bridge. On-site gauge the river downstream of the bridge. **Caution:** the one-lane dirt road to the Lower Silver takeout at Silver Falls Park (south off Skanee Rd.) is sometimes too snowy or muddy to pass. Alternate takeout at the Skanee Rd. Bridge (continue on Skanee Rd. about 0.5 mile past the turn off for Silver Falls).

Mad City

MADISON IS KNOWN for its progressive politics, a great farmer's market, and a top-flight university. But the Mad City happens to be mad about whitewater paddling. Credit one part geography: the city is surrounded by twin lakes Mendota and Monona and is just a few hours drive from Wisconsin white water like the Wolf and Peshtigo. And add one part Hoofer: the University of Wisconsin's Hoofer Outing Club. According to lore, the outing club's whitewater group started in the 1950s after a quietwater trip blundered onto a section of rapids (the canoes were shot, but the boaters were stoked).

By the '60s, the club's boat shop was the place to find the hottest new fiberglass molds from Europe. And members started traveling across the country to national races, bagging awards like the first American medals (C-1 wildwater team) at the world championship wildwater races. By the '70s, Hoofers like Illinoisan Fred Young were in the thick of river exploration—"Fearless Fred" routinely put 100,000 miles a year on his Mercury Marquis station wagons—notching first descents throughout the region. Hoofer Gordy Sussman opened Rutabaga Paddlesport Shop in Madison, a mecca for all things paddling.

Today the Hoofer Outing Club is one of the country's largest outdoor collegiate clubs with 3,500 members (whitewater boating is just one part of it; there are hang gliding, mountaineering, equestrian, sailing, scuba, and ski and snowboard clubs, too). Most members are university affiliated, but anyone can join by joining the Wisconsin Union.

Whitewater Hoofers are a tight-knit group, holding regular reunions that are "like going to a Neil Diamond concert," Young says. Today Fearless Fred, now in his late 50s and running the family business outside Rockford, IL, is more into fly-fishing than whitewater boating. But he's a hard-core Hoofer. He and his wife, Wendy, a Minnesota Cascader, paddled down the "aisle" to their wedding ceremony in 1981 on the banks of the Wolf. Young's run some 400 rivers, hairy stuff his specialty. And he relishes memories of long Hoofer road trips, passing the time discussing black holes with astrophysics graduate students.

"It was the best, just all about being ready for adventure," Young says. "We were fearless."

Where to Connect

The Basics: Instruction

- Chicago Whitewater Association winter pool classes, mid-October to mid-March. Great way to get fundamentals. City classes usually at New City YMCA (1515 N. Halsted St. at North Ave., 312-266-1242) plus several suburban locations. Instructional spring trips to DuPage, Vermilion, and Wolf Rivers. See www.northstarnet.org/eakhome/cwa/. Or contact Sigrid Pilgrim at (847) 328-0145.

- Bear Paw Outdoor Adventure Resort (715-882-3502, www
  .bearpawinn.com) in White Lake, WI, runs weekend whitewater paddling classes and private instruction on the Wolf
  and area rivers. Paddlesport gear, rentals, and lodging.

- Wolf River Guides (715-882-3002, www.wolfriverguides
  .com) in White Lake, WI, runs a canoe and kayak school
  on the Wolf and area rivers. Whitewater classes for most
  levels, including freestyle play and swiftwater rescue.
  Private instruction.

- Kayak and Canoe Institute at the University of Minnesota
  in Duluth (218-726-6177, www.umdoutdoorprogram.org)
  offers a full range of summer whitewater courses on the St.
  Louis, from river-running fundamentals to rodeo freestyle
  clinics.

- Nantahala Outdoor Center (800-232-7238, www.noc.com)
  in Bryson City, NC, runs a full range of whitewater paddling courses held on area rivers as the Nanty and Ocoee.

- Wausau Kayak/Canoe Corporation runs summer whitewa-
  ter training camps for beginners and intermediates on the
  Wausau Whitewater Course and nearby rivers. Contact
  Julie Walraven at (715) 845-5664 or e-mail wkcc@dwave.net.

Clubs

- Chicago Whitewater Association. You need to join.
  Instruction. Informal and formal trips throughout the
  Midwest and Appalachian range. See contacts above.

- Wisconsin's Badger State Boating Society (www.bsbs.org), or
  BS-squared, runs whitewater trips and clinics.

- Hoofers Outing Club at the University of Wisconsin-
  Madison (608-262-1630, www.hoofers.org/outing
  /Whitewater/index.html) offers boating gear for member
  use. Trips to Wisconsin waters, Appalachia, out West, and
  spring runs to the U.P. and points along the Lake Superior
  shore (club uses a strict rating system to decide who's qualified to go on what trips).

- Twin Cities–based Cascaders (612-452-8328) do plenty of Minnesota North Shore runs, among other trips.

Shops

- Chicagoland Canoe Base (4019 N. Narragansett Ave., 773-777-1489, www.chicagolandcanoebase.com), owned by lifetime paddler Ralph Frese (see "Sea Kayaking & Canoeing," page 44), carries a range of whitewater boats and gear.

- Moosejaw (1445 W. Webster Place #9, 773-529-1111, www.moosejawonline.com) has whitewater boats and gear.

- Rutabaga Paddlesport Shop (800-I-PADDLE or 608-223-9300, www.paddlers.com) in Madison, WI, founded by Hoofer whitewater addict Gordy Sussman, carries a full range of whitewater boats and gear.

Events

- Paddling in the Park (www.paddlinginthepark.com). Two-day canoe and kayak festival in July at Twin Lakes Recreation Area in Palatine. Low-cost clinics including white water. Meet vendors, test-drive new boats, and network with Chicago-area paddlers.

- Wausau Whitewater Park (715-845-8200, www.home .dwave.net/~wkcc) is a great place to see world-class paddlers. Wausau hosted the U.S. Slalom National Championships and World Cup Finals in 2001. WACKO Citizens Slalom in late June. Rodeo last weekend in August.

- East Race Waterway (574-233-6121 or 574-299-4765, www.ci.south-bend.in.us/PARKS/index.htm) in South Bend, IN, holds the Mid-America Slalom in late August and at least one international kayak race each year.

- Wolfman Triathlon (715-882-3502) in early September mixes a 3-mile whitewater paddle through Section II of the Wolf River, a 13-mile mountain bike, and 3.5-mile trail run.

- University of Wisconsin Hoofer Outing Club rodeo on the Menominee (608-262-1630, www.hoofers.org/outing/Whitewater/index.html) in August.

- Butter Cup slalom series, cumulative point series in Wisconsin and Minnesota. Starts Mother's Day on the Apple River in Somerset, WI, and ends mid- to late September on the Wolf River near Langlade, WI. Races draw Joe Boater as well as top-notch talent (Olympic paddler Rebecca Giddens and junior up-and-comer Gwen Greeley, both from Green Bay, WI, have raced the series). Appropriately, plastic dairy cow trophies. Contact Scott Stalheim at (715) 748-0647 or stalheim@tds.net.

Books

- Breining, Greg. *Paddling Minnesota*. Guilford, CT: Globe Pequot Press, 2001. Includes St. Louis, Baptism, and Brule.

- Dennis, Jerry, and Craig Date. *Canoeing Michigan Rivers: A Comprehensive Guide to 45 Rivers*. Davison, MI: Friede Publications, 2001. Flatwater and whitewater routes.

- Palzer, Bob, and Jody Palzer. *Whitewater, Quiet Water: A Guide to the Wild Rivers of Wisconsin, Upper Michigan, and Northeast Minnesota*. 8th ed. Birmingham, AL: Menasha Ridge Press, 1998.

- Svob, Mike. *Paddling Northern Wisconsin*. Black Earth, WI: Trails Books, 1998.

    ———. *Paddling Illinois*. Black Earth, WI: Trails Books, 2000.

    ———. *Paddling Southern Wisconsin*. Black Earth, WI: Trails Books, 2001.

Links

www.americanwhitewater.org

http://water.usgs.gov for USGS gauges

Cameron Lawson Photography

Fishing

CAST FOR SMALLMOUTH downtown in summer as they cruise the rocks along Lake Michigan's shore before you hit the outdoor film fest in Grant Park. Stalk walleye in the Skokie Lagoons under the watchful eye of a great blue heron. Throw a chunk of Spam on a line and haul a 4-pound channel catfish out of Lincoln Park Lagoon. Hop a fishing charter out of Burnham Harbor to battle a monster Chinook 10 miles offshore. The options inside the city and backyard alone are dizzying—small inland lakes, urban lagoons, riffly rivers, Lake Michigan. Widen the lens to tack on a few hours drive and they're seemingly endless.

The Big Lake offers up a bounty of salmon, trout, steelhead. Years back, commercial fishing

183

and sea lamprey virtually exterminated the native lake trout, triggering an alewife explosion. So Lake Michigan was stocked with Pacific salmon and steelhead (rainbow trout), migratory predators that spend part of their life in salt water, part in freshwater, to keep fish like the alewife in check. Turns out the game fish adapted remarkably well to a purely freshwater existence, making Lake Michigan prime sportfishing waters. And when the brawny lake-run salmonids make their migratory runs up coastal tributary rivers to their spawning grounds in spring and fall, anglers haul out the 9.5-foot fly rod or 10-foot spin-caster and flock to spots like the Root River in Racine for a chance at hand-to-hand combat with Some Seriously Strong Fish.

You're likely to see more people spin- and bait-casting around these parts, but fly-fishing is alive and well (and this chapter includes all three, though purists may gasp). Matt Mullady, who's been guiding anglers for 25 years on the Kankakee River, says people are just starting to realize how good its smallmouth fly-fishing is, just 60 miles south of the city. "I don't get it. People from Chicago will fly 1,200 miles to Montana to catch a cutthroat 8 inches long, but they can fish on the Kankakee for a smallmouth with the potential of taking an 18-inch fish with twice the fight."

Jon Uhlenhop of Chicago Fly Fishing Outfitters danced his first fly in the Skokie Lagoons at age 9. Urban fly-fishing, he says, is not a contradiction in terms. "Six years ago I'd go down to the lakefront and not see anyone else with a fly rod. That's not true anymore." He's hit CTA buses hauling down Lake Shore Dr. on a long back cast from Belmont Harbor. In spring and fall he casts from the lakefront harbors and piers for steelhead, coho, and brown trout. "We all go down there with dreams of 4- and 5-pound smallies and wind up hitting bluegill, perch, and rock bass just because they're more abundant and closer to shore," Uhlenhop says. "It's not always the most effective way to fish; sometimes it's just chuck and chance, but you still get the hand-to-hand combat. It's something to cure the itch."

And within a 3- to 4-hour drive of the city you can be dancing a fly for wild brown trout on a narrow, watercress-lined cold spring creek straight out of fly-fishing central casting in southwestern Wisconsin, whose limestone creeks are said to rival the fabled waters of central Pennsylvania.

If you already fish, you know that the sport is a specialized, complex alchemy of art and science. Equipment, technique, and approach all rely on the mercurial mix of wind, light, temperature, and so on. Happily, Chicago is home to several expert shops, like the veteran Henry's Sports & Bait Shop—and just plain experts, like Fishing Guy Bob Long, Jr.—that are your best source for the kind of detailed, nuanced information that can't be provided here. Consult the fishing reports in the two local papers, check out the barrage of local radio and TV fishing shows, and pick up

The Fishing Guy

HAVE A QUESTION about metro-area fishing but don't know who to ask? Try Bob Long, Jr., the Park District's angling point man, better known as The Fishing Guy. He runs a ton of urban fishing programs, getting some 12,000 kids out fishing every summer. He's also a lifelong Chicagoan (he lives in the same South Side house he grew up in), a lifelong angler ("I'm 52 years old and I've been fishing 47 years"), and a font of wisdom on area waters, having fished most of them. Fly-fishing smallmouth is his passion. "Put me on a kayak on the Kankakee at sunset and I'm a happy man." If he can't answer your question himself, he'll know who can. Call (312) 742-4969.

one of the many monthly fishing mags (like *Outdoor Notebook* or *Midwest Outdoors*).

Heads up: you won't find catch and size limits and special regulations here for each waterway because they change most every year. See *Before You Fry*, page 206, for contact info to check the latest with state officials.

City Limits

LAKE MICHIGAN SHORE

Location: Up and down 29 miles of Chicago lakefront

Fish: King and coho salmon, smallmouth bass, yellow perch, smelt, steelhead, among others

Seasons: Shore and harbor fishing year-round, some ice fishing allowed in the harbors depending on winter freeze conditions. City charters run April–October, sometimes early November (more on charters later).

Charters: Captain Al Skalecke (312-565-0104, www.captainalscharters.com) of Captain Al's Charter Service in Burnham Harbor has been guiding anglers on Lake Michigan for 30 years. Other established city charters from Burnham Harbor include Salmon Seeker Charters (773-267-9033) and Delila Sue Charters (630-837-7152). From Diversey Harbor, Kingfisherman Charters (630-897-5352) and Captain Randy's Charter Service (312-718-1995).

Tackle: Park Bait (773-271-2838) is on the east end of Montrose Harbor at Montrose Ave. and Harbor Dr.

Licenses and permits: $13 annual Illinois sportfishing license and $6.50 salmon stamp, or $5.50 daily license, available at Chicago Park District field houses and lagoons and most local bait shops. Note: no casting allowed within 100 feet of moored vessel or vessel underway.

Map and books: "Let's Go Fishing, Chicago" booklet from Chicago Park District (312-742-4969 or 742-7529) shows designated fishing areas in harbors and lagoons and includes bait tips. *Chicagoland's Top 30 Fishing Trips; Northern Illinois Fishing Map Guide.*

Description: Chances are, at one time or another a fisherman has dipped his rod along most every inch of Chicago's 29 miles of shoreline. Superb urban angling, off piers and breakwalls and in the city harbors. Though the lake's stars are salmon and trout, the variety of fish venturing close to shore has increased in recent years. Winter brings perch, panfish, and trout. Spring brings coho and smelt runs. Yellow perch are good all summer long (though the season is closed in July), as are smallmouth. From about September to December, king and coho salmon show up to lay eggs in the harbors, along with brown trout and steelhead chasing lake shiners and minnows. Where two decades ago smallmouth were a rarity along the city shoreline, now 5-pounders are caught every season.

So many spots to hit, but plenty of local anglers consider Montrose Harbor the city's best all-around shore fishing spot, with a pier that juts out into 20-foot depths and a shoreline full of riprap. Try inside the harbor or along the shore from the point to the harbor entrance. Or ask one of the locals. The harbor is on my regular run, and I've yet to hit a day when there aren't at least a few fishermen out.

Other productive spots: Navy Pier near downtown, Burnham Harbor by the Museum Campus, and Jackson Park's inner and outer harbor by 63d St. For fly-fishing, Jon Uhlenhop of Chicago Fly Fishing Outfitters likes Belmont and Diversey Harbors, checking out the smallmouth bed in the inlet by "Dog Beach" at Belmont Harbor, wading thigh-to waist-deep along a series of gravel bars lining the harbor's west shore or casting full sinking lines for kings or steelhead in fall and spring. Check out Lincoln Park

Lagoon, too (city lagoons have early-season bluegill and crappie in March/April, plus largemouth bass and stocked bluegill and catfish later in the season).

Directions: For Montrose Harbor, 4400 N, exit Lake Shore Dr. at Montrose Ave. Go east on Montrose; there's parking all along Montrose and lots east by the beach. By transit, take the Red Line L to the Wilson Ave. stop. It's a mile-plus walk: east on Wilson to N. Marine Dr., south to Montrose, east to the harbor. Or take the 78 bus to Marine Dr. and walk east on Montrose to the harbor.

For Jackson Park inner and outer harbors, 6400 S, take Lake Shore Dr. south to 63d St. Turn east at the light into the beach lot. By transit, take the Green Line L to E. 63d St (Red Line stops at 63d farther west). From there, take the 63 bus east to the harbors.

Bright Lights, Smelt City

A S THE CHILLY April evening starts to fold into darkness, fishermen's lanterns pop on around Montrose Harbor. Folding chairs are staked out by the edge of the water. A family chattering in Spanish, two small kids in pj's reluctantly tucked into sleeping bags on the grass, readies their nets. At 7 P.M., it's smelting time.

The city has a thing for smelts. Each April, when water temperatures run in the low 40s (and air temps can be equally or more frigid), the diminutive, anadromous, silvery fish migrate toward the shoreline to spawn at night. Most rainbow smelt caught during the spawning runs are about 6 inches long. Some say a big haul of smelt smells faintly of fresh cucumber, but most fishermen aren't snagging huge amounts these days. The smelt aren't native to Lake Michigan; their origins in the Big Lake are credited to escapees from a 1912 stocking of Crystal Lake in Michigan. Turns out they were good eats for resident lake trout, walleye, burbot, and yellow perch. And good eats for fishermen (see *Before You Fry*, page 206).

Dave Jesse of Hagen's Fishmarket (5635 W. Montrose Ave., 773-283-1944), a family-owned smelt purveyor since 1946, recommends rolling smelt in cracker crumbs and pan-frying 3 minutes or so. "The bones pretty much just melt out when you cook them so you can eat the whole thing—minus the head."

Smelting season runs 7 P.M.–1 A.M. throughout April. As the night wears on, the party picks up with the inevitable suitcases of Old Style and fires blazing in garbage cans around the harbors (for the record, both the beer and the fires are illegal). Other popular smelting spots are Belmont, Diversey, and Burnham Harbors, as well as 31st St. Pier and 95th St. Smelt stalkers need a state fishing license before dipping net.

Backyard

TAMPIER LAKE

Location: About 20 miles SW of Chicago

Fish: Largemouth bass, crappie, and bluegill tend to be most abundant, but lots of locals say it's the best metro-area walleye fishing hole around. Also northern pike, catfish, perch, sunfish, carp, white (striped) bass.

Seasons: Year-round action, but spring and fall are tops.

Tackle: Seasonal on-site bait and tackle shop (708-448-9809) at the lake's northeast end off 131st St., rowboat rentals April–end of October. Dee's Bait Shop (708-460-3337) in Orland Park is about a block from Tampier, just west of 135th St. and Wolf Rd.

Licenses and permits: Illinois fishing license. See "Fishing Guide" below for Cook County Forest Preserve's special catch and size regulations.

Maps and books: "Fishing Guide" from Cook County Forest Preserve District (708-366-9420) has depth maps. *Chicagoland's Top 30 Fishing Trips; Northern Illinois Fishing Map Guide.*

Heads up: Try to come during the week; summer weekends can be a mob scene. Wheelchair access and fishing wall at launch ramp (no gas motors).

Description: A 160-acre gem tucked into the sprawling 14,000-acre Palos and Sag Valley Forest Preserves. Fairly shallow, with depths to 15 feet, Tampier warms up fast in spring. Translation: early-season bass and panfish action along the shoreline cover. After spawning, the bigger panfish settle across midlake flats. Try for northern pike in the shallow bay north of 131st St. soon after ice-out; largemouth bass, crappie, and bluegill use the shallows for spawning from late April through June. Since yearly stocking of walleye fingerling at Tampier started in the mid-1980s, the gamefish has thrived here. Pick an overcast drizzly evening—walleye are notoriously light averse—and you might even pick one up as close as 5 to 8 feet from shore. In summer, work the edge of the old creek channel with deep-diving crankbaits for largemouth and walleye. Come on a weekday, rent a rowboat to ply the turbid waters, and feel the city melt away.

Directions: Take I-55 south to LaGrange Rd. (exit 279). Go south on La Grange/US 45 through the forest preserves. Turn right (west) on 131st St. From Wolf Rd. it's less than 0.5 mile to the parking lot and concession buildings. Additional parking a little farther west on the north side of 131st St. and on Lake-Cook Rd. just south of the intersection with 131st St.

BUSSE LAKE

Location: About 25 miles NW of Chicago

Fish: Largemouth bass, bass, bass. Also northern pike, walleye, bluegill, bullhead, catfish, sunfish, crappie, pumpkinseed, carp, and sucker.

Seasons: Year-round action, but spring and fall are best.

Tackle: Seasonal on-site shop (847-640-1987 or 847-437-0201) and canoes, rowboats, electric motors, and paddleboats for rent April–end of October. Quick Stop Food Pantry (1193 Biesterfield Rd., 847-923-1943) in Elk Grove Village carries the basics and limited tackle.

Licenses and permits: Illinois fishing license. See "Fishing Guide" below for Cook County Forest Preserve's special catch and size regulations.

Maps and books: "Fishing Guide" from Cook County Forest Preserve District (708-366-9420) has depth maps. *Chicagoland's Top 30 Fishing Trips; Northern Illinois Fishing Map Guide.*

Heads up: Shore and boat fishing; windy lake may make you wish you had rented an electric trolling motor with your rowboat (no boats in North Pool or the marshy pond north of Higgins Rd.).

Description: Bass-o-matic along some 20 miles of shore. The 590-acre Salt Creek impoundment is the county's biggest inland lake, divvied up into the 25-acre North Pool, 146-acre South Pool, and 419-acre Main Pool. Part of the heavily wooded Ned Brown Forest Preserve, this greenspace is an oasis in a suburban desert that includes the sprawling Woodfield Mega-Mall and convention-center-sized Ikea. Not surprisingly, the park sees a lot of strip mall escapees looking to run, blade, bike, boat, and fish (see "Running," page 461). When the weather's fine, you'll see sailboats and canoes out on the Main and South Pools.

For bass, some locals swear by the North Pool, usually

clearer and higher—and less busy—than the main lakes. Separated from the main lake by a spillway, the fish are corralled in their 25-acre home. Massive fertile weedbeds by late spring make it a happy home. North Pool has walleye and channel catfish. Late spring through summer, look for 5- to 10-foot depths and steep drop-offs for wily walleye. In summer, try below the main dam for walleye, crappie, bass, and catfish. There's a warm-water discharge just past the dam for year-round use—catch bass with just a minnow and hook there in early spring and late fall. The pond north of Higgins Rd. is an important pike-spawning area. Check out the resident elk herd in the pasture at the northwest corner of Arlington Heights and Higgins Rds.

Directions: Take I-90 west to Arlington Heights Rd. south. Stay on Arlington Heights until Higgins Rd./IL 72. Go right (west) on Higgins until you see the sign for Busse Lake. Turn left (south) and follow the road to the boat rental/tackle shop parking.

SKOKIE LAGOONS

Location: About 20 miles N of Chicago

Fish: Bass, walleye, northern pike, as well as panfish and catfish

Seasons: Year-round action, but spring and fall are best.

Tackle: Ed Shirley Sports (5802 W. Dempster St., 847-966-5900) in Morton Grove

Licenses and permits: Illinois fishing license. See "Fishing Guide" below for Cook County Forest Preserve's special catch and size regulations.

Maps and books: "Fishing Guide" from Cook County Forest Preserve District (708-366-9420) has depth maps. *Chicagoland's Top 30 Fishing Trips; Northern Illinois Fishing Map Guide.*

Heads up: Bike up the North Branch Trail from the city (see "Biking," page 219).

Description: In the Bad Old Days, carp and bullhead dominated this neglected dam-laced series of pools that the Potawatomi called the Chewab Skokie, "big wet prairie," before it was transformed into a network of lagoons that eventually feed into the North Branch of the Chicago River. But since the fishery got rehabbed in the early 1990s, it's become a first-class bass, pike, and walleye spot. Five-pound walleye lurk in the dam tailwaters. Plenty of anglers stake out a spot along the ample shoreline; try the west bank of Lagoon 6 just past the dike. But in my mind, the 190-acre shallow lagoons are best explored by canoe (see "Sea Kayaking & Canoeing," page 46). There's a boat launch at Tower Rd. You'll see guys dipping poles from the bridge. Come at dusk. Deer forage on the wooded islands. Great blue herons and kingfishers stalk the shoreline (see "Bird-watching," page 311).

Directions: Take I-94 west to Willow Rd. east. Continue on Willow and turn left (north) on Forestway Dr. Turn left (west) on Tower Rd. Cross the bridge (often full of people dangling fishing rods). Turn left (south) into the boat launch lot. Or pick one of the obvious gravel pull-off parking areas along Forestway Dr. on the lagoons' eastern edge.

Going Charter

APTAIN AL "THE fisherman's pal" Skalecke knows the waters off Chicago, with three decades of guiding sport-fishing charters on Lake Michigan. Though there's always some kind of fish to be caught along the city's shoreline, you can target your fish of choice and cover more ground on the open water. Equipped with temperature probes to check the thermocline and depth sonar to track schools, Skalecke says "I can do everything but open a fish's mouth."

He gets bookings for families, bachelorette parties, hotel guests. "Then there's the hard-core guys who want to get out early so they can be at their desks downtown by 9 A.M."

Charter season usually kicks off April 1 and runs through the end of October. Novices and seasoned anglers alike go charter. You don't need any equipment. Skalecke will even net, clean, gill, gut, and fillet whatever you catch (or you can practice catch and release). Depending on conditions, he may travel as far as 17 miles offshore. "You get 10 miles or so offshore, the city's just gorgeous," he says. Word to the easily seasick: 5- to 6-foot waves are usually too high, but Skalecke will go out in 4 footers.

In early April the coho are just starting to run; they're small—3 or 4 pounds—but manic. They're schooled up and feeding in large groups, putting on an average of a pound a week to beef up for the spawn. "They're scrappers," Skalecke says. "They're jumping a lot, rolling around and surface feeding this time of the year. It can be pretty dramatic." As the water temperature warms up, the fish move out deeper. "April, May, June, part of July—that's when you come out to catch a lot," Skalecke says. "I like June, it's not uncommon to come back with 20–30 fish—100 pounds of fish. You get some good action and some great battles." By midsummer, fish can be down 100–150 feet, especially lake trout. ("I've had lots of clients who catch a lake trout and high tail it down to Chinatown for their favorite restaurant to serve it up. It's tasty stuff, yellow flesh kind of like perch.")

"Most people who come later in the season, say September and October, they're going for the big ones. The Chinook aren't feeding, they're protecting their nests. And they're not easy prey. But you can get kings from 15 to 30 pounds." His boat's record heavyweights include a 33-pound Chinook, 28-pound brown trout, and 23-pound steelhead.

So what keeps Captain Al going after so many years plying the city's front-yard waters? "There are no two days alike out there. I love the fish, I respect them. Like steelhead, they're just solid muscle, they've got a thick, square base of the tail. They come out of the water and do a flip, they twirl and turn toward you, looking for slack in the line, and they just straighten out the hooks on the bait. Amazing. And it's so peaceful out there. People unplug from the city and leave the stress back on shore."

Short Hops

FLY-FISHING THE KANKAKEE RIVER, KANKAKEE RIVER STATE PARK

Location: About 60 miles S of Chicago

Fish: Smallmouth bass and channel catfish dominate. Also largemouth bass, walleye, croppie, bluegill, grass pickerel, freshwater drum, among others

Seasons: Year-round, but not many winter anglers. Fall best for fly-fishing smallmouth. Tributary Rock Creek stocked with rainbow trout in spring.

Tackle: Lanny's Live Bait and Tackle (815-935-1661) in Kankakee has been in business for some 20 years and is a font of information. For a guide, especially smallmouth fly-fishing, call Matt Mullady, (815) 932-6507. He's been guiding a quarter century on the Kankakee, since age 19. His dad, Ed, publishes the "Sportsmen's Letter," started in 1958, and wrote the book on the Kankakee.

Licenses and permits: Illinois fishing license

Maps and book: Lanny's has detailed river maps. *Kankakee River Fisherman's Atlas, Illinois.*

Heads up: Camp with a river view at Kankakee River

State Park (815-933-1383)—head for Potawatomi camp-ground to ditch the RV crowd. Call Reed's Canoe Trips (815-932-2663) in Kankakee for riffly canoeing along the glacial-scoured river.

Description: From its source near South Bend, IN, the Kankakee crosses into Illinois and flows 62 miles before joining the Des Plaines near Channahon to form the Illinois. One of the Midwest's cleanest rivers, listed on the federal Clean Streams Register, it's home to some unusual species, like the ironcolor shiner and the rare river red-horse. The river runs 11 riffly miles along the wooded and limestone-etched banks of Kankakee River State Park. Perfect for shore angling and wading. Dance a fly for smallies from Labor Day to mid-October. Most smallmouth average 10–12 inches, but 3- and 4-pounders are taken regularly (they reproduce naturally here). Too shallow for big bass boats. The park's nice and quiet after the summer crush. Limestone outcroppings. Wooded islands with even more shoreline. Tricky currents, rocky shoals, and eddies in the narrow stretch downstream of Rock Creek. Rocky bottom and many drop-offs. Try out the shoals around Warner Bridge. Hike the 3-mile creek trail for a limestone canyon and a small waterfall. Guide Matt Mullady says "you can see the fish from the suspension bridge over Rock Creek. So if the river's high and stained, you always have the cold, spring-fed creek. And the mouth of the creek's good, too." Cast your fly among the red-breasted mergansers and goldeneyes in November.

Directions: Take I-94 east to I-57 south to exit 315 (Bradley/Bourbonnais). Go right off the exit ramp to the first stoplight, Armour Rd. Take a right on Armour and follow to IL 102. Turn right (west) on IL 102 and go about 5 miles until you see the park on your left. Note: it's a shorter walk to the river from the Kankakee's north banks off IL 102 than from the south side off IL 113. But you'll see fewer anglers from the south bank.

FOX RIVER

Location: About 45 miles W of Chicago

Fish: Smallmouth, yellow, white bass (some large-mouth), channel and flathead catfish, northern pike, bluegill, carp, crappie, walleye

Seasons: Year-round, best in spring and fall

Tackle: Emerald Bait & Tackle (847-697-0193) in South Elgin on the west side of the river, not far from the dam, also carries some flies. Riverside Sports (630-232-7047) in Geneva carries a range of conventional and fly tackle.

Licenses and permits: Illinois fishing license

Map and book: "Fox River Access Areas & Fishing Guide," Illinois DNR (312-814-2070, www.dnr.state.il.us). *Northern Illinois Fishing Map Guide.*

Heads up: Bring a bike; paved Fox River Trail runs 32 riverside miles from Algonquin to Aurora.

Description: Along the broad Fox's 115-mile course from Antioch near the Wisconsin border to where it flows into the Illinois at Ottawa are 15 major dams that create tail-water areas and impound the water into pools. Eleven of those dams are sandwiched into a 22-mile, island-dotted stretch from riverside towns Elgin to Aurora, paralleled by the multiuse Fox River Trail and loads of riverside parks and forest preserves. Great fishing around each dam, some with channels, like the west side of the river at upper Batavia Dam, chock full of crappie. Ideally, by the time you read this, Metra will have gotten its act together and come up with a reasonable bikes-on-trains policy so you can catch a train from downtown to Elgin or Aurora, hop on your bike, and cruise the Fox River Trail (see "Biking," pages 218 and 232) to scout a quiet spot to call your own.

Jon Uhlenhop of Chicago Fly Fishing Outfitters likes the South Elgin dam, where he catches smallmouth in spring with his fly rod. (He says you'll probably catch more with a rod and reel: "People look at us like we're crazy swinging a fly rod out here.") "The dam's right by the police station. You can fish downstream of it for about a mile before it starts to flatten out and become featureless. Smallmouth like to hold in the oxygenated water there. Spring's great, like late April, for smallies. There's more water and the fish are more lethargic, more skittish in fall when the water's lower. There's lots of rock that helps hold the forage, some soft bottom. It's nice because the area's kind of shallow in the middle so I cast back to the sides for the first couple hundred yards below the dam. And there's a series of islands that are good to fish from, too. The banks are fairly covered with trees or parkland so you can fish from shore. There's some traffic noise from the road bridge—it's not Montana, but it's pretty serene, suburban serene. In spring you're wading knee- to waist-deep. I've done well on yellow and white squirrel tail Clousers, about 1–1.5 inches, chartreuse and white Clousers, olive and white Clousers, crayfish flies, all along the Fox." St. Charles and North Aurora dams are popular spots. And you can always fish from a canoe along one of the state's prettiest river stretches, on the Lower Fox from Sheridan to Wedron (see "Sea Kayaking & Canoeing," page 54).

Directions: Take I-90 west to IL 31 south for about 5 miles. Go left on Spring St., which takes you right to the river. The dam is about a block north of Spring St.

By transit, take Metra's Milwaukee District/West Line to the Elgin station. The South Elgin dam is just over 2.5 miles south.

FLY-FISHING THE ROOT RIVER, RACINE, WISCONSIN

Location: About 80 miles N of Chicago

Fish: Steelhead, brown trout, Chinook, coho, and the occasional, elusive brookie

Seasons: Year-round fishing, fall and spring best. Chinook run early/mid-September through the end of October; Skamania strain is more hit or miss, from early/mid-August through October, with fish hanging around through the winter; steelhead spring run often peaks around March.

Tackle: Jalensky's Sports Headquarters (262-554-1051) in Racine has been around for 20-plus years; they do some guiding, but most anglers go it alone. Racine has a dozen-plus charter boats that run trips onto Lake Michigan; for details call Fishing Charters of Racine (800-475-6113 or 262-633-6113).

Licenses and permits: $10, 2-day nonresident Wisconsin license. The $15, 4-day, $20, 15-day, and $34 annual licenses require $7.25 trout and salmon stamp.

Map: Best advice, grab a local city map and talk to the guys at Jalensky's.

Heads up: Stop for pizza at Wells Brothers Italian Restaurant (262-632-4408), a Racine institution.

Description: Fly-fishing on this riffly urban river runs an intense 6-mile stretch from Racine Harbor to Horlick Dam. It's something of a regional rarity with three steelhead runs—spring, summer, and fall/winter, though the Root depends on rain for decent water levels and flow. When the water's high enough, kayakers hit the short series of playspots around Quarry Lake Park (see "White Water," page 162).

Spring is the biggie—try to come midweek for a shot at tranquility; weekends can be shoulder-to-shoulder from the dam to the country club. You'll probably be wading no more than waist-deep, though you may find yourself up to your chest in deeper holes in the rocky riverbed. Try yarn eggs, wooly buggers, or egg sucking leeches for spring runs. As the end of the road for migratory fish, Horlick Dam is often most packed with anglers wading from the Root's steep banks. There's wading and shore fishing to be had from Island Park, Lincoln Park, and Colonial Park (you can walk upstream along the banks from Lincoln to Colonial). Check out the fish ladder at Lincoln Park, where the DNR collects eggs and fish for the hatchery at its trap-and-transfer facility.

Directions: Take I-94 west. Exit WI 20 east. Take 20 east about 6 miles until you hit WI 31. Turn left (north) on WI 31. Take the right split (east) onto County MM. You'll see the Horlick Dam and a Days Inn. Turn right (east) onto Northwestern Ave./WI 38. Cross the bridge over the Root; stay in the right lane. You'll pass Quarry Lake Park on the right. For Lincoln Park and the steelhead facility, take WI 38 to Spring St./County C just before the intersection with State St. Turn right (west) on Spring St. and take the first right on Domanik Dr. down to the river.

ST. JOSEPH RIVER, BERRIEN SPRINGS, MICHIGAN

Location: About 95 miles E of Chicago

Fish: Walleye, steelhead, smallmouth, Chinook, crappie, catfish, brown trout

Seasons: Fall and spring are best; steelhead peak in October/November and February/March, but you can catch them year-round.

Tackle: B-J's Sports (616-429-8271) just south of St. Joseph in Scottdale carries conventional and fly-fishing bait and gear. Goldeneye Charters (616-471-7162, www.goldeneyecharters.com) in Berrien Springs specializes in walleye trips. Ripple Guide Services (574-272-7453, www.ripplequideservice.com) in South Bend, IN, runs St. Joe trips on the Indiana side.

Licenses and permits: Daily nonresident all-species license $7, season license $41

Book: *Fish Michigan: 50 Rivers.*

Heads up: Check out Dowagiac Creek in neighboring Cass County for fly-fishing trout. Good warm-water fly-fishing on the St. Joe above Mendon.

Description: You want it, the St. Joseph probably has it. "It's one of the most diverse fisheries around," says Bob Long, Jr., The Fishing Guy at the Chicago Park District. You can fly-fish, spin, or bait cast. Wade, boat, or fish from shore. Though the river is best known for its migratory metalheads and salmon, there's also trophy walleye—some 14-plus pounders—and trout hanging out in tributary pools. All a mere 2-hour drive from the Loop. One of Michigan's biggest rivers, the St. Joe averages a quarter- to a half-mile wide. Depths change dramatically; be sure to stay to the outside of bends. A good overall spot for fly or conventional angling is right below the dam and fish ladder at Berrien Springs. Shore fish from Shamrock Park on the north bank; there's a good gravel bottom, easy to wade, plus a boat launch. Show up in early September for the healthiest kings, while they're still silver and putting up a good fight.

Directions: Take I-94 east to US 31. Take US 31 south into Berrien Springs. Turn left on Ferry St., then right (southeast) onto North Mechanic to run into the DNR parking lot at the dam and fish ladder. For the boat launch and Shamrock Park, cross the bridge and take the first left.

Meccas

FLY-FISHING THE PERE MARQUETTE RIVER, MICHIGAN

Location: About 268 miles N of Chicago

Fish: Steelhead, king salmon (Chinook), brown and rainbow trout—all wild

Seasons: Year-round fishing. Spring is best for steelhead (starting early March), fall run peaks late October/mid November, and the fish stay in the river all winter. Salmon start spawning in mid-August and peak around mid-September/early October, but fishing is good through the end of October. Brown trout peak May–October, with epic summer hatches, but can be found year-round.

Tackle: Baldwin Bait and Tackle (231-745-3529, www.fishbaldwin.com) and Pere Marquette River Lodge (231-745-3972, www.pmlodge.com) in Baldwin are among the many informed shops. Both offer guides and fly-fishing schools. To float on your own, try Baldwin Canoe (800-272-3642, www.baldwincanoe.com) or Ivans Canoe (231-745-3361, www.invanscanoe.com).

Licenses and permits: Daily nonresident all-species license $7, season license $41

Books: *Trout Streams of Michigan; Great Lakes Steelhead; River Journal: Pere Marquette.*

Heads up: Blue-ribbon trout waters with serious pedigree: in 1884 it was the country's first river to be successfully planted with German brown trout.

Description: The Pere Marquette's tea-colored water offers some 70 miles of first-class fishing, much of it flowing through Manistee National Forest. Baldwin guide Herb Jacobsen says the steelhead and salmon runs along the National Wild and Scenic River are like Washington State's of 40 years ago (he used to guide around the Olympic Peninsula). Chinook average 12–16 pounds, but fish over 30 pounds are caught each year. Steelhead average 6–8 pounds but can reach 20. Brown trout average 10–14 inches but can reach 20-plus. It's enough to whip seasoned anglers into a giddy lather. Since 2000, the 8-mile, fly-only stretch from MI 37 to Gleason's Landing has been catch-and-release only on all species year-round— locals say they've already noticed bigger brown trout as a result. The intimate stretch looks like a small intestine, all bends and holes, and holds superb steelhead fishing. Legendary spots like Bawana's Bend, Miss Smith's, The Whirlpool. "You can roll half a mile and look across the river and see where you were at the beginning because it's so winding," Jacobsen says. White pine, oaks, and maples line the banks (late September brings peak color), dotted with the occasional cabin. You'll see anglers shore fishing, wading, and drifting.

The river's upper section has great trout fishing—it's wilder and often less crowded than the fly-only stretch. The lower river from Gleason's Landing to its mouth at Lake Michigan is truly big water with some truly big fish (floating advised). Great Hex hatch—granddaddy of the trout buffet with 2-inch-plus wingspans—for monster trout in June/July.

Directions: For the Green Cottage in Baldwin, a popular access along the fly-only section on the south bank of the river, take I-94 east toward Indiana and Michigan. In Benton Harbor take I-196 north to Holland, then US 31 north to Ludington. At Ludington, take US 10 east to MI 37. Take MI 37 south to 72d St. (just south of the bridge). Turn west on 72d. Turn right at Peacock Rd. You'll see the river and parking area in 0.25 mile.

FLY-FISHING TROUT IN THE DRIFTLESS AREA, SOUTHWEST WISCONSIN

Location: About 285 miles NW of Chicago (to Coon Valley, WI)

Fish: Brown trout, some rainbow and brookies—mostly wild

Seasons: Early catch-and-release season starts in March, major hatches run April–June, throw hopper patterns

August–September. Trout season ends at the end of September.

Tackle: Madison Outfitters (608-833-1359, www.wisconsindrifters.com) in the Mad City covers the Driftless Area and runs a comprehensive fly shop. Veteran fly-fisherman Bob Blumreich (608-637-3417) in Viroqua guides on the West Fork and Timber Coulee, among others. For gear and wisdom, hit the General Store in Avalanche (608-634-2303) in the heart of the West Fork's artificials-only, catch-and-release section, owned by local conservationist and trout angler Roger Widner.

Licenses and permits: Nonresident Wisconsin license: $15, 4-day, $20, 15-day, and $34, annual, plus $7.25 inland trout and salmon stamp. Call Wisconsin DNR (608-266-2621 or 608-266-1877) for a free copy of "Wisconsin Trout Fishing Regulations and Guide"—many streams and creeks have special regulations on designated sections.

Maps and books: Vital maps in DNR trout fishing guide above. *Trout Streams of Wisconsin and Minnesota; Fly Fishing Midwestern Spring Creeks; Exploring Wisconsin Trout Streams.*

Description: Dubbed the Montana of the Midwest, Wisconsin has 10,000-plus miles of trout water. Except Phil Miller of Madison Outfitters says, "I used to guide in Montana, and there's no way you could drag me back out there with all that we've got right here."

Sure, there's epic fishing to be had in the state's northern reaches. But a good chunk of those 10,000-plus trout miles are within a half-day drive of Chicago, winding through the state's achingly scenic southwest corner—the Driftless Area, a zone untouched by the glaciers, with rivers zigzagging a landscape of verdant valleys, or "coulees." Amish enclaves, rugged hills, tidy dairy farms, fields of trillium and bee balm, and rolling apple orchards abound. The area is rich in hard, cold, fertile, alkaline waters bubbling through the limestone. Most of its spring creeks are less than 25 feet wide, lined with watercress and wild mint. Many rivers and streams are limited or no kill, artificials only. Brown trout predominates—much of it wild—with some rainbow and brookies. Great hatches— peak runs April–June—draw the faithful. Excellent public access.

Waaaay too many streams to detail, but a few gems to note. Miller, who guides on some 30 area streams, says, "Lots of days I don't cover more than 200 yards of water all day because the density is so good." Timber Coulee Creek is Exhibit A with up to 5,000 fish per mile along an 8-mile stretch. The Vernon County creek hosts some wild brookies in addition to browns and has made its way into *Trout* magazine's list of top 100 U.S. streams. Superlative fishing during the little black caddis hatch from mid-May to mid-June.

The West Fork of the Kickapoo River, nestled in the Kickapoo Valley's organic farming mecca, has 24 miles of mostly browns with some wild brookies in spring heads. Loads of narrow tributaries. Work your way up and down County S. Closer to the city, in Grant County, the Big Green River's wild browns lurk in long pools in the lower portion of an 11-mile stretch. Fish from low, wet meadows and cow pastures farther upstream. Hard-core anglers flock to spots like Black Earth Creek, just an hour west of Madison, for nocturnal angling among the mosquitos, bats, and muskrats during the legendary Hex hatch. "It's a real elusive hatch. It's 'the evening primrose is in bloom, the Hex is going to come off' kind of thing," Miller says. "Usually you can kind of smell it in the air. Fishing it is a real adventure. You can't see a rise, so you just listen. You hear a slurp and you set the hook and then, bang! You've got it."

Directions: For Coon Valley and the Timber Coulee, take I-90 west past Madison to Sparta. Take WI 27 south to US 14 west to Coon Valley.

Before You Fry

NFORTUNATELY, MANY FISH in Lake Michigan and its tributaries, as well as other regional rivers, are contaminated with PCBs and other toxins. Anglers are advised to limit their consumption of certain (sometimes all) species. To get details on recommendations for a given waterway, contact the offices below. Children and women of childbearing age—and especially pregnant women—must be particularly careful. Officials generally recommend choosing smaller fish and fish with lower fat content, cutting away fatty deposits (where the toxins accumulate) before eating.

- Chicago office of the Illinois Department of Natural Resources (312-814-2070, www.dnr.state.il.us)
- Michigan Department of Community Health (800-648-6942) or Michigan DNR (616-685-6851, www.dnr.state.mi.us)
- Wisconsin Bureau of Fisheries Management and Habitat Protection (608-267-7498) or Wisconsin DNR (608-266-2621 or 266-1877, www.dnr.state.wi.us)

Where to Connect

Clubs and Organizations

These groups are involved with angling, water-quality improvement, or public-access issues—or a mix of the above. For more species-specific clubs, call Henry's Sports & Bait Shop (312-225-8538) or The Fishing Guy (312-742-4969).

- Trout Unlimited's Chicago chapter (www.edtu.org); or call Kent Carlson at (312) 663-9601.

- Chicago Angling and Casting Club (www.christophermerrill.com/ACA/) traces its roots to 1892 when it was the

Chicago Fly Casting Club, with a Lincoln Park clubhouse where the Peggy Notebaert Nature Museum now sits (there's still a casting platform there). Check the Web site for a schedule of local and regional competitions.

- Prairie Rivers Network (217-344-2371, www.prairierivers .org)

- Lake Michigan Federation (312-939-0838, www .lakemichigan.org)

- Chi-Town Bassmasters (www.chitownbass.com)

- Great Lakes Sport Fishing Council (www.great-lakes.org)

Shops
- Henry's Sports & Bait Shop (3130 S. Canal St., 312-225-8538, www.henryssports.com) is a city institution, open since 1952 and run by the Palmisano family, anglers all. Grab a bait menu when you walk in the door. The shop runs a local fishing report that's updated religiously, (312) 225-3474 (FISH).

- Dan's Tackle Service (2237 W. McLean Avenue, 773-276-5562)

- Chicago Fly Fishing Outfitters Ltd. (1729 N. Clybourn Ave., Store 4, 312-944-3474, www.chicagoflyfishingoutfitters.com) runs fly-fishing classes and clinics in the city and beyond, organizes regional and international trips, and hosts a steady stream of speakers and demo days.

- Orvis Company Store (142 E. Ontario St., 312-440-0662, www.orvis.com) also offers fly-fishing classes and clinics, beginner–advanced, plus seminars and private lessons.

Events
- Chicago Carp Classic (www.carpecarpio.com) in late September on the main stem of the Chicago River down-town. Anglers battle for the honor of being crowned

Chicago Carp King, among other titles. Sponsored by the Carp Anglers Group, which aims to promote the oft-maligned species as a worthy sporting fish.

- Henry's Sports & Bait Shop runs several derbies in the city throughout the year, including ice fishing in February, coho in April, and perch in summer/fall.

- Salmon-A-Rama (www.salmonarama.com) in Racine, WI, in July. A week-plus of tourneys, live music, and cheese fries. Dubbed the world's largest freshwater fishing event, drawing anglers from 30 states and crowds of 100,000.

Books

- Born, Steve, Jeff Mayers, Andy Morton, and Bill Sonzogni. *Exploring Wisconsin Trout Streams: The Angler's Guide.* Madison, WI: University of Wisconsin Press, 1997.

- Brich, Steve, Jay Christianson, and Brian Vaughn. *Chicagoland's Top 30 Fishing Trips.* Rhinelander, WI: Fishing Hot Spots, Inc., 1994.

- Huggler, Tom. *Fish Michigan: 50 Rivers.* Davison, MI: Friede Publications, 1996.

- Humphrey, Jim, and Bill Shogren. *Trout Streams of Wisconsin and Minnesota.* Woodstock, VT: Backcountry Guides, 2001.

- Linsenman, Bob, and Steve Nevala. *Great Lakes Steelhead: A Guided Tour for Fly-Anglers.* Woodstock, VT: Backcountry Guides, 1995.

  ———. *Trout Streams of Michigan: A Fly-Angler's Guide.* Woodstock, VT: Backcountry Guides, 2001.

- Mueller, Ross A. *Fly Fishing Midwestern Spring Creeks.* Appleton, WI: R. Mueller Publications, 1999.

- Mullady, Ed. *Kankakee River Fisherman's Atlas, Illinois.* Kankakee, IL: Sportsman's Letter, 2002.

- Sportsman's Connection. *Northern Illinois Fishing Map Guide*. Superior, WI: Sportsman's Connection, 2000.

- Supinski, Matthew. *River Journal: Pere Marquette*. Portland, OR: Frank Amato Publications, vol. 2, no. 4, 1994.

Links

www.chicagofishing.org

www.illinoisfishingnews.com

www.lakemichiganangler.com

outsidepix.com

MID-SEPTEMBER. MAGIC HOUR, when the sun bathes the landscape in an Indian summer evening's last-ditch golden light and transforms an abandoned lot, a phone booth, the 151 bus into something cinematic. The sky goes purplish somewhere around Monroe as I pedal my way north along the Lakefront Trail.

Just after the bend around Oak St. Beach, a gaggle of cyclists is stopped, staring out into the lake. I slow. An enormous harvest moon hangs close enough to touch, just over the horizon. We stand, silent, for several minutes as it inches up, becoming level with the trees in Olive Park by the water filtration plant, traffic buzzing oblivious, incessant behind us on Lake Shore Dr. One by one, the bikers peel off. The whole way home I ride with the path lit by the giant pearl at my right shoulder.

We are so lucky.

Riders use the Lakefront Trail as a two-wheeled Lake Shore Dr. to commute to work, to train, to just ride. Over the years, Chicago has gained a reputation as a bike-friendly city; the Second City earned the #1 spot among big U.S. cities in *Bicycling* magazine's 2001 ranking. Biking here is easy, flat, and fast. Just watch for epic rim-crushing potholes and ride defensively. And despite Chicago's reputation for ass-kicking winters, it's fairly easy to ride year-round. See www.bikewinter.org for tips.

We have a mayor who's an avid cyclist. The city transportation department's bike coordinator, Ben Gomberg, says he gets notes from Daley "easily once a month," including a recent one requesting more bike racks outside City Hall. City bike ambassadors troll community meetings and festivals promoting safe cycling. Chicago leads the nation in bike parking, with 6,000-plus bike racks. The city has 150-plus miles of bike paths, lanes, and signed on-road routes. With plans to add 150 more miles in the next year or so, the landscape will have changed by the time you read this. And the Chicagoland Bicycle Federation (CBF) keeps the pressure on; watch their excellent Web site at www.biketraffic.org for the latest.

Gomberg's office hands out a plethora of free city cycling literature, including the "Chicago Bike Map," updated each year to show city trails and the best on-road routes (312-742-2453, www.ci.chi.il.us/Transportation/Bikes/). Armed with the city map and CBF's regional seven-county "Chicagoland Bicycle Map" ($7 in most bike shops and book stores, or free if you join CBF), it's pretty straightforward to devise your own routes.

Those listed here include road rides and off-road rides on

paved or crushed limestone trails. Some are built for speed, others take in scenic rolling hills, orchards, farmland, and suburban swaths of prairie.

For the most part, trails are out and back. Don't be put off by the big mileage numbers: on any trail you can easily shorten a ride by turning back early. Where practical, we've listed CTA and Pace transit options here, with Metra as a choice of last resort. Unfortunately, as of this writing, Metra had a tenuous, mind-bendingly complex and restrictive bike policy (see *Have Bike, Will Travel*, page 217, for details). If and when it improves, it will be infinitely easier to get to area trails without a car—and to ride one-way routes (Metra stations are marked on CBF's regional map). Be sure to check the latest before you set out.

Biking is among the best ways to explore our "City of Neighborhoods," a moniker the Chicago Cycling Club celebrates every summer with its Ultimate Neighborhood Ride. I love riding the broad, brownstone-lined boulevards around Logan Square, Humboldt Park, and the University of Chicago. The city supports a lively bike scene. Clubs, races, and group rides abound. So ride on.

Critical Mass

THE NAME CRITICAL MASS becomes clear by 6 P.M. or so on a late August Friday night. Daley Plaza is like a queen bee nest for bikers, homing in from LaSalle, Madison, and Washington for a pre-ride gathering under the looming Picasso.

There's a cluster of choppers. One middle-aged guy on a modified penny farthing. A couple on a tandem with toddler twins in a trailer. The Plant Man, whose bike is festooned front and back with elaborate ferns and succulents tucked tastefully into baskets lined with mounds of Spanish moss. He's wearing a T-shirt that reads "Depave Lake Shore Drive." A guy with a scraggly gray beard hands out leaflets for an anti-Boeing demonstration. I get handed a neon orange flyer for the 7th Annual Nude Swim at North Ave. Beach.

Somewhere out of the festival-like chaos, order assembles. Two riders mount the base of the Picasso to offer competing ride routes tonight. We vote to ride south to the Sears Tower, then north to Urban Bikes in Uptown. After a few laps around Daley Plaza, we're off.

The rides are intended to raise awareness, promote an alternative to car culture, and push for bike transportation improvements. Plenty of drivers are none too happy with this "two wheels good, four wheels bad" demonstration; horns blare as we take over State St. at rush hour.

When a white stretch SUV limo tries to turn right into our path, two riders get the driver to roll down the window and hand him a Critical Mass leaflet as the crowd cheers. At intersections, a few riders post themselves to form a human roadblock and let the mass ride on, embodying the Critical Mass coda: "We're not blocking traffic, we *are* traffic."

Along the route, I meet a high-school math teacher, a graphic artist, a viola player with the Chicago Symphony Orchestra. As we pedal down Clark St. and it's thick with bikes, literally hundreds of riders reclaiming the streets on two wheels, I realize I'm grinning like an idiot. I'm not sucking exhaust. I'm not looking over my shoulder for a road-rager whose Navigator commands the entire lane. Tonight, we are powerful. Liberation feels good.

Theme rides include the Halloween Ride, Polka Ride, and Santa Rampage. Costumes and bedecked bikes abound. Monthly rides gather the last Friday of every month (yes, year-round) at 5:30 P.M. in Daley Plaza. Summer rides draw several hundred riders. See www.criticalmasschicago.org.

City Limits

LAKEFRONT TRAIL

Location: 5800 N (Ardmore Ave.) to 7100 S (South Shore Cultural Center)

Length: 36 miles out and back (use L for one-way route)

Difficulty: Paved, flat, and easy (except when fighting strong lake-fed headwinds)

Maps: "Chicago Bike Map"; Chicago Park District's (312-747-2474) "Chicago's Lakefront" map.

Heads up: For speed, ride early in the morning, especially in summer. Four-season trail, plowed (usually) in winter. Watch road crossings; cars are supposed to yield but often don't. If you're continuing north to Evanston, follow the green lakefront on-road route signs—riding the sidewalk on Sheridan Rd. is a big no-no ($250 fine and a zip-tie handcuff around your back wheel).

Description: Urban salvation. The trail hugs the shoreline, cutting through a continuous ribbon of lakefront parks and beaches. It's what keeps a lot of Chicagoans sane. It's also the most popular place in the city to ride, blade, run, and walk (see "Running," page 443). Sunny summer weekends are packed; prepare to dodge small children and dogs and ride handlebar-by-jowl on some North Side stretches, especially around Oak St. and North Ave. Beaches. Come early if you seek anything approaching Zen. Or stick to the less used section south of McCormick Place, in the throes of a major facelift at this writing. Fall's tops—beach throngs (and thongs) are gone. Great night riding, but you need a strong light. A cinder running path parallels the northern sections to about North Ave.

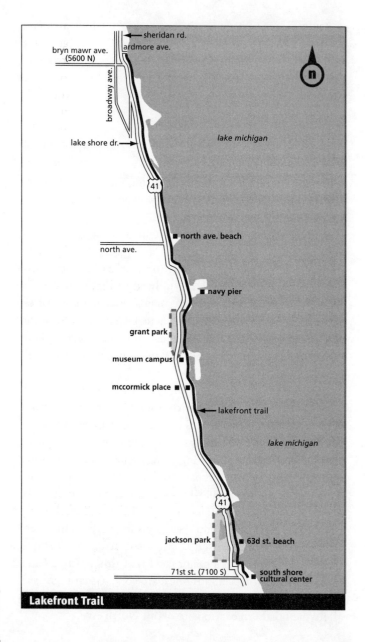

sheridan rd.
ardmore ave.

bryn mawr ave.
(5600 N)

broadway ave.

lake shore dr.

41

lake michigan

■ north ave. beach

north ave.

■ navy pier

grant park

museum campus ■

mccormick place ■ ■

← lakefront trail

lake michigan

41

jackson park

■ 63d st. beach

71st st. (7100 S)

■ south shore
cultural center

Lakefront Trail

Route: Ride from Ardmore Ave. south to the trail's end at 71st St. and the South Shore Cultural Center (good pit stop). Turn around and hope for a tailwind. Of course, you can start a ride virtually anywhere. In addition to direct street access in spots, underpasses and bridges let you pick up the trail at multiple points along its length (see "Chicago Bike Map"), with more underpasses in the works on the South Side. If you head east to Lake Shore Dr. and find yourself blocked by eight lanes of traffic, you generally don't have to ride more than a few blocks in either direction to gain safe access across to the path.

Option: for a one-way route, ride to 63d St., then go about 1 mile west to the E. 63d St. Green Line L.

Directions: By car, take Lake Shore Dr. north to the Bryn Mawr exit. Go right (east) into the beach parking lot. Several other beaches along the trail have parking.

By bike, best choice is the path itself, but if you want to save it, ride Dearborn or Wells Sts. north to Clark St. Ride Clark to Balmoral Ave. Turn right (east) on Balmoral. Turn left (north) on Kenmore Ave. and ride to Hollywood Ave. Turn right (east) on Hollywood and cross Lake Store Dr. to the trail.

By transit, the Red Line L Bryn Mawr stop is closest to the path's north end; Green Line L E. 63d St. stop is closest to the path's south end. Ride east from L stops to pick up the trail.

Have Bike, Will Travel

UST A FEW short years ago, the idea of being able to take your bike on board a train or bus in Chicago was just that—an idea. "We were nowhere 3 years ago," says Chicagoland Bicycle Federation executive director Randy Neufeld.

Thankfully, that's changing. CTA has even added indoor bike

parking in scores of L stations. As of this writing, Metra had a complicated, restrictive policy for bikes. Here's hoping that by the time you read this, it will be just as easy to hop a train out of the city as it is to travel within it. Of course, a folding bike offers the ultimate in portability (talk to the guys at Rapid Transit in Bucktown if you're interested). Now, the skinny.

- **CTA** (836-7000 city or burbs, no area code needed; www.transitchicago.com)

   On the L, bikes allowed anytime weekends; weekdays, all hours except 7–9 A.M. and 4–6 P.M. rush hours. Limit two bikes per car. On buses, by summer 2002 CTA had equipped four routes with bike racks: 72 North Ave., 63–63d St., 65 Grand Ave., 75–74/75th St. No day/time restriction for use. As of this writing, CTA planned to add racks on its entire bus fleet, rolling out routes gradually.

- **Pace Bus** (847-364-7223, www.pacebus.com)

   By the time you read this, the six-county suburban bus system expected to have racks on all buses, all routes.

- **Metra Rail** (312-322-6777 weekdays 8–5 P.M., 836-7000 evenings/weekends, www.metrarail.com)

   In summer 2001, Metra launched a bike program with many strings attached. Cyclists with advance reservations could bring bikes on board for $5 (on top of regular fare) from August to October, Saturdays only, one line only (it changed from week to week), and only during specific inbound and outbound runs. The good news? CBF has been negotiating with Metra to expand the program. Ample bike parking at most stations.

- **South Shore Line** (800-356-2079, www.nictd.com) to northern Indiana

   Bikes have to be taken apart and carried on board "in a bag or container expressly designed for such purposes" and stowed in the overhead luggage rack.

- **Amtrak** (800-872-7475, www.amtrak.com)

   Bikes must be boxed and checked in baggage cars for a

small fee; boxes available for $10. Some shorter routes in the Midwest allow roll-on service on certain trains for a reservation fee of $5 or $10, depending on space availability.

- **Van Galder Bus** to Madison and other Wisconsin stops (800-747-0994 or 608-752-5407 www.vangalderbus.com)

  Bikes go with checked baggage; $5 boxed, $10 unboxed (you'll likely have to take off the front wheel).

- **Greyhound** (800-231-2222, www.greyhound.com)

  Bikes are checked with luggage for $15 and must be boxed or packed in "wood, leather, canvas or other substantial carrying case and securely fastened." Boxes available for $10.

Backyard

NORTH BRANCH TRAIL

Location: Starts within city limits (6400 N/5600 W) and ends N in Glencoe

Length: 40 miles out and back

Difficulty: Easy, paved, winding—at times perceptibly rolling—trail

Maps and book: Cook County Forest Preserve (708-771-1330) "North Branch Bicycle Trail Map," North Branch and Skokie Divisions trail maps. *Hiking and Biking in Cook County, Illinois.*

Heads up: Fuel up at Chicago Botanic Garden café at the trail's northern end; nab a seat on the outdoor deck. Beaucoup picnic potential around Skokie Lagoons. Or, definitely post-ride, chow a Chicago hot dog classic at Superdawg Drive-In (6363 N. Milwaukee Ave.). Ride east along Lake-Cook Rd. for easy connection with the Green Bay Trail (see page 222).

Description: Shimmy north along a slender swath of forest harboring the North Branch of the Chicago River in its most natural, unchannelized state. Come for the trout lilies, restored prairie, silver maples, and meandering river, not the speed (though plenty of riders ignore the ban on speed training and racing—and the molasses 8-mph limit). Bird while you bike, especially for great blue herons and kingfishers along the Skokie Lagoons, carved out of ancient marshes (see "Bird-watching," page 311). While you pedal, you may see others paddling (see "Sea Kayaking & Canoeing," page 48). Expect to share asphalt with runners and in-line skaters. Several road crossings.

Route: From the southern trailhead at Caldwell Woods, head north. Stay right at the path's first fork around the 10-mile mark (the spur heads out to Winnetka Rd.). At Tower Rd. the path splits to loop around the Skokie Lagoons; both ways lead to Dundee Rd. Cross Dundee to enter Chicago Botanic Garden. If you want a break but don't have time to linger, duck into the diminutive Pullman gardens behind the bathrooms on the service road shortly after you enter from Dundee Rd. Hit a bench. And breathe in. No riding on the garden's paths and trails; follow the service road about 1 mile to the trail's end at Lake-Cook Rd. Turn around and ride back the way you come.

Directions: By car, take I-94 west to the US 14/Peterson-Caldwell exit (west). Go northwest along Caldwell Ave. about 0.5 mile to Devon Ave. Turn left (west) onto Devon. Park in the Caldwell Woods lot on the right, just east of Milwaukee Ave.

By bike, take the Elston Ave. bike lane north to Devon. (Elston joins Milwaukee around Peterson Ave.). Turn right (east) on Devon. There's a trail entrance on the north side of Devon.

By transit, take the Blue Line L to the Jefferson Park sta-

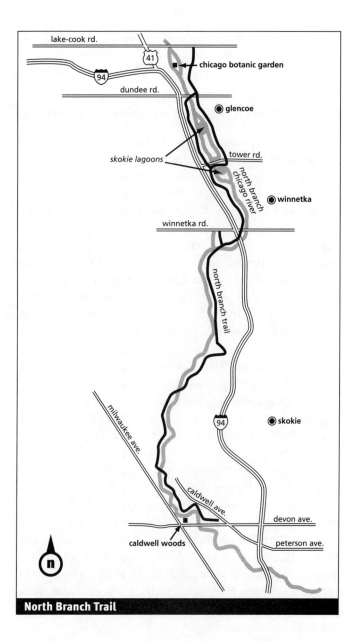

lake-cook rd.

41

94

chicago botanic garden

dundee rd.

glencoe

skokie lagoons

tower rd.

north branch
chicago river

winnetka

winnetka rd.

north branch trail

94

skokie

milwaukee ave.

caldwell ave.

devon ave.

caldwell woods

peterson ave.

n

North Branch Trail

tion. Ride north on Milwaukee to Devon. Turn right (east) on Devon. Use the same trail entrance as above.

GREEN BAY TRAIL/ROBERT McCLORY BIKE PATH

Location: About 20 miles N of Chicago

Length: 36 miles out and back

Difficulty: Easy, ramrod-straight trail. Mostly crushed limestone, some paved and on-road sections.

Map and book: CBF's "Chicagoland Bicycle Map." *Hiking & Biking in Cook County, Illinois.*

Heads up: Pick up the trail at virtually any Metra station in the towns along the Union Pacific North Line. Fuel: do not pass go, do not collect $200 without sampling prairie berry or fresh peach ice cream at Homer's on Green Bay Rd. just south of the trailhead in Wilmette. Ride west along Lake-Cook Rd. to connect with the North Branch Trail (see page 219).

Double heads up: Name games. Green Bay Trail now includes only the 6-plus miles in Cook County, from Wilmette to Lake-Cook Rd., but used to cover more. Once you cross into Lake County, it turns into the Robert McClory Bike Path, but many still call it the Green Bay Trail or North Shore Path.

Description: Bike through a string of swank suburbs, leafy parks, and elegant town train stations along what was once a well-worn Native American footpath between Fort Dearborn in Chicago and Fort Howard in Green Bay, WI, later the North Shore Line electric rail to Milwaukee, and now Metra's Union Pacific North Line. Starting from Wilmette, you'll pass Ravinia and Fort Sheridan, a former army base shuttered in 1993, with historic lakeside limestone officer mansions being rehabbed into yet another upscale North Shore community.

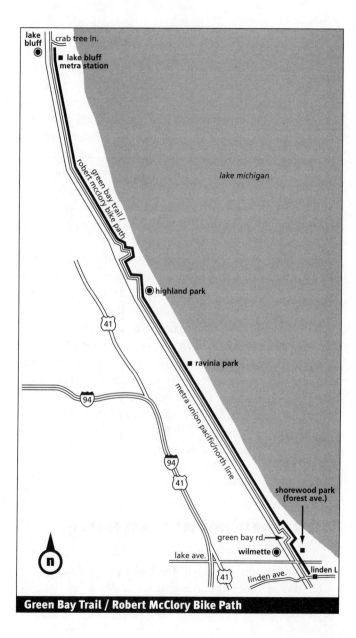

lake bluff

crab tree ln.

■ lake bluff metra station

green bay trail / robert mcclory bike path

lake michigan

● highland park

41

■ ravinia park

94

metra union pacific/north line

94

41

shorewood park (forest ave.)

green bay rd.

lake ave.

wilmette ●

linden L

linden ave.

41

n

Green Bay Trail / Robert McClory Bike Path

Route: Trail is well signed; when it gets interrupted, like around downtown Highland Park, follow the green on-road trail signs. From Shorewood Park in Wilmette, follow the trail north through tiny, tony Kenilworth and onto Winnetka, Glencoe, Highland Park, Highwood, Fort Sheridan, Lake Forest (Timothy Hutton flashback—you'll pass Lake Forest High School, one of several local spots shot in '80s Academy Award–winner *Ordinary People*), and Lake Bluff. About 0.5 mile past the Lake Bluff Metra station, turn around at Crab Tree Lane and ride back the way you came.

Option: continue north for roughly 19 miles of increasingly secluded, quiet trail (plus a few not-so-nice urban stretches) to 89th St. in Kenosha, WI.

Directions: From Chicago take I-94 west to Lake Ave. Head east on Lake to Green Bay Rd. Turn left (north) on Green Bay and almost immediately turn right (east) onto Forest Ave. Shorewood Park is on your left on the east side of the RR tracks. Most days/times you can park on Forest.

By transit, take the Red Line north to Howard St. Transfer to the Purple Line and take to the Linden L stop in Wilmette. Ride Linden Ave. west to Green Bay. Turn right (north) on Green Bay to Shorewood Park off Forest.

By bike, see Sheridan Road directions below. From Gillson Park, just north of Linden it's under a 2-mile ride west to Shorewood Park. Follow transit directions above from Linden to Shorewood Park.

SHERIDAN ROAD (WILMETTE-LAKE FOREST-WILMETTE)

Location: About 20 miles N of Chicago
Length: 36 miles out and back
Difficulty: Moderate

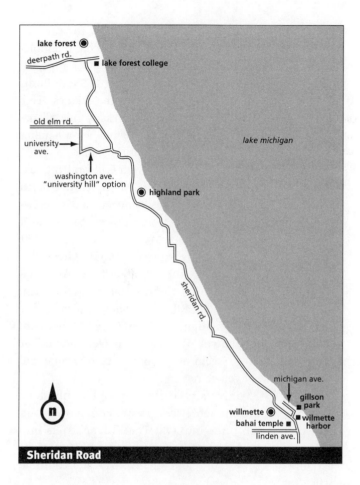

Map: CBF "Chicagoland Bicycle Map"

Heads up: Talk to the guys at Higher Gear or Turin for advice, wisdom, and more hills. No bikes on the ravines between Tower and Scott around Glencoe. Start from the city to rack up training miles and quality scenery along Chicago and Evanston lakefront paths.

Description: Sheridan Rd. is the Lycra Highway. Group

rides and racers flock here to train (start early to beat traffic). The lakefront manse-filled ribbon of road has manhole-flat straightaways and twisty-windy rolling sections, all through moneyed, tree-lined, bucolic North Shore burbs threaded with quaint stone bridges over the ravines. This route stops in Lake Forest, but you can easily ride all the way to Wisconsin. Flat to rolling road with just a handful of stoplights and a hill-sprint option at the end.

Route: Start from Wilmette's lakefront Gillson Park, just northeast of Linden Ave. and the Bahai Temple. Ride north on Sheridan Rd. to Tower Rd. Bikes banned on a corkscrew-like stretch through ravines between Tower Rd. (about 4 miles into the ride) and Scott Ave. To detour, turn left (west) at Tower Rd., turn right (north) on Old Green Bay Rd. (east of the RR tracks), turn right on Scott Ave., and turn left back on Sheridan Rd. Continue north on Sheridan. Follow the green Sheridan Rd. signs when it jogs farther north, like around Highland Park. After Fort Sheridan, you're in for more curves. When you hit Deerpath Rd. at Lake Forest College's gem of a campus, turn around and ride back the way you came.

Option: hit "University Hill," a popular mile-long sprint hill by turning left (west) on Washington Ave. in Highwood, which turns into Old Trail Rd. and runs into University Ave. Ride north up University Ave. Turn right (east) on Old Elm Rd. to rejoin Sheridan Rd. and continue north.

Directions: By bike, hop on the Lakefront Trail (see page 215) and ride north until it ends at Ardmore Ave. Ride west on Ardmore to Kenmore Ave. Follow the green bike route signs to Evanston (you'll rejoin Sheridan Rd. at N. Rogers Ave., then pick up the trail that hugs the lake around Calvary Cemetery into Evanston). Continue on the Evanston lakefront trail around Northwestern University. After the beachfront sports/aquatic center, the trail hits Lincoln St. Take Lincoln west to Ridge Ave. Ride north on Ridge (it merges with Sheridan Rd.) around the Bahai Temple. Gillson Park is off Michigan Ave. to your right after the harbor. By car, take Lake Shore Dr. north to Sheridan Rd. Take Sheridan north to Michigan Ave. at Wilmette's Gillson Park. Turn right onto Michigan and park or scout limited spots on area side streets. (Don't park inside Gillson Park unless you have a sticker.)

By transit, take the Red Line L to Howard. Transfer to the Purple Line and take to the Linden stop in Wilmette. It's a 0.5-mile ride east on Linden Ave. to Sheridan Rd. Turn left (north) on Sheridan Rd. Ride on.

PALOS-AREA ROAD RIDE (WILLOW SPRINGS-LEMONT-LOCKPORT-WILLOW SPRINGS)

Location: About 22 miles SW of Chicago

Length: 45-mile loop

Difficulty: Moderate

Maps: CBF "Chicagoland Bicycle Map;" Cook County Forest Preserve (708-771-1330) Palos and Sag Valley Divisions Map.

Heads up: Umpteen spots for pre- or post-ride picnic in the Palos preserves, beloved backyard fat-tire mecca (see "Mountain Biking," page 271). Expect horse trailers on the road.

Description: Surprisingly quiet single-lane roads through forest preserves, an historic town on the bluffs of the Des Plaines, new development McMansions, horse stables, and threatened farmland. Chris Dimick of Turin Bicycles in Evanston, who lives in Pilsen, loves this area: "It's got nice climbs and rolling hills. Just grab the CBF map—you can

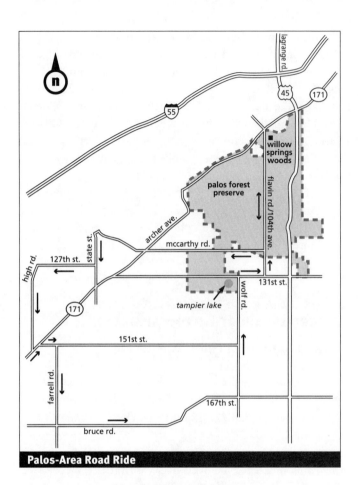

Palos-Area Road Ride

easily put together a 100-mile loop. And it's only a 20-minute drive from the Loop." Thanks to Dimick for the route below.

Route: From the Willow Springs Woods lot, ride south on winding Flavin Rd./104th Ave. through Palos's abundant ponds and sloughs with a longish climb around Teasons Woods. Turn right (west) on McCarthy Rd., which starts out wooded and rolling and flattens out a bit before a fun

Biking

downhill into Lemont. McCarthy runs into Stephen St. as Lemont's Main St. comes into view at the bottom of the hill. Hang left (west) onto Illinois St., quick left onto State St. Crank up State to 127th St. Turn right (west) on 127th and prepare for a stepped downhill past massive oil vats; you'll probably smell the refinery. Happily, you'll ride above it. Slow down to make a sharp left (south) onto High Rd. (unmarked), the last left you can take before 127th St. runs out at the bottom of the hill. After a long stretch of hills and climbs, High Rd. ends at what's marked as 171st St. (IL 171). Turn left (northeast) on IL 171 and ride about 0.25 mile to 151st St. Turn right (east) on 151st. Turn right (south) on Farrell Rd. Turn left (east) on Bruce Rd.; new subdivisions gradually give way to farmland. When the road bends right, stay straight on Bruce Rd., which turns into Hadley Rd. and then 167th St. as you cross from Will to Cook County. Turn left (north) onto Wolf Rd. Turn right (east) on 131st St. by Tampier Lake. Turn left (north) onto 104th Ave. and ride back north.

Directions: Take I-55 south to LaGrange Rd. (US 45) exit south. Go south on LaGrange to Archer Ave./IL 171. Turn right (southwest) on Archer. Take Archer to Flavin Rd./104th Ave. Turn left (south) on Flavin/104th. Park in the Willow Springs Woods lot on the east side of the street.

By transit, take the Orange Line L to Midway. Transfer to Pace bus 831, which drops you at the corner of Flavin Rd./104th Ave. and Archer Ave.

DES PLAINES RIVER TRAIL (HALF-DAY ROAD TO THE WISCONSIN BORDER)

Location: About 35 miles N of Chicago
Length: 60 miles out and back (includes roughly 5-mile on-road connector each way)

Difficulty: Easy. Crushed limestone with occasional dirt patches on well-marked trail.

Maps and book: Lake County Forest Preserve Des Plaines River Trail maps at trailheads and online (847-367-6640, www.co.lake.il.us/forest). *Hiking & Biking in Lake County, Illinois.*

Heads up: See maps for multiple trail access points. Easy to break up into 11-mile north and 14-mile south section (one way). On-road connector is very busy—ride defensively.

Description: Multiuse trail with few street crossings meanders alongside the Des Plaines and through the river valley. Gradually morphs from narrow oak-, hickory-, and maple-filled valley into prairie, savanna, and cattail-choked wetlands. Ride past stables around Old School Rd. Gets quieter the farther north you pedal. Popular horse trail. The county is working to join the south and north sections for a seamless trail—check in for the latest.

Route: Follow clearly marked signs to the south trail from the Half Day Rd. parking lot. Ride north to the south trail's end at River Rd. To link to the north trail, ride north on River Rd. to IL 120/Belvidere Rd. Ride west on Belvidere to Milwaukee Ave./IL 21. Ride north on Milwaukee to Washington St. Pick up the north trail on Washington and follow the trail north until it ends at Russell Rd. Ride back the way you came.

Directions: Take I-94 west to Half Day Rd./IL 22. Go 2 miles west on Half Day. Turn right (north) on Milwaukee Ave./IL 21 and follow about 1 mile. Turn right (east) into the Half Day Forest Preserve lot for the south section. For the north section, take I-94 west to the Grand Ave./IL 132 exit. Go east on Grand Ave. to Kilbourne Rd. Turn left (northeast) on Kilbourne. Parking lot is just south of US 41 on your left.

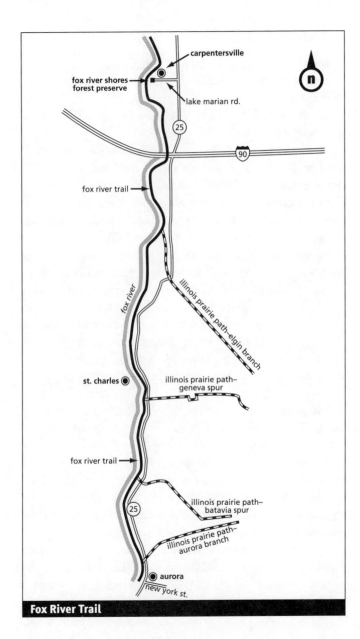

carpentersville

fox river shores
forest preserve

lake marian rd.

25

90

fox river trail

fox river

illinois prairie path–elgin branch

st. charles

illinois prairie path–
geneva spur

fox river trail

25

illinois prairie path–
batavia spur

illinois prairie path–
aurora branch

aurora

new york st.

Fox River Trail

FOX RIVER TRAIL

Location: About 44 miles NW of Chicago

Length: 64 miles out and back (loop options with Illinois Prairie Path)

Difficulty: Easy. Some rolling hills. Paved trail with on-road sections.

Map and book: Kane County Forest Preserve's Fox River Trail map (630-232-5980, www.co.kane.il.us/forest/). *Hiking & Biking in the Fox River Valley.*

Heads up: As of this writing, trail work was underway to extend 8 miles south to Oswego. Easy, signed connections with the Illinois Prairie Path (see page 233).

Description: Trail runs along or near the broad Fox River (see "Fishing," page 197) from Algonquin in the north to Aurora in the south. Pedal through several historic riverside towns, forest preserves, and parks; pick up a yupped-up sandwich in downtown St. Charles or Geneva and head for Old Mill Park and Island Park around State St./IL 38 crossing. Nice, long climb to Tekakwitha Woods (walk the trails there for a break). Trail gets increasingly winding as you ride south.

Route: From the Fox River Shores lot, ride south along the trail. In Elgin, Geneva, Batavia, and Aurora you'll see connections with the Illinois Prairie Path (from the river's east bank; the trail runs on both sides from around Geneva to North Aurora). Around Fabyan Parkway and the 68-foot windmill, take the bridge across the Fox to ride the trail's west bank to its southernmost point at New York St. in Aurora. Turn around and ride back the way you came.

Options: for a 39-mile loop, ride south from Fox River Shores lot to Geneva. Pick up the Illinois Prairie Path Geneva spur and ride east. When the spur ends in Winfield, ride back northwest on the IPP Elgin branch. In Elgin, pick up the Fox River Trail and ride back north to your car at Fox River Shores. More miles: once the Fox River Trail crosses the McHenry County line to the north, it melds into the Prairie Trail, running 26 miles (mostly paved) away from the river to Richmond, just shy of the Wisconsin line. After Crystal Lake, it gets real quiet.

Directions: Take I-90 west to IL 25. Take IL 25 north to Lake Marian Rd. Go left (west) on Lake Marian. Turn right at Williams Rd. and watch for signs to the Fox River Shores Forest Preserve lot. (Parking's tougher at the northern trail-head in Algonquin, about 2 miles north of Fox River Shores.)

By transit, take the Metra Union Pacific Northwest Line to the Fox River Grove station. Ride south on Algonquin Rd. to River Rd. Follow River Rd. south (water's on your right) and watch for signs to the Algonquin trailhead. For one-way route option, take Metra Burlington Northern Line from downtown Aurora (about a block north of New York Ave. on the east side of the river) back to the city.

ILLINOIS PRAIRIE PATH (WHEATON-ELGIN-WHEATON)

Location: About 28 miles W of Chicago

Length: 32 miles out and back (loop options, too)

Difficulty: Easy. Flat and straight crushed limestone path.

Map and book: Nonprofit, all-volunteer Illinois Prairie Path (630-752-0120, www.ipp.org) sells a detailed color map for $6. Well-signed with trailboards at most major junctions. *Hiking & Biking in DuPage County, Illinois.*

Heads up: Easy, signed links with other area trails for several route options—no sweat to patch together a century. See www.ipp.org for route suggestions and mileage. Nation's first rails-to-trails conversion, established in 1966, along former Chicago, Aurora & Elgin Railway.

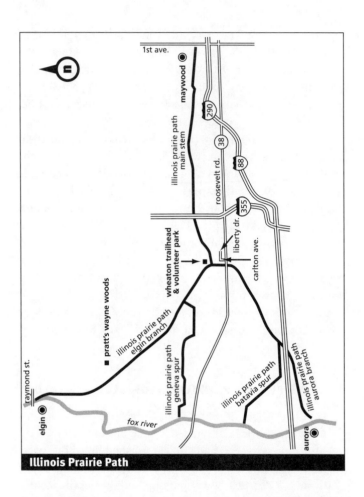

Illinois Prairie Path

Description: IPP covers 61 miles across three counties in the western burbs and intersects with the Fox River Trail to the west. Main stem runs 15 miles straight west from 1st Ave. in Maywood to the Wheaton trailhead. There the trail splits into two branches: one stick-straight northwest to Elgin with a spur to Geneva, the other southwest to

Aurora with a spur to Batavia. Wheaton-Elgin out and back starts off suburban (one yucko stretch past a pungent landfill) through tree tunnels and grows increasingly rural with wetlands, marshes, savannas, cornfields. Sandhill cranes sometimes nest along the route in Pratt's Wayne Woods from March through September. Last time I rode here, in mid-November, I saw four red-tailed hawks catching thermals over a Brewster Creek pond.

Route: From the Wheaton trailhead, ride across Volunteer Bridge and stay north along IPP's Elgin branch. When the IPP hits the Fox River Trail, continue north about 2 miles on the mix of on- and off-road trail. The northern IPP trailhead is at Raymond St. in Elgin. Turn around and ride back the way you came.

Option: Wheaton-Elgin-Geneva-Wheaton is a roughly 30-mile triangle. Pick up the Fox River Trail when the IPP crosses it in Elgin, head south on the Fox River Trail to pick up the Geneva spur, and ride east back to the Wheaton trailhead.

Directions: Take I-290 west to I-88 west to I-355 north. Follow I-355 north to Roosevelt Rd./IL 38 and go west on Roosevelt about 3 miles to Carlton Ave. Turn right (north) on Carlton and follow about 0.3 mile to Volunteer Park and the Wheaton trailhead (corner of Carlton and Liberty Dr.). Park in the garage on Liberty Dr. ($1 weekdays, weekends free). See www.ipp.org for parking areas (mostly free) along the main stem and branches.

By bike, ride west on Washington Blvd. about 12 miles. Turn left (south) at 17th Ave. in Maywood and ride to the IPP main stem trail. From there, it's about 14 miles to the Wheaton trailhead.

By transit, take the Metra Union Pacific West to the Wheaton station. Ride west on Liberty Dr. to the Wheaton trailhead.

Short Hops

GRAND MERE TRAIL ROAD RIDE, THREE OAKS, MICHIGAN

Location: About 76 miles NE of Chicago

Length: 50-mile loop

Difficulty: Moderate

Map and book: "Backroads Bikeway Map" from the Three Oaks Spokes Bicycle Club has 11 road rides from 5 to 60 miles (888-877-2068 or 616-756-3361, www.applecidercentury.com), available at Three Oaks Bicycle Museum. *Cycling Michigan.*

Heads up: Easy to ride over 2 days and start from your campsite at Warren Dunes State Park in Sawyer (616-426-4013; 800-44PARKS for reservations), less than 10 miles east of Three Oaks. Hit Three Oaks Bicycle Museum for local wisdom from Bryan Volstorf (former longtime Three Oaks mayor and creator of the Backroads Bikeway), plus reasonable bike rental rates and antique bikes like the 1870s "Boneshaker."

Description: For a full day's scenic ride, the 50-mile Grand Mere loop is hard to beat, with mostly flat, quiet country roads punctuated by a few hilly stretches. You'll pass an ostrich farm, sprawling apple and cherry orchards, a vineyard, several dune-studded lakefront state parks, and Warren Woods State Forest, 311 acres of primeval beech and maple, the oldest tree dating back 450 years. Several small towns for fuel, but I like to hit the pit stop off Hills Rd. at Tabor Hill vineyard for lunch (800-283-3363, www.taborhill.com; panko-crusted crab cake, anyone?) and/or liquid refreshment. Routes are signed with the green Backroads Bikeway symbol. The Apple Cider Century in late Septem-

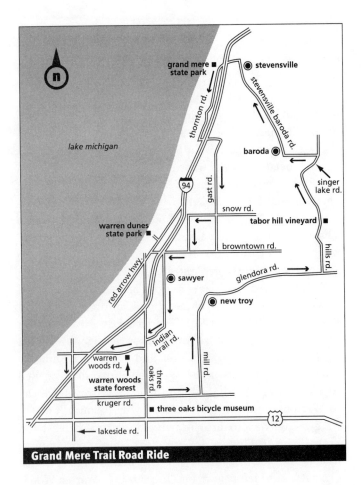

Grand Mere Trail Road Ride

ber draws 6,000-plus riders to this corner of southwestern Michigan.

Route: From Three Oaks Bicycle Museum, head west on Southcentral St. to Elm St. Turn right (north) on Elm St./Three Oaks Rd. to Kruger Rd. Turn right (east) on Kruger to Mill Rd. Turn left (north and east) on Mill to New Troy. From New Troy, ride straight east on Glendora Rd. to Hills Rd. You'll start to climb on Glendora, with rolling hills most of the way from here to Baroda. Turn left (north) on Hills Rd. to Snow Rd. You'll see signs for Tabor Hill vineyard before you hit Snow. Turn left (west) on Snow Rd./Hills Rd. Stay right on Hills to Singer Lake Rd. Turn right (east and north) on Singer Lake to Lemon Creek Rd. Before you hit the inland Singer Lake, watch for the sprawling ostrich farm on your left. Turn left (west) on Lemon Creek to Baroda. Turn right (north) on Stevensville-Baroda Rd. to Stevensville. Continue straight on St. Joseph Ave. to the flashing light at John Beers Rd. (Cycle Path Bicycle Shop on your left). Turn left (west) on John Beers and continue across Red Arrow Highway and I-94 overpass to Thornton Rd. Continue straight to enter North Grand Mere State Park or turn left (south) on Thornton Rd. to South Grand Mere State Park entrance (the popular birding park has three inland lakes tucked behind the dunes and massive blowouts). Stay straight on Thornton and follow the signs to Livingston Rd. Turn left (east) on Livingston to Gast Rd. Turn right (south) on Gast through Bridgeman to Snow Rd. Turn right (west and south) on Snow to Browntown Rd. Turn right (west) on Browntown to Red Arrow Highway. Turn right (north) on Red Arrow Highway to Warren Dunes State Park. Turn right (south) on Red Arrow Highway to Browntown Rd. Turn left (east) on Browntown to Flynn Rd. Turn right (south) on Flynn to Indian Trail Rd. Turn right (west) on Indian Trail to Three Oaks Rd. Turn left (south) on Three Oaks to Warren Woods Rd. Turn right (west) on Warren Woods to Warren Woods State Forest. Stay straight on Warren Woods Rd. to Lakeside Rd. Turn left (south) on Lakeside to Kruger Rd. Turn left (east) on Kruger to Three Oaks Rd. Turn right (south) on Three Oaks Rd./Elm St. back to the Bicycle Museum.

Directions: Take I-94/-90 east. Stay on I-90 east at the split. Get back on I-94 east at exit 21. Take exit 4a, US 12 east, to Three Oaks. After about 5 miles, turn left on Three

Oaks Rd. to the Three Oaks Bicycle Museum, housed in the 1898 Michigan Central Depot. FYI: as of this writing, Amtrak didn't stop in Three Oaks, but there were murmurs about a future Chicago-Three Oaks route geared toward weekend bike trippers.

Get Lapped

LANCE ARMSTRONG FANTASY? You're in luck. Chicago has two velodromes within easy reach, one in Northbrook, the other in Kenosha, WI. Both have U.S. Cycling Federation-sanctioned races. In Northbrook, Thursday is race night; in Kenosha, it's Tuesday.

Even if racing's not your gig, for a few bucks you can try out track riding in low-key citizen races held Friday nights in Northbrook, Monday nights in Kenosha. Just bring your bike and a helmet. You'll literally see everything from heats with toddlers riding their Green Machines (Northbrook's open to riders 5 and up, Kenosha 2 and up) to Masters on custom-built track bikes.

Northbrook's Ed Rudolph Velodrome (847-291-2974 ext. 646, www.northbrookvelodrome.com) was named for a local parks commissioner and speed-skating trainer whose protégé brought home several Olympic medals over the years. Rudolph's son Gordon trained on the 382-meter bike track for the '63 Pan Am Games, where he nabbed several medals. Kenosha lays claim to the nation's oldest operating velodrome; the 333-meter Washington Park Velodrome (262-653-4080, www.333m.com) opened in 1927. Heritage aside, it's in great shape.

To get to the Northbrook track, take I-94 west to Willow Rd. west. Take Willow to Waukegan Rd. Go north along Waukegan about 3 miles. Meadowhill Park is on the left (west) side of the street at Maple Ave. For Kenosha, take I-94 west to WI 142 east. Go east on WI 142 to 22d Ave. Turn right on 22d; park entrance is at the bottom of the hill on the left.

I&M CANAL STATE TRAIL

Location: About 50 miles SW of Chicago

Length: 102 miles out and back

Difficulty: Easy. Mostly flat, some rolling sections on crushed limestone trail.

Maps and book: Trail maps from I&M Canal State Trail center in Morris (815-942-0796, www.imcanal.org) and the visitors center in Channahon. *Hiking & Biking the I&M Canal National Heritage Corridor*.

Heads up: Good option over a weekend or long weekend with trailside camping (see *Pitching Tent*, page 242). Off-trail camping options in nearby state parks. Easy to shorten up for a day trip; many access points from towns lining the canal. Washouts in spots. Watch for hikers.

Double heads up: Map and trail mile markers start from the original eastern canal terminus in Bridgeport at the South Branch of the Chicago River. Route starts in Channahon around mile 45 and ends around mile 96.

Description: Pedaling through serious history along the former Illinois & Michigan towpath, where drivers used to guide horses and mules hauling barges crammed with corn and grain east to Lake Michigan for shipping to the East Coast. Finished in 1848, the canal established Chicago as a shipping powerhouse connecting Lake Michigan to the Mississippi via the Illinois. Today, water runs along only half the 61-mile-long trail, from Morris east and Utica west with marshy wetland patches in between. And the trail, lined with several state parks, quiet farmland, and historic river towns, is horse and mule free (but you may see wild turkey). Limestone cliffs abound from Ottawa to LaSalle. Part of the coast-to-coast American Discovery Trail.

Route: Trail begins at Brandon Rd. in Rockdale, but it's best to start in Channahon State Park. Check out the locks and restored locktender's house, then pick up the trail and

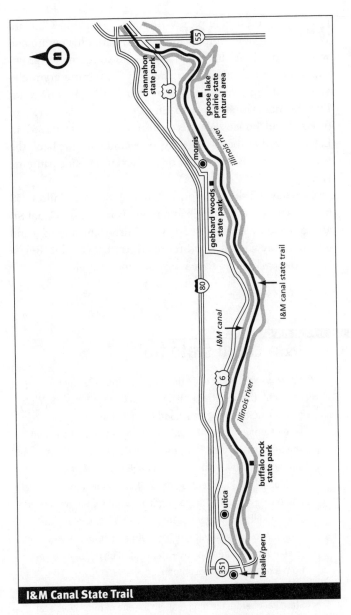

I&M Canal State Trail

ride west. You'll ride past William G. Stratton, Gebhard Woods, Illini, and Buffalo Rock State Parks for picnic and water stops along the way. Easy access to towns for provisions. In Seneca, check out the only remaining grain elevator from the canal's early days, built in 1861–1862 to let local farmers ship in bulk to Chicago. In Ottawa there's an original toll house. When you reach the end at IL 351 in LaSalle/Peru at locks 14/15, turn around and ride back the way you came. Bed down at one of seven trailside camping sites.

Directions: Take I-55 south to exit 248/US 6. Follow US 6 west about 3 miles to Channahon. Turn left on Canal St. and go about 0.25 mile to Story St. Turn right on Story and follow to the Channahon State Park trail access lot. Register in the park office to leave your car overnight.

i&m canal state trail

F YOU WANT decent odds that you'll be the only one camping at a spot, the primitive walk-in sites along the Illinois & Michigan Canal State Trail are a good bet. Most of the seven sites spread along the 61-mile trail are designed for just one tent. The best part? Officials say they're underused, even in summer and fall when bikers, hikers, and anglers hit the trail hard.

Most sites, just steps off the trail, are fairly wooded, private and quiet, with a fire ring and grill top. Bring your own water (you can fill up in several state parks and towns along the canal). Avoid the site at Aux Sable Aqueduct unless you want to sleep to the sound of semis along Dellos Rd. behind you from a nearby trucking company.

If you're up for riding some 43 miles out from Channahon State Park before pitching tent, go for one of three sites scat-

Biking

tered within a few miles west of Buffalo Rock State Park (the two around mile 88 are near a pond that's a shocking turquoise, thanks to nearby silica mines). Crank up the bluff to check out the two resident bison across from the baseball diamond and pick up your camping permit. If you want to pitch tent sooner, head for the site east of Seneca, about 22 miles out from Channahon, shaded by burr oak and cottonwood. Save room in your panniers for a rod to tangle with bass, crappie, bluegill, carp, catfish, and bullhead.

Details: Trailside campsites are first-come, first-served. They can be found around mile markers 53, 57, 61, 67, 87, and two around 88 (Channahon State Park is at mile 45). You'll need a $6-a-night camping permit; head for the state park closest to the site you want or settle up in Channahon State Park at the start of your ride if you know where you want to camp. Register your car with park officials in Channahon to leave it there overnight. Questions? Contact the I&M Canal State Trail center at (815) 942-0796.

Longer than a Short Hop

ELROY-SPARTA STATE TRAIL, ELROY, WISCONSIN

Location: About 225 miles NW of Chicago

Length: 64 miles out and back (car shuttles available for one-way ride)

Difficulty: Easy, mostly flat, some gradual climbs. Crushed limestone trail.

Maps: Pick up trail maps from any of the following: Elroy Commons (888-606-2453 or 608-462-2410, www.elroywi.com); Elroy-Sparta State Trail headquarters in Kendall (608-463-7109, www.elroy-sparta-trail.org); Sparta Area Chamber of Commerce (888-540-8434 or 608-269-4123).

Heads up: Wisconsin state trail pass, $3 day, $10 year. Biking-cum-spelunking: bring flashlight or headlamp for long, dark RR tunnels. Weekend ride made easy; primitive first-come, first-served trailside walk-in camping in Elroy and Sparta. Car shuttle service and bike rental from Elroy Commons trailhead.

Double heads up: Easy connections to roughly 80 more miles of trail from Elroy and Sparta. Rolling road rides through Amish country around Sparta and between Ontario and La Farge off WI 131.

Description: Beloved classic rail-to-trail path along former Chicago Northwestern railbed parallels WI 71, surrounded by wooded valleys and small towns and crisscrossed by the Baraboo and Kickapoo Rivers (plus several trout-stuffed streams; see "Fishing," page 203). Three limestone tunnels, dug out by pick ax in the 1870s and capped by enormous double doors built to protect them between trains from cracking (and falling) during the Wisconsin winter's freeze and thaw, are what draw the crowds. The first two are 0.25-mile long; the third stretches 0.75 mile. It's just you, the dark, and the drip-drip of natural springs coursing through the rock walls and ceiling. Dismount in tunnels. Don't expect speed; families and hikers abound.

Route: From the trailhead at Elroy Commons, ride the trail west. You hit Kendall (trail HQ) at 6 miles out, tunnel 1 at 9 miles, tunnel 2 at 18 miles, and after a gradual 150-foot climb, tunnel 3 (the biggie) at 24 miles. Check out the old tunnelkeeper's shack (the lucky guy got to open and shut the massive doors between trains from November to April). In Sparta, claim one of 13 trailside camping spots. If you ride the roughly 3.5 miles from the campground toward downtown Sparta, head to the corner of E. Wisconsin St. and S. Water St. to see the town's claim to the "world's largest bike," a 30-foot-high fiberglass mustached rider atop a penny farthing. The next day, ride back to your car at Elroy Commons.

Directions: Take I-90 west past Madison to Mauston and WI 82. Turn left (west) onto WI 82. Stay west on WI 82 about 14 miles into Elroy (WI 82 joins WI 80). In Elroy, turn left (east) on Franklin St. Elroy Commons will be on your left in a few blocks.

FRANK LLOYD WRIGHT ROAD RIDE, SPRING GREEN, WISCONSIN

Location: About 190 miles N of Chicago

Length: 20-mile loop

Difficulty: Moderate. Several steep hills.

Maps: Free "Wisconsin Biking Guide" (800-432-8747, www.travelwisconsin.com) has a map and elevation guide. For help with longer routes around Spring Green, contact Bike Wisconsin (608-935-7433, www.bikewisconsin.org).

Heads up: Frank Lloyd Wright Taliesen tours (608-588-7900, www.taliesinpreservation.org). Show up early to nab one of the 15 first-come, first-served camping spots at Tower Hill State Park (608-588-2116, about 0.3 mile east of Frank Lloyd Wright visitors center on County C. Fuel: at the visitors center café, pick up sandwiches or eat in the only Wright-designed restaurant still in use—stellar river views.

Description: Cycle through the pastoral wrinkling, rolling landscape that inspired architect-egotist Frank Lloyd Wright to set up his Taliesen studio complex just south of Spring Green on the homestead of his Welsh ancestors. Perfectly weathered barns. Lush green hills. Wright buildings. And a Wisconsin ode to the outrageous, House on the Rock. (Built atop a 60-foot rock chimney, the house is merely the center of a conglomeration of themed

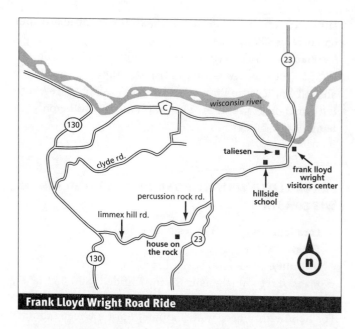

Frank Lloyd Wright Road Ride

structures—Heritage of the Sea, Pizza, Weapons, and the all-glass Infinity Room jutting out 200-plus feet to levitate above the valley floor. File under Must See to Believe.) Epic paddling journeys on the Wisconsin River from Spring Green (see "Sea Kayaking & Canoeing," page 57).

Route: From the Frank Lloyd Wright visitors center at the intersection of WI 23 and County C, turn left (south) onto WI 23 and start to climb as the road veers west. You'll pass Wright's Hillside School, built in 1902, on your right. Follow WI 23 as it turns south at Lower Wyoming Rd. Turn right (west) onto Percussion Rock Rd., another climb. After a nice downhill to the intersection with Sneed Creek Rd., stay left. Cross the creek and continue straight. Bear right on Limmex Hill Rd. Continue straight on Limmex Hill Rd. onto WI 130. Go right (north) on WI 130 to Clyde Rd. Turn right on Clyde and follow to High Point Rd. Go right on High Point. Climb again approaching Sneed Creek Rd.; go left at Sneed Creek. Stay left at the next junction. Turn left on Lower Wyoming Rd. and follow to County C. Turn right (east) on County C. Lost Hill is your last as Taliesen comes into view. Cross WI 23 to get back to your car.

Directions: Take I-90/-94 west. Stay on I-90 west at the split. Take the west exit for US 12/US 18 to loop around Madison. Take US 14 west to Spring Green. Turn left (south) onto WI 23. Cross the Wisconsin River. The Frank Lloyd Wright visitors center is on your left (east) on County C. Park in the visitors center lot.

Mecca

HOOSIER HILLS AND HILLY HUNDRED (ROAD RIDE), BLOOMINGTON, INDIANA

Location: About 233 miles S of Chicago

Length: 115 miles over 2 days (two loop rides)

Difficulty: Moderate-difficult. Rolling terrain and some bona fide breathtaking hills.

Maps and book: Hoosier Hills Tour, Bloomington Bicycle Club (812-332-6028, bbc@bloomington.in.us, www .bloomington.in.us/~bbc) sells map packets of 27 Bloomington loop rides (including Hoosier Hills Tour routes) for $10; Hilly Hundred, Central Indiana Bicycling Association (317-767-7765, www.cibaride.org, www.hillyhundred.org); general maps and info from visitors centers in Bloomington/Monroe County (800-800-0037) and Brown County (800-753-3255). *Best Bike Rides Midwest*.

Heads Up: Classic 1979 cycling-inspired flick *Breaking Away* was filmed in and around Bloomington, home of Indiana University and hoards of die-hard bikers. Route combines two legendary cycling events sponsored by local clubs: Hoosier Hills Tour in mid-September and Hilly Hundred in early October through south-central Indiana hill country.

Description: Two-wheeled touring nirvana. Quiet, tree-lined country roads roll through small-town and rural Monroe, Lawrence, and Brown Counties. Names like Strain Ridge Rd., Ramp Creek, and "The Alps" are the tip-off that you're in for enough 250- to 300-foot quad-burning climbs to make for Jell-O legs around the campfire at night. Circle Hoosier National Forest and 10,750-acre Lake Monroe the first day; plenty of spots to take a dip. Check out Heltonville's limestone monument to Hoosier basketball madness. The next day is a slightly easier ride skirting dairy farms, peach and apple orchards, Yellowwood State Forest, and the south shore of Lake Lemon. Stop in Nashville, an artist colony ever since impressionist T. C. Steele fell in love with the landscape and set up shop in the early 1900s.

The Hoosier Hills ride usually starts at Jackson Creek School in town. Since you're likely to drive to Bloomington the night before you ride, for simplicity's sake the route below starts and ends at the campground at Paynetown State Recreation Area (812-837-9490), 0.25 mile off the route along IN 446. But there's a bounty of gorgeous places to choose from to pitch tent, hike, sail, and fish—Hoosier National Forest, Yellowwood State Forest, and Brown County State Park among them. Thanks to both Bloomington Bicycle Club and Central Indiana Bicycling Association for sharing their routes. Pack some snacks for the ride— you've got long stretches between towns. For the first day, grab sandwiches at Heltonville's country store on IN 58— your next chance is Holts Grocery around Judah. On the second day, Nashville has a slew of options, but for traditional Brown County fare (fried chicken, mashed potatoes, green beans, and Brown County biscuits, something like a

jelly donut minus the jelly) head to the Brown County Inn
(812-988-2291).

Route, Day 1, 65-mile Hoosier Hills ride: Exit Paynetown
SRA and turn right (south) on IN 446.

13.2   Right (west) on IN 58 at blinker light
21.8   Right (north) at Mt. Pleasant Rd. (look up for the
       hills)
24.1   Right (east) at unsigned "T"
26.1   Left (north) at unsigned "T" (stop sign)
30.4   Left (west) at unsigned "T" (stop sign)
30.5   Yield left (west) at unsigned road, follow main
       road
32   Yield left (south) at unsigned road—across the
       small bridge
32.6   Right (west) at unsigned "T" (stop sign)
33.1   Left (south) at unsigned "T" (stop sign)
33.4   Right (NW) unsigned at pig pen
35.7   Yield right (north) unsigned at yield sign
37.8   Yield right (NW) at Old IN 37 (unsigned) at stop
       sign
38.1   Right (north) unsigned at "To Guthrie" sign
40.9   Straight (north) at Valley Mission (unsigned)
41.4   Yield left (NW) unsigned at Valley Mission
       Church (you're in "The Alps")
43.5   Left (west) at Lake Monroe Dam Rd.
44   Straight (north) at Lake Monroe Dam Rd.
44.8   Right (north) at Strain Ridge Rd.
46.2   Left (north) at Strain Ridge Rd. after Lakeview
       School
48.9   Right (east) at Smithville Rd. at stop sign
49.1   Straight (east) on Ram Creek—cross Fairfax Rd.
       at stop sign
51.4   Left (NW) at unsigned "T" (stop sign)
53.2   Left (west) at Moffett Lane at "T" (stop sign)

53.5	Right (N) at Harrell Rd.
55	Left (west) at Rhorer Rd. at "T" (stop sign)
55.7	Right (north) at Sare Rd. at bottom of hill
55.8	Left (west) at Jackson Creek School (end of original ride)
57.1	Right (east) on David Dr.
57.3	Left (north) on Forrester Dr. at "T" (stop sign)
57.4	Right (east) on Olcott Blvd.
58.3	Right (east) at Moores Pike at "T" (stop sign)
59	Right (south) at IN 446 at stop sign
64.2	Straight (south) on IN 446 to Paynetown Rd.
64.4	Right (east) on Paynetown Rd. to Paynetown SRA

From Paynetown SRA, drive north on IN 446. At IN 46/3d St. go left (west) to Walnut St. Turn right (north) on Walnut St. and follow to Kinser Pike. Go left (west) on Kinser Pike; Bloomington High School North is on the right side of the street.

Route, Day 2, 50-mile Hilly Hundred ride: From Bloomington High School North, go straight on Kinser Pike.

0.3	Left into golf course, slow for steep hill
0.9	Left at Old IN 37 (stop sign)
1.6	Cross Walnut St. (stop sign)
2.6	Right on Bethel Lane
6.1	Left at IN 45 (stop sign)
13.7	Yield right onto Lanam Ridge Rd. (to Yellowwood State Forest)
17	Right at Owl Creek
19.1	Right at Helmsburg Rd. (stop sign), caution for killer downhill
21.5	Left at Greasy Creek Rd.
23.5	Yield right onto Bear Wallow Rd.
26.5	Left at Gatesville Rd.; be careful crossing IN 135 at stop sign a few miles down
30.9	Left at IN 45 (at stop sign)

35.2	Right at South Shore Dr.; caution at railroad a mile down
39.4	Left at Tunnel Rd. (stop sign)
40.8	Right at Robinson Rd.
44.8	Left at Old IN 37 (stop sign)
48	Cross Walnut St. (stop light)
48.7	Right at Cascade Shelter
49.3	Right at Kinser Pike
49.5	Straight into Bloomington High School North

Directions: Take I-90/-94 east. Stay on I-90 east to Indiana. Take the I-65/US 12/Dunes Highway/US 20 exit 17 toward Indianapolis. Continue on I-65 south for 140 miles. Take exit 123 for I-465 south toward the Indianapolis airport. Follow I-465 south to the Harding St./IN 37 south exit. Follow IN 37 south. About 4 miles north of Bloomington, take the Walnut St./College Ave. exit south into downtown. Go south on Walnut St. about 3 miles to the IN 45/46 bypass. Go left (east) on the bypass; you'll cross IN 45, then hit IN 46. Go left (east) on IN 46 to IN 446. Go right (south) on IN 446 to Paynetown Rd. Turn right on Paynetown Rd. to the state recreation area campground.

Community Re-Cycling

MATT BERGSTROM HAS a thing for Chicago alleys. They have been good to him.

The 32-year-old graphic artist long toyed with the idea of building a bike out of trash. A few years ago, he and a few friends started prowling the alleys around Bergstrom's Uptown neighborhood by bike, reclaiming discarded parts.

"I was feeling bad about all those usable pieces gone to waste. I wanted to rescue them," Bergstrom says. "It took a while to get enough parts to build one bike. And pretty soon we started finding stuff all over the place."

Eventually, the storage stall by Bergstrom's apartment building laundry room was crammed ceiling-high with discarded bike parts. From this stockpile was born the Rat Patrol. Bergstrom, his roommate, and a crew of like-minded friends in Wicker Park created a squadron of "99%" recycled bikes, several choppers among them, with names like Neon Girl, Abigail the Chicken (my personal favorite, check it out at www .geocities.com/RatPatrolHQ), Zapruder, and Gimpy Trailer, a reworked wheelchair designed to haul treasures back to the Rat Laboratory—usually Bergstrom's apartment.

When the siren call of the alley beckons, the Rat Patrol responds with a decidedly urban group ride. Bergstrom and friends troll the city's alley maze atop their handmade creations, dumpster-diving for parts, trying to beat The Scrappers (independent metal scavengers whose trucks are an ode to "Sanford and Son") to the best discarded loot. Watch for their telltale "Rat Droppings"—red stickers with the Rat Patrol logo— on the backs of street signs and dumpsters.

Bergstrom's ridden his recycled choppers and had people stop him on the street to ask where he bought it, how much it cost. But Rat Patrol members build bikes for their own use and amusement, not to resell.

"And that's part of the point, too, you can't buy it," says Bergstrom, who inherited a family 10-speed and has yet to actually *buy* a bicycle. "You have to use your own hands to build it. You have to make some kind of personal connection to it. There's a lot of excess people feel they need to buy into; we're trying to get across that it's really not necessary."

Though the Rat Patrol fleet isn't for sale, two Chicago bike shops, one in Uptown on the city's North Side, the other in Woodlawn on the South Side, specialize in recycled bikes made of donated or salvaged parts, with a big dose of community service to boot. Both Urban Bikes and Blackstone Bicycle Works run apprenticeships for neighborhood residents (mostly kids) who learn bike repair and other skills and can earn their own bike through the shops' barter systems.

You can easily walk away with a bike from either shop for under $100.

"We're a hunter-gatherer bike shop," says Tim Herlihey, a self-described lifelong dumpster-diver, bike mechanic, and founder of Urban Bikes, which he started a decade ago in the garage of the Uptown Catholic worker shelter where he was living.

Blackstone Bicycle Works is a subsidiary of the Resource Center, the city's oldest and largest not-for-profit recycler. You'll see plenty of University of Chicago students pedaling around campus on converted 3- and 10-speeds bought through the nonprofit's retail shop. Manager Andy Gregg, besides being an amateur cyclist and professional bike mechanic, has a degree in fine art and makes furniture out of rejected bike parts (check out his Vector lounge chair, crafted from professional-level road and off-road racing rims).

Urban Bikes (4653 N. Broadway, 773-728-5212) and Blackstone Bicycle Works (6100 S. Blackstone Ave., 773-241-5458, www.blackstonebike.com) offer bike repair and sell new bike parts and accessories in addition to recycled bikes and wares. Donations welcome.

Inexpensive recycled bikes can also be had at the Giant Humanitarian Bike Sale in Pilsen, 1406 W. Cullerton St., Saturdays 10 A.M. to 3 P.M. Proceeds benefit the Chicago-based Working Bikes Cooperative, an all-volunteer nonprofit group that sends discarded and donated bikes overseas to humanitarian projects in Africa, Central America, and the Caribbean. Details at www.workingbikes.org.

EXPLORATION EXTRA
in-line scene

HEIDI GOLDWATER, DIRECTOR of the Chicago chapter of National Skate Patrol, says Chicago is a great in-line city. She ought to know. She doesn't own a car; her blades are her wheels.

"As long as you obey the bike laws you can skate on the street. There are tons of bike lanes. Pretty much all the parks have water fountains. And the lakefront path is just amazing," Goldwater says.

It's tough to miss the in-line crowd at Oak St. Beach. From Memorial Day to Labor Day, red-shirted volunteers from Chicago Skate Patrol give free clinics on the level concrete paralleling the Lakefront Trail every Saturday and Sunday from 11 A.M. to 4 P.M. Lots of incredibly skilled skaters hang out there and practice moves; it's a great spectator spot.

For group skates, the skate patrol runs an intermediate/advanced skate of about 10 to 12 miles on Wednesday spring, summer, and fall evenings, leaving from the Londo Mondo on Dearborn Ave. (see below) at 6:30 P.M. Post-skate, the mob—anywhere from 25 to 75 skaters—usually rolls on to Melvin B's, a skate-friendly bar on State St.

"Rave Master" Tom Grosspietsch organizes Road Raves the first and third Friday of the month, June through September, leaving from the Picasso statue at Daley Plaza at 7:30 P.M. The 11- to 16-mile advanced street skates have a different theme each month. Favorite past routes include The Riot Rave, blading to the scene of the Haymarket Square Riot, the Chicago Police Academy, and the Grant Park statue where the '68 Democratic National Convention riots started. Or The Candy Rave, hitting Blommer's Chocolate, Margie's Candies, the Fannie Mae factory, and the Wrigley Building.

Biking

To get on the Road Rave listserve, e-mail chicagoroadrave @hotmail.com. To hook up with other skaters and learn more, see www.chicagoblader.com, www.thirstydog.net, www .getinlinechicagoland.com, and www.teamrainbo.com.

For rentals and gear:

- Windward Sports (3317 N. Clark St., 773-472-6868, www.windwardsports.com)
- Londo Mondo (1100 N. Dearborn Ave., 312-751-2794; 2148 N. Halsted St., 773-327-2218; 444 W. Jackson Blvd., 312-648-9188; www.londomondo.com)
- Rainbo Sports Shop (4107 W. Oakton St., Skokie, 847-982-9000, www.rainbosportsshop.com) sells but doesn't rent; its Chicago store on the 4800 block of N. Clark St. shut down after 45 years.

Where to Connect

Clubs and Organizations

- Chicagoland Bicycle Federation (312-427-3325, www .chibikefed.org) is the city's bike-advocacy powerhouse. Web site and monthly newsletter, "Bike Traffic," are best ways to stay up-to-date on city bike scene. Updated regional ride calendar, bike repair school, maps. Their annual semiformal fundraiser, Bike Town Bash, in 2002 was held at A. Finkl & Sons Co. steel works and dubbed "Where Steel Meets Style." One word: join.

- League of Illinois Bicyclists (630-978-0583, www.bikelib .org) offers statewide advocacy. Good online trail links.

- Chicago Cycling Club (773-509-8093, www .chicagocyclingclub.org) runs multiple weekly rides from April through October with pace and distance tailored to beginners through serious roadies. New riders encouraged to join "get acquainted" ride the fourth Wednesday of each month. Most rides start from Waveland clock tower, 3700 N, off the Lakefront Trail just south of the golf course. Training rides and off-road and weekend trips.

- Cycling Sisters (773-252-8102, www.cyclingsisters.org/) runs monthly rides the first Friday of every month at 5:30 P.M. from Daley Plaza at Washington and Clark to share cycling wisdom and encourage more women bikers.

- Windy City Cycling Club (312-458-9841, www.brisknet.com/wccc/) is a recreational club with primarily gay and lesbian participation. Regular group rides.

- Critical Mass (www.criticalmasschicago.org) rides the last Friday of every month at 5:30 P.M. from Daley Plaza; active listserve.

- Evanston Bicycle Club (847-866-7743, www.evanstonbikeclub .org) runs group rides for novice and experienced riders, most in northern Cook and Lake Counties starting from Evanston; remote starts, too. Show-and-go rides year-round. The long-time club hosts the North Shore Century in mid-September.

Shops

- Rapid Transit Cycleshop (1900 W. North Ave., 773-227-2288, www.rapidtransitcycles.com/) is among the city's best bike shops, definitely the place to test-ride a wide range of recumbent and folding bikes. Commuter-minded, but full stash of road and mountain bikes, too. Quality mechanics. The Bucktown shop's hard to miss: its Wolcott Ave. mural says "Don't sit in traffic, ride your bike to work," and a bike with a constantly rotating front wheel dangles over the shop's sign.

- Yojimbo's Garage (1310 N. Clybourn Ave., 312-587-0878) is a hub for the city's bike-messenger community—who else opens at 8 A.M. weekdays?—and cyclists in the know. Owner and star wrench Marcus Moore, a former messenger, helped found local team XXX Racing (road, mountain, cyclo-cross, track). City's best selection of track bikes and parts.

- Upgrade Cycleworks (1130 W. Chicago Ave. at Milwaukee Ave., 312-226-8650, www.upgradecycle.com) has a huge inventory, from top-end road and track bikes to tandems and adult trikes. Knowledgeable staff. Special orders in 2 days.

- Higher Gear (1435 W. Fullerton Parkway, 773-472-7433, www.highergearchicago.com) is all about road bikes, medium to high-end stuff. Group rides from the Lincoln Park store: Saturday 8 A.M. moderate pace 40-miler to the Highland Park store and back; Wednesday 6 P.M. ride follows same route but draws serious racers. Racing team. Owner John Olin runs regular hill rides off Sheridan Rd. heading north from Wilmette.

- The nonprofit Blackstone Bicycle Works (6100 S. Blackstone Ave. 773-241-5458, www.blackstonebike.com) in Woodlawn is the place to go for your $60 converted 10-speed with upright handlebars (most bikes below $120). Specializes in used/recycled bikes.

- Urban Bikes (4653 N. Broadway Ave., 773-728-5212) in Uptown also specializes in used/recycled bikes, from $45 to $250.

- On The Route Bicycles (3146 N. Lincoln Ave., 773-477-5066, www.ontheroute.com) has fat-tire emphasis but rents and sells mountain, hybrid, and high-end road bikes.

- Johnny Sprocket's Bicycles (3001 N. Broadway Ave., 773-244-1079; 1052 W. Bryn Mawr Ave., 773-293-1695) sells full range of bikes and runs 25-mph training rides from the Bryn Mawr store, geared toward triathletes.

- Kozy's Cyclery and Fitness (601 S. LaSalle St., 312-360-0020; 1451 W. Webster Ave. in the Webster Place strip mall at Clybourn Ave., 773-528-2700; 3712 N. Halsted St., 773-281-2263; www.kozy.com) is a family-owned local mini-chain. Full range.

- Village Cycle Center (1337 N. Wells St., 312-751-2488, www.villagecycle.com) sells a full range.

- Alberto's Cycles (952 Green Bay Rd. in Winnetka, 847-446-2042), open since the mid '70s, is for roadies and racers; weekend group rides average 20 mph.

- Turin Bicycle (1027 Davis St. in Evanston, 847-864-7660, www.turinbicycle.com) is another veteran, specializing in road bikes. Road and mountain bike racing teams. Sunday winter rides for all levels. Wednesday evening rides average 25 mph. Rents tandems, hybrids, and the occasional road racer.

Rentals

- Bike Chicago (312-755-0488, www.bikechicago.com) rents mountain, hybrid, and road bikes—plus tandems, cruisers, in-line skates, and push scooters—from three spots along the lakefront, April–November. Free tours from Navy Pier to Lincoln Park, Grant Park, and Hyde Park. Rentals include helmet and lock; kids' bikes and seats available. You save 10% if you make reservations online. Locations: Navy Pier, 600 E. Grand Ave., (312) 755-0488; North Ave. Beach, (773) 327-2706; 63d St. Beach, (773) 324-3400. On The Route in Lincoln Park and Turin in Evanston are other rental options.

Events

- Bike Chicago (312-744-3370, www.ci.chi.il.us /Special Events/) is a month-long bike event sponsored by the mayor's Office of Special Events with group rides, Bike-to-Work Day, free bike checkups, seminars, and clinics from mid-May to mid-June. League of American Bicyclists named it the nation's top cycling event in 2001.

- Chicago Bike Winter (773-486-9015, www.bikewinter.org)
  runs free classes on winter cycling and maintains a calendar of winter bike events, from how-to clinics on dressing
  for winter biking and winter bike maintenance to bike sledding outings.

- Boulevard Lakefront Tour (www.RideBLT.com) around
  Labor Day has a 10- and 35-mile route and drew 6,000-plus
  cyclists in 2001. Supports Chicagoland Bicycle Federation;
  contact them (see above).

- Bike the Drive (www.bikethedrive.org) in early June is the
  only (legal) chance you'll get to ride on LSD. That's Lake
  Shore Dr. The ride, with 15- and 30-mile routes, debuted in
  2002. Supports CBF; contact them.

- LATE ride (312-857-2757, www.lateride.org) in mid-July is
  a nocturnal 25-mile, non-competitive ride through the city
  starting at 1:30 A.M. from Buckingham Fountain in Grant
  Park with a mass breakfast in the park post-ride. Supports
  nonprofit advocacy group Friends of the Parks. About 9,000
  riders in 2001.

- Chicago Bike Show and Fitness Expo (847-675-0200 ext.
  203, www.chicagobikeshow.com) runs 3 days in late March
  at Navy Pier.

- Ultimate Neighborhood Ride in summer, usually July, traverses neighborhoods and ferrets out some of the lesser-
  known historic landmarks through the city's north and
  northwest sides. Guided tour option. From 20 to 35 miles;
  routes change yearly. Contact Chicago Cycling Club (see
  above).

- Monsters of the Midway Criterium (http://ucvc.uchicago
  .edu/) runs Mother's Day on Midway Plaisance at the
  University of Chicago campus. Run by U of C Velo Club,
  beginner–elite riders.

- Chicago SuperCup (617-454-1170, www.kirongroup.com)
  November/ December. Part of USCF-sanctioned national

cyclo-cross series. Held in Washington Park on Chicago's South Side. Draws elite and amateur riders nationwide. Turin in Evanston is the local contact (see above).

- U.S. Pro Criterium Championships (www.sportsgrandprix .com) draw top-flight riders in mid-August to Downers Grove. Also handcycling, in-line skating events.

- American Cancer Society Walk and Roll (312-372-0471, www.walkandrollchicago.org) draws several thousand the Sunday after Mother's Day for a 10-mile skate, 5-mile walk, and 15-mile bike route.

- Four Bridges of Elgin (www.bridgesofelgin.com) in early July draws international competitors with top in-line skaters, bikers, and handcyclists; amateur races, too.

- Calumet Ecological Park Association (CEPA) fall ride (www.lincolnnet.net/cepa), usually in October, showcases little-visited corners of the city through the Lake Calumet area and Chicago's East Side. See remnant marshes filled with slag from area mills' spent steel. Nike missile pads. The city's last remaining sawmill. Flames from the coke plant off the Calumet River. Prairie. And smell the oddly sweet air wafting from the Cerestar corn syrup processing plant. But what makes the ride are guides John Pastirik and Cory Glasen, native East Siders brimming with tales of the area's political, natural, and industrial history. Contact CEPA (773-646-4773) or Pastirik (773-768-4663) for details.

Books
- Gentry, Karen. *Cycling Michigan: The 30 Best Routes in Western Michigan*. Lansing, MI: Thunder Bay Press, 2000.

- Glowacz, Dave. *Urban Bikers' Tricks and Tips: Low-Tech and No-Tech Ways to Find, Ride and Keep a Bicycle*. Chicago, IL: Wordspace Press, 1998.

- Hochgesang, Jim. *Hiking & Biking in Lake County, Illinois*. Lake Forest, IL: Roots & Wings, 1994.

————. *Hiking & Biking in DuPage County, Illinois*. Lake Forest, IL: Roots & Wings, 1995.

————. *Hiking & Biking in Cook County, Illinois*. Lake Forest, IL: Roots & Wings, 1996.

————. *Hiking & Biking in the Fox River Valley*. Lake Forest, IL: Roots & Wings, 1997.

————. *Hiking & Biking the I&M Canal National Heritage Corridor*. Lake Forest, IL: Roots & Wings, 1998.

• Van Valkenberg, Phil. *Best Bike Rides Midwest: Road Rides for the Serious Cyclist*. Guilford, CT: Globe Pequot Press, 1997.

L **ET'S GET THIS** straight from the get-go. You can't take the "mountain" in mountain biking too literally in Chicago.

What follows are off-road areas, predominantly dirt trails. Most have a degree of technical challenge or ruggedness that separates them from the off-road trails in the "Biking" chapter. These are some of the best-loved places Chicagoans go for their fat-tire fix. And as creative riders like Eric Anderson demonstrate, mountain biking is as much a state of mind as a (literal) state of trail (see *Urban Assault*, page 269).

That said, the state of trail in the Chicago area is a tenuous one. In the mid-1990s, in the wake of complaints by other trail users, Cook County officials moved to ban mountain biking on forest preserve trails. The then-fledgling Chicago Area Mountain Bikers (CAMBr, formerly TURF) countered with 25,000 signatures against the move and won a reprieve from the blanket ban. Still, some trails were closed—and continue to be closed—in many areas. And turf wars continue for over-loved, under-funded, finite urban green space.

Bottom line: it's more critical than ever to ride responsibly (see *IMBA Rules of the Trail*, page 266) and support groups like CAMBr to avoid losing the precious metro-area trail that remains open.

Virtually all the *City Limits* and *Backyard* routes here are Cook County Forest Preserve trails. They're multiuse trails: don't spook horses, don't blow past hikers and runners. As of this writing, the county says it's legal to ride in less heavily biked places like LaBagh Woods, Indian Boundary, and Des Plaines Divisions, but the trails are largely unmarked (hence the very general route descriptions). In classic bureaucratic catch-22, county officials say the only legal trails are those marked on the county's brown trail maps, but both the maps and signage are woefully lame and outdated. If you're unsure about a trail's status, ask. Getting caught riding an illegal county trail gets you a $100 fine and a mandatory court appearance.

The good news? Chicago riders have a real backyard gem in the Palos preserves just 20 miles from downtown, packed with tight, twisting singletrack (good enough to compel a reverse recreational commute—check out the Wisconsin plates in the parking lot on weekends). And Deer Grove is Palos' northerly—though much smaller—cousin. The state had plans to add hundreds of miles of trail by the time you read this book. And if you're willing to travel a few hours to places like Michigan's Yankee Springs Recreation Area, you'll be rewarded with enough knobby track to make the trip worthwhile.

A few final thoughts. Where practical, CTA and Pace bus options are listed here as a car alternative, with Metra as a choice of last resort. Sadly, as of this writing Metra had a summer-only, less-than-user-friendly bike policy (see "Biking," page 218 for details), but it's included in the hopes that the commuter train line's policies will improve. Check the latest before setting out.

You'll want two maps for general navigation: the city transportation department's free "Chicago Bike Map" for city trails and best on-road routes (312-742-2453, www.ci.chi.il.us/Transportation/Bikes/) and the Chicagoland Bicycle Federation's regional seven-county "Chicagoland Bicycle Map" ($7 in most bike shops and book stores or free if you join CBF). For more area options, check out *Chicago Mountain Bike Trails Guide*, a labor of love from Peter Strazzabosco (aka P. L. Strazz).

"Length" for the rides in this chapter is approximate total trail miles in an area—you can tailor your ride by cutting away on smaller loops, turning around on out-and-back trails, or obviously, log more miles by running loops multiple times. Now go forth and hammer.

Let It Snow

YEAH, IT'S COLD HERE. Miserable cold sometimes. But Chicago Bike Winter exists to help people cope with— nay, revel in—winter biking.

For information on free classes on winter cycling and a calendar of winter bike events, from how-to clinics on dressing for winter biking and bike maintenance to bike sledding outings, check out Chicago Bike Winter (773-486-9015, www.bikewinter.org). Also see www.icebike.com, an ode to winter biking with all sorts of groovy cold-weather, snow, and ice tips, including step-by-step plans to make your own studded tires.

Eric Anderson, for one, celebrates the arrival of the white stuff. It means new terrain. New challenges. And a shift in the city's horizontal monotony.

"Hills get taller with snow," says Anderson, who rides in mountain bike and cyclo-cross races with local team XXX Racing. "Throw on your studded tires. You can ride up walls when the snow's packed tight enough against the concrete. Ride up a snowbank over a guardrail. Dive off your bike into a snowbank. Throw yourself down sledding hills—I like Humboldt Park. In snow, you downshift and keep spinning and just grind through it. It can be total masochism. And total fun."

IMBA
Rules of the Trail

ELOW IS A shortened-up version of the International Mountain Bicycling Association's trail rules (full text at www.imba.org). These rules represent a global standard code of conduct for mountain bikers.

1. Ride on Open Trails Only

    Respect trail and road closures (ask if uncertain); avoid trespassing on private land; obtain permits or other authorization as may be required.

2. Leave No Trace

    Practice low-impact cycling. Wet and muddy trails are more vulnerable to damage. When the trailbed is soft, consider other riding options. This also means staying on existing trails and not creating new ones. Don't cut switchbacks. Be sure to pack out at least as much as you pack in.

3. Control Your Bicycle

    Inattention for even a second can cause problems. Obey all bicycle speed regulations and recommendations.

4. Always Yield Trail

Let your fellow trail users know you're coming. A friendly greeting or bell is considerate and works well; don't startle others. Show respect when passing by slowing to a walking pace or stopping. Anticipate other trail users around corners or in blind spots.

5. Never Scare Animals

Give animals extra room and time to adjust to you. When passing horses use special care and follow directions from the horseback riders (ask if uncertain).

6. Plan Ahead

Know your equipment, your ability, and the area in which you are riding—and prepare accordingly. Keep your equipment in good repair, and carry necessary supplies for changes in weather or other conditions. Always wear a helmet and appropriate safety gear.

City Limits

LABAGH WOODS–GOMPERS PARK

Location: About 5200 N on the city's northwest side
Length: 5-plus total miles
Physical difficulty: Easy to moderate
Technical difficulty: Moderate
Terrain: Dirt. Mix of singletrack, doubletrack, and wide stretches. Trails throw up some tight turns, roots, tree fall, and short climbs.
Book: *Chicago Mountain Bike Trails Guide.*
Heads up: Ridiculously muddy when wet; best in dry summer and fall months or when the ground's frozen hard in winter. Trails are unmarked. Use the river as your guide

to avoid getting lost. For fuel, hit Taqueria El Ranchito, 5151 N. Cicero Ave., for great tamales and homemade pico de gallo.

Description: These wiry trails winding along the North Branch of the Chicago River offer sustenance for carless city bikers looking for a quick and easy fat-tire fix. With trail connections to LaBagh Woods, 39-acre Gompers Park is divided by Foster Ave. Bike action is in the park's wooded swath north of Foster, though the newly restored 2-acre wetland in the park's southern section is worth a look; in summer it's a butterfly magnet and kids catch fingernail-sized frogs along the floodplain's tallgrass edge. RR tracks cut through Gompers and LaBagh. Joggers and hikers threaded the surprisingly quiet trails the last time I was here.

Route: Easiest start is from the LaBagh Woods lot off Cicero Ave. just north of Foster Ave.; go left at the fork and follow to the picnic shelter. Pick up the trail just behind the shelter; it plunges into the woods a bit before splitting north and south along the river's west bank (there's more trail to be had on the river's east banks too). Alternative start from Gompers Park: pick up the trail from the north-ernmost corner on the north side of Foster by the fenced-in asphalt area on the river's west side (there's some trail on the river's east side, but it's shorter and a bushwhack). Follow the main trail north (river is on your right) as it hugs the river's northwesterly meander. Following that trail will take you from Gompers Park through LaBagh Woods (across Cicero) and into the forest preserve's North Branch Division.

Directions: LaBagh Woods is on Cicero Ave. (4800 W) just north of Foster Ave. By bike or car, follow the Elston Ave. bike lane northwest until you hit Cicero. Go north on Cicero, turning right (east) into the LaBagh Woods entrance. After you cross the highway overpass, stay left at the fork to the parking lot. There's a trailhead behind the picnic shelter. Gompers Park is at the intersection of Pulaski (4000 W) and Foster. Parking is just south of Foster on the west side of Pulaski.

By transit, take the Blue Line L to the Jefferson Park stop. Ride northwest on Milwaukee Ave. Turn right (east) on Foster. Continue to Cicero. Turn left (north) on Cicero. Follow above directions to the trailhead.

Urban Assault

THERE'S A GREAT frontier out there in the city, as wild and unpredictable as any Rocky Mountain acreage. And on a semiregular, semisecret basis, a handful of intrepid riders mount their ATBs to explore it on an Urban Assault, a late-night journey through the city's underbelly, its forgotten spaces.

They ride over jagged broken pavement and looming concrete piles in a vacant lot. Churn through a railbed's heavy gravel. Hammer through a brownfield. Catch air off lakefront boulders. Speed up parking garage or loading dock ramps. Create an industrial archaeology lesson of Goose Island's scrap-metal yards and hulking boxcars. Traverse downtown's below-grade parallel universe. Sometimes they'll lock up their bikes to climb a train bridge or rappel off the side of a water tower. Or organize races à la bike messengers' alley cats.

Sure, danger is part of the allure (this is mountain biking, after all); trespassing tends to come with the territory. Riders have been harassed, or chased down, by cops, security guards, guard dogs, homeless people. But Eric Anderson, a longtime Critical Masser who went on his first Urban Assault ride 4 years ago and now is a regular, says for him it's all about exploration.

"It's transplanting cross-country mountain biking into an urban setting," he says. "It's about getting on your mountain bike and deliberately going out and seeing places you never would've seen if you hadn't gotten on a bike and deliberately decided not to ride on the street. It's about finding new terrain. You start to link things together to make a patchwork of the city. You really start to understand how it all fits. . . . It's the spirit of finding things that are unique to this city. Chicago is so industrial and has such a different feel from a city like San Francisco. Here you have to really seek out things that out there are so easy to find. So maybe you discover a sweet piece of singletrack along a highway here. You work at it."

Anderson credits Urban Assault rides with getting him back into mountain biking. Sometimes he makes solo trips, giving himself a simple challenge of "how close can I get to home without riding on a street."

"It's made Chicago livable," says the Joplin, MO, native who used to ride the mossy cliffs and pines of the Ozarks. "It just opens up the possibilities in a city I thought of as a concrete, desolate place." The 31-year-old recalls an early Urban Assault ride, weaving through urban prairie and a thick swath of trees along a lonely stretch of the South Branch of the Chicago River, within sight of the Loop's architectural behemoths. "I just remember looking up and thinking, 'No way. I'm in these woods and I'm in downtown Chicago, fucking staring up at the Sears Tower through the leaves.' That's when I realized that this is not about just going for a ride, it's about seeing a place no one else really sees. There's a sense of mystery about that."

 Backyard

PALOS AND SAG VALLEY FOREST PRESERVES

Location: About 20 miles SW of Chicago

Length: 35-plus total miles

Physical difficulty: Moderate to difficult

Technical difficulty: Moderate to difficult

Terrain: Dirt, roots, and rocks

Maps and books: Rough trailboard at Bull Frog Lake parking lot; Cook County Forest Preserve Palos and Sag Valley Divisions trail map (708-839-5617 or 708-771-1330, see www.cambr.org). *A Guide to Mountain Bike Trails in Illinois; Mountain Bike! Midwest.*

Heads up: Backyard mecca. Chicago area's longest, toughest trails through 14,000 acres of rolling pawpaw, black, red, and white oak dotted with upland meadows, small lakes, ponds, and sloughs. Only gray-marked trails are open to bikes. Some are marked "ride only when dry."

Description: Thank the last glacier for carving out hills (some 50-plus feet) and canyons here, welcome respite from the city's unrelenting horizontal plane. Despite closure of several miles of prime singletrack, Palos remains a fat-tire treasure with hills, rolling doubletrack, and tight twisty singletrack. To fully appreciate the bounty, hook up with experienced riders who know their way around, at least for a first foray. Be sure to ask regulars for any recent trail closures. Active patrolling and ticketing for biking on no-bike, closed, or dry-only trails. Monthly trail work days here through Chicago Area Mountain Bikers (CAMBr) from Bull Frog Lake parking lot. See www.cambr.org or call Ed Bartunek at (708) 749-8488. In spring, masses of hawthorn and crabapple bloom. Funny how my hands take on a purple hue in July when the blackberry and raspberry patches ripen. . . .

Route: These will get you started, but check with CAMBr for a new, much-improved trail map they were drafting at press time. From Bull Frog Lake parking lot trailhead, take the doubletrack loop around the lake, with some quick downhills followed by a long uphill. Single-track trails like 3 Ravines (follow junction markers 5, 9, and 16) and Turf 1 (follow markers 4, 7, and 12) radiate from the loop. Roots and rocks abound. If you stick to the doubletrack it strikes out east (markers 39, 37, and 36) to the Little Red School House Nature Center. No biking on nature center trails. Pick up the doubletrack east of Willow Springs Rd. to explore a maze of country roads converted to multiuse trails. From Swallow Cliff Woods parking lot there's 15 miles of great doubletrack. You'll be tempted to pick up the singletrack: resist, it's closed. Head east from the lot and ride under LaGrange Rd. to pick up a roughly 7-mile loop that climbs up Swallow Cliff. Once you cross back under LaGrange Rd. you'll hit another parking lot; trails branch out from this grove. Remember where the cliff ridge is to avoid getting lost (always a distinct possibility in Palos).

Directions: From I-55 south exit LaGrange Rd. (US 45) south. Go south on LaGrange about 3.5 miles. Turn right (west) on 95th St. and follow about 1 mile. The entrance to Bull Frog Lake parking lot is just beyond Maple Lake, to your left. Stay left (south) as 95th veers right. If you hit the stop sign at Archer Ave. you missed it. Park in the first lot at Bull Frog Lake; you'll see a mountain bike staging area sign. By transit, take the Orange Line L to Midway. Catch Pace bus 831 and take it to the intersection of Archer and 95th. Ride east on 95th to the Bull Frog Lake trailhead.

For Swallow Cliff Woods, follow instructions to

LaGrange Rd. Stay south on LaGrange about 6 miles. After crossing the Calumet-Sag Channel, turn right at the exit for IL 83. Go left (west) on IL 83. Take a quick left (south) into the Swallow Cliff toboggan run parking lot.

DEER GROVE FOREST PRESERVE

Location: About 30 miles NW of Chicago

Length: 8-plus total miles (mostly loop)

Physical difficulty: Easy to moderate

Technical difficulty: Moderate

Terrain: Mostly dirt, some rock and gravel

Maps and book: Online map at www.cambr.org; Cook County Forest Preserve's Deer Grove trail plan map (708-771-1330). *Chicago Mountain Bike Trails Guide.*

Heads up: The northerly (much smaller) answer to Palos. Only gray-marked trails are open to bikes. Some are marked "ride only when dry."

Description: Deer Grove's 1,800 hilly acres are more straight-ahead than Palos, especially since the county closed singletrack winding through the delicate ravine areas to all but foot traffic because of erosion. The remaining doubletrack perimeter loop still makes for a solid workout. You'll have to share this rare open space carved out of intense suburban sprawl with horseback riders, runners, hikers, and cross-country skiers. Play nicely. Small creek and bridge crossings along the wooded trails. CAMBr has monthly trail work days. Contact Wayne Mikes at Mikes Bike Shop in Palatine (847-358-0948).

Route: Hit the loop trail west of Quentin Rd. From the parking lot, ride the paved trail west across Quentin for 50–75 yards until you hit the marked trailhead to your right. Follow the loop trail. On the east side of Quentin (in addition to a 4-mile paved loop), there's 1 mile or so of off-

Deer Grove Forest Preserve

road trail that runs through swamp, ridable when it's dried out in late summer.

Directions: Take I-94 west to Dundee Rd. Go west on Dundee to Quentin Rd. Turn right (north) on Quentin for about 0.5 mile. Park in the lot on the east side of Quentin.

By transit, take Metra's Union Pacific Northwest line to the Palatine station. Ride north on Northwest Highway to Quentin Rd. Turn right (north) on Quentin, crossing Dundee Rd. Follow directions above.

INDIAN BOUNDARY-DES PLAINES DIVISION FOREST PRESERVES

Location: About 11 miles W of Chicago
Length: 23 total miles (one way)
Physical difficulty: Easy to moderate

Technical difficulty: Easy

Terrain: Dirt, some roots, twists, and bumps

Maps and books: Cook County Forest Preserve Indian Boundary and Des Plaines Division maps (708-771-1330). *Chicago Mountain Bike Trails Guide; A Guide to Mountain Bike Trails in Illinois.*

Heads up: Another solid option for carless riders

Description: Tame, but a chance to rack up riverside miles. Hop on your nubbies from the Loop, pedal some 11 miles west along Madison or Washington Sts., and pick up the unmarked trail as it winds its way through cottonwoods, elms, blue beech, and silver maples hugging the Des Plaines River's east bank to the county line. Prime flight-path territory (the trail runs just east of O'Hare for a stretch). Last time I biked here, I saw a crowded collage of prints—raccoon, deer, and beaver—dried in the mud along the riverbank. Great blue heron sightings, too. Personal favorite stretch: from Irving Park Rd. north. Best single-track tends to stick close to the river. Construction blocking some sections (like North Ave. to Fullerton Ave.) was due to be finished by the time you read this. Best to keep an open mind and check the latest with CAMBr.

Route: Indian Boundary Division runs from Madison St. to Touhy Ave. From Madison, pick up the trail in River Forest just west of Thatcher Ave. on the north side of the street (a split-post fence marks the entrance). Just before North Ave., the trail abruptly dumps you between the guardrails onto Thatcher. Heavy street traffic here. Go north along the east side of Thatcher. Cross North Ave. About a block and a half past Russell's Barbecue, take the forest preserve entrance on the west side of Thatcher. There's a small parking lot and a multitrack trail by the water pump that leads to the river trail again. Farther north, near Higgins Rd., the singletrack goes under the expressway and runs into a cemetery. Head east 0.25 mile or so to pick up the trail on the other side of the cemetery. At Touhy Ave., the Des Plaines Division starts and continues north another 12 miles to the county line (Lake-Cook Rd.) in Northbrook-Wheeling. Ride east on Lake-Cook Rd. to Waukegan Rd. to catch the 212 Pace bus (no Sunday service) to the Davis St. L stop in Evanston.

Option: for more miles, trails continue along the Des Plaines through Lake County (see "Biking," page 229), but there's a 4-mile gap between the two counties' trails. When Cook County's dirt trails dead-end at Lake-Cook Rd., ride north along the Milwaukee Ave. shoulder—beware heavy traffic—until you can pick up Lake County's mostly crushed limestone trail off Riverside Rd. (one-lane road east off Milwaukee).

Directions: By car or bike, head west on Madison or Washington Sts. to the Des Plaines River, or check the "Chicago Bike Map," for another westbound street to pick up the trail. See forest preserve maps for parking lots scattered along the route.

By transit, take the Green Line L to Harlem/Lake stop. Ride west on Lake St. about 10–12 blocks to the trail.

WATERFALL GLEN FOREST PRESERVE

Location: About 25 miles SW of Chicago

Length: 9-plus total miles (loop)

Physical difficulty: Easy to moderate

Technical difficulty: Easy

Terrain: Mostly crushed limestone, gradual climbs

Maps and books: Trailboard at the trailhead parking lot; DuPage County Forest Preserve map (630-933-7248); online map at www.cambr.org. *Chicago Mountain Bike Trails Guide; A Guide to Mountain Bike Trails in Illinois.*

Heads up: Ideal nontechnical—but scenic—intro to

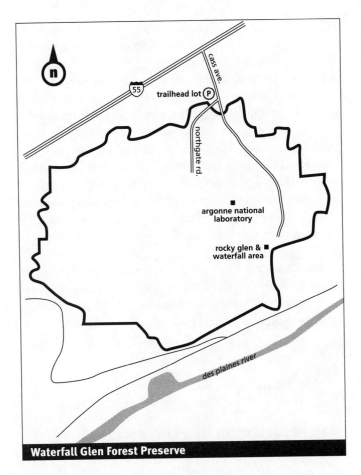

Waterfall Glen Forest Preserve

mountain biking. Bikers of all levels come for speed and scenery. Good place to come when dirt trails elsewhere are mucked out.

Description: Rolling trail through pine groves, oak and maple woods, wetlands, savanna, and prairie chock full of big bluestem, mountain mint, and yellow foxglove. In summer the air is sweet with Queen Anne's lace; butterflies feast on purple clover. Man-made waterfall built in the

1930s by the Civilian Conservation Corps, but the preserve is actually named for an early forest preserve leader, Seymour "Bud" Waterfall. Only fleeting views of encroaching subdivisions. The main 9-mile multipurpose trail, 8–10 feet wide, loops around Argonne National Laboratory (you won't see it) and offers gradual climbs and zigzags. Trail is popular with runners, cross-country skiers, and to a lesser extent, horseback riders (see "Running," page 460).

Route: Take the main multipurpose loop from the trailhead parking lot. Abundant singletrack beckons off the main trail but is off limits to bikes. DuPage County strictly enforces its ban on riding trails less than 8 feet wide. Officials here say most mowed fire lanes are wide enough to ride.

Directions: Take I-55 south and exit at Cass Ave. south. Continue south on Cass Ave. less than 0.25 mile and then turn right (west) onto Northgate Rd. Make another right into the trailhead parking lot.

Short Hops

JUBILEE COLLEGE STATE PARK, BRIMFIELD, ILLINOIS

Location: About 183 miles SW of Chicago
Length: 30-plus total miles (intersecting loops)
Physical difficulty: Moderate
Technical difficulty: Moderate
Terrain: Dirt, grass
Maps and book: Trailboard at the trailhead; rough trail map from Jubilee State Park (309-446-3758); see Peoria Area Mountain Bike Association, www.pambamtb.org. *A Guide to Mountain Bike Trails in Illinois.*

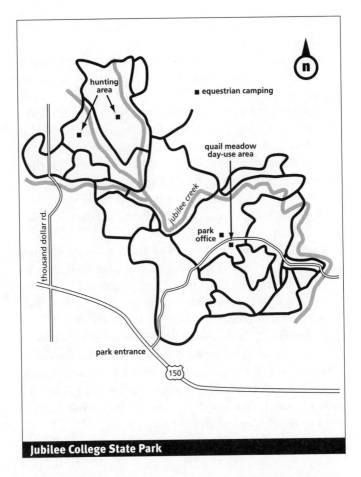

Jubilee College State Park

Heads up: Year-round camping. For turbo-technical rides under an hour drive from Jubilee, talk to Mike Antonini at Little Ade's bike shop in Pekin (309-346-3900) for the skinny on a handful of under-the-radar gems he's helped develop. Dirksen Park is a local favorite, great for honing free-riding skills with 10 miles of rugged, tight, technical singletrack, including stick and board trail, ladders, ramps, log piles, and jumps (bonus: no horses). Antonini can help you with maps and routes and, if things are slow, might show you the trails himself.

Description: Central Illinois conjures images of pancake-flat cornfields—of which there are plenty—not fat-tire tread. But the Peoria area's rolling hills have quietly emerged as a staple of the mountain bike scene, with 3,200-acre Jubilee College State Park the biggest of a handful of areas worth the trek from Chicago. Gully crossings abound in the woods and prairies of Jubilee, bisected by riffly Jubilee Creek (fishing for bluegill and smallmouth bass, but no swimming). Bikers share the multiuse trails with horseback riders, hikers, cross-country skiers, and the occasional wild turkey.

Route: Best biking is south of Jubilee Creek, farthest from hunting areas and equestrian center in the park's northwest quadrant. Start from Quail Meadow day-use area and plot out which unnamed loop you want to follow; trailboard is behind the shelter next to the trailhead.

Directions: Take I-55 south about 125 miles to I-74 west. Follow I-74 west through Peoria and take the Kickapoo-Edwards exit (exit 82). Go north about 1.5 miles to Kickapoo. Turn left (west) onto US 150. Follow US 150 about 3 miles to the park entrance on your right. Follow the park road to Quail Meadow day-use area.

JOHN MUIR AND EMMA CARLIN TRAILS, KETTLE MORAINE SOUTH; EAGLE, WISCONSIN

Location: About 90 miles N of Chicago

Length: 40 total miles (intersecting loops)

Physical difficulty: Moderate to difficult. Stick to trails that match your level. Expect grinding climbs.

Technical difficulty: Moderate to difficult. Connector and Emma Carlin trails are most technical.

Terrain: Dirt, sand, roots, rocks, washboards on wide single- and doubletrack

Maps and book: Trail maps available at John Muir and Emma Carlin parking lots; see www.worba.org. for Southern Kettle Moraine chapter link. *Mountain Biking Wisconsin.*

Heads up: Fans call it "Moab of the Midwest." Call ahead for the state forest's trail conditions (262-594-6202), especially in winter and spring. Camping at Whitewater Lake, spots go fast (888-947-2757 for reservations, 262-493-6200). Self-registration boxes for trail passes and vehicle stickers in the John Muir and Emma Carlin parking lots. Nonresident vehicle sticker $30 annual, $10 day; trail pass $10 annual, $3 day. Trail wisdom and fuel: LaGrange General Store (262-495-8600, www.backyardbikes.com) mountain and road bike rental and repair at US 12 and County H.

Description: Jaded city bikers say these well-traveled state forest trails are overrated. Whatever. If you can't find something to love here, sell your mountain bike and leaf through the rest of this book to get hooked on something new. Crowded? Yes. But hit the trails early on weekend mornings and you'll be heading to LaGrange General Store for a portabella burger and yogurt smoothie when the masses are just finishing their warm-up on the Red Loop. Emma Carlin's three loop trails, a bit farther north, tend to get less use than John Muir's five loops. Namesake kettles (giant glacier-induced potholes) and moraines (hilly masses of rock, gravel, and sand deposited beneath the ice) offer varied terrain in a pristine pine and hardwood forest dotted with leatherleaf bogs. Most climbs are in the 20- to 30-foot range, but several are 60-plus feet. Mountain biking allowed only on designated Muir, Carlin, and Connector trails; hikers use trails on both sides of County H. Popular ski and horse trails north in the forest (see "Winter Sports," page 419, and "Horseback Riding," page 493).

Route: All trails are one way except for the brutal 5-mile

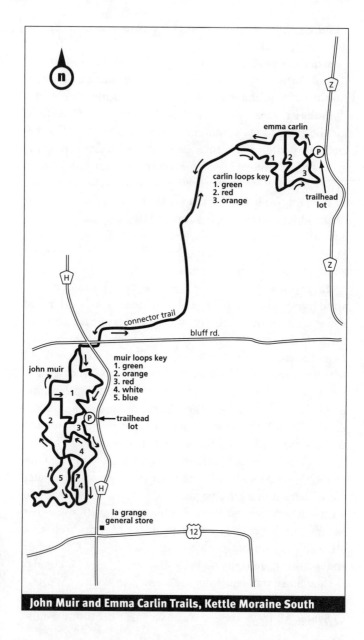

emma carlin

carlin loops key
1. green
2. red
3. orange

trailhead lot

connector trail

bluff rd.

john muir

muir loops key
1. green
2. orange
3. red
4. white
5. blue

trailhead lot

la grange
general store

John Muir and Emma Carlin Trails, Kettle Moraine South

Connector between John Muir and Emma Carlin; some riders consider the Connector, with switchbacks, steep climbs, wide-open singletrack, and rocky descents, a highlight itself. Your route depends on your skill and stamina; hard-core riders can cover Muir and Carlin for a full day of bone-rattling riding. Advanced riders favor Green and Blue trails. From easiest to toughest, John Muir's loop trails are: Red (1.5 miles; good warm-up with one small downhill), White (4 miles; switchbacks and climbs), Orange (5.3 miles; killer 1-mile climb and steep descent dubbed "frame breaker"), Green (6.8 miles; technically demanding), and Blue (10 miles; custom designed for biking, frequent finesse areas and washboards). Emma Carlin loops—loose, rocky, hilly, and narrow—are considered more technical: Red (2 miles; steep hogback ridge), Orange (2.4 miles), and Green (4 miles; gear-grinding uphill—Connector trail leads you to this loop).

Directions: Take I-94 west to WI 50 at Kenosha. Go left (west) on WI 50 to US 12, just before Lake Geneva. Follow US 12 north to County H by the LaGrange General Store. Turn north (right) onto County H. The John Muir trailhead parking lot is about 1.5 miles on the left. Emma Carlin trails are about 5 miles north. From John Muir's lot, go north on County H to Bluff Rd. Turn right (east) on Bluff Rd. until County Z. Turn left (north) on County Z to the Emma Carlin trailhead lot on your left.

GREENBUSH RECREATION AREA AND NEW FANE TRAILS, KETTLE MORAINE NORTH; CAMPBELLSPORT, WISCONSIN

Location: About 150 miles N of Chicago (New Fane's about 20 miles closer)

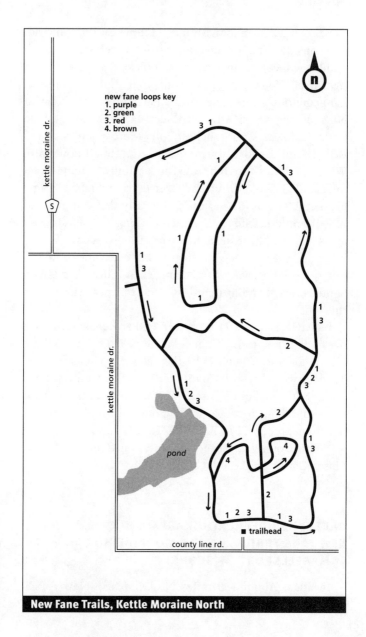

new fane loops key
1. purple
2. green
3. red
4. brown

pond

■ trailhead

county line rd.

kettle moraine dr.

kettle moraine dr.

New Fane Trails, Kettle Moraine North

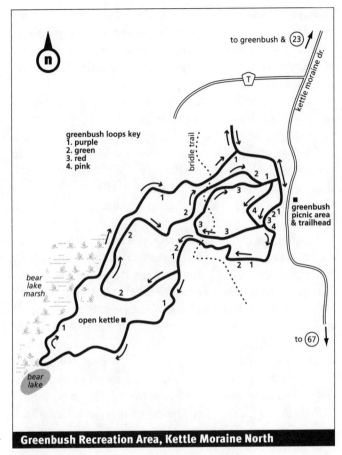

Greenbush Recreation Area, Kettle Moraine North

Length: 11 miles at Greenbush; 8 miles at New Fane (intersecting loops)

Physical difficulty: Moderate to difficult

Technical difficulty: Easy to difficult. Greenbush has tougher trails.

Terrain: Dirt, sand, roots, and rocks. Lots of hardpack, wide singletrack at New Fane. Single- and doubletrack at Greenbush.

Maps and book: Trailboards at Greenbush and New Fane trailheads; stop by Ice Age Visitors Center on WI 67, about 3 miles east of WI 45, for trail maps or call (262) 626-2116; see www.worba.org for Fat Kats Mountain Bike Club. *Mountain Biking Wisconsin.*

Heads up: Kettles minus the heavy crowds. Trails usually open late April–early November, but always call ahead for conditions (262-626-2116). Self-registration at Greenbush and New Fane trailheads for required vehicle stickers and trail passes. Nonresident vehicle sticker $30 annual, $10 day; trail pass $10 annual, $3 day. Trailside camping at Greenbush Group Camp. Individual sites at Mauthe and Long Lakes.

Description: Father from major metro areas, the Kettles' 30,000-acre northern unit sees less traffic than its southern sibling but still offers biking through the geological equivalent of Swiss cheese. Skiers and hikers tend to outnumber bikers on the well-marked trails here (see "Winter Sports," page 422, and "Hiking & Backpacking," page 345). Horse trails cross Greenbush cluster trails at several points but don't share trail (see "Horseback Riding," page 494). Greenbush trail cluster is made up of two ridges with a valley cutting through the middle. Each loop from the main trail starts high on the south rim, drops into the valley, and climbs back to the north rim. The town of Greenbush is worth a stop for historic white clapboard buildings. New Fane trails are a hair over 20 miles south and offer beginner to advanced terrain.

Route: Hit Greenbush first while your legs are fresh, then do what you like of New Fane on your way back to the city. Stop for a summer dip at Mauthe Lake. Pick up Greenbush's main Purple trail (5.1 miles) from the picnic area. The smaller loops (Pink 0.7, Green 3.6, Red 1.5 miles) cut away from the Purple trail, which runs along the ridgetops passing through pines, diminutive Bear Lake, and Bear Lake

Marsh. Fast bumps, jumps, and turns. The Pink loop—
powder puff name notwithstanding—is tough, with rapid-
fire descent and quick cutbacks. New Fane has four loops:
Purple, 3.1; Red, 2.4; Green, 1.5; and Brown, 0.7 miles.
Brown is considered beginner. Greenbush and New Fane
trails are one way.

Directions: Take I-94 west to Milwaukee. In Milwaukee,
take I-43 north to Sheboygan. At Sheboygan, take WI 23
west to County T. Turn left (south) on County T/Kettle
Moraine Dr. and follow a little over 1 mile through the town
of Greenbush. After County T splits off, stay south on scenic Kettle Moraine Dr. and follow about 2 miles to the
Greenbush picnic area and trailhead on the right (west) side
of the road. To get to New Fane from Greenbush, follow Kettle Moraine Dr. south to County Line Rd. Turn left (east) on
County Line Rd.; parking lot and trailhead are on the left.

YANKEE SPRINGS RECREATION AREA,
MIDDLEVILLE, MICHIGAN

Location: About 175 miles NE of Chicago
Length: 13 total miles (loop)
Physical difficulty: Moderate to difficult
Technical difficulty: Moderate to difficult
Terrain: Dirt, soft sand, rocks, and roots

Maps and books: Maps at trailhead; call rec area (616-795-
9081) for trail conditions and hunting closures. See Michigan Mountain Biking Association at www.mmba.org.
*Chicago Mountain Bike Trails Guide; Mountain Biking the
Great Lakes States.*

Heads up: Pumping through sand can make trail feel a
whole lot longer; some come a few days after a hard rain
packs it down. First-come, first-served rustic camping at

Deep Lake, just yards from the trailhead. Bring your rod for rainbow trout and northern pike in the 34-acre lake (just one of eight in the park). Park fee $4 day, $20 annual.

Description: Popular for a reason; these trails are just plain fun, with enough terrain to keep them interesting for more advanced riders. Switchback through the pines 40 miles north of Kalamazoo on 5,200 acres of onetime Algonquin hunting grounds. Palefaces seem to dig hunting here, too; local bikers report close encounters with bow hunters stalking wild turkeys in early fall. Seems like the perfect time to pull out that vintage '80s orange neon shirt crumpled in the back of the closet. Watch for hikers, too. If you're spending some time in the area, Fort Custer Recreation Area, with 15-plus miles of more mellow trail (Red and Green are tops), is less than an hour drive from here.

Route: Pick up the trailhead by the lot just east of Deep Lake campground. Ride counterclockwise on the one-way trail; several shortcuts available. Trail starts on flat to gently rolling hardpack singletrack through tight oak forest (watch those handlebars) with occasional short, steep dips through streams and ravines, as well as roots and rocks. As you ride northeast to higher ground, the hills kick in steady and steep (some 100-plus feet). Around the 10-mile mark, look for Devil's Soup Bowl, a glacial kettle more than 100 feet deep.

Directions: Take I-94 east through Indiana and into Michigan. In Kalamazoo, take US 131 north to exit 61. Go east on County A 42. After about 8 miles turn right (south) on Gun Lake Rd. Park HQ is less than 1 mile on the right (pick up park sticker and map). Continue on Gun Lake Rd. to the intersection with Yankee Springs Rd. Turn left (north) on Yankee Springs and follow less than 1 mile to the entrance, left, for the Deep Lake campground parking area.

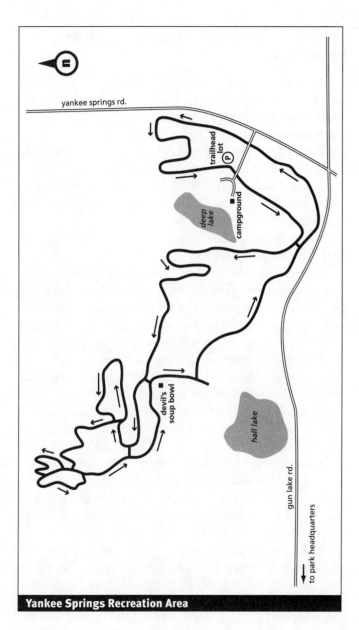

Yankee Springs Recreation Area

yankee springs rd.

trailhead lot
P

campground

deep lake

devil's soup bowl

hall lake

gun lake rd.

to park headquarters

DEVIL'S HEAD RESORT SKI AREA, MERRIMAC, WISCONSIN

Location: About 173 miles N of Chicago

Length: 12 total miles

Physical difficulty: Moderate to difficult

Technical difficulty: Moderate to difficult

Terrain: Dirt, grass, rocks, blowdowns, ruts, and the closest you'll get to a mountain in these parts

Map and book: Devil's Head Resort (800-338-4579, www .devilsheadresort.com) has a seriously rough trail map. *Chicago Mountain Bike Trails Guide.*

Heads up: Mountain bikes take over from skiers mid-May through mid-October.

Description: Here for one reason alone: elevation. The popular ski resort offers climbs of 500-plus feet. Period. The place was better before they built a new golf course and knocked out about half of the available mountain bike trails (they still charge $7 for a daily trail pass). Management seems largely indifferent to mountain bikers; they haven't drawn a decent map or done much in the way of trail maintenance. They used to host mountain bike races but apparently didn't make much money off them, so they stopped. But if you need to climb and want screaming downhills, this is your place. Expect to get slashed by thorns.

Route: Go up. Come down. Repeat. Ride over the top and find Ghost Rock singletrack trail, best in the place. Or run a 5-mile loop from Mile Climb to Deer Run to Max's Run to Shady Climb to Top of the Hill to Dylabob to Mid Mountain and down Mile Climb again.

Directions: Take I-90 west about 160 miles. Stay on I-90/94 past Madison. Take exit 108a for Merrimac. Follow WI 78 south about 8 miles. Take a right on County DL. After about 4 miles, you'll hit a four-way stop. Go right on Bluff Rd. The resort is about 0.25 mile on the right.

Mecca

CAMBA TRAILS, CHEQUAMEGON NATIONAL FOREST, CABLE, WISCONSIN

Location: About 440 miles NW of Chicago

Length: 300-plus total miles

Physical difficulty: Something for everyone. Easy to expert.

Technical difficulty: Ditto

Terrain: Dirt, gravel, sand. Everything from big climbs and technical singletrack to gently rolling scenic cruising in big wilderness.

Maps and books: Chequamegon Area Mountain Bike Association (CAMBA) maps (800-533-7454, www.cambatrails .org) are a must and an amazing deal: $5 gets you an overview map, detailed topo trail maps, and route narratives for all six clusters. Pick them up—along with Forest Service stickers for parking at trailhead lots, $3 day, $10 annual—at area bike shops. *Mountain Biking Wisconsin; Mountain Biking Chequamegon.*

Heads up: Thought you died and went to fat-tire heaven. Chance to ride the 52-km Birkebeiner Trail, host to the legendary ski race (see "Winter Sports," page 427). Most trails ridable May–November. Chequamegon Fat Tire Festival in mid-September. Idyllic camp-and-bike journey (see *Pitching Tent*, page 293).

Description: Long drive from the city, but the trade-off's well worth it when you're rewarded with nearly a mile of trail for every mile you drive. Some consider this 1,600-square-mile knobbydrome carved out of the Chequamegon National Forest wilderness (plus tracts of Bayfield and

Sawyer County Forests) the mountain bike capital of the Midwest. Trails are organized in six clusters around the towns of Cable (HQ for CAMBA), Delta, Drummond, Hayward, Namakagon, and Seeley. Each cluster has one or more trailheads and 40–100 miles of trail. Though the trail system's sheer size can be overwhelming, it's unlikely you'll get lost in the sea of fragrant pine and hardwood if you're armed with the essential CAMBA maps; trails have frequent reassurance markers, and major trail intersections carry "You are here" markers with a corresponding land marker number on the CAMBA maps. In addition to single- and doubletrack, trails include logging roads, fire lanes, snowmobile trails, and ski routes.

Ron Bergin of CAMBA recommends two classic routes: Cable's Short and Fat and Namakagon's Rock Lake Trail. The Short and Fat is a 15-mile, intermediate roller-coaster point-to-point from Cable trailhead to Telemark Resort trailhead—part of the fall fat-tire festival. It covers gravel road, singletrack, doubletrack, and a sliver of paved road through mixed hardwood and pine. You'll need to clean off your granny gear for the 9.9-mile Rock Lake Trail. The tough loop covers 100% singletrack through brutal uphills and screaming downhills, skirting the edge of several lakes. Sound good? Get the maps.

Directions: Take I-90 west to Madison. Stay on I-90/I-94 past Madison and take I-94 to Eau Claire. At Eau Claire, take US 53 north to Trego. At Trego, take US 63 into Cable.

For Cable trailhead, turn right (east) on County M. After two blocks, go right (south) on Randysek Rd. Drive one block to First St. Turn right (west), go half a block, and park behind the former Cable Grade School in downtown Cable.

For Rock Lake trailhead, from Cable go 7 miles east on County M. Turn right (south) at Rock Lake trail sign and park in the lot. Forest Service parking fee here; self-register in the lot for $3 daily sticker if you haven't picked one up. Note: a 5- or 6-mile bike ride down Rock Lake Rd. will take you to the Cable and Seeley clusters.

chequamegon national forest, wisconsin

MIDWESTERN WILDERNESS WRIT large. With a whopping 860,000 acres, Chequamegon National Forest (pronounced "Shuh-WAH-muh-gun") in Wisconsin's North Woods covers more ground than the state of Rhode Island.

About 16 miles northeast of Cable, home turf for the Chequamegon Area Mountain Bike Association, Namekagon campground is well positioned for easy trail access. Nab a hemlock-sheltered site by Namekagon Lake (sailing and boating), headwaters of the Namekagon and the north fork of the St. Croix National Scenic Riverway. Cut through your hard-earned bike grime with a dip in the 3,227-acre lake. Gorge yourself on crazily abundant wild strawberries, raspberries, blueberries, and blackberries from June to September. Bring binos for 229 species of birds.

If you don't want any neighbors to mar your views of the aspen, birch, and maple, strike out for the backcountry. You can camp virtually anywhere in the national forest. The black bear population here is the state's largest; consider yourself lucky if you spot a rare timber wolf or elk.

With Chequamegon's 800 lakes, 74 coldwater trout streams, and 100-plus "warm-water" rivers and streams with umpteen acres of marshes and bogs, you'd be a fool not to bring your lures along. Muskie is akin to religion around here, celebrated in a mid-June Muskie Festival. On that note, don't leave town without checking out the 144-foot-tall fiberglass muskie, in whose hollow gut is the National Freshwater Fishing Hall of Fame. It's in Hayward (as is the Muskie Festival), about 17 miles south of Cable.

Details: Namekagon campground has 34 primitive sites for $12 a night (vault toilet, water pumps, swimming beach, fishing pier, no showers). All sites have fire grates and picnic tables. Reservations at (877) 444-6777, www.reserveusa.com. No permits, no fees for backcountry camping; pitch tent at least 50 feet from any trail or water body. Closest National Forest office is in Hayward (715-748-4875), north of town off US 63. To get to Namekagon campground, take I-90 west to Madison. Stay on I-90/I-94 past Madison and take I-94 to Eau Claire. At Eau Claire, take US 53 north to Trego. At Trego, take US 63 into Cable. At Cable, go east on County M about 11 miles to County D. Turn left (north) on County D and go just over 5 miles to FR 209. Turn left (west). You'll hit the campground in about 0.3 miles.

Lakefront Rental

ESIDES THE HANDFUL of bike shops listed later that rent as well as sell mountain bikes, Bike Chicago (312-595-9600, www.bikechicago.com) rents mountain, hybrid, road, tandem, and kids' bikes April–November. Rent by the hour, day, week, or month (a 3-day weekend special runs $14.99 a day, including helmet and lock). In-line skates and scooters, too. Three lakefront spots: North Ave. Beach (773-327-2706), Navy Pier (600 E. Grand Ave., 312-755-0488), 63d St. Beach (773-324-3400).

Where to Connect

Clubs and Organizations

- Chicago Area Mountain Bikers (CAMBr; P.O. Box 444, Oak Forest, IL 60452; atb@cambr.org; www.cambr.org) runs monthly trail work days at Palos and Deer Grove. Also races, poker ride, National Mountain Bike Patrol.

- Chicago Cycling Club (773-509-8093, www .chicagocyclingclub.org) sponsors regular group rides, including local and overnight off-road trips.

- Chicagoland Bicycle Federation (312-42-PEDAL, www.chibikefed.org) is the area's primo advocacy group. Publishes "Chicagoland Bicycle Map," including off-road for seven-county area. CBF's Randy Warren coaches local team XXX Racing.

- Peoria Area Mountain Bike Association (www.pambamtb .org; contact Terry Carter at terry@pambamtb.org)

- Wisconsin Off-Road Bicycling Association (P.O. Box 1681, Madison, WI 53707; www.worba.org)

- Michigan Mountain Biking Association (866-889-MMBA, www.mmba.org)

- Chequamegon Area Mountain Bike Association (800-234-6635, www.cambatrails.org)

Shops

- On The Route Bicycles (3146 N. Lincoln Ave., 773-477-5066, www.ontheroute.com) has fat-tire emphasis. Rents and sells mountain, hybrid, and road bikes.

- Johnny Sprocket's Bicycles (3001 N. Broadway Ave., 773-244-1079; 1052 W. Bryn Mawr Ave., 773-293-1695). Zero attitude in this neighborhood shop.

- Kozy's Cyclery and Fitness (601 S. LaSalle St., 312-360-0020; 1451 W. Webster Ave. in the Webster Place strip mall at Clybourn Ave., 773-528-2700; 3712 N. Halsted St., 773-281-2263; www.kozy.com). Family-owned local mini-chain. Full range of mountain, hybrid, and road bikes.

- Village Cycle Center (1337 N. Wells St., 312-751-2488; www.villagecycle.com). Huge inventory; full range.

- Turin Bicycle (1027 Davis St., Evanston, 847-864-7660, www.turinbicycle.com). Road bikes are Turin's pedigree, but they carry everything, have been around forever, and are a fixture in the area bike scene. Mountain bike and road racing teams (Aside: five of the eight mountain bike team members are women.) Bike club. Some weekend mountain bike trips. Tandems, hybrids, and the occasional road racer for rent.

- Yojimbo's Garage (1310 N. Clybourn Ave., 312-587-0878) is a no-nonsense shop owned by Marcus Moore, star wrench and former Chicago bike messenger. If you're interested in racing, talk to Moore, who helped found, and races with, local team XXX Racing (mountain bike, cyclo-cross, road, and track).

Events

- Chicago SuperCup in November/December draws elite and amateur riders from around the country as part of a USCF-sanctioned national cyclo-cross series, held in Washington Park on the South Side. Turin Bicycle is local contact, or see www.kirongroup.com.

- 12 Hours of Palos Mountain Bike Challenge in August on the rugged Palos trails. Proceeds go toward trail maintenance. Contact CAMBr for details.

- Fall Color Festival on the John Muir trails of Wisconsin's Kettle Moraine State Forest south unit held in late September flame-out. Tune-up clinics, demos, single speed,

8-, 20-, and 30-mile rides; proceeds go to trail development. (414) 529-6600, www.worba.org.

- 12 Hours at John Muir in August is part of the Wisconsin Endurance Mountain Bike Series. www.12hoursjohnmuir .homestead.com.

- Pedro's Mountain Bike Festival Midwest in late June–early July in Hatfield, WI, has clinics, night rides, games, and a big bike expo. (262) 549-6801 ext. 81, www.pedrosfest.com.

- Chequamegon Fat Tire Festival in mid-September is a weekend-long happening in Cable and Hayward featuring the Chequamegon 40-miler and 16-mile Short and Fat races. The fest started in 1983 with 27 local riders. Today it's capped at 2,500 riders from around the country. Plus a half-mile criterium, Rough Stuff Rendezvous (orienteering), clunker bike toss, hill climb, and kids' bike rodeo. Highly coveted race slots are doled out by lottery. In 2002 registration had to be postmarked by March 15. (715) 798-3594, www.cheqfattire.com.

Books

- Hochgesang, Jim. *Hiking & Biking in Cook County, Illinois*. Lake Forest, IL: Roots & Wings, 1996.

- Johnson, Steve. *Mountain Biking Chequamegon*. Helena, MT: Falcon Publishing, 1998.

- Ries, Richard, and Dave Shepard. *Mountain Bike! Midwest*. Birmingham, AL: Menasha Ridge Press, 2000.

- Strazz, P. L. *Chicago Mountain Bike Trails Guide*. Chicago, IL: Big Lauter Tun Books, 1998.

- Van Valkenberg, Phil, and Jack McHugh. *Mountain Biking the Great Lakes States*. Birmingham, AL: Menasha Ridge Press, 1995.

- Waller, Colby Thor. *Mountain Biking Wisconsin*. Helena, MT: Falcon Publishing, 1998.

- Zyznieuski, Walter G., and George S. Zyznieuski. *A Guide to Mountain Bike Trails in Illinois*. Carbondale, IL: Southern Illinois University Press, 1997.

Links

www.mtbr.com

www.imba.org

www.illinoismtbr.com

PEREGRINE FALCONS SHRED prey on the 34th-floor ledge of 125 S. Wacker. Snowy owls cruise Meigs Field along the lake as planes take off. Lime sherbet-hued monk parakeets build their condolike nests on light poles by the Jackson Park driving range. Threatened grassland birds breed in increasingly rare prairie on the metro area's outer edge.

There's incredibly rich birding within city limits, with more than 300 species seen in Chicago throughout the year. Some 7 million birds pass through the city on their migratory routes. City parks and county forest preserves offer up remarkably diverse terrain, from savanna and prairie to oak-maple forest and wetlands. Magic Hedge at

Montrose Point and Wooded Island at Jackson Park, both benefiting from recent habitat face-lifts, are legendary hotspots in fall and spring. Plenty of local birders wouldn't dream of leaving the city in May, when a carpet of migrating flycatchers, thrushes, warblers, and tanagers alight like tiny jewels along the lakefront parks, though increasingly birding is becoming a year-round addiction.

What makes Chicago special? It's a key stopover on the Mississippi flyway. "Historically, in this state, we're at the place where the eastern deciduous forest and the prairie came together," says Doug Stotz, conservation ecologist and ornithologist at the Field Museum of Natural History. "By being centrally located we get a flavor from everybody. We're not boreal forest, but we get a taste of it when snowy owls and northern shrikes show up. We're not in the forests of the southeast but we still get Kentucky warblers." Many migratory birds fly over Lake Michigan at night; when morning comes, they need a place to land and pile up along the lakefront. Inland birds get pushed along by southwest winds in spring and northwest fronts in fall. And Chicago is an oasis at the northern end of what Stotz calls "the great corn and soybean desert. From southern Illinois until you get to Chicago there's very, very little for the birds to use."

The distinct advantage of city birding is that birds are concentrated in relatively compact, accessible urban patches of green, making them a lot easier to see—especially notoriously difficult-to-spot species like the Connecticut warbler.

Birding may be one of the less physically demanding pursuits in this book, but rest assured, it's one of the most competitive sports around, with dedicated adherents constantly adding species to their life list. The city's birding clubs are open to novices and obsessives alike. If you're a beginner, hook up with one of the many guided bird walks in the metro area; many of the state parks listed here run walks,

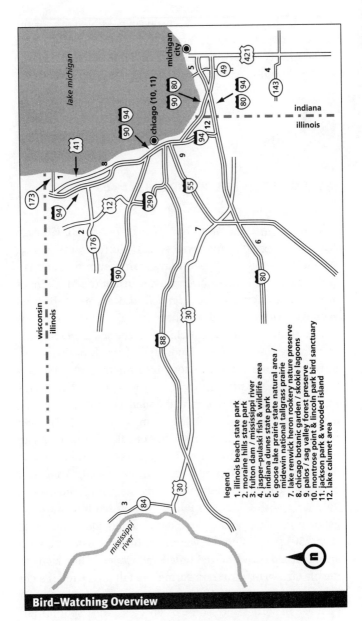

Bird–Watching Overview

lake michigan

wisconsin
illinois

indiana
illinois

michigan city

chicago (10, 11)

mississippi
river

legend
1. illinois beach state park
2. moraine hills state park
3. fulton dam / mississippi river
4. jasper-pulaski fish & wildlife area
5. indiana dunes state park
6. goose lake prairie state natural area /
   midewin national tallgrass prairie
7. lake renwick heron rookery nature preserve
8. chicago botanic garden / skokie lagoons
9. palos / sag valley forest preserve
10. montrose point & lincoln park bird sanctuary
11. jackson park & wooded island
12. lake calumet area

too. This chapter would not have been possible without the help of Sheryl DeVore, author of *Birding Illinois*, and Lynne Carpenter, co-author of *A Birder's Guide to the Chicago Region*. You'll need their books to exploit the riches.

City Limits

JACKSON PARK AND WOODED ISLAND

Location: 6400 S

Contact: Chicago Park District (312-747-6187); Chicago Audubon Society runs twice-weekly bird walks 7 A.M. Wednesdays and 8 A.M. Saturdays spring, summer, and fall at the Clarence Darrow bridge just south of the Museum of Science and Industry (see *Island Bird Man*, page 303, and *Where to Connect* for details).

Description: Landscape architect Frederick Law Olmsted transformed a sand ridge landscape of scrub oak and cottonwood into a forested showpiece for the 1893 World's Columbian Exposition, carving out a 16-acre island that's an urban birding phenom. "Wooded Island" is, in fact, densely and diversely wooded, from weeping willows and green ash to gingko and six species of oak and maple. As an island, formally the Paul H. Douglas Nature Sanctuary, it offers exhausted migrants—and the 55 species that nest here—built-in protection from predators. Doug Anderson, a volunteer with Chicago Audubon who's led bird walks in Jackson Park for nearly three decades, has identified more than 250 species here. Rewarding birding year-round, with great horned owls and red-tailed and Cooper's hawks picking off rabbits in winter. In spring and fall migration it's not unheard of to tick off 100 species in a few hours. Warbler paradise in spring with some 34 species. Great spot for rarities, too, like Townsend's and Swainson's warblers. Anderson's also seen lesser black-backed gulls and a magnificent frigatebird blown in by a remnant hurricane. Loop around the island, then walk through Bobolink Meadow on the east side. Check the lightpoles by the driving range for monk parakeet (see *Political Parrot*, page 305). Though the park's gotten a lot safer in recent years, it's still best to bird in the A.M. and go in multiples.

Directions: Take Lake Shore Dr. south to the Museum of Science and Industry. Just past 57th St. make your first right (west) onto Science Dr. and head for the parking lot in the southwest corner. Note: you can only access the free lot heading south on Lake Shore Dr. For street parking check west of the museum.

By transit, the 6 and 10 buses from downtown stop near the museum.

Island Bird Man

DOUG ANDERSON KNOWS every inch of Jackson Park: the cottonwood tree where a raccoon family has nested for the past 8 years, the dead limb that's a favored perch of Cooper's hawks, the stand of meadow-cup flowers whose curved leaves collect rainwater and offer small birds a place to bathe and drink. Little wonder. Anderson, who's led several Chicago birding organizations over the years, has been running bird walks at the gem of a park since 1974. A lifelong Hyde Parker, as a kid Anderson used to climb the park's 271-year-old burr oak and still lives within shouting distance, in a red brick building that overlooks the urban sea of green that's listed on the National Register of Historic Places.

The 67-year-old with the Harry Caray-esque glasses started birding after his biology teacher at Hyde Park High took the class out to Jackson Park's Wooded Island. Since then he's birded coast-to-coast, through South and Central America, India, and Africa. But Jackson Park—"a birders paradise since 1893"—always beckons.

Anderson started the walks as a joint effort with a local alderman to try to reclaim the parks from rival gangs. Birders had been mugged, so people were steering clear. He figured people would feel safer in groups, and as a Cook County juvenile court probation officer, Anderson knew some of the local gang members. "Plus I needed a hobby that took me away from the enormous people problems I faced during the week."

On this October Saturday morning, eight of us have shown up for the walk, including loyal regulars like 95-year-old Hyde Parker Dale Pontius, a retired political science professor who's birded with Anderson since his first walks (Pontius is walking around with his bike helmet affixed to his head; he still rides over to the park). During peak migration, Anderson draws groups of 30 to 40, with birders from across the Midwest, as well as listers on holiday from Japan and Europe.

We wind through the Japanese garden, along the island path, and into the rose garden-turned meadow (the roses were there for the 1893 World's Fair), a favorite spot for hawks and owls, scanning for warblers and rabbits foraging in the tall grasses. As if on cue, crows start squawking in a nearby maple, eventually flushing out a great horned owl.

Anderson peppers the walk with tales of Chicago's natural, ecological, and cultural history. As a pair of cedar waxwings flit about, he points out the white snakeroot in the underbrush, which he says used to kill people who drank the milk of cows who'd grazed the stuff, casually mentioning that Abraham Lincoln's mother met her maker this way.

We stalk the big bluestem, Indian grass, and 73 other native prairie species in the 8-acre Bobolink Meadow along the lagoon's eastern edge, "a piece of what Chicago looked like 200 years ago." Anderson points out the anomalous stubby pine where he's spotted the occasional northern saw-whet owl.

Though he lost a battle to save Bobolink Meadow from an encroaching driving range—the meadow used to stretch from the lagoon all the way to Lake Shore Dr. and was the only place the bobolink nested in the city—he helped win the fight to protect the beloved monk parakeet (see *Political Parrot,* below). And he managed to get Wooded Island named for Paul H. Douglas, the progressive environmentalist Illinois senator who taught for nearly three decades down the street at another Hyde Park landmark, U of C. When Douglas died in 1976, his ashes were spread over Wooded Island.

"He loved this island," Anderson says. "And so do I."

Political Parrot

S O THE STORY goes, former mayor Harold Washington swore that as long as the monk parakeets continued to nest on the tree by his Hyde Park apartment he would never lose an election (he never did). After Washington died in office in 1987, the U.S. Agriculture Department made noises about relocating the non-native birds, saying they were a threat to crops. City parrot lovers clamored to the birds' defense, establishing the Harold Washington Memorial Parrot Defense Fund and threatening to fight the move in court. Eventually, the feds backed down.

Doug Anderson, a member of the monk defense team, says while the birds are considered an agricultural pest in their native South America, eating grain and fruit crops, "here they eat weed seeds, shrub berries, and in the winter, seed from neighborhood bird feeders. I've seen them alight on lawns and snip off dandelion tops." An estimated 200 monk parakeets are spread across more than a dozen nesting sites on the city's South Side. Sightings of the Hyde Park parakeets go back a few decades. Some say the birds escaped from a cage at O'Hare; others say the population more likely stems from pets that escaped or were set free (monks fall short on mimicking skills but do chatter loudly).

"I've been their protector because they fit in very well with our native species; they don't compete with them for space," Anderson says, pointing out one of the Jackson Park parakeets' enormous communal nests, with separate entranceways for the different nesting pairs, wrought from a thicket of twigs. And, he adds, they fill an ecological niche that was left vacant when the Carolina parakeet, Illinois' only native parakeet, became extinct in the early 1900s.

MONTROSE POINT/LINCOLN PARK BIRD SANCTUARY

Location: 4400 N (Montrose Point)–3600 N (bird sanctuary)

Contact: Chicago Park District (312-747-2474); Montrose Ave. Beach (Memorial Day–Labor Day, 312-742-0600); Chicago Ornithological Society runs weekly Wednesday 7 A.M. bird walks at the North Pond in Lincoln Park a few miles south of the bird sanctuary, near the Peggy Notebaert Nature Museum.

Description: Jutting out into the lake, windswept Montrose Point scoops up waves of weary migrants at the site of a former Nike missile base, dismantled in the 1970s. The Magic Hedge is a legendary hotspot, a 150-yard collection of dense shrubs and trees that grew up along the base's border—start your birding there. Meander the mown paths through burr oak, jack pine, plum, and hawthorns. More than 300 species have been sighted around the point, including rarities like the secretive black rail, groove-billed ani, reddish egret, and Kirtland's warbler.

In early August thousands of purple martins gather before taking flight en masse for southerly climes. Check the beach for shorebirds or head out to the fishing pier: sanderlings, greater yellowlegs, and spotted sandpipers in summer, plovers and terns in early fall, loons, ducks, and grebes later in fall. Snowy owls have been spotted at Montrose Harbor in winter. Easy enough to hit the 5-acre Lincoln Park Bird Sanctuary, about 1 mile south of Montrose Point behind the totem pole off the Lakefront Trail. A trail circles the densely wooded, fenced-in spot with a viewing platform and benches at the wetter, marshy east end (look for rails). Though it's not as active, Lincoln Park's diminutive North Pond is worth visiting with Geoff Williamson on his regular COS walks—great skyline views, too.

Directions: Take Lake Shore Dr. to the Montrose Ave. exit. Follow Montrose east. Turn right (south) at the bait shop and water fountain on the corner. Park along the road before it turns to wrap around the harbor. For the bird sanctuary, exit Lake Shore Dr. at Irving Park Rd. Go east on Irving Park, cross under Lake Shore Dr., and turn south on the park road. The sanctuary is just south of the tennis courts by the totem pole.

By transit, for Montrose Point take the Red Line L to Montrose Ave. Walk east along Montrose, or take the 78 bus, about 1 mile to the point. For the bird sanctuary, take the Red Line L to Addison St. Walk about 0.5 mile east along Addison, through the Lake Shore Dr. underpass to the sanctuary.

New
Dune

SOMETIME AROUND 1999, Montrose Beach regulars spotted a few green stems with bright red bases sprouting up from the shoreline sand. Turns out it was the lakeshore rush and the first time the plant had been found on the city's lakefront since 1946. Now, thanks in part to historically low lake levels, the plants have started colonizing a new dune on the beach's south end. Sharp-tailed sparrows and others are finding refuge in the new plants, fenced off to protect the emerging dune from dogs and beach throngs. One more stop to make on the Montrose birding circuit.

LAKE CALUMET AREA

Location: About 11500 S

Contact: Calumet Ecological Park Association (773-646-4773, www.lincolnnet.net/cepa) for a general area map. Chicago Ornithological Society usually runs area bird walks in spring, summer, and winter.

Description: From the high-speed vantage of I-94, the way most city dwellers see this southeastern corner of the city, the Lake Calumet region looks like pure urban industrial blight. True enough, slag heaps, chemical plants, and scrap-metal yards abound. It can smell. Your eyes may water. But tucked among the Rust Belt detritus are remnants of what was once a vast, rich zone of wetlands, prairie, and dunes. And these tenuous remnants offer a shot at exceptional shore and marsh bird viewing, with some 200 species living or migrating through the area, including 30 species of shorebirds and 20 state-endangered or threatened species, like little blue heron, yellow-headed blackbird, and common moorhen. The area regularly holds one of the state's largest colonies of black-crowned nightherons. Unfortunately, great spots dot a complex maze of private industrial property. The best way to see this area is with Walter Marcisz, the undisputed Lake Calumet area expert who's birded here since he was a 10-year-old in Hegewisch, on his COS bird walks.

A good public access spot is Eggers Woods Forest Preserve, hard against the Indiana line and a regular nesting area for yellow-headed blackbird, common moorhen, pied-billed grebe, and the occasional least bittern. Yellow-crowned night-heron if you're lucky. April through August is best. Great egrets, coots, and marsh wrens are regulars. From the entrance, drive south until the road dead-ends. Walk the unmarked trail south into a rough slag area; you'll eventually hit a huge marsh on your left. When Deadstick Pond is good, it's very good, especially July through September. Bird the pond and area marshes (on private property) from the side of the road along 122d St. and Stony Island Ave.

Directions: For Eggers Woods Forest Preserve, take I-94 east to 103d St. Head east on 103d to Torrence Ave. Go south on Torrence to 106th St. Take 106th east to Ewing Ave. Take Ewing south to 112th St. and follow to the preserve entrance.

Lights Out

OR THE LAST few years, Doug Stotz and his colleagues at the Field Museum have taken on the rather unsavory task of counting dead birds at the foot of McCormick Place in the name of science. They have been studying the link between building lights and bird mortality during fall and spring migration and have concluded that whether lights are on or off has a huge effect on bird deaths. In all, nearly 1,300 birds died over a 2-year period after hitting lighted windows at the massive glass-front expo hall on the lake; only 192 died from hitting unlighted ones.

Many migratory species fly at night to avoid airborne predators and navigate by the light of stars and the moon, as well as geographical markers such as rivers and lake shorelines. The high-rise wattage apparently can confuse birds' navigation systems. The city, meantime, is urging downtown buildings to dim or turn off their lights in spring and fall as part of the Urban Conservation Treaty for Migratory Birds, signed with the U.S. Fish and Wildlife Service in 2000.

Backyard

PALOS AND SAG VALLEY FOREST PRESERVES

Location: About 27 miles SW of Chicago

Contact: Little Red Schoolhouse Nature Center (708-839-6897) has guided early morning bird walks some Saturdays in spring; some winter walks, too. Naturalists at Camp Sagawau (630-257-2045) lead walks in the county's only natural rock canyon.

Description: Loads of birding throughout the county's largest tract of open space, 14,000 acres of rolling forest studded with upland meadows, small lakes, ponds, and sloughs. Check in at the Little Red Schoolhouse for the latest sightings. Hit the area trails, meadow, and handful of neighboring sloughs for migrating songbirds and waterfowl, like the prized Connecticut warbler and American black duck in spring and fall. Breeders include marsh wrens and soras and a long list of edge and field birds, like cedar waxwings. Summer brings grebes, swallows, orchard orioles, yellow-breasted chats, and ruby-throated hummingbirds (check nests in the center garden).

For ducks, head to Saganashkee and McGinnis Sloughs. In her indispensable book, *Birding Illinois*, Sheryl DeVore reports sightings of 19 duck species at Saganashkee in a single fall day and says it's one of the most reliable spots for western species like the diving canvasback and dabbling northern pintail. Loons and other waterfowl in spring and fall. Best in March/April and October/November. Follow the rough path along the slough's southern edge. Breeding pied-billed grebe and common moorhen at McGinnis Slough. In fall watch for clouds of great egrets in the trees. Sightings of the rare red-necked phalarope and American avocet along the water's edge.

Directions: Take I-55 south to LaGrange Rd./US 45. Head south on LaGrange Rd. to 95th St. Turn west (right) on 95th and go about 1 mile to 104th Ave. The Little Red Schoolhouse parking lot is under 1 mile on your right. To get to Saganashkee Slough, continue south on 104th Ave./Flavin Rd. past 107th St. Parking lot is on your right. McGinnis Slough is just south of 135th St. on LaGrange Rd.; parking is on the west side.

CHICAGO BOTANIC GARDEN/SKOKIE LAGOONS

Location: About 25 miles N of Chicago

Contact: Chicago Botanic Garden (847-835-5440) runs occasional bird walks.

Fee: $7.75 parking at the garden

Description: Within 385 acres, the Chicago Botanic Garden packs a slew of habitats: lagoons, oak woodlands, restored prairie, and conifers, attracting 250-plus bird species—everything from migratory waterfowl and songbirds to breeding woodpeckers, swallows, and orioles. Especially good in fall and spring migrations. In May, check the prairies for clay-colored and Nelson's sharp-tailed sparrows. Past rarities have included scissor-tailed and vermilion flycatchers. Head to the dwarf conifer garden for winter finches and nuthatches. Even in coldest winters there's usually some duck life to see, with at least some water kept open to protect aquatic plants. McDonald Woods nature trail in the garden's northeast corner is a reliable spot for migrating thrushes and warblers. Watch for shorebirds at Marsh Island.

Walk south through the garden, across Dundee Rd. to the North Branch Trail lining the Skokie Lagoons. The 190-acre chain of islands and lagoons draws waterfowl in early spring; later it's a magnet for migrants like yellow-bellied sapsuckers, swallows, kinglets, cuckoos, thrashers, and flycatchers. Some 70 species breed or stick around in summer. Come early to beat the angler crowds.

Directions: Follow I-94 west to US 41 north. Take the Lake-Cook Rd. exit and go east 0.5 mile to the garden entrance. For the lagoons, exit I-94 at Tower Rd. east. Park at the Tower Rd. boat launch lot or on Forestway Dr. along the east side of the lagoons.

By transit, take Metra Union Pacific North Line to the Braeside station. Walk west about 1 mile to the garden entrance. Or bike up the North Branch Trail (see "Biking," page 219), which cuts through the lagoons and the garden.

LAKE RENWICK HERON ROOKERY NATURE PRESERVE

Location: About 38 miles SW of Chicago

Contact: Will County Forest Preserve's Lake Renwick Heron Rookery Nature Preserve (815-727-8700, www.fpdwc.org/renwick/cfm) in Plainfield is open May–August, 8 A.M. to noon on Saturdays, 10 A.M. Wednesdays for a 1-hour tour.

Description: The only spot in the state where five species, including three that are state endangered or threatened, nest together: great blue heron, great egret, black-crowned night-heron, cattle egret, and double-crested cormorant. Birds and their young nest on islands in the

200-acre lake, sandwiched in layers by species (great blues and cormorants in treetops, great egrets in the middle, night-herons and cattle egrets near the ground). Other migrant water birds, like teals and shovelers, use the lake, including some rarities like white pelicans, tundra swans, and tricolored herons. During tour hours, forest preserve staff are usually on hand and set up scopes for better viewing. You can always bird from the shoulder along US 30 north of Renwick Rd., but beware heavy traffic.

Directions: Take I-55 south to US 30. Head northwest on US 30 for about 1 mile. Turn right at Renwick Rd. The rookery entrance is about 0.25 mile on the left.

 Short Hops

GOOSE LAKE PRAIRIE STATE NATURAL AREA AND MIDEWIN NATIONAL TALLGRASS PRAIRIE

Location: About 60 miles SW of Chicago

Contact: Midewin National Tallgrass Prairie (815-423-6370, www.fs.fed.us/mntp/) in Wilmington runs birding tours in spring and fall. Goose Lake Prairie State Natural Area (815-942-2899) in Morris runs occasional birding programs.

Description: With the state stripped of much of its native grasslands, these spots offer rare swaths of prairie and reclaimed agricultural lands harboring grassland species tough to see in the rest of the region. Goose Lake's 2,537 acres of prairie cordgrass, big bluestem, northern prairie dropseed, and wetlands are prime in late spring and early summer for prairie and marsh birds like the eastern meadowlark and state-endangered king rail. Seven miles of trail. Watch for Henslow's sparrow where the Tallgrass Nature

Trail and Marsh Loop trails merge. Check Marsh Loop for blue-winged teal and belted kingfishers. Cattails shelter Virginia rails and American bitterns. Sedge wrens abound. Owls in winter.

Less than 10 miles east, Midewin National Tallgrass Prairie—actually a 19,000-acre mix including sedge meadow, oak woods, and prairie—shelters more than 100 breeding species, including some of the Midwest's most endangered birds, according to Chris Whelan, an avian ecologist with the Illinois Natural History Survey. Midewin is home to the state's largest breeding population of state-endangered upland sandpipers. Other breeders include Henslow's sparrow, Bell's vireo, blue grosbeak, dickcissel, northern mockingbird, and bobolink. Northern bobwhite are more often heard than seen. A former munitions site, Midewin is still a work in progress (see "Hiking & Backpacking," page 332), with 3 miles of provisional trail open to the public and plans for 48 miles total. Guided tours highly recommended.

Directions: For Midewin, take I-55 south to exit 241 (Wilmington). Go left back over I-55 and stay on North River Rd. until IL 53. Turn left (north) onto IL 53 and follow to the entrance on your right. For Goose Lake Prairie, take I-55 south to Lorenzo Rd. Head west about 3 miles and turn right (north) onto Jugtown Rd. at the Goose Lake sign. Follow to the visitors center parking lot.

INDIANA DUNES STATE PARK, INDIANA

Location: About 51 miles SE of Chicago

Contact: Indiana Dunes State Park in Chesterton (219-926-1952, www.state.in.us/)

Fee: $5 day, $26 annual pass for out-of-state cars; $1 if you walk or bike in.

Description: In spring, this park virtually explodes with birds savvy enough to avoid the industrial soup that hems in the lakefront dunescape. All but one of the 39 warbler species ever recorded in the dunes have been seen at this park. Take trails 2, 10, and 9 encircling the big marsh east of the nature center. Watch for prothonotary warbler, Louisiana waterthrush, and a rare colony of nesting prairie warblers. Don't expect to cover much distance before repetitive binocular-raising-stress syndrome kicks in. Though spring is superlative, there's quality birding year round with 70-plus species cataloged around the park in winter. In summer, you'll often see nesting veery, white-eyed vireo, ovenbird, and cerulean, hooded, and blue-winged warblers; fall brings shorebirds, warblers, and waterfowl. See "Hiking & Backpacking," page 333.

Directions: Take I-94 east to IN 49 north. Follow IN 49 north to the gatehouse. Take the first main road branching east and follow past the campground to the nature center trailhead.

By transit, take the South Shore Line train (800-356-2079, www.nictd.com) from downtown to the Dune Park station. Walk north on IN 49 (just west of the station) about 0.5 mile to the gatehouse. From there, it's about 0.75 mile to the nature center trailhead.

ILLINOIS BEACH STATE PARK

Location: About 53 miles N of Chicago

Contact: Illinois Beach State Park (847-662-4811) in Zion

Description: Raptors' delight. Vic Berardi runs a hawk-counting spot here for the Hawk Migration Association of North America. He says 20 birds an hour is a slow day; he and his fellow counters tallied about 4,000 hawks over 90 days in a recent fall with poor migrating weather. His best one-day count so far: 735 raptors. You can expect to see about 14 species, from merlins, kestrels, and rough-legged hawks to northern harriers, goshawks, and a shot at such rarities as Swainson's or ferruginous hawks. Occasional bald and golden eagles. Good owl-watching, too. "Generally, any day with westerly winds you're going to see hawks here, just about any day from mid-September to mid-November. Hawks generally migrate on days following a cold front in the fall," Berardi says, adding that birds get conveniently concentrated along the shoreline because most hawks don't migrate over water. Head over to the North Unit pavilion to hook up with Berardi and Co. Lots of birders hit the South Unit trails in the morning for fall migrants like American redstarts and join the hawk-watchers in the afternoon (see "Hiking & Backpacking," page 341). The observation deck off the South Unit's trails is another prime raptor-viewing site. Miles of beachfront to comb for shorebirds; gulls in winter.

Directions: Take I-94 west to IL 173. Go east on IL 173 to IL 137. Turn left (north) onto IL 137 and take it about six blocks to 17th St. Turn east onto 17th St., the North Unit's main entrance, and follow it past the pond on your right until you hit the sailing beach sign. Turn right and park in the first parking area you come to. Go up the short walk to the hawk-watching pavilion. For South Unit trails, turn right (south) onto IL 137 from IL 173. Turn east on Wadsworth Rd., the South Unit's main entrance. Park in the lot before you hit the resort and conference center.

By transit, take Metra's Union Pacific North Line to the Zion station. It's about a 1.5-mile walk to the North Unit pavilion. Pick up the Zion bike trail on the west side of the tracks and follow it north to 17th St. From there, follow car directions above. It's a roughly 2.5-mile walk to the South Unit trails. Walk east on Shiloh Blvd. to Deborah Ave. Go south two blocks to the bike trail. Follow the bike trail east and south past the campground and resort and conference center to the trailhead.

MORAINE HILLS STATE PARK

Location: About 50 miles N of Chicago

Contact: Moraine Hills State Park (815-385-1624) in McHenry

Description: More than 100 species, including some of the state's rarest wetland breeders, at this rolling 1,690-acre park, best from March through October. Head to the McHenry Dam day-use area on the park's western border by the Fox River early in the morning to search for songbirds before the angler crush descends. Take the Fox River Trail around Black Tern Marsh to the wooden deck lookout and scan for breeding state-endangered yellow-headed blackbirds and black terns, as well as grebes and common moorhens, from late April through mid-July. Black Tern Marsh draws migratory waterfowl and herons and egrets in late summer. Prothonotary warblers nest in boxes in the Fox River backwaters. Bluebirds, rough-winged swallows, and sedge wrens around Lake Defiance. Least bitterns have bred around Pike Hills Marsh. If you've got time, check out nearby McHenry County's Glacial Park along the recently restored Nippersink Creek.

Directions: Follow I-90 west to IL 53 north. Stay on IL 53 north until the US 12/Rand Rd. exit. Turn left (west) on Rand Rd. At IL 176/Liberty St. turn left (west). Stay on IL 176 until you hit River Rd. Veer right onto River Rd. and follow it to the second state park entrance, off McHenry Dam Rd. Park at the far end of the dam by the concession building.

Meccas

JASPER-PULASKI FISH AND WILDLIFE AREA, INDIANA

Location: About 90 miles SE of Chicago

Contact: Jasper-Pulaski Fish and Wildlife Area (219-843-4841)

Description: Sandhill crane spectacle about an hour drive south of Indiana Dunes. My first October trip here was surreal, cranes with 6-foot wingspan flying in V-formation from every point on the compass, trumpeting wildly, swooping onto the marshy field like the plastic parachute men I played with as a kid, spindly legs dropping down, heads up, and a flap or two of the wings to slow before touching ground. The ground was a wall-to-wall crane carpet. More sandhills gather at Jasper-Pulaski in Indiana than anywhere else east of Nebraska (32,000-plus staged here in fall 1992). The up to 3.5-foot-tall birds leave their nesting grounds in the Upper Midwest's marshy wetlands in late summer and start arriving here in mid-September with peak numbers—up to 15,000 or so—in late October, early November. Smaller concentrations arrive in March and April, but that's when you're more likely to witness their frenzied, leaping courting ceremonies. Come at dawn or early dusk; most cranes leave the refuge to feed in area fields during the day. There's primitive camping if you want to check out the birds at sunrise.

Directions: Take I-94 or I-90 east to Indiana past the dunes. Around Michigan City, take US 421 south to IN 143 west. The first Fish and Wildlife Area sign on the north side of the road is for the headquarters building and camping area. The second sign is the turnoff for the crane observation tower, about 0.25 mile along County 1650W. Continue north along County 1650W to hit the parking area and trailhead for the waterfowl observation tower.

FULTON DAM/MISSISSIPPI RIVER CORRIDOR

Location: About 140 miles W of Chicago

Contact: Thomson Park Rangers (815-259-3628) runs a bald eagle watch at Fulton's Lock and Dam 13 in early January; Mississippi Palisades State Park (815-273-2731); Lost Mound National Wildlife Refuge/Savanna Army Depot (815-273-3184).

Description: As northern waters freeze up in winter, eagles cruise the Mississippi River flyway in search of open water. In early spring, more bald eagles can be seen along the Mississippi in Illinois than almost anywhere else south of Alaska. Wintering eagles tend to congregate around dams, which keep the water turbulent and tend to stun shad and other fish so they float to the surface and make for easy picking. Just north of Fulton, IL, the observation deck at Lock and Dam 13 offers a front-row seat with as many as 400 birds congregating for a few weeks in December. "It's ideal because they roost in the trees across from you and they're fishing right in front of you," says Ed Anderson of the nascent Lost Mound National Wildlife Refuge just north of Savanna. You may see the occasional golden eagle, too. Dress like you mean it; the platform is exposed and the overlook building is often closed. Mild winters tend to make the eagles more dispersed and tougher to find along the river.

Combine a trek to Fulton with Mississippi Palisades State Park, about 20 miles north near Savanna, with just under 200 species. Especially good in invasion years when several species of winter finches take up residence. Nuthatches and creepers in the pines, winter wrens in wooded creek bottoms. Hopefully by the time you read this the Lost Mound National Wildlife Refuge, formerly the Savanna Army Depot, will be open to the public. It offers spectacular eagle viewing along the river, plus a slew of other species among the floodplains, backwater bays, and uplands. See *Birding Illinois* for details on more eagle spots up and down the Mississippi.

Directions: Take I-290 west to I-88 west. Stay on I-88 west about 100 miles to US 30 west. Stay on US 30 until you hit IL 84. Go right (north) on IL 84, paralleling the river. Lock and Dam Rd. is a few quick miles north off IL 84 on your left. Mississippi Palisades State Park is about 20 miles north off IL 84.

Rare
Bird
Alert

F YOU'RE DESPERATELY searching for a particular bird to add to your list, you can narrow your search by calling the Chicago Audubon Society's rare bird alert (847-265-2118) to find out where species have been seen in recent days. Call (847) 265-2117 to report a sighting.

Where to Connect

Clubs and Organizations
• Bird Conservation Network (847-965-1150) www.iit.edu /~cos/BCN/), a coalition of Chicago-area birding organizations, promotes the conservation of bird habitat, coordinates bird monitoring, and is the best one-stop-shop birding

Bird-Watching

site with a hugely comprehensive calendar of area bird walks, field trips, and other events.

- Chicago Ornithological Society (312-409-9678, www.chicagobirder.org) runs regular bird walks at North Pond in Lincoln Park and under-birded Grant Park downtown and offers Birding for Beginners programs.

- Chicago Audubon Society (773-539-6793, http://homepage .interaccess.com/~stephenc/index.html) holds regular bird walks at North Park Village Nature Center and Jackson Park's Wooded Island.

- Evanston North Shore Bird Club (847-864-5181 through the Evanston Ecology Center; www.ensbc.org) runs regular field trips to Chicago birding hotspots and other area sites.

- Illinois Audubon Society (217-446-5085, www .illinoisaudubon.org) has been around since 1897.

- Illinois Ornithological Society (www.illinoisbirds.org)

Shops
- Wild Birds Unlimited (www.wbu.com) and Wild Bird Centers (www.wildbirdcenter.com) have several suburban locations, but as of this writing, none in the city.

Events
- Christmas Bird Counts are held in December at sites around the metro-area; Spring Counts in May. Field volunteers always needed. Contact area bird clubs for details.

- Crane Fest the Saturday before Mother's Day at the International Crane Foundation (608-356-9462, www .savingcranes.org) in Baraboo, WI. The foundation works on breeding and reintroduction programs and has captive cranes on exhibit, including the 6-foot-tall sarus and the federally endangered whooping crane. Check out the chick exercise yard.

- Chicago Audubon Society Birdathon in May; teams compete to see how many species than can find in a single day. Contact CAS.

- Great Lake Migratory Bird Fest in Lake County, IN, (219-663-8170, www.lakecountyparks.org) includes field trips, speakers, seminars, and a birding gear expo over 3 days in May.

Books

- Brock, Kenneth J. *Birds of the Indiana Dunes*. Michigan City, IN: Shirley Heinze Environmental Fund, 1997.

- Campbell, Marilyn F. *Finding Bald Eagles in Illinois*. Danville, IL: Faulstich Printing Company, 2002. Available through the Illinois Audubon Society.

- Carpenter, Lynne, and Joel Greenberg. *A Birder's Guide to the Chicago Region*. DeKalb, IL: Northern Illinois University Press, 1999.

- DeVore, Sheryl. *Birding Illinois*. Helena, MT: Falcon Press, 2000.

- Powers, Tom. *Great Birding in the Great Lakes: A Guide to the 50 Best Birdwatching Sites in the Great Lakes States*. Flint, MI: Walloon Press, 1998.

Links

http://home.xnet.com/~ugeiser/Birds/Birding.html is a good Illinois site with links to pages in neighboring states.

www.ci.chi.il.us/Environment/BirdMigration/sub/main.html from the city's department of environment has good migration information.

SOMETIMES STATE OF mind is the only thing that differentiates a hike from a walk. Case in point: I caught flak from my husband, Geoff, when I strapped on my Camelback and tucked in a peanut butter Powerbar as we set out one fine fall day to hike the downtown canyonlands along the Chicago River Trail. (For the record, he happily sucked at the plastic tube later on as we tramped along Ogden Slip.)

That said, the city has several spacious, leafy parks for a quick-and-dirty hoof—Jackson Park, Washington Park, Columbus Park, Lincoln Park—that you won't find here. Nor will you find routes through city streets, though I heartily encourage you to craft your own urban thru-hike of, say,

Clark St. or Milwaukee or Lincoln Aves. and watch the dizzying landscape of taquerias, Polish bookstores, seedy '50s neon motels, and uber-hip art galleries and boutiques unfold.

Hikes here run the gamut from a 4-mile loop in glacier-carved forest 20 miles from downtown to dune scrambles an hour's train ride away to a multiday backpacking trip on rugged, remote Isle Royale.

The backpacking *Meccas* have too many trails and route possibilities to detail here. Thoughts on "Don't Miss" trails or routes are included in an overview of what you're likely to find in an area, but this isn't the book to guide you through the backcountry wilderness. Luckily, great guide-books like Jim DuFresne's bibles on Isle Royale and the Porcupine Mountains are.

We aren't blessed with bona fide mountain peaks to scale, though the Porkies in Michigan's Upper Peninsula come as close as you'll find in the region. Dunes are our mountains. Chicago poet and writer Carl Sandburg stated it clearly: "The Dunes are to the Midwest what the Grand Canyon is to Arizona and the Yosemite is to California. They constitute a signature of time and eternity." Happily, the Indiana Dunes are practically in the city's hip pocket, offering easy escape into a national lakeshore that ranks seventh among national parks in native plant diversity.

This chapter is fairly short, because *virtually all the trails in this book make good hikes*. Maximize your options by referring to the "Running," "Mountain Biking," "Biking," and "Winter Sports" chapters. You just may have to turn back earlier on foot. In particular, keep in mind metro-area trails like the Illinois Prairie Path, North Branch Trail, Waterfall Glen, Indian Boundary Division, and I&M Canal State Trail. Cook County forest preserves alone have 200 miles of trail winding through nearly 68,000 acres of open space. And the Lakefront Trail straddles the space where the concrete ends and the city's front-yard, roadless, watery wilderness begins.

City Limits

CHICAGO RIVER TRAIL

Location: Downtown

Length: About 5 miles one way

Difficulty: Easy. But wear good shoes; concrete's tough on the feet—lots of stairs, too.

Map and book: Friends of the Chicago River downtown river trail map (312-939-0490, www.chicagoriver.org). For historical inspiration, check out *The Chicago River: An Illustrated History and Guide to the River and Its Waterways.*

Dogs: Yes

Heads up: Urban canyon views. Prepare to detour around Wacker Dr. construction, designed to produce a continuous river trail along the south bank of the river's Main Stem downtown, scheduled for completion in 2004. Fuel: pick up supplies for a riverside picnic at foodie haven Fox and Oble market off McClurg Court by the Ogden Slip.

Description: Friends of the Chicago River is working to create a continual Chicago River Trail along the urban stream's 156 miles. Though that's a long way away, recent improvements downtown along the Main Stem and South Branch give a taste of what such a trail might look like— and of how the City of Big Shoulders got started. Walk across Wolf Point, a patch of open land wedged behind the sprawling Merchandise Mart, named for an 1820s tavern serving the trappers and traders of frontier Chicago. Hike through Pioneer Court, marking the area where Marquette

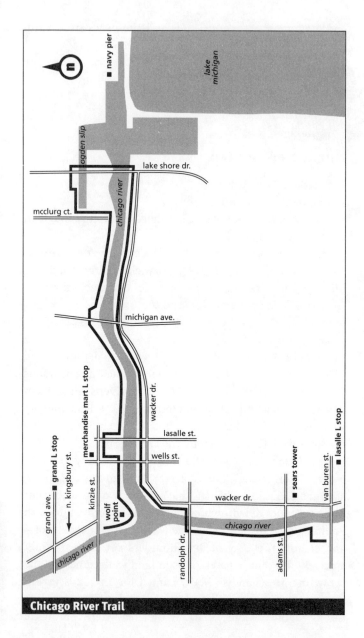

Chicago River Trail

and two voyageurs in 1674 became the first Europeans to pitch tent on Chicago soil and where Jean Baptiste DuSable (considered the city's first permanent settler) built his home and trading post along the river's swampy banks in 1779. And ponder the jarring juxtaposition to the city's man-made vertical grid.

Route: From the west side of the Kinzie St. Bridge, check out the flurry of new or revived riverfront buildings and the venerable East Bank Club. Go east across the bridge and turn right (south) at the parking garage behind the Merchandise Mart. Follow the riverside path/sidewalk along Wolf Point, where geese feed on a rare swath of downtown green. When the path abruptly ends, take the stairs to Orleans St. Walk along the Mart (stairs going down to the river are for private docks). Note the Oz-like heads—four-times life size—of early merchandising titans like Marshall Field and Edward A. Filene. Cross Wells St. and jog north to a narrow walkway. Cut through the parking garage onto the LaSalle walkway. Take the stairs up to Dearborn St., site of the city's first moveable bridge in 1834 (current bridge is the fourth). Walk behind the bridge plaque through Marina City (looks like a Space Age honeycomb) parking to the State St. Bridge. Walk through IBM plaza, past the Sun-Times building, through the Wrigley Building outdoor courtyard. Cross Michigan Ave. and cut through Pioneer Court (pay homage to Marquette and DuSable). Go down the stairs and follow the riverwalk to Centennial Fountain and McClurg Court. Turn left (north) on McClurg. Turn right (east) at Ogden Slip, walking on the north side. Take the stairs up to lower Lake Shore Dr. and walk north to the light at Illinois St. Cross to the east side of the bridge and walk south on lower LSD (check out the locks and Coast Guard station, watch for kayakers and rowers). Go down the stairs (west side of the street) heading back to the river along Lower Wacker Dr. Follow the south bank path west (until the city finishes the south bank river trail, you'll be forced up to street level). At 360 N. Michigan Ave., pass the site of Fort Dearborn, set up by the feds in pre–Louisiana Purchase 1803 to defend the country's then-western boundary at the Mississippi. Continue along Wacker, crossing west over the river at Randolph Dr. Follow the South Branch on the west bank past the art deco Civic Opera, Riverside Plaza, Chicago Mercantile Exchange, Sears Tower. At Van Buren St., go east across the river and walk three blocks to the Red Line and Brown Line LaSalle L stop (closed Sundays; walk east to the Library L stop).

Directions: From the Brown Line Merchandise Mart L stop, walk west on Kinzie St. to the bridge. Go west across the bridge to start the route. From the Red Line Grand Ave. L stop, walk west on Grand about seven blocks to N. Kingsbury St. Turn left (south) on Kingsbury and walk to Kinzie St. Walk west across the bridge.

Backyard

MORTON ARBORETUM

Location: About 25 miles W of Chicago

Length: 8.5-mile loop

Difficulty: Easy. Heritage and Woodland Trails have mellow uphills.

Fee: $7 per car for nonmembers, $3 Wednesdays

Map and book: Morton Arboretum visitor map (630-968-0074, www.mortonarb.org). *Country Walks Near Chicago.*

Dogs: No

Heads up: Free weekend and Wednesday walking tours. Plethora of tree species means superb fall colors, but good year-round.

Hiking & Backpacking

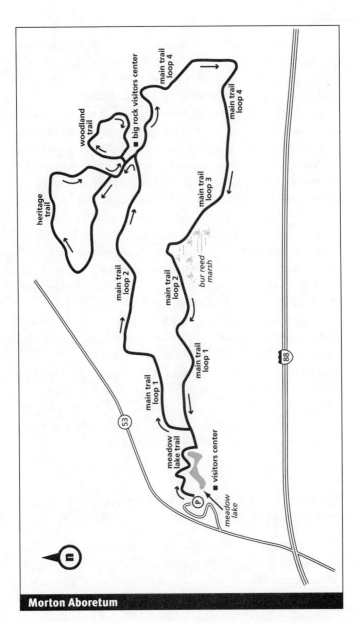

Morton Aboretum

Description: From salt sprout trees. Thank Jay Morton, founder of Morton Salt, who bought up land for a country estate around Lisle and established the arboretum in 1922. Some 12 miles of trail thread the 1,700 acres, with 3,300-plus plant types from around the world, dotted by meadows and marshland. Sticking to the eastern section's outer trails, hike through red sumac, beech, spruce, 43 types of oak, 60-plus types of maple. Funky ginkgo and cashew family groves. Easy to shorten up by taking fewer loop trails.

Route: From the visitors center parking lot, walk the north side of the short, paved Meadow Lake Trail to pick up Main Trail Loop 1. You'll follow the north sections of Loop 1 and Loop 2. At Big Rock visitors station, go left and follow the Heritage Trail loop clockwise through open oak woodlands and meadow. Then pick up the Woodland Trail loop through yellow linden and elms and follow clockwise. Turn left from the loop, past Big Rock visitors station, to pick up Loop 4 through purple American ash. Follow to Loop 3, returning to the visitors center via the south part of Loop 2, passing Bur Reed Marsh, and Loop 1.

Directions: Take I-290 west to I-88 west. Exit I-88 west onto IL 53 north. Turn right (east) into the arboretum entrance off IL 53. Park in the main visitors center lot. For shorter hikes away from the main center, follow the park road east to Big Rock visitors center.

SWALLOW CLIFF, PALOS AND SAG VALLEY FOREST PRESERVES

Location: About 20 miles SW of Chicago

Length: 4.25-mile loop (out-and-back and loop extensions possible)

Difficulty: Easy. Rolling terrain.

Map and book: Rough trail map from Cook County Forest Preserve Palos and Sag Valley Divisions (708-839-5617 or 708-771-1330). *Country Walks Near Chicago*.

Dogs: Yes

Heads up: Backyard treasure. Good post-work hike. Watch for bikers and horses. Generally unmarked and several illegally cut trails. Nearby Camp Sagawau (630-257-2045) runs guided hikes through the county's only natural rock canyon.

Description: Hike through Sag Valley's rugged glacial debris, littered with hummocks and hollows, part of the Palos and Sag Valley Preserves' 14,000 forested acres studded with upland meadows, small lakes, ponds, and sloughs. Gradually climb the bluff that backs the 100-plus-foot-high Swallow Cliff toboggan runs. Watch for nesting eastern phoebes, broad-winged hawks, and ospreys, especially if you opt to continue west beyond the 4-mile loop into one of the state's largest nature preserves, 1,520-acre Cap Sauers.

Route: From the parking lot, walk west toward the woods along the well-trodden trail crossing the bottom of the toboggan runs. The path takes you onto an unmarked counterclockwise loop trail. Follow the wide bridle path along the bottom of the bluff. You'll cross 104th Ave. by the Teasons Woods parking lot (to your right). After 104th, it cuts through ravines with several rolling hills. At the junction with another unmarked, wide path heading west, stay left as the path goes downhill to continue the loop. (Option: follow the westerly out-and-back path through Cap Sauers; one 2-mile spur roughly parallels Ford Rd. west to Will-Cook Rd., the other goes 1 mile north to IL 83.) From here the rolling trail winds. Before crossing back over 104th you'll pass another unmarked trail spur that dead-ends at McCarthy Rd. Cross 104th and pass Horsetail Lake to your right. Ignore the spur after the lake. Stay straight at the next major junction (forest preserve map is misleading here); walk past the wooden fence. (Option: trail branching right loops around Laughing Squaw sloughs, with an eastern spur to an underpass that picks up a 3.5-mile loop trail east of 96th Ave.) Go left (north) on the broad trail; you'll eventually wind up at the top of the toboggan chutes. Go down the stairs to the lot.

Directions: By car, take I-55 south to LaGrange Rd. (US 45) south. Go south on LaGrange about 6 miles. After crossing the Calumet-Sag Channel, turn right at the exit for IL 83. Go left (west) on IL 83. Take a quick left (south) into the Swallow Cliff toboggan run parking lot.

State of Prairie

OR A PLACE dubbed the Prairie State, Illinois has precious little prairie: less than 0.01% of the state's original 21 million acres remains. But the 19,000-acre Midewin National Tallgrass Prairie raises the specter of someday being able to hike through an endless sea of grass browsed by bison and littered with native wildflowers in spring and summer—just 60 miles southwest of downtown.

In the 1940s, the military built the world's largest munitions plants in Joliet, pumping out a billion pounds of TNT and loading hundreds of millions of bombs, shells, mines, and detonators. By the late 1970s, the Joliet Arsenal was largely defunct. In 1997 the military transferred the huge tract of land to the Forest Service to create the first national tallgrass prairie.

Though several grassland bird species that are tough to see in the rest of the state breed here, most of Midewin's landscape today isn't prairie; several thousand acres are grazed by cattle or planted in corn, soybeans, alfalfa, oats, or hay (see "Bird-Watching," page 313). But prairie restoration efforts are underway and should bear fruit over the next decade. Scores of volunteers are helping to plant and maintain seed production beds—it turns out the concrete igloos used to house explosives also harbor prime conditions for storing prairie forbs and seeds. And by the time you read this, work will have started on a 48-mile trail network—including 20 hiking-only miles—for hikers, bikers, horses, and cross-country skiers.

Two 1.5-mile interim loops through former farm fields and past old bunkers are already open to the public. For details, or to volunteer, see www.fs.fed.us/mntp/ or call (815) 423-6370.

Short Hops

INDIANA DUNES, CHESTERTON AND PORTER, INDIANA

Location: About 51 miles SE of Chicago

Length: Route 1: 4.4-mile loop on Indiana Dunes National Lakeshore Cowles Bog Trail. Route 2: 10-mile loop on Indiana Dunes State Park Trails 8, 9, and 10.

Difficulty: Easy to moderate. Scrambling up dunes and humping through sand make trails feel longer.

Fee: For state park, $5 day, $26 annual pass for out-of-state cars; $1 if you walk or bike in. National park trails free. Warning: keep your state park receipt with you. State patrols for hikers trying to enter the state trails via the lakefront without paying fee at the gatehouse (i.e., linking Cowles Bog Trail to state trails).

Maps and books: Trail maps from Indiana Dunes State Park in Chesterton (219-926-1952, www.state.in.us/) and Indiana Dunes National Lakeshore in Porter (219-926-7561 ext. 225, www.nps.gov). *Dune Country; Sacred Sands* documents the 80-year fight, led by many Chicagoans, to save the dunes from industrial encroachment (and helps explain why you see a steel mill and power plant in the middle of the national lakeshore).

Dogs: Yes (but prohibited on swimming beaches or on shared horse trails).

Heads up: Carfree hiking, camping, swimming, biking (if you don't mind boxing your bike). Ecological lollapalooza. Quality birding. Spectacular sandhill crane migration hot spot about an hour south of here (see "Bird-Watching," page 314).

Description: Retreating glaciers left a trail of contradictory plant life here; arctic bearberry grows next to prickly pear cactus, and southern dogwoods grow one dune over from northern jack pines. Sandwiched between Gary and Michigan City, interrupted by a pocket of power plants and down-on-their-luck steel mills, the state and federally protected dunescape is packed into a narrow ribbon along 14 miles of windswept beach.

Though small, the dunes are big on plant and habitat diversity. You get a sampler—from stands of yellow beech and chokeberry-lined marsh to sandy black oak forest and a walk on a lonely beach with paper-thin stones itching to be skipped—on Cowles Bog Trail, named for a pioneering University of Chicago ecologist who studied the area around the early twentieth century as a natural laboratory for plant succession. Stitching together several state park trails takes you along sand trails to the summits of three dunes (no, the air is not thinner atop the tallest, 192-foot Mt. Tom), past living dunes—so named for their slow inland march, burying trees along the way—tree graveyards, steep-sided valleys, "blowouts" studded with cottonwoods, and juniper-topped ridges. Warbler paradise in spring; early summer brings red-headed woodpeckers and barred owls. Indigo lake views abound. Wildflower bonanza.

Route 1, Cowles Bog Trail: From the trailhead on the west side of Mineral Springs Rd., follow the well-marked trail through a flat stand of white birch and around the edge of a

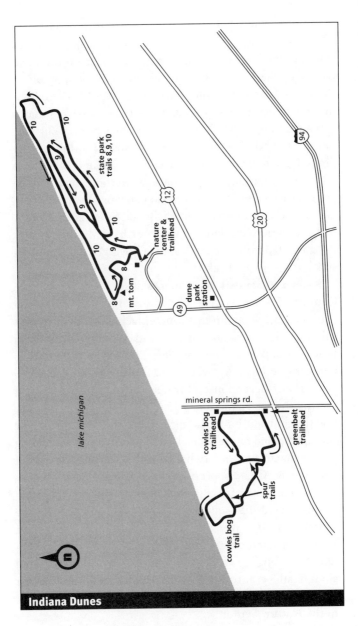

lake michigan

state park
trails 8,9,10

nature
center &
trailhead

mt. tom

dune
park
station

mineral springs rd.

cowles bog
trailhead

greenbelt
trailhead

spur
trails

cowles bog
trail

Indiana Dunes

big marsh. You'll pass two spur trails to the south (for shorter loops) as you hike deeper into the oak forest and start to scramble up the dune ridge. Hike down the dune face onto the Lake Michigan shoreline. Walk west along the beach. After 0.2 mile, look for the trail leading back into the dunes, past a wetland full of Dr. Seuss–like plumes waving on tall stems. You can sometimes hear the distant hum of the NIPSCO power plant as you pass through the pines. Option: if you take the second trail spur on your hike back and turn right (east) onto the main trail, you'll retrace your steps and wind up at your car (shaving about 0.3 mile). Otherwise, continue straight and you'll finish at the Greenbelt Trailhead. Turn left and walk north on Mineral Springs Rd. about 0.5 mile—steer clear of annoyingly abundant poison sumac—to get back to your car.

Route 2, State Park Trails 8, 9, and 10: From the Nature Center, pick up Trail 9 and follow the 3.75-mile loop counter-clockwise through sandy black oak and blueberry thickets. Stay straight on the trail, passing the spur to Beachhouse Blowout on your left. Follow the ridge trail to Furnessville Blowout, where the trail loops west, eventually passing Beachhouse Blowout. Turn right (west) when the trail hits a T-junction. When Trail 9 comes to a V, follow the spur south to pick up Trail 10. Follow Trail 10 east through upland forest of black oak and sassafras, paralleling a long marsh on your right. Pass the scattered stands of white pine. After a short boardwalk, the trail goes north—past a tree graveyard, Big Blowout, up and down a basswood-covered hill—and then loops west and follows the shoreline a little over 2 miles. Look for the Trail 8 marker among the sand cherry and marram grass. Hump up 192-foot Mt. Tom, down the wooden stairs, wading in sand along Trail 8 east to 184-foot Mt. Holden and onto 176-foot Mt. Jackson. From there it's less than 0.25 mile south back to the Nature Center.

Directions: By car, take I-94 east to Indiana. For Cowles Bog Trail, exit US 20 northeast. Turn left (north) on Mineral Springs Rd., cross US 12 east, and continue to the trailhead parking on the east side of the road. (The NPS Dorothy Buell Memorial Visitors Center is a few miles east off US 12.) For state park trails, exit I-94 east to IN 49 north. Follow IN 49 north to the gatehouse. Take the first main road branching east and follow past the campground to the Nature Center trailhead.

By transit, take the South Shore Line train (800-356-2079, www.nictd.com) from downtown to the Dune Park station. For Cowles Bog Trail, follow signs to Calumet Trail (rough bike trail) paralleling the RR tracks. Walk west along Calumet Trail a little over 1 mile to Mineral Springs Rd. Turn right (north) on Mineral Springs. Pass Greenbelt Trailhead on your left. After about 0.5 mile you'll hit the Cowles Bog trailhead on the west side of Mineral Springs Rd. For state park trails, walk north on IN 49 (just west of the station) about 0.5 mile to the gatehouse. From there, it's about 0.75 mile to the trailhead. Follow car directions above.

PITCHING TENT

indiana dunes, indiana

YOU'VE GOT TWO solid options for dunescape camping, both with beach access, just over an hour's train ride from downtown.

If your heart is set on sleeping flanked by a Midwestern mountain, head for the state park's oak-covered campground. You're also a short walk from the area's best trails. Some sites are nestled against the lee side of the dunes. As the sky darkens, I like to scramble up Mt. Holden off Trail 8. Lie on your back on the cool sand for quality stargazing. Watch the moon turn the sand and water pearly. And pay homage to the downtown skyline across the lake, surging upward like a lit cluster of Legos.

You can't hug a looming dune at the National Park Service Dunewood campground, but you get fewer crowds, bigger sites, and more privacy. Go for one of 25 walk-in sites, tucked away in a mixed oak forest. No wolves howling at night, but somehow the moody call of the train feels perfect.

If you come without a car and want a long day's hike—about 16 miles—from Dunewood, head west to the Dunewood Trace Trail, Ly-co-ki-we Trail, across US 12 to the state park trails, east along the lakefront to Mt. Baldy (watch for hang gliders), back along the Calumet Bike Trail to Broadway, and across US 12 to your tent. You've got 16-plus miles of state trails, roughly 27 miles in the national lakeshore.

For swimming, Porter Beach is a short walk from the state campground, Kemil Beach from Dunewood. Launch your kayak from the national lakeshore, but carry it, don't drag it on the beach—there's a lot of life you can't see going on amid the singing sands.

Details: State campground has 168 non-electric sites for $13 a night. Half the sites are reservable by mail (add $6 fee; reservation forms online) by writing Indiana Dunes State Park, 1600 North 25 East, Chesterton, IN, 46304-1142. No booze at the state campground, but it's OK by the feds. Dunewood campground has 25 walk-in sites, 54 drive-in sites, all first-come, first-served. $10 a night. There's a convenience store 0.25 mile north of the campground at US 12 and Broadway. You know you're not in the city anymore when you can buy a soft-serve cone for under a buck. See hiking entry directions for the state park, above. For Dunewood, by car follow US 20 north-east to Kemil Rd. Turn left (north) on Kemil. Turn right on US 12. At Broadway, turn right and follow to the campground.

By transit, take the South Shore Line to the Beverly Shores station. Campground is 0.25 mile south across US 12.

STARVED ROCK STATE PARK, UTICA

Location: About 92 miles SW of Chicago

Length: 8 miles out and back

Difficulty: Easy-moderate. Some short uphills.

Maps and books: Overview trail map from Starved Rock State Park (815-667-4868, www.dnr.state.il.us)—grab one for adjacent Mathiessen State Park trails, too. *Hiking Illinois; Illinois Hiking and Backpacking Trails.*

Dogs: Yes

Heads up: Solid year-round option. Camping (815) 667-4726, for lodge and cabin reservations (800) 868-7625. Fuel: nab sandwiches from the café in the park's 1930s stone-and-log lodge and sit on the broad stone deck overlooking the Illinois River.

Description: You'll cover a dozen canyons carved out of porous St. Peter sandstone hiking from the park's visitors center to Kaskaskia Canyon and back. I think a lawyer designed these trails; you'll encounter handrails and stairs in parts. Great hike for a hot early summer day; cool off in waterfalls at canyon heads, surrounded by fern-choked walls. By late summer, most falls are sucked dry. Ice climbers tackle frozen waterfalls in winter (see "Rock Climbing," page 376). The main trail follows the Illinois River, meandering riverside at points, but mostly scrambles up and down dry, sandy bluffs topped with black oak, red cedar, and white pine. Watch for red-tailed hawks seeking sustenance from voles and field mice. Starved Rock has 13 miles of trail; if it's a mob scene here, less-visited neighboring Mathiessen State Park has 5 miles.

Route: Yellow dots mean you're hiking away from the visitors center/lodge (east), white dots mean you're returning (west). Brown markers or posts show the Bluff Trail, red the River Trail. Following either gets you back to your car. From the visitors center parking lot, hike east along the

Hiking & Backpacking

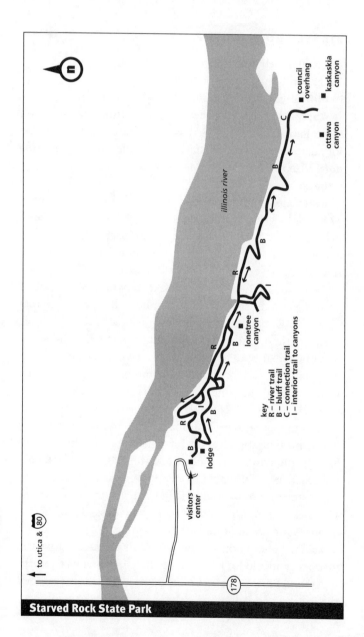

Starved Rock State Park

to utica & (80)

(178)

visitors center

lodge

illinois river

lonetree canyon

ottawa canyon

council overhang

kaskaskia canyon

key
R – river trail
B – bluff trail
C – connection trail
I – interior trail to canyons

N

Bluff Trail (for the most part, after Lonetree Canyon there's only one main trail, which alternates between River and Bluff). Whenever you're given the option to follow a green Interior Trail, do. They lead to canyons off the main trail. After Ottawa Canyon, follow the green Connection Trail to Council Overhang and continue on to Kaskaskia Canyon. When you reach Kaskaskia Canyon, turn around and hike back west. Around Lonetree Canyon on the return, take the River Trail back to your car.

Option: if the main parking area looks packed, start from one of several parking areas at the eastern end off IL 71 and hike west.

Directions: Take I-94 east to I-57 south to I-80 west. Follow I-80 west to Utica. Take IL 178 south to the park entrance.

ILLINOIS BEACH STATE PARK, ZION

Location: About 53 miles N of Chicago

Length: 5-mile interconnected loops (plus 6.5 miles of beach walking)

Difficulty: Easy and flat

Maps and books: Maps from Illinois Beach State Park (847-662-4811, www.dnr.state.il.us). *Hiking Illinois; Illinois Hiking and Backpacking Trails.*

Dogs: No

Heads up: Bonus: carfree hiking, swimming, camping, and biking along 10-mile paved bike trail—all via Metra. Bummer: Zion nuclear power plant divides the park's north and south sections. Avoid during May camping show and late July/early August national jet ski championships. Fall camping's quiet. Several launch and land sites for kayakers along the Lake Michigan Water Trail.

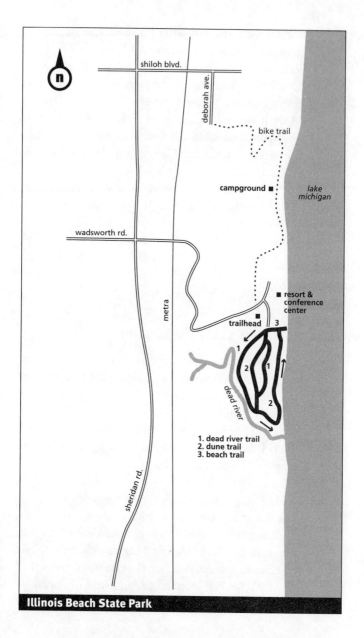

shiloh blvd.

deborah ave.

bike trail

campground ■

lake michigan

wadsworth rd.

metra

■ resort &
conference
center

■

trailhead   3

1

2   1

dead river

2

1. dead river trail
2. dune trail
3. beach trail

sheridan rd.

Illinois Beach State Park

Description: Short-but-sweet trails in a designated state nature preserve jammed with 650-plus plant species, from creeping juniper to blazing stars. This is the only place you'll catch a glimpse of natural ridge shoreline in Illinois; Land o' Lincoln duneland. The Dead River looks more like a long pond; it's a stream (very much alive) blocked by a sandbar most of the year. When the water rises high enough, it breaks through the sand and drains the surrounding marshes—a few times a year it jumps its banks to flow into Lake Michigan. In fall, west winds carry a slew of airborne hunters (see "Bird-Watching," page 315). Quiet beach walks, too.

Route: The Dead River Trail and Dune Trail make two concentric circles. From the parking lot, take the sandy Dead River Trail along the river through marsh and prairie. Pick up the Dune Trail outer loop and hike north toward the resort and conference center. There, hike the short Beach Trail back to the trailhead and parking lot to finish the trails' inner loop through black oak forest, fragrant pine, and sand ridges.

Directions: Take I-94 west and exit IL 132 east. At the first stop light, Dilleys Rd., go left and continue 4 miles to Wadsworth Rd. Turn right on Wadsworth and follow about 8 miles, crossing Sheridan Rd. into the park. Park in the lot before you hit the resort and conference center.

By transit, take Metra's Union Pacific/North Line to the Zion station. From there, it's a 2.5-mile walk to the trailhead. Walk east on Shiloh Blvd. to Deborah Ave. Go south two blocks to the bike trail. Follow the bike trail east and south past the campground and resort and conference center to the trailhead.

Ice Age Primer

SCORE ONE FOR the good guys. Back in the 1950s, ardent trekker and erstwhile natural historian Ray Zillmer of Milwaukee came up with the idea of a 1,000-mile linear national park winding through Wisconsin, connecting primo examples of the state's textbook glacial terrain and making the outdoors accessible to the masses.

Congress approved the Ice Age National Scientific Reserve, a cluster of nine units dotting the state, in 1964 (sadly, Zillmer died in 1960), but the National Park Service rejected the trail as logistically too complex. Volunteers through the Ice Age Park and Trail Foundation Zillmer founded doggedly kept adding miles to existing trails, and finally, in 1980 the Ice Age National Scenic Trail won a presidential signature.

Today, managed by a conglomeration of local, county, state, and federal authorities, the trail covers roughly 600 miles in disjointed sections; the long-term plan is completion of a 1,000- plus-mile continuous trail following the terminal moraine of the last glacier. The Ice Age Trail runs within 100 miles of 18 million people.

It's been thru-hiked by a dedicated few using roads to connect the trail. Happily, Kettle Moraine State Forest, just a few hours north of Chicago, has two of the longer, and best maintained, trail segments. (Other top-notch segments run through Langlade and Taylor Counties several hours north of Kettle Moraine.) The Ice Age Park and Trail Foundation in Milwaukee (800-227-0046, www.iceagetrail.org), with 22 regional chapters divvied up to cover every inch of trail, is the single best source of information.

Below, thanks to info from the Ice Age Park and Trail Foundation, a glacial glossary to enlighten your journey.

Moraine: Ridge formed by the gravel, sand, and boulders toted along the edge of the glacier and dumped as it melted back.

Esker: Serpentine ridge of gravel and sand created by debris-laden streams flowing through tunnels under stagnant ice sheets.

Erratic: Boulder that hitched a long-distance ride on the ice and therefore bears no resemblance to the bedrock and soil where it now sits.

Kettle: Surface depression 20 feet deep or more, formed as sand and gravel settled over a melting ice block, forming V-like hollows.

Drumlin: Elongated hill that looks like the upside-down bowl of a teaspoon, usually found in groups—sometimes by the hundreds—and parallels the direction the ice was moving.

Kame: Conical hill plunked down—not thrust up, like most hills—by debris deposited by meltwater running into funnel-shaped holes in the ice.

ICE AGE NATIONAL SCENIC TRAIL, KETTLE MORAINE NORTH; CAMPBELLSPORT, WISCONSIN

Location: About 150 miles N of Chicago

Length: 29-mile one-way backpack over 2 long days (12-mile one-way day-hike option). See maps for loads of trail-heads to shorten up.

Difficulty: Moderate to difficult. Lots of up and down on loose glacial till and roots, punctuated by flat stretches on top of esker ridges. Max elevation change 300 feet.

Fee: $10 day, $30 annual nonresident vehicle, good for all Wisconsin state parks.

Maps: Kettle Moraine State Forest hiking, camping, and overview maps (262-626-2116, www.dnr.state.wi.us); segment trail maps from Ice Age Park and Trail Foundation (800-227-0046, www.iceagetrail.org); Ice Age visitors center (920-533-8322) on WI 67 just southwest of Dundee has maps and same-day shelter permits.

Dogs: Yes

Heads up: High demand for the five year-round, Adirondack-style shelters along the trail. Reserve ahead or aim for a midweek trek in summer. Fall is best; no bugs, flame-out in early October. Not all shelters have water; check segment maps for drinking water access along route. Shelter 3 makes a good midpoint for a weekend thru-hike; otherwise camp at Long Lake (better) or Mauthe Lake campground. Shelter and campground reservations at (888) 947-2757, www.wiparks.net.

Double heads up: Fat-tire forest trails (see "Mountain Biking," page 283). Swimming in Crooked Lake, Butler Lake, Mauthe Lake (sand beach). Good panfish and large-mouth bass fishing in Crooked Lake.

Description: Trail runs 31-plus miles through the length of the forest's stellar glacial terrain. Pothole and kettle lakes. Bogs. Prairie meadows. S-shaped esker ridges. American beech and sugar maple forest dotted with pine plantations. The forest's north unit is wider, less crowded, and less intruded upon by creeping housing than its immensely popular (some say overused) southern twin. Though the trail is never farther than about 3 miles from a road—and you'll cross many—it still feels remarkably unspoiled. Kevin Thusius, the Ice Age trail's eastern field coordinator, who's hiked here since he was 12, sums it up: "I bike the south, I hike the north." From Dundee Mountain, a 1,100-foot-high kame, you get westerly views of the Campbellsport drumlin fields that look like hundreds of terra firma waves. For a serious day hike, Thusius favors Mauthe Lake to Parnell Tower, built on top of a kame. On a clear day, Parnell gives views of Milwaukee, kame fields, and Holy Hill, a Romanesque church and monastery atop a 1,300-foot kame snuggled between the state forest's north and south units. Deer, red fox, and the occasional badger or mink. Red-shouldered hawks breed here.

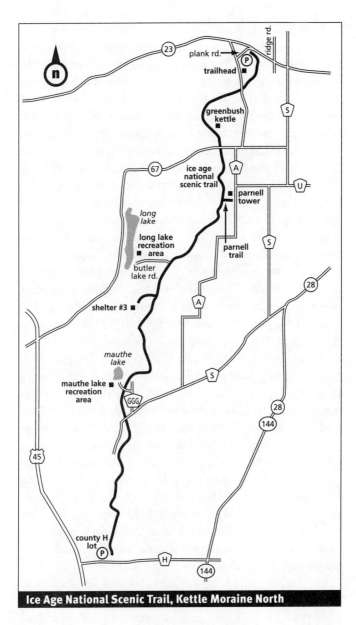

Ice Age National Scenic Trail, Kettle Moraine North

Route, day 1: Pick up the trail from the parking lot at WI 23 and Plank Rd. (trail formally starts about 2.9 miles north on County P but makes for a really long first-day hump to shelter 3 if you're hiking over a 2-day weekend). Follow the yellow-blazed trail south; major trail intersections are posted with the Ice Age Trail woolly mammoth logo. You'll cross paths, but not share trail, with mountain bikes and horses. Pass Greenbush camping area, shelter 5, Greenbush kettle. After passing shelter 4, you'll see the Parnell Trail. Take it to the 60-foot Parnell Tower for views. Back on the Ice Age Trail, continue south to Butler Lake and the start of 4-mile Parnell Esker. If you're pitching tent at Long Lake (12-plus miles into your hike), or want to check out views from Dundee Mountain, walk along Butler Lake Rd. west to Long Lake campground. Take the nature trail south of the campground to Dundee Mountain. Retrace your steps to get back to the main trail and continue south to the spur for shelter 3 (about 15 miles into the hike), tucked among the beeches. Listen for coyotes.

Day 2: Continue south past Crooked Lake, Forest Lake, Mauthe Lake (campground is 19-plus miles into the hike). From here, the trail roughly parallels the Milwaukee River through wooded hillsides. Pass shelter 2 and the New Fane trail area. About 0.3 mile after shelter 1, the trail ends at County H parking lot. For Mauthe Lake-Parnell Tower day hike, see directions below for trailhead parking.

Directions: Take I-94 west to Milwaukee. In Milwaukee, take I-43 north to Sheboygan. At Sheboygan, take WI 23 west. After you cross County S and Ridge Rd., look for Plank Rd. Turn left onto Plank Rd. and park in the lot. Unless you've arranged a car shuttle, park a second car at the County H lot, about 1 mile east of US 45.

For the day hike, follow above to Milwaukee. From I-43 exit west to WI 28. Take WI 28 southwest to County S. At County GGG, turn right (north). In under 1 mile you'll hit the left turnoff for Mauthe Lake visitors center. Park in the lot; the trailhead is right there. Park a second car at the end of your hike at Parnell Tower; the lot is just west of the intersection of County A and County U.

Meccas

ISLE ROYALE NATIONAL PARK, MICHIGAN

Location: There are several jumping off points in Michigan and Minnesota for trips to the island. Grand Portage, MN, is about 610 miles N of Chicago (plus a 2- to 3-hour ferry ride to Windigo on the island's west end; see Directions for ferry launch options).

Length: 165 miles of trail

Difficulty: Moderate to difficult. Stellar 28-mile Minong Ridge Trail is the island's toughest.

Fee: $4 day, $50 annual pass

Outfitters: Northwest Passage in Wilmette (847-256-4409 or 800-RECREATE, www.nwpassage.com) runs backpacking trips. Glacier Valley Wilderness Adventures (608-493-2075, www.glaciervalley.com) and Uncommon Adventures (231-882-5525 or 866-882-5525, www.uncommonadv.com) run kayaking trips with some hiking. Contact the park for guided backpacking through the Isle Royale Institute.

Maps and book: "Trails Illustrated" map, 1:62,500, available from nonprofit Isle Royale Natural History Association (800-678-6925, www.irnha.org). Isle Royale National Park (906-482-0984, www.nps.gov/isro) sells some USGS topo maps, same scale. *Isle Royale National Park Foot Trails and Water Routes* is the island bible.

Dogs: No

Heads up: Park open mid-April to late October. Prepare

for mercurial weather. Just getting to the island is an adventure—advance planning is key. Reservations accepted starting December 1 for the National Park Service ferry to Rock Harbor. Free camping permits; sites are first-come, first-served. Water taxis from Rock Harbor Lodge (906-337-4993 in season, off-season 270-773-2191) offer pick-up/drop-off service for various trailheads/campgrounds.

Double heads up: Portages connect nine inland lakes; coastal kayakers brave Momma Superior. Angler haven on dozens of motorfree lakes.

Description: For urbanites craving roadless topography, this 210-square-mile wilderness island plunked 22 miles offshore in the world's largest freshwater lake is healing salve. White spruce and balsam fir cover the fog-draped Lake Superior basalt shoreline; sugar maples and yellow birch thrive in the warmer, drier interior. Snack trailside on dwarf raspberries and thimbleberries. In mid-June/early July, 100-plus types of wildflowers blanket the island after the mainland show is dying down.

The 45-mile-long island, 8.5 miles wide at its broadest, has everything from straightforward day-hike loops to multiweek backpacking treks. See Jim DuFresne's must-have guidebook for more details. The much-loved, classic 40-mile Greenstone Ridge Trail runs along the park's backbone from Windigo to Lookout Louise, taking in the island's highest point, 1,394-foot Mt. Desor.

But for lots of backpackers, the wildlife clinches the deal. And no trail gives better odds for a moose safari than the rugged Minong Ridge Trail. The 28-mile, 4- or 5-day trek lacks the boardwalks and bridges of other island trails (expect soaked boots) and follows an unrelenting up-and-down path over bare-rock ridge. Good map-reading skills are essential; moose paths are easily mistaken for trail. Veterans recommend hiking the trail east to west. Your reward for the knee-grinding route? Sweeping views over Lake

Superior and Canada. Camping in quiet coves and harbors. Watching beaver, loons, and moose feed at dusk. And listening for the call of eastern timber wolves.

Directions: For Grand Portage, MN, take I-90 west to Madison. In Madison, take I-94 west to Eau Claire. Take US 53 north to Duluth. In Duluth, take I-35 north about 4 miles to MN 61 north. Stay on MN 61 up the Minnesota shore to Grand Portage. In Grand Portage, follow signs for Grand Portage National Monument and the ferries. Grand Portage offers simplest logistics to hike Minong Ridge Trail east to west.

Other launching points, in Michigan: Houghton, about 418 miles from the city, has seaplane service and a 6-hour National Park Service ferry to Rock Harbor on the island's east end. Copper Harbor, about 453 miles from Chicago, also has a Rock Harbor ferry. Some ferries run daily, others just a few days a week. For transport details go to www.nps .gov/isro and click on "in depth" option. Or contact the park at (906) 482-0984.

PORCUPINE MOUNTAINS WILDERNESS STATE PARK, MICHIGAN

Location: About 455 miles N of Chicago

Length: 90-plus miles of trail

Difficulty: Moderate to difficult

Fee: $4 day, $20 annual pass for out-of-state vehicles

Maps and book: Porcupine Mountains Wilderness State Park (906-885-5275, www.dnr.state.mi.us) sells trail maps. Pair with USGS topos for Thomaston, White Pine, and Carp River sections. *Porcupine Mountains Wilderness State Park: A Backcountry Guide for Hikers, Campers, Backpackers and Winter Visitors*

Dogs: Yes

Heads up: Chance for cabin-to-cabin backpacking complete with wood stove, bunks, mattresses and—at three lakeside spots—boats. Reserve one of 16 trailside cabins through the park starting the first business day in January. Sites at two of six campgrounds reservable through DNR (800) 447-2757. Black fly season mid-May to mid-June. Big Carp River is thick with spawning Chinook and coho in fall, but remote enough to keep most anglers at bay. Snowshoeing, alpine and cross-country skiing in chest-high snow (see "Winter Sports," page 432).

Description: OK. Technically the Porkies aren't mountains—the park's highest point, 1,958-foot Summit Peak, falls 42 feet shy by geological definition. But it's one of the loftiest crests going between South Dakota's Black Hills and New York's Adirondacks. So savor it. (FYI: apparently Native Americans thought the ridges sloping down to Lake Superior looked like crouched porcupines. And yes, porcupines do inhabit the park.)

With 60,000-plus acres, this is serious U.P. wilderness, home to an enormous swath of virgin hardwood-hemlock forest. Four lakes, trout-choked streams, major rivers (Presque Isle draws skilled whitewater boaters), dozens of falls, and 25 miles of pristine Lake Superior shoreline to explore. Bed down in one of three Adirondack shelters, pitch tent trailside or in 50 first-come, first-served backcountry campsites with fire rings and bear poles. River otters, coyote, bobcat, beaver, peregrine falcons, and bald eagles abound. Black bear lumber through heavy woods, but you're more likely to see tracks and scat.

Two "Don't Miss" trails: 9-mile Big Carp River and 4-mile Escarpment (both easily linked with others for multi-day loops). Ogle Shining Cloud Falls, twin 35-foot cascades jammed into a sheer gorge as Big Carp River Trail winds toward the river's mouth at Lake Superior. Escarpment Trail tops out at 1,600 feet along the rocky bluff with views into Big Carp River valley and Lake of the Clouds, 300 acres of indigo ink—one of most photographed images in Michigan. Snag the oh-so-sweet backcountry campsite near the edge of the bluff after Cuyahoga Peak for serious tent-flap vistas.

Directions: Take I-90 west past Madison. Take I-39 north about 100 miles to US 51 north. Follow US 51 north for roughly 130 miles. At the Wisconsin-Michigan border, take US 2 east about 12 miles. At Wakefield, take MI 28 east for 20 miles to Bergland. Turn left (north) on MI 64 at the blinking light. Follow MI 64 north for 18 miles to MI 107. Go left (west) on M 107 and follow signs to the visitors center. Pick up trailheads for Big Carp River and Escarpment Trails from Lake of the Clouds.

RIVER TO RIVER TRAIL, SHAWNEE NATIONAL FOREST, ILLINOIS

Location: About 320 miles S of Chicago

Length: 176 miles of linear trail (22-mile weekend backpack option)

Difficulty: Moderate to difficult. Rugged dirt and sand trail through dense woods, along blue-green hill ridges, some steep climbs (max elevation change 150 feet). Thru-hike includes about 20 miles of blacktop.

Map and book: *River to River Trail Guide Across Southern Illinois* from the River to River Trail Society (618-252-6789, www.rivertorivertrail.org) has section-by-section trail narratives and overlays the trail on 1:32,000 contour maps. John O'Dell, the society's founder and chairman, is a font of wisdom—he marked virtually the entire trail. Don't expect much help from Shawnee National Forest; they'll likely just wind up referring you to O'Dell, who also happens to head the Illinois Hiking Society and serves as the American Discovery Trail coordinator for southern Illinois.

Dogs: Yes

Heads up: Car shuttles and guided hikes through River to River Trail Society. Poison ivy, copperheads, and rattlesnakes. Southern Illinois' temperate climes make for year-round backpacking possibilities; winter temps average 35-40°. Snow doesn't stick around long. Fall brings ripe persimmons and leaf-peeping in oak and hickory forest dotted with beech and gum. Avoid late summer: it's hot as balls and water is tough to come by. Hikers and horses are encouraged to travel east-west along the trail. Climber paradise (see "Rock Climbing," page 372).

Description: One of the joys of the River to River Trail: spring shows up here early. In mid-April, when the city and northerly *Meccas* like the Porkies are still in late winter's clutch, dogwood and redbud are in bloom and the forest floor is wall-to-wall with spring beauties, shooting stars, and sweet William. Clear creeks crisscross the trail. Waterfalls abound. The woods positively hum with birds (250-plus species).

The 176-mile point-to-point trail runs from Battery Rock on the Ohio to Grand Tower on the Mississippi through the Shawnee Hills—otherwise known as Illinois Ozarks—in a part of Illinois spared by glacial steamrolling. Most of the trail, which forms a chunk of the coast-to-coast American Discovery Trail, cuts through 270,000-acre Shawnee National Forest, the state's largest swath of public land, dotted with wooded hollows, rock escarpments, and a wildlife roster that counts the elusive bobcat. Straddling an ecological transition zone, the forest harbors both eastern and western bluebirds, northern and southern garter snakes, hardwood hills and marshland bayou.

Hike the trail's far western end and you may get to witness spring and fall migration of some 35 snake species, including water moccasins and cottonmouths (the Forest Service bans cars from a major road for months to allow safe slithering).

Thru-hikers generally take 14 days. O'Dell's pick for a weekend trip: a roughly 22-mile hike from Garden of the Gods to Lusk Creek Wilderness Areas. Make the 5.5-hour drive Friday night to pitch tent at one of a dozen first-come, first-served sites at Garden of the Gods' Pharaoh campground (Elizabethtown ranger district, 618-287-2201). Take spur trails to check out sandstone outcroppings like Camel and Anvil Rock. At One Horse Gap you can spend the night under one of several rock overhangs and listen to the waterfalls. Pristine Lusk Creek is jammed between 100-foot-high cliff walls; orchids and ferns grow on one side, cacti on the other. You could easily spend an entire day exploring the creek canyon (canoe when the water's up) and nearby Salt Peter Cave.

Directions: For Garden of the Gods trailhead and Pharaoh campground, take I-94 east to I-57 south. Take I-57 south through umpteen cornfields to Marion. Take exit 52 and go east on IL 13 to Harrisburg. At Harrisburg take US 45 south to IL 34. Take IL 34 south and east to Herod. At Karber's Ridge Rd. go left (east) to Garden of the Gods. Follow the signs to Garden of the Gods Wilderness Area. Pick up the trailhead from the parking lot or campground.

SLEEPING BEAR DUNES NATIONAL LAKESHORE, MICHIGAN

Location: About 320 miles N of Chicago
Length: About 100 miles of trail
Difficulty: Easy to difficult
Fees: $7 vehicle pass good for up to 7 days, $15 annual
Maps and book: Sleeping Bear Dunes National Lakeshore (231-326-5134, www.nps.gov) in Empire has basic trail

maps (mileage underestimated on some trails); USGS topo maps—for Platte Plains Trail use Beulah section, for North and South Manitou Islands use said sections. *50 Hikes in Lower Michigan* gives Sleeping Bear Dunes lots of ink.

Dogs: No

Heads up: Prime sailing and kayaking grounds (see "Sailing," page 89). Hang-gliding hot spot (see "Hang Gliding," page 479). Good snowshoeing in winter—watch for snowshoe hares. Bring a rod for summer largemouth bass, coho and Chinook in fall, rainbow and lake trout in spring.

Description: Chippewa legend holds that a forest fire drove a mother bear and her two cubs into Lake Michigan. As the mother reached the opposite shore and climbed to the top of a bluff to wait for the cubs, they drowned. Sleeping Bear dune marks where the mother waited; her cubs are North and South Manitou Islands. The national lakeshore's 71,000 acres cover 34 miles of shoreline and the Manitou Islands.

Prevailing westerlies gusting across Lake Michigan have built dune drama, with steep perched dunes plunging 460 feet to the water. On the mainland, sand-filtered lakes, birch-lined streams, and bleached cottonwood skeletons half-smothered by sand dot beech-and-maple-covered hills. Top day hikes include Empire Bluff (great sunset spot) and the Dunes Trail. For mainland backpacking, hit the 15-mile-loop Platte Plains Trail with a backcountry camping jewel at White Pine, tucked into a narrow ravine.

But for serious trekking, head for the islands, onetime logging and farming outposts. North Manitou boasts bona fide wilderness, a 23-square-mile roadless refuge with some 25 miles of marked trail, camping allowed virtually anywhere. From the east-side ferry dock, savvy backpackers hoof 5 miles to the island's west side to bed down at Swenson's Clearing or Fredrickson Place, both with tent-flap views of brilliant sunsets. A 3-day, 17-mile loop takes you past abandoned barns and orchards, along rugged sand bluffs, and through beech-maple forest. South Manitou, roughly a third smaller, sees more day trippers. Camping is restricted to three spectacular rustic shoreline campgrounds—Weather Station's a favorite. Take two days for a challenging 9-mile loop past the Francisco Morazan wreck, virgin 500-year-old white cedars, and 300-foot perched dunes. Strong hikers can cram it into a day before the afternoon ferry leaves, but why rush?

Directions: Take I-94 east to Benton Harbor. At Benton Harbor take I-196 north to Grand Rapids. From there, take US 131 north toward Cadillac. Before Cadillac, exit north onto MI 115. Take MI 115 north to MI 22. Take MI 22 north into the park. Ferries for the Manitous leave from Leland, about 30 miles north of park headquarters on MI 22. Manitou Island Transit in Leland (231-256-9061, www.leelanau.com/manitou/) runs ferries across tricky Manitou Passage to the islands, late May–October for South Manitou, until November for North Manitou.

▲

◀ ᵃᵗⁱᵒⁿ
 ₒ EXTRA
 ⁰ₓₑ
 ▼ o-games

ARL AND MARIE Larsson started orienteering as kids in their native Sweden, home of the world's biggest orienteering event, the O-Ringen. Now the transplants flex their navigational muscles in metro-area forest preserves through the Chicago Area Orienteering Club.

For the uninitiated, orienteering involves using a detailed map and compass to navigate around a course with designated control points, which are drawn on the map. Some competitive orienteers run the course, others walk it. The navigational skills honed in orienteering are a natural boon for serious hikers.

"Even our kids seem to have an easy time finding things," Marie Larsson says (the whole family competes in orienteering). "When Emma was 10 she could navigate to Canada from

Chicago by herself, figuring out what roads to take. And that
definitely came from the orienteering, otherwise she wouldn't
have had a clue about maps. A lot of our friends can't believe
we let our kids walk around in the woods alone. But they know
what they're doing and how to find backcountry paths when
there aren't trails."

The group hosts around 12–15 meets a year (and posts a
calendar of regional meets on its Web site) in spots like Deer
Grove, Waterfall Glen, Busse Woods, and Palos Forest Preserves. Meets usually include courses for all levels and draw
an average of 250 competitors. First-timers are welcome;
meets are generally held Sundays from 10 A.M. to noon with
beginner instruction a half hour before start time. In 2002 the
club hosted the Bramble Ramble Extreme, an A-meet and designated World Ranking Event. The next A-meet will probably be
held in 2004. For details, call the O-phone hotline at (847)
604–4419 or see www.chicago-orienteering.org.

Where to Connect

Clubs and Organizations

- Chicago Group of the Sierra Club (312-251-1680, www
  .illinois.sierraclub.org/chicago/) runs local and regional
  outings.

- The Nature Conservancy's Volunteer Stewardship Network
  (312-346-8166 ext. 22, www.nature.org /Illinois) trains citizen conservationists to work on ecological restoration projects around the metro-Chicago area. Great way to meet
  hiking partners.

- Chicago Wilderness (www.chicagowilderness.org) is a coalition of more than 140 public and private groups working to
  protect, restore, study, and manage the region's ecosystems.

Hiking & Backpacking

Good volunteer links and a great namesake quarterly magazine with local and regional news and events.

- Calumet Park Ecological Association (www
  .lincolnnet.net/CEPA/) runs occasional walks through
  urban wilderness in a little-visited corner of the city around
  Lake Calumet, hemmed in by steel mills and slag heaps.

- Illinois Hiking Association (618-252-6789, www
  .rivertorivertrail.org) helps organize hiking clubs around the
  state, runs guided hikes in Shawnee National Forest, and
  sells the *River to River Trail Guide Across Southern Illinois*.

- The Prairie Club (630-516-1277, www.prairieclub.org),
  established in 1908, was instrumental in the protection of
  the Indiana Dunes and other regional spots. The group runs
  walks and other outings for members. Members have
  access to two club camps with cottages and campsites in
  Harbert, MI, and McHenry County, IL.

Shops

- Uncle Dan's Great Outdoor Store (2440 N. Lincoln Ave.,
  773-477-1918, www.udans.com) stocks—and more importantly, knows how to fit—hiking boots and carries camping
  supplies.

- Eastern Mountain Sports (1000 W. North Ave., 312-337-
  7750, www.ems.com) stocks and rents all manner of hiking
  and camping gear. Check for clinics and guided trips.

- Erehwon Mountain Outfitter (1800 N. Clybourn Ave. above
  Goose Island in the mall just north of EMS, 312-337-6400,
  www.erehwonoutdoors.com) also stocks the full range.

- Moosejaw (1445 W. Webster Pl. at Clybourn Ave., 773-529-
  1111, www.moosejawonline.com) carries mountaineering,
  hiking, and camping gear.

- Active Endeavors (55 E. Grand Ave., 312-822-0600, and 935
  W. Armitage, 773-281-8100; www.activeendeavors.com)

- REI (8225 Golf Rd. in Niles, 847-470-9090, and 17 W. 160 22d St. in Oakbrook Terrace, 708-574-7700; www.rei.com) carries a full range; regular clinics and events. Niles store carries clearance items—sometimes you get lucky.

Books

- Daniel, Glenda. *Dune Country: A Hiker's Guide to the Indiana Dunes*. Athens, OH: Swallow Press, 1984.

- DuFresne, Jim. *Isle Royale National Park: Foot Trails and Water Routes*. Seattle, WA: The Mountaineers, 1991.

  ———. *Porcupine Mountains Wilderness State Park: A Backcountry Guide for Hikers, Campers, Backpackers, and Winter Visitors*. Holt, MI: Thunder Bay Press, 1999.

  ———. *50 Hikes in Lower Michigan: The Best Walks, Hikes, and Backpacks in the Lower Peninsula*. Woodstock, VT: Backcountry Guides, 1999.

- Engel, J. Ronald. *Sacred Sands: The Struggle for Community in the Indiana Dunes*. Middletown, CT: Wesleyan University Press, 1983.

- Fisher, Alan. *Country Walks Near Chicago*. Baltimore, MD: Rambler Books, 1987.

- Post, Susan. *Hiking Illinois*. Champaign, IL: Human Kinetics, 1997.

- River to River Trail Society. *River to River Trail Guide Across Southern Illinois*. 3d ed. Harrisburg, IL: River to River Trail Society, 2002.

- Solzman, David M. *The Chicago River: An Illustrated History and Guide to the River and Its Waterways*. Chicago, IL: Wild Onion Books, an imprint of Loyola Press, 1998.

- Zynieuski, Walter, and George Zynieuski. *Illinois Hiking and Backpacking Trails*. Carbondale, IL: Southern Illinois University Press, 1993.

outsidepix.com

THE LAND ITSELF may be manhole flat, but Chicago is a city defined by its vertical landmarks. Simply witness the local outrage over Malaysia's Petronas Towers trumping the Sears Tower as the world's tallest building and you see what I mean. Despite the fact that Chicago suffers from ACS—that's Acute Crag Shortage—the city supports an avid, growing climbing community, a storied mountaineering club, and plenty of opportunities to learn to climb.

"It's a really mellow scene in this city," says Dave Hudson, manager of Hidden Peak rock gym. "I've worked at gyms in southern California, Utah, Ohio, and Chicago is by far the friendliest climbing community I've been in." He adds, "Here, you have to really make the effort if you want to be into climbing."

With the closest rock just shy of 3 hours away, city climbers scour the urban landscape for potential routes. I've talked to climbers who surreptitiously ascend bridges on the Chicago River, Lincoln Park statues, and University of Chicago science buildings (not that I'm recommending any of the above, this being an official guidebook and all). Even a lone boulder with one, sad, single route in front of Cook County Hospital gets a mention. Happily, the Harbor Wall in Jackson Park—a favored spot of U of C students and Hyde Parkers—offers free lakefront bouldering. Of course, there are several artificial climbing walls in the city, but they're a breed apart, detailed in the "Climbing Walls" chapter.

For Tony Berlier, one of the city's strongest climbers, world-famous Red River Gorge in Kentucky is the local crag—about a 7-hour drive. He leaves the city Friday night, climbs all day Saturday, all day Sunday. If he's back before midnight after a weekend trip, he's pumped. "I know my friends out West think we're nuts. I tell them where I go for a weekend and they say, 'Man, I don't even go that far for a week.' But to me, it just makes me that much more moti-vated to climb hard once I hit the rock." And long road trips have a way of forging tight bonds with other climbers.

Midwest climbs tend to be short; you're not going to find seven-pitch climbs in the city's backyard. But you will find a quartzite gem in Devil's Lake in Wisconsin and gor-geous sandstone bouldering and climbing in southern Illi-nois at spots like Jackson Falls in Shawnee National Forest. And when conditions are right, there's quality ice climbing on frozen falls just 2 hours west of the city in Starved Rock State Park.

This isn't the place for route descriptions, which are

highly technical, so these entries include general descriptions of the areas, kinds of climbing you'll find, and directions to the main parking areas. For each spot I've listed the best guidebook, where you'll find detailed route descriptions, safety cautions, gear recommendations, climbing history, regulations, and more. You'll absolutely need these books to climb well.

Remember, routes close; new ones are developed all the time. Network with local climbers and take advantage of the free flow of beta (climber-speak for advice). See www .climbingcentral.com. Check out *Vertical Jones*, a climbing mag covering the Midwest. And most of all, chalk up, have fun, and play safe.

City Limits

South Side Bouldering

CONSIDER IT THE adopted urban crag in the backyard of University of Chicago's Hyde Park campus. Tucked on the south face of the Jackson Park Harbor channel below a picnic area, the 650-foot-long rough-cut granite and mortar wall reaches about 16 feet high at its tallest point. Known simply as The Harbor Wall, it's an outdoor bouldering oasis in a rock-starved city a mere 8 miles from downtown.

Bouldering is the art of climbing without ropes, altitude, or protection—a kind of freeform gymnastics. It's a low-tech affair: all you need is a pair of climbing shoes, a bag of chalk, and a bouldering pad to cushion a landing if you fall (a buddy to spot you is never a bad idea either). Most bouldering "problems," short routes or traverses across rock face, take you no more than 30 feet or so off the ground. But make no mistake: bouldering requires great physical power. John Gill, a mathematician and the patron saint of bouldering, was known for his ability to do a chin-up while hanging from a single finger.

Jeff Elam wrote an informal bouldering guide to the Harbor Wall after climbing there in the early '90s while working on his Ph.D. in chemistry at U of C. The guide's problems are named for the rock-face graffiti marking the start ("Toni-n-Grant," for example, is a 5.10b with sharp holds). Elam got hooked on climbing after a lab buddy took him to Devil's Lake. Back on campus, determined to hone his skills and get a vertical fix, after finishing lab work in the research institute building he'd rappel the five-story stairwell at night or lead-climb the brick-latticed geophysical sciences building or make up bouldering problems on the underside of the campus gym stairs.

Eventually, he and some friends started hitting the Harbor Wall (Elam says rumor was Gill had flashed the wall when he did a stint at U of C in the late '50s). "In summer when we were all just fanatical about climbing we'd hit the wall just about every afternoon. I got to know every crevice it seemed. Usually it was pretty mellow there, but every once in a while someone threw a bottle over the side. One guy almost got hit by a car battery someone lobbed over. But it was fun."

Greg Johnson, a Harbor Wall regular and Colorado native who worked on the guide with Elam while earning a doctorate in religion, adds, "I'd get little black kids yelling down at me 'Mister, mister, you can get up over here, there's stairs.' I knew they're thinking 'Here's another helplessly dumb white guy who doesn't understand he can just walk around.' People really had no clue what we were doing down there. I spent a stupid amount of time at the Harbor Wall. You can spend endless hours picking apart a piece of rock, taking out this piece, adding that one. Climbing wise, it helped make the city less of a wasteland for me."

I ask Jeff Elam if the Harbor Wall is to Chicago what Central Park is to New York City bouldering. Elam chuckles on the line from Boulder where he's doing a postdoc and can look at the clock at 4:30 P.M. and decide to go climb world-famous Eldorado Canyon. "Central Parkers would probably laugh at us, the same way people here in Boulder would laugh at [Central Park's] Rat Rock. It's all about making do with what you have."

HARBOR WALL

Location: Jackson Park Harbor (6400 S)

Book: Not a book, but an online bouldering guide by U of C alum Jeff Elam at www.oac.uchicago.edu/climbing/. It has hand-drawn maps with 26 problems. Numbered problems work their way from the iron fence to the concrete stairs.

Description: It's the beginning of December. The Hawk is ripping in off the lake. Though he's far too kind to tell me, I think David Clifford hates me. The 24-year-old doctoral candidate in statistics heads up University of Chicago's outdoor club; he caught the climbing itch in college back in Cork, Ireland. Clifford bought a car when he moved to Chicago just so he could climb. But when he needs a quick fix, he comes here. Just not usually in December.

He's toting crucial Harbor Wall gear: a bouldering pad (many of the problems run along a concrete landing—no soft bed of pine needles to fall on here), climbing shoes, and a broom to sweep up the mosaic of broken glass. From the shards, it looks like Corona and Icehouse are the drinks of choice. An abandoned left half of a pair of size 11 Air Jordans is wedged between the breakwater rocks.

The graffiti used as markers in Elam's guide has been sandblasted, but most of his routes are still easy enough to make out. Some problems have what Clifford dubs "credit card holds" because the ledges are about as thin as an Amex. The Wall's face is riddled with dimples and pockets. "There's no mystery to it in a gym, everything's all nice and neat and color coded, but here, see I just found this hold here, perfect," Clifford says, jamming his index finger into a barely-there dimple to haul up 0+00, a 5.8 problem by the flagpole.

Elam's guide lays out a few rules to extract maximum challenge from the wall (if you follow the rules, no climb is below a 5.8). One, moves are static—no lunging. Two, climb high enough to put your hand on the cement slab on top of the wall. Three, use only features on the block faces as holds—ledges, cracks, blobs of mortar *not* on the face are considered off route. But everything is on for the descent. Clifford encourages would-be Harbor Wall junkies of all levels to get creative and make up their own problems. Plenty of local climbers (mostly Hyde Parkers and U of C students) hit the wall just to traverse end to end and build strength. The wall's assets are clear: it's free, it's rarely crowded, and it's got killer lake views and breezes to boot. It could be just you, the gulls, the slap of the water against the breakfront, and the sailboats gliding in and out of the harbor.

Directions: By car, take Lake Shore Dr./US 41 south. Pass the 63d St. beachhouse. Right after Jackson Park Harbor, US 41/South Shore Dr. swings east. Take the first left into the entry for La Rabida Hospital. Drive to the northern-most point and park at the picnic area/roundabout. Walk down the stairs at the southeast corner and go left. Bouldering problems start where the breakwater rocks begin.

By bike, ride south on the Lakefront Trail and follow directions from La Rabida above.

By transit, take the Green Line L to E. 63d St. (Red Line stops at 63d farther west). From there, take the 63 bus east to 63d St. Beach and walk south to La Rabida.

Chicago Mountaineering Club

YOU MAY HAVE to choose among 32 kinds of breakfast cereals, but for climbing, the Chicago Mountaineering Club holds a virtual monopoly.

Founded in 1940 by three University of Chicago students who met in the Grand Tetons, the CMC started out as a local group of hard-core mountaineers who used Midwest spots like Devil's Lake as a training ground to pioneer first ascents up and down serious peaks out West. (The Stettner brothers, Joe and Paul, brought true alpine-style climbing to the lake from their native Bavaria in the 1920s after immigrating to Chicago. Their name is attached to a landmark climb— Stettner's Ledges—they made on Colorado's Longs Peak with hemp rope and nail boots in 1927.)

Today the club's 240 members include high-altitude climbers, mountain climbers, ice climbers, and rock jocks (the club's oldest member is in his 80s and still climbs regularly). Some have climbed Everest, others are newbies; most climb in the 5.6–5.11 range, according to treasurer Chris Young. "We've played in about just about every mountain range in the world." The club sponsors monthly local climbing outings from April to October and a handful of trips out West each year.

Many local climbing outings, seminars, and the club's annual dinner in March—which draws world-class climbers and mountaineers like Royal Robbins and Jim Donini, known for his leading-edge ascents in Patagonia—are open to nonmembers. Check the schedule and details at www.cmcwebsite.org. To join you have to attend one Western outing or go on three local climbs and be sponsored by two club members. Members get access to two extraordinary resources: a members-only campground at Devil's Lake and a library with some 4,000 mountaineering and climbing titles.

Short Hop

MISSISSIPPI PALISADES STATE PARK, SAVANNA, ILLINOIS

Location: About 165 miles NW of Chicago

Outfitter: Apex Adventure Alliance (847-234-1000 or 877-ON-CLIMB, www.apexadventurealliance.com) guides and offers instruction here.

Camping: Mississippi Palisades State Park (815-273-2731, www.dnr.state.il.us) has first-come, first-served camping.

Book: *River Rock*

Heads up: Climbers congregate for grub and beta at CJ's bar in Savanna (815-273-2050), with a guidebook and New Route notebook at the bar. There were rumblings of a Palisades-area bouldering guide in the works.

Description: This band of pocket-laden dolomite limestone towers jutting above the Mississippi River is the closest real crag to Chicago, with 100-plus routes ranging from 5.0 to 5.12. Lots of midrange climbs. Most climbing is concentrated in the park's south end, with the Sentinel—the park's largest freestanding tower, dropping 120 feet to the river—a main draw with expansive views over the rolling river valley. Hawks, harriers, and kestrels are regulars.

The Quadrangle, a platform area sandwiched behind the Sentinel and the Sentinel's Main Wall, is climbing central with access to most of the Sentinel Area's 30-plus routes. Scramble up the gully/chimney on the Sentinel's north side to reach the Quadrangle. Twin Sisters area is another route-packed zone, popular with beginners (there's a short practice wall nearby for warm-up or bouldering) but with some challenging climbs of its own.

River Rock includes lead and top-rope climbs, though leading can be a challenge on the soft stone (unstable rock is an issue). Several areas, like Forgotten Wall and Sun Buttress, have been closed to climbers. Unfortunately, Amphitheater Wall, with the park's greatest continuous vertical rise and loads of long, challenging routes, was closed as of Fall 2001 because of rock fall. As of this writing the parking area holds two truck-sized boulders.

Directions: Take I-290 west to I-88 west. Around Dixon, take US 52 northwest to Savanna. In Savanna, pick up IL 84 and follow it north to the park entrance. Use the south entrance for the Sentinel Area and park in the lot at the shelters. On the far side of the picnic area, cross the bridge over the gully and turn west to hike to the Sentinel.

Longer than a Short Hop

DEVIL'S LAKE STATE PARK, BARABOO, WISCONSIN

Location: About 200 miles N of Chicago

Fee: $10 day out-of-state vehicle pass, $30 annual

Outfitters: Dairyland Expeditions (920-734-0321, www.climbwithus.com) in Appleton, WI, guides and runs classes here. They have an office in Wheeler's campground just outside the park. Apex Adventure Alliance (847-234-1000 or 877-ON-CLIMB, www.apexadventurealliance.com) guides and offers instruction here.

Camping: Devil's Lake State Park (608-356-8301; 888-947-2757 or www.wiparks.net for reservations) has three campgrounds that fill fast; reserve up to 11 months ahead. Plenty of rock jocks head to Wheeler's campground (608-356-4877, www.wheelerscampground.com), replete with small pro shop and run by climber Mark Wheeler.

Book: *Climber's Guide to Devil's Lake*

Heads up: Devil's Lake quartzite has close to zero friction. Humidity and rain make the rock more evil. Virtually every rating in the park is a sandbag.

Description: Climbers throughout the Midwest praise Mother Nature for creating a geological exception to the rule—hard-as-nails red-purple quartzite cliffs and talus in a region dominated by sandstone. Without question, Devil's Lake is the place Chicago climbers flock to most. It's gorgeous, with bluffs up to 400 feet high forming a big bowl around mile-long Devil's Lake. It's also immensely popular.

Clean-fractured angular features, thin edges, and cracks abound on the almost shellacked-shiny rock. Way too many gems to mention here: 1,500-plus climbs from 5.4 to 5.13b divided among the East Bluff and West Bluff, most between 5.8 and 5.11. East Rampart, a 0.25-mile-long band of summit buttresses on the East Bluff off the CCC Trail, is most popular. No bolts, it's traditional climbing with scattered bouldering. Paul Kuenn of Dairyland Expeditions encourages beginners to head to The Pillow area on the West Bluff or Lichen on the East Bluff. If crowds get to be too much (summer weekends are packed; bees are nasty), head north of Lost Face. "If you're willing to keep on walking, there's always something quiet," Kuenn says.

The entire East Bluff faces south; winter usually brings at least 10 solid climbing days. On hot days, regulars climb the East Bluff's west- and north-facing routes in the morning, swim in the lake, then hop to the West Bluff's east-facing climbs in the afternoon. Giant white pines and oaks offer shade. Endless views in mid-April before spring buds. Hiking, swimming, mountain biking, fishing, scuba diving, and cross-country skiing when your fingers hit tilt.

Directions: Take I-90 west past Madison. Take exit 106 to WI 33. Go west on WI 33 for 15 miles to Baraboo. In Baraboo, go south on WI 123 and follow it straight to the park.

Rock Climbing

For East Bluff, follow the park road south along the lake and park at the South Shore picnic area or the beginning of the CCC Trail.

WILD IOWA

Location: About 212 miles W of Chicago

Camping: Pictured Rocks Park (563-487-3541) has first-come, first-served primitive camping.

Book: *Wild Iowa*

Description: Egad. Iowa peaks along the Maquoketa River near the quiet town of Monticello. Sport climbing central on nicely overhanging faces, popular with collegiate climbers from University of Iowa and University of Northern Iowa. Wild Iowa includes three areas: Pictured Rocks, Indian Bluffs, and the Ozarks. Most action is in Pictured Rocks with some 70 routes on 40- to 80-foot-high cliffs. (Officials are not keen to see climbers at Indian Bluffs, a prime hunting area.)

The heavily pocketed dolomite carries lots of vertical cracks with a texture akin to fine sandpaper (though some route edges have been rubbed smooth from use). No fun in the rain. Comet Gallery and Wild Iowa Wall have a dozen or more climbs each; most of the better ones are 5.10–5.11 with a few fun—busy—5.8 and 5.9s. Some short traditional stuff, but nothing to write home about, says Shawn Kintzle, author of *Wild Iowa*. Oak and walnut forest with smatterings of wild ginger. Plenty of shade in summer—Pictured Rocks' walls run north to south with mostly eastern exposure. But the nettles are beastly.

All Pictured Rocks crags line the river, most concentrated within 0.5 mile upstream of the parking area on the west bank, though they stretch about 3 miles. More—and quieter—climbs on the east bank across the mellow

Maquoketa (it usually runs about 3 feet deep). Canoes glide by in fine weather. Would-be spelunkers can head to nearby Maquoketa caves (see "Caving," page 399).

Directions: Take I-55 south to I-80 west to the Quad Cities. Take I-61 north to Maquoketa. From Maquoketa, take IA 64 west to IA 38. Take IA 38 north toward Monticello. A few miles south of town look for signs for the east turnoff to Camp Courageous. Follow the road about 2 miles until it dead-ends in Pictured Rocks Park. Once you hit the river the road splits. Take the road that forks left to a small pavilion and parking area. Walk upstream (north) of the parking area to the crags. Note: in winter and early spring the Camp Courageous gate is often locked and you have to hoof it in (or head to Monticello and follow signs from there).

SOUTHERN ILLINOIS

Location: About 320 miles S of Chicago

Outfitter: Eric Ulner, regional coordinator for the Access Fund, runs Vertical Heartland climbing school and guiding service (618-995-1427, www.verticalheartland.com) at his private cliff, Draper's Bluff.

Camping: At Jackson Falls, climbers camp out of their cars and walk under 1 mile to hit the cliff. No public camping at Cedar or Draper's Bluff; closest is Ferne Clyffe State Park (618-995-2411). Also Giant City State Park (618-457-4836) and Shawnee National Forest (800-699-6637).

Book: *Vertical Heartland*

Description: Southern Illinois hill country offers some of the best sandstone climbing (sport and traditional protection) in the Midwest. The area's fast becoming a regular stop on coastal climbers' road trips out west or down south. Fans liken the top-notch bouldering here, especially in Shawnee National Forest's Jackson Falls, to France's fabled Fontainebleau forest. "It's very slopey and bulbous," Eric Ulner says. "Great textured sandstone, grippy, with lots of cool features, sloping swirls and little iron edges and pockets."

Jackson Falls alone has some 300 routes, mostly tough sport routes (lots of 5.12) with some traditional stuff on cliffs up to 65 feet high, tucked into a beech-maple-stuffed cloverleaf-like canyon—the 35-foot main waterfall cascades into a Grade A swimming hole. About a half-hour drive west, Draper's Bluff is the next largest area with about 100 routes (most in the 5.6–5.10 range), offering a shot at multipitch climbs—two, maybe three pitches if you meander—on the 120-foot-tall cliff. Ulner's clients can get used to camping on the wall before heading out to places like Yosemite. Ulner, who developed much of the area climbing, bought most of Draper's south face in '96 and keeps it open to climbers. Sign in and out at his kiosk and donate what you can to support the effort.

Cedar Bluff, with 70- to 90-foot cliffs about 0.5 mile east of Draper's, also has sport and trad climbing and a small but high-quality bouldering area. Other area spots: Ferne Clyffe and Giant City State Parks. Both are good places to top-rope as a beginner; the latter has some great bouldering and is about 10 minutes from SIU's campus in Carbondale. Milder climes than Chicago mean year-round climbing options; winter sun on Draper's south face adds a good 10–15°. See "Horseback Riding," page 495, and "Hiking & Backpacking," page 353, for other Shawnee-area diversions.

Directions: To Jackson Falls, take I-94 east to I-57 south. Follow I-57 south past Marion. Take I-24 east toward Nashville for about 7 miles. Exit at Tunnel Hill Rd. and go east until the road ends at a stop sign. Turn left on US 45 and follow it northeast about 3 miles. Turn right on Ozark

Rd. and go east about 5 miles. Follow the road as it curves sharply left around a cemetery. Turn right on the first gravel road past the cemetery (it looks like the farmhouse driveway, but it's not). Follow the gravel road about 1 mile. At end of the road, drive down a big hill. You'll hit the main parking area with a vault toilet on the right before you cross the creek. A kiosk and signboard are just inside the woods on an obvious trail. It's under 0.25 mile from the lot to the cliff.

To Draper's Bluff, take I-57 south past Marion to exit 36/Lick Creek Rd. Turn left (east) on Lick Creek (watch for tractors and farm animals on the road). You'll see Draper's Bluff on your left after about 2.5 miles; keep driving until you see the parking area and kiosk on your left. Sign in and follow the trail to the cliff.

Mecca

RED RIVER GORGE, STANTON, KENTUCKY

Location: About 417 miles SE of Chicago

Outfitters: Red River Outdoors (606-663-9701, www.redriveroutdoors.com) has guided climbing and instruction and limited gear, climbing shoe rentals. Apex Adventure Alliance (847-234-1000 or 877-ON-CLIMB, www.apexadventurealliance.com) guides and offers instruction here. Climb Time in Lexington (859-253-3673, www.climbtime.net) has gear and indoor climbing if you get skunked by lousy weather.

Camping: See Red River Gorge Climbers' Coalition (www.rrgcc.org) for full options and rules. Crowded, free camping at Roadside Crag parking area.

Books and link: *Red River Gorge Climbs* is the bible;

Selected Climbs at the Red River Gorge. Also see www
.rrgcc.org for updates and info.

Heads up: Miguel's (606-663-1975), just across the street
from Natural Bridge State Park, is the Red's version of
Yosemite Camp 4 with a climber kiosk in the parking lot,
good pizza, cheap camping, and some gear. Access is always
an issue; closures/restrictions in force throughout the area.
For the latest check with Red River Gorge Climbers' Coalition and Daniel Boone National Forest (606-663-3852,
www.southernregion.fs.fed.us/boone/rockclimb.htm).

Description: About an hour drive east of Lexington, the
Red offers hard-core Chicagoans world-class climbing
within reach for a weekend pilgrimage. Jammed with natural arches, pinnacles, and cliffs, the Red is a series of high
ridges along the up to 1,300-foot Pottsville Escarpment in
the Appalachian foothills. The Red's namesake rusty red
color comes from limonite, a kind of iron oxide that
cements the Corbin sandstone's pebbles and sand. Rock
quality ranges from crumbly sand to near-granite toughness.

Besides the embarrassment of riches, with 1,000-plus
traditional and sport routes and an emerging bouldering
scene, what makes the Red such a standout is the area's
wildly overhanging rock faces. Classic multipitch and
crack climbs. More than 700 miles of cliffline in the Stan-
ton ranger district in Daniel Boone National Forest, where
most routes are found—though several killer areas, like
Roadside Crag, aren't in the gorge itself. Most routes are 5.8
and up, making this an intermediate-advanced area. Year-
round climbing, but after June it can really cook. Cliffs harbor several rare plant and animal species, including the
white-haired goldenrod and endangered Virginia big-eared
bat. Other area diversions include hiking, horseback riding,
paddling (on the Red River snaking through the gorge), and
caving.

Directions: Take I-90 east to I-65 south. Stay on I-65 to

Louisville. Take I-64 east toward Lexington. Take exit 98 for the Bert T. Combs Mountain Parkway/KY 402 and follow to exit 33 (Slade). From here your choices are many. To get into the gorge itself, turn left at the bottom of the exit ramp and take another left on KY 11/15. Go about 1 mile on KY 11/15 to KY 77. From KY 77 follow signs for the park. For Roadside Crag, from exit 33 turn right (south) on KY 11 and go about 6 miles (you'll pass Miguel's on the left). Parking area is right, crag is left.

Ice Queen (or King)

SO WHAT, EXACTLY, is the allure of climbing the equivalent of a vertical ice rink?

"Rock is rock," says Paul Kuenn of Dairyland Expeditions. "Ice changes every 2 feet. It's riskier. And it's the closest thing you can get in the Midwest to a real alpine experience."

Midwestern ice is known for its spindly, chandelier-like texture—tough, temperamental stuff made up of little tendrils that sometimes form overnight and haven't quite thickened up. Kuenn recommends getting comfortable with basic rock climbing skills before tackling ice.

To learn how to handle the slick stuff, would-be ice masters head about 3.5 hours north to Kuenn's Ice Pit, a former quarry with 90- to 110-foot vertical ice set with prehung top ropes. Weekends December–March, Kuenn offers beginner-advanced instruction (gear and boot rental provided) as well as open ice climbing (bring your own gear or find a friend with the same shoe size; lots of people share the pricey gear). Basic ice gear includes tools (hammers or an adze), a helmet, goggles or some form of eye protection (you don't want Frisbee-sized chunks of ice taking out your cornea), mountaineering boots, and crampons.

Pictured Rocks National Lakeshore in Munising, MI, is a rugged gem with nearly 200-foot routes and night views of the aurora borealis. Climbers snowshoe or ski in hip- to chest-high powder past stunted hemlocks to the longer climbs. "You get that feeling of being on a big mountain that you can't get anywhere else," says Kuenn, who's been guiding since 1980 and runs classes at Pictured Rocks. "It's isolated. And Lake Superior is like being at altitude—you're not sucking wind, but your body is pushed" by climbing in temps of -15 to -20° and being whipsawed by brutal lake-fed winds. Munising proves its frozen mettle with a 3-day ice-climbing festival the first weekend in February.

A few Wisconsin state parks, like Governor Dodge, Lone Rock, and Wyalusing, have a handful of routes. Minnesota North Shore areas like Tettagouche State Park are especially popular with Twin Cities climbers. And hard-core climbers hit Lake Superior's Ontario shore in spots like Orient Bay, Agawa Canyon, and the Montreal River Harbor. North of Superior Climbing Company (www.northofsuperiorclimbingcompany .com) in Thunder Bay offers instruction and guiding in Ontario. For the most comprehensive Midwest ice guide to date, see *Superior Ice*.

Some of the best ice climbing around is closer to home, about 2 hours west of Chicago in Starved Rock State Park's steep, vertical-to-overhanging sandstone caverns (no rock climbing; certain canyons are open to ice-only by truce with park officials). Increasingly mild winters of late have made for iffy ice, but when it's good, it's very good with pillars up to 85 feet. It's also where headliner ice climber Raphael Slawinski cut his teeth while studying at U of C (he was also a regular at the Harbor Wall on the South Side). French Canyon, a 35-footer, tends to form early in the season; great for novice crampon practice with or without an ice axe. Talk to Mark and Tom at Starved Rock Outfitters (888-580-5510, www.starvedrockoutfitters.com) in Utica for gear and wisdom. Call the park at (815) 667-4868 and hit 1 for basic ice conditions.

Where to Connect

See the "Climbing Walls" chapter for instruction from the indoor gyms—the walls are great places to network. And some indoor gyms also have pro shops that carry gear.

Schools and Guides

- Dairyland Expeditions (920-734-0321, www.climbwithus .com) in Appleton, WI, offers extensive beginner–advanced rock and ice instruction, guiding at Devil's Lake and Pictured Rocks National Lakeshore, among other sites.

- Apex Adventure Alliance (847-234-1000 or 877-ON-CLIMB, www.apexadventurealliance.com) guides and offers beginner–advanced instruction at spots including Mississippi Palisades, Devil's Lake, and Red River Gorge.

- Vertical Heartland (618-995-1427, www.verticalheartland .com) is a climbing school and guiding service in southern Illinois.

- Red River Outdoors (606-663-9701, www.redriveroutdoors .com) has guided climbing and instruction in Kentucky's Red River Gorge.

Shops

- Moosejaw (1445 W. Webster Pl. at Clybourn Ave., 773-529-1111, www.moosejawonline.com)

- Erehwon Mountain Outfitter (1800 N. Clybourn above

Goose Island brewery in the mall just north of EMS, 312-337-6400, www.erehwonoutdoors.com)

- REI (8225 Golf Rd. in Niles, 847-470-9090, and 17 W. 160 22d St. in Oakbrook Terrace, 708-574-7700; www.rei.com)

- Active Endeavors (55 E. Grand Ave., 312-822-0600, and 935 W. Armitage, 773-281-8100; www.activeendeavors.com)

- Eastern Mountain Sports (1000 W. North Ave., 312-337-7750, www.ems.com)

Books
- Bronaugh, John H. *Red River Gorge Climbs: A Comprehensive Rock Climbing Guide to Kentucky's Red River Gorge.* 2d ed. Lexington, KY: Geezer Press, 1998.

- Collett, Bill, and Gary Taylor. *River Rock: A Climber's Guide to Mississippi Palisades State Park.* Madison, WI: Granite Publishing, 1991.

- Farris, Mike. *Rock Climbing Minnesota and Wisconsin.* Helena, MT: Falcon Guides, 2000.

- Hynek, Don. *Superior Ice: Ice Climbs of the Lake Superior Region, a Compendium.* Madison, WI: Granite Publishing, 2001.

- Jarrard, Porter, and Chris Snyder. *Selected Climbs at the Red River Gorge.* Lexington, KY: El Rancho Relaxo, 1997.

- Kintzle, Shawn. *Wild Iowa: Sports Climbs of the Central Maquoketa.* Monticello, IA: Self-published, 1997. An updated version was in the works as of this writing.

- Swartling, Sven Olof. *Climber's Guide to Devil's Lake.* Madison, WI: University of Wisconsin Press, 1995.

- Ulner, Eric. *Vertical Heartland: A Rock Climber's Guide to Southern Illinois.* 2d. ed. Carbondale, IL: Falcon Press, 1996. A third edition was in the works as of this writing.

Links

www.climbingcentral.com

www.verticaljones.com

www.rockclimbing.com

www.accessfund.org

INDOOR CLIMBING MEANS instant gratification for a vertical fix. It's the boiled-down essence of Life In The Big City: Want to see the latest Iranian film masterpiece? OK. Eat crazy-fresh ahi tuna in a sushi bar 2,000 miles away from the Left Coast? You got it. Climb a nicely overhanging route in T-shirt and shorts in a February snowstorm in the middle of the city? No problem.

For Chicagoans, who face about a 3-hour drive to the closest real crag, climbing walls are a godsend. They make it possible to integrate climbing into daily life. Climb at lunch, after work, at night. This is separate from the "Rock Climbing" chapter because climbing artificial walls indoors is an animal apart from outdoor climbing on real rock, where there are far more variables.

Besides being a blast, artificial walls offer the chance to learn and hone climbing skills whether you ever plan to climb outdoors or not. The gyms are also ideal places to connect with other city climbers. Most of the gyms in this chapter offer intros to rock climbing, continuing instruction, and have gear to rent. Except for Hidden Peak, which is purely a rock gym, all of the city walls are part of a larger health club. If you've never visited a climbing wall, you'll likely be blown away by the seeming chaos of colors, shapes, and textures hewn into the varied terrain—and the fluid elegance of climbers dissecting and making sense of the madness. You may be able to hear climbers' clipped commands, if the music isn't pumping too hard.

If you're new to climbing, most gyms will make you take, and pay for, an orientation class to get certified in safe belaying and climbing techniques before you chalk up to hit the routes. Call the gyms for specifics. A drop-in daypass can be pricey; it's usually a better deal to get a 10- or 20-punch pass—or check out membership rates if you get hooked.

Below are four climbing walls in the city, three in the burbs, and one indoor *Mecca* in Bloomington, IL, that inspires Chicago road trips. Two top-notch Wisconsin gyms not detailed here but worth mentioning (Chicago climbers make pit-stops there en route to spots like Devil's Lake): Adventure Rock (262-790-6800, www.adventurerock.com) near Milwaukee and Boulders Gym (608-244-8100, www.bouldersgym.com) in Madison. Boulders' annual February Barn Burner competition is a favorite. See the "Rock Climbing" chapter for *Where to Connect* info.

HIDDEN PEAK

937 W. Chestnut St.

(312) 563-9400, www.lakeshoreacademy.com.

Location: NW of downtown (900 N)

Description: The climber's climbing gym. Hidden Peak is the closest thing the city has to a climbers' hub. In a building hard by the Chicago River, you walk past balance beams and mats in the Lakeshore Academy gymnastics school to get to the climbing. Primarily a bouldering gym, with most action taking place 14 feet and under over a compact 2,000 square feet with up to 80% overhang—practically horizontal. Problems run the gamut up to mid-5.13. Creative route-setters keep it lively. Campus board for building finger strength. And though many of the city's best climbers are here, the vibe is decidedly low key.

"You have to enjoy the sport and the movement to want to climb here for an extended period of time," says manager Dave Hudson. "Some climbers are hard core. Some are just recreational climbers but definitely incorporate it in their lives. We try to get people introduced right away so it's not intimidating. If you're bouldering, there's always someone working on a V-0 or V-1."

Custom-built wall with great texture. And rates are among the city's most reasonable; a day-pass is $10 (add $6 for full gear), 10-punch pass $80. Climb on your lunch hour, 12–2, when it's quiet and the price drops to $7. Tuesday and Thursday evenings and Saturdays are busiest. If you want to rope up, there are eight ropes on a slab wall and six on a wall running vertical to 40-degree angle. For $35, newcomers get a 1.5-hour class in top roping, including a free day-pass card and equipment. Not the best place to lead. And not necessarily the best place on a sweltering day—although the basement gym stays pretty cool, there's no air conditioning. Big kids program. Bouldering comps.

Directions: By car, take I-90/-94 west to the Milwaukee/Augusta exit. Turn left on Milwaukee Ave. Take Milwaukee to Chicago Ave. At Chicago turn left (east) and follow to Sangamon St. Turn left on Sangamon, which dead-ends into the parking lot (banner says Lakeshore Academy).

By transit, take the Blue Line to Chicago Ave. Walk east on Chicago and follow directions above.

LINCOLN PARK ATHLETIC CLUB

1019 W. Diversey Parkway

(773) 529-2022, www.lpaconline.com

Location: About 4 miles N of downtown (2800 N)

Description: If the thought of holing up inside the gym on a glorious day makes you cringe, this urban Entre Prises crag is your spot. (If it's a *really* nice day, come early to beat the throng.) As of this writing, the city's only open-air wall. And it's a beauty: 70 feet high and 35 feet wide with 11 top ropes, each with 4 to 10 routes, stocked with overhangs, roofs, dihedrals, arêtes, and gullies. Lit for night climbs. Routes range from 5.6 to 5.12. Newly added synthetic ice sections (think foam on steroids). A $20 ice orientation includes use of crampons and tools (for certified climbers). Leadable on all but ice sections. Open year-round, but call ahead; they usually close the wall if it's below 48° or raining heavily.

Indoors there's the equivalent of a treadmill for climbers, a computerized, rotating climbing wall; plug in the speed and steepness from less than vertical to fully horizontal roof. You can campus and boulder on it, good endurance training. Beginner-advanced classes on the outdoor wall May–October. Otherwise, climbing classes at the sister club in Evanston (with two feature-filled indoor walls and a 500-square-foot bouldering cave), easily accessible by L. Competitions and games at Friday Night Flash, first Friday of the month. Both the city and the Evanston gym offer (separate) 10- or 20-punch passes to climb.

Directions: By car, take Clark St. north to Diversey Parkway. At Diversey turn left (west) and follow to the gym, just west of Sheffield Ave.

By transit, the Brown Line Diversey L stop is across the street.

LAKESHORE ATHLETIC CLUB

211 N. Stetson Ave.

(312) 616-9000, www.lsac.com.

Location: Downtown

Description: One of the city's first climbing walls. And the tallest, topping out at 100 feet—that's seven stories high. Great for endurance, though some rock rats complain it's too narrow (about 20 feet). Six top ropes with about 30 routes, most in the 5.9–5.10 range, plus a beginner section with extra holds. Some overhangs. Lead climbing Thursdays only. There was talk of adding a bouldering section in the racquetball court—stay tuned.

Prices reflect the real estate: the wall is smack downtown across the street from the Illinois Center in a posh health club. It's $20 a visit, including chalk and harness; shoes are extra. Experienced climbers may qualify for a discount on the orientation fee. Lessons.

Directions: By car, why bother? If you must, take Lake

Shore Dr. to Randolph St. Take Randolph west to Stetson Ave. Turn right on Stetson and follow to Lake St. and the gym.

By transit, take the Red Line L to the Washington and Lake stop. Walk east on Lake St. to Stetson Ave. Turn left on Stetson to the gym.

FITPLEX EXTREME FITNESS

1235 N. LaSalle St.

(312) 640-1235, www.multiplexclubs.com

Location: About 1.5 miles N of downtown

Description: Lots of terrain, from slabs to faces to overhangs, on a 30-foot-high, 40-foot-wide Eldorado wall. Eight to ten top ropes, about 10 to 12 routes from 5.5 to 5.12. Leading on a few routes over about half the wall, bouldering on the same wall. Climbing 101 class. $12 day-pass, including all gear but shoes (add $4). Usually hosts one competition a year.

Directions: By car, take Lake Shore Dr. to the North Ave. exit. At LaSalle St. turn left (south) and follow to the gym, on the east side just north of Division St.

By transit, take the Red Line L to the Clark and Division stop. Walk one block west on Division St., then less than a block north on LaSalle St.

The Shop

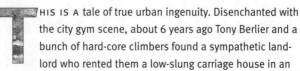

THIS IS A tale of true urban ingenuity. Disenchanted with the city gym scene, about 6 years ago Tony Berlier and a bunch of hard-core climbers found a sympathetic landlord who rented them a low-slung carriage house in an

un-yuppie neighborhood and let them gut the place to con-
struct a dream bouldering playhouse from pure sweat equity.

They created a climbing co-op dubbed The Shop (so named
because the building was a onetime cabinet shop). Members—
usually anywhere from 12 to 18—contribute modest monthly
dues and pitch in to clean up, change routes, and build addi-
tions and improvements, like heat. (I promised not to divulge
The Shop's location because members, dedicated climbers all,
prefer to climb rather than field unannounced visitors.)

Prospective members usually get referred by friends or staff
from area climbing gyms, many of whom themselves climb at
The Shop. It's not a place for beginners. "Problems are short
and hard here," Berlier says. "This is a very humbling place. It
keeps the ego in check. We all just seem to get better and just
feed off each other."

Though he's too modest to say so, Berlier is widely
acknowledged as one of the best climbers in the city. All his
vacations are climbing vacations, mostly out West. In season,
he spends pretty much every weekend at the Red in Kentucky
or in southern Illinois. And if he's not out on the crag or at
work (he's a systems analyst), he's probably here.

Berlier started out in 1993 with a small "garbage wall" in
his basement in Wicker Park. Friends would drop by to train. It
was fun, but it quickly became clear they needed more space.
He and his climbing friends weren't crazy about the gyms: they
had limited hours, they were pricey, and they weren't that challenging. "They just didn't meet our idiosyncratic needs,"
Berlier says. "The mission was to have a fun place to climb, a
place with really positive energy."

With The Shop, there are no set hours. Members have keys
and come and go as they like. Dogs are occasional visitors, as
are young children. One former member, an Art Institute professor, used to come grade papers on the floor while others
just climbed around him.

The Shop covers some 1,400 square feet of contoured overhang with a clearance of 9 or 10 feet. You can climb-through everywhere, there's no dead space. Every surface is so plastered with technicolor holds and electric tape I can barely make out specks of plywood underneath. There's a campus board for beefing up fingers. And three van loads' worth of discarded mattresses lining the moon-walk-like floor, covered by a multi-hued hodgepodge of poly shag carpet. No flash, all function.

When I drop by one cold Tuesday night, a few people are ordering in pad Thai noodles. Funky jazz plays in the background. There's a candy kitty full of Skittles. A jumbo size bottle of Tylenol. A few hammers. Chalkbags dangling from nails. A Scrabble board. The co-op is a mixed crowd: carpenters, traders, baristas, firemen, teachers, doctoral students.

Jill Domke, a physical therapist and dancer, dangles spider-like from the ceiling. "Climbing here is like going to someone's house, it's more personal here," Domke explains, as she stems a corner. "There's a real community feel."

As for Berlier, the Cincinnati native has lived in the city since 1993. And The Shop has a lot to do with why. "I fully expected to be gone out West by now. I never thought I'd last here in the city this long. But as a climber, this place has made living in Chicago completely bearable."

Suburban Gyms

CLIMB ON

18120 Harwood Ave., Homewood, IL 60430
(708) 798-9994, www.climbon.net
Location: About 25 miles S of Chicago
Description: This south suburban rock gym, accessible

by Metra from downtown, has about 4,800 square feet of climbing. Anywhere from 20 to 60 bouldering problems set throughout the gym, plus a 400-square-foot bouldering cave above the locker rooms that runs from 45 degrees to roof. The U-shaped 32-foot-high, 160-foot-wide Eldorado wall has real rock texture. Some 25 top ropes and about 50 routes. Roughly 40% of the gym is overhung, and all of it's leadable. Limited climbs on a 35-foot-high outdoor wall in the back. Tuesdays half-off for the superior sex (that'd be women). Full instructional program and a youth team. Plans were in the works to add a new lead wall with serious overhangs. Reasonable membership fee in addition to day-pass and 10-pass options. Routes change frequently; the gym strips down and resets routes for several bouldering competitions every year. Loaded pro shop.

Directions: By car, take I-94 east to I-80/-294 west. Take I-80/-294 west to Halsted St./IL 1 exit south. Follow Halsted St./US 1 south about 1 mile to Ridge Rd. At Ridge, turn right (west). Follow Ridge to Harwood Ave. Turn left on Harwood. The gym is about a half-block on the left.

By transit, take Metra Electric University Park line to the Homewood station. Gym is about a half-block south of the station.

VERTICAL REALITY

732 Prairie St., Aurora, IL 60506
(630) 892-1109, www.verticalreality.net
Location: About 43 miles W of Chicago
Description: Don't let this gym's location inside Luigi's Pizza & Fun Center put you off. "This is a climber's gym," says owner Jeff Larsen. Between 60 and 100 routes packed into 8,000-plus square feet of climbing on a plywood wall that averages 36 feet with slabs, vertical, and overhangs.

Thirty-seven top ropes. Totally overhung roof to lead; more than half the gym is open to leading with plans to make the entire gym leadable. Friendly vibe.

There's a rappelling ledge and bouldering throughout the gym, with some 800 square feet of dedicated bouldering space. Seven-inch-thick padded floor feels mighty nice if your spotter fails to brace a fall. Larsen hopes to add a new 1,200-square-foot overhung cave: "It'll be like climbing in a tube basically." Reasonable fees for orientation, classes, and drop-in passes. Pro shop. Full range of classes. Outdoor climbing trips to spots like Mississippi Palisades or Devil's Lake (see "Rock Climbing," pages 368 and 369). The gym runs comps through the American Bouldering Series, as well as its own.

Directions: By car, take I-290 west to I-88 west to IL 31/Lake St. south. Take IL 31/Lake St. south to Prairie St. Turn right (west) on Prairie to the gym, inside Luigi's Pizza & Fun Center.

By transit, the gym is 2 miles south of the Aurora Metra stop. Take Metra's Burlington Northern Santa Fe line to the Aurora station. On foot, cross west over the Fox River and walk south down Lake St. to Prairie St. Turn right on Prairie to the gym. Or take Pace bus 524.

VERTICAL ENDEAVORS

28141 Diehl Rd., Warrenville, IL, 60555
(630) 836-0122, www.verticalendeavors.com
Location: About 31 miles W of Chicago
Description: Flashy monster gym with some 80 routes spread over 18,000 square feet of climbing on three walls ranging from 30 to 42 feet high, including Nicros surfacing that mimics natural rock features and texture. Lots of crack systems for jamming, overhang, slab, chimneys, arêtes,

dihedrals galore. Catwalk for rappelling. Lead climbing, 40 routes, over just under half the gym; 120 top ropes plus 19 auto-belays so you don't need a partner. Pricey walk-in, about $23 with gear. The gym runs outdoor rock and ice classes and guides to places like Minnesota's North Shore and Devil's Tower in Wyoming. Hosts a few climbing comps a year. Full range of instruction.

Directions: By car, take I-290 west to I-88 west. Take the Winfield Rd. exit south toward Naperville. Winfield Rd. dead-ends at the gym's front door, at Diehl Rd.

By transit, the gym is about 3 miles north of the Naperville Metra stop. Take Metra's Burlington Northern Santa Fe line to the Naperville station. From there, take Pace bus 676 north to Diehl and Winfield Rds. On foot, walk north on Washington St. to Diehl Rd. Turn left (west) on Diehl and follow to Winfield.

Mecca

Against the
Grain

FORGET THAT THERE'S nary an outcropping on the 2-hour drive through the cornfields from Chicago to Bloomington. Climbers make the flatland trek to a looming cluster of concrete grain silos that Chris and Pam Schmick transformed in 1995 into a shrine of tendon-popping bliss at their rock gym, Upper Limits.

At first the climber couple tried to find space in Chicago but had little luck. They stumbled across the Bloomington silos, convinced the bank that no, they weren't crazy, and started work. They spent 3 months in agricultural fallout hell, cleaning out scrap steel and 6 tons of rotten soybeans (Funk Bros. Seed

Company had abandoned the silos about a decade earlier). "It was pretty gnarly," Chris says. "It smells like the worst thing in the world, like rotting carcasses." Pam jumps in, cradling their 3-month-old son, Spencer. "Yeah, Spencer's diapers smell better than that."

Then came 3 months of wall construction. Only problem was the silos weren't accessible from the bottom. We go upstairs to a room with massive grain chutes feeding into the silos. Chris lifts up a square of cement from the floor; suddenly we're looking down at top ropes, climbers methodically scaling one of the 65-foot cylinders. Chris fixed bolts in the ceiling and rappelled down each silo to drill holes for bolts and holds. As part of my Silo 101 lesson, he shows off a huge brass grain scale.

Grain tunnels became conduits for heat. A grain elevator now shuttles adrenaline junkies to a 120-foot rappel from a dusty attic overlooking a flat blanket of trees, houses, and railroad tracks. Chris grins. "This is the best part of owning a silo. I get my own elevator."

Though the Schmicks now spend most of their time in St. Louis, where they opened a second Upper Limits, they still keep a home in Bloomington. It's conveniently located next door to their gym—inside a 110-foot silo. "We just laugh when the tornadoes come through," Chris says.

UPPER LIMITS ROCK GYM

1304 W. Washington, Bloomington, IL 61701
(309) 829-8255, www.upperlimits.com
Location: About 137 miles S of Chicago
Description: Think Disney World for climbers. Where else are you going to get to scale the inside of a grain silo? From the inspired minds of Chris and Pam Schmick come

20,000-plus square feet of climbing—almost all of it lead-able—with about 100 routes up to 5.14d.

Main area has eight top ropes on a 30-foot wall, 70% overhung with slabs, roofs, arêtes. Campus boards near the 2,000-square-foot bilevel bouldering loft, all roof and steep angles (45 degrees or more). Leadable wave wall. Some 40 ropes inside 5 leadable silos: stretch out on 3 65-foot round silos, 2 silos with dihedrals, chimneys, stems. A 110-foot outdoor wall in season. Ice climbing and classes on a 30-foot man-made frozen waterfall in winter.

Rappel down the side of a 120-foot silo (take the old grain elevator up). Full array of climbing classes. The place draws a wide range of climbers: Chicago rock nuts, local families, Boy Scouts, college kids from U of I and neighboring Illinois Wesleyan and Illinois State. Plans for weights, treadwall, and an expanded lounge area. Supremely stocked pro shop. Annual Hangdog Jamboree in November draws competitors from across the Midwest.

Directions: By car, take I-55 south through the cornfields to Bloomington. Take Market St./exit 160a. Turn right (south) on Dinsmore St. Turn left on Washington St. The gym is just ahead on the right. You'll see the logo atop the silos.

By transit, Amtrak (800-872-7475, www.amtrak.com) and Greyhound (800-231-2222, www.greyhound.com) run regular service between Chicago and Bloomington.

WHEN I TALK to Fred Schumann, he's just gotten back from doing survey work at Mammoth Cave in Kentucky. He casually mentions that he spent 18 hours straight underground. "It was awesome," the 29-year-old says. "I lost total connection with the world above for a while. When I'm down there, nothing else exists for me but the cave."

Chicago cavers like Schumann are unfazed by the fact that there are no caves here. "Caving Chicago-style means if you want to cave, you have to drive," Schumann says. "The glaciers pretty much made us cave-deprived here."

No matter. Chicago has two groups, called grottos, affiliated with the National Speleological Society. Grottos can take you to caves throughout the region (southern Illinois, Indiana, and Kentucky are popular destinations). That's a good thing, because without the grottos you won't find the caves—except for "show" caves, caverns developed for tourists with paved paths and lights, or a handful of public "wild" caves without such amenities. Grottos will also teach you to cave safely and, often, loan you equipment. Plus cavers scout new caves, watching for plumes of steam rising from the ground in winter.

Many wild caves are on private land and are accessible only to those in grottos; the grottos have relationships with landowners and have cave maps. Cave locations are closely guarded, both to protect people from caves—you definitely don't want to get trapped—and caves from people. The underground ecosystems are incredibly fragile; it takes thousands of years for geological formations to form. A mere smudge of oil from a human finger can halt their growth altogether.

Below you'll find a handful of wild caves on public lands open to explorers. If you've never been caving before, stick to the beginner areas or—better yet—hook up with a grotto trip. There are also several show caves: Indiana's Marengo and Wyandotte Caves and Mammoth in Kentucky offer strenuous guided wild caving trips that require plenty of crawling, squeezing, and generally muddying up.

Urban Spelunking

T'S AROUND 10:30 P.M. on a brutal 17° January night. In the shadow of a vacant lot packed with hulking cranes, "OttoRepo" swiftly lifts up the metal grate that serves as a portal to the underground city. We hoist our backpacks and climb down a metal ladder, 40 feet below downtown. The air is moist and, at

50° or so, feels downright balmy. I don the fluorescent orange knee-high rubber boots my husband wore tromping around the Latin American bush, a hard hat, and a headlamp, and our group of five sets off down a dark tunnel.

Let me be clear: I'm not with any grotto. I'm with Chicago Urban Exploration (CUE), a group that relishes exploring the hidden corners of the city and its fringes—abandoned factories, forgotten cemeteries, steam tunnels, sewers.

Chicago may not have any caves, but it definitely has a subterranean universe. We're in one part of it, a 40-plus-mile warren of onetime freight tunnels that wind under the Loop and beyond. Officially, they're off-limits (which is why CUE members insist on being referred to by their code names). For urban explorers, infiltration is part of the thrill and the challenge. The point is to observe, explore, and learn—the club abhors vandalism, which is why you won't see destination details or maps on their Web site, www.chicagourbanexploration.com. Several members are also into film or photography and post a record of their missions online.

"Basically, we're like modern-day urban anthropologists," explains 31-year-old "Jhereg."

The Chicago freight tunnels are one of the club's favored haunts. Starting around the turn of the century, workers hand-dug blue clay under the burgeoning city to eventually create a 60-mile tunnel system for small electric trains to deliver mail and coal to downtown businesses. The trains were shut down in 1959; the roughly 6-foot-wide, 7.5-foot-tall tunnels have since been used for fiber-optic and other cable networks. In 1992 a construction crew accidentally punched a hole in a tunnel that ran under the Chicago River, flooding City Hall and scores of buildings throughout the Loop.

Though the flood has long since drained, tonight we're sloshing through mid-shin water in parts of the labyrinth, thick sucking mud in others (several times it nearly swallows my boot). "ShyX," who works for a construction company, quickly instructs me in the finer points of grate-walking; the water's deepest in the middle of the tracks, hiding lots of ankle-twisting pits and holes, so we scale close to one side of the wall, then another to avoid cramping up on one side.

A few stretches are lit by bulbs, but most places it's deep darkness punctured only by our thin flashlight beams. The musty, slightly acrid tunnels are marked with the same standard-issue green street signs used above ground—here's Franklin, there's Van Buren—which only emphasizes the feeling of having walked through the looking glass to find a parallel universe, a below-ground grid.

We pass bolted or cemented-in doors to Loop businesses. My senses are on overdrive; the Blue Line L's rattling feels very close. I'm jumpy every time a car drives over a grate somewhere above our heads, triggering an echoing boom through the concrete caverns. After a while, I lose all sense of direction and time. Up ahead, "Derailer" calls us to catch up. He flashes a beam on stalactites dripping from the ceiling, on nascent, stumpy stalagmites in a grayish lump surrounded by cottonlike crystals.

"OttoRepo," a 30-year-old graphic artist who works in the Loop, sees a lot of parallels between the city tunnels and the natural caves he's explored. "The sense of exploration, of finding something new every time you descend, is definitely the same. And there's an inherent draw in being underground. It makes you realize, when you're walking around above ground, just how much is going on right underneath you. In these tunnels, you kind of disappear for a while. What's great is a lot of people know about the tunnels, but no one's really been in them. And it's right under everybody's noses. Plus, there's something special about crawling around underneath the office where you work."

We push on, passing a poem scratched on the wall, presumably penned by a Com Ed worker about his "dead-end" (pun intended?) job. An elaborate, frightful portrait of The Tunnel Beast (fictional, I'm hoping) rendered in white chalk. A rusted-out dolly that looks like it was probably left behind when the trains became obsolete. "OttoRepo" takes a cigarette break and asks us all to click off our flashlights; we stand silent in total darkness watching the alien red glow move up as he takes a drag, then down again.

Around 1 A.M., filthy ("Derailer," a 22-year-old computer consultant clad in black who travels with an industrial steel-encased laptop, declares: "Filth is good"), we clamber back up the metal ladder, pop open the street grate, and haul ourselves out into the cold air. "Just like that—we're back to the grid," grins "OttoRepo."

Read more about the freight tunnels, if you can get hold of Bruce Moffat's (now out of print) 1982 book *Forty Feet Below: The Story of Chicago's Freight Tunnels*.

Wild Caves

MAQUOKETA CAVES STATE PARK, MAQUOKETA, IOWA

(563) 652-5833

www.state.ia.us/parks/maqucav.htm

Location: About 185 miles W of Chicago

Description: A great place to try out wild caving with some 13 caves to explore, from 30 to 800 feet long. Self-guided. Get a copy of the slightly dated *A Guide to Maquoketa Caves State Park* by Thomas Henry from the park office. Beginners without claustrophobia should try Barbell Cave; it's a fairly tight crawl but eventually opens into a room filled with small formations and big spiders.

Dancehall Cave, the largest, with several offshoots and tight, muddy passages, is mostly even-floored and usually lit in warm weather (the lights are switched off when bats start hibernating in fall and winter). Legend has it the cave got its name because square dances were held there several generations back in the large room at the southern end. Watch for rappellers. Rugged limestone landscape above ground is good for scrambling and hiking. Camping here, too.

Directions: Take I-290 west to IL 64 west. Stay on IL 64 for about 95 miles until US 52. Bear right on US 52 (northwest), continuing 32 miles. At IA 64, go left (west) for 35 miles. At US 61 go right (north) about 1 mile, then left on IA 428 until it runs into the park entrance.

SPRING MILL STATE PARK, MITCHELL, INDIANA

(812) 849-4129

www.in.gov/dnr/parklake/parks/springmill.html

Location: About 287 miles S of Chicago

Description: Bronson, Donaldson, and Twin Caves are all part of the same cave system—home to the endangered pinkish-white northern blind cave fish—with water flowing from Twin Caves through Bronson into Donaldson. The dry side of Donaldson, a large open room with the requisite stalactites and stalagmites, can be explored. Prepare for mud, especially in warmer months. Watch for bright orange cave salamanders near the cave mouths. Bronson is a technical, wet cave prone to flooding and is open by permit only to experienced cavers. Camping. En route to Spring Mill, you'll pass Bluespring Caverns in Bedford, a show cave that offers boat rides down a cave river.

Directions: Take I-90/-94 east. Stay on I-90 east toward Indiana. Take the I-65/US 12/Dunes Highway/US 20 exit

(exit 17), toward Indianapolis. Continue on I-65 south for 140 miles. Take I-465 south past the Indianapolis airport and pick up IN 37 south. Stay on IN 37 south to Mitchell. Turn on US 60 east. Park entrance is about 3 miles on the left.

ILLINOIS CAVERNS STATE NATURAL AREA, WATERLOO, ILLINOIS

(618) 458-6699

www.dnr.state.il.us/lands/Landmgt/PARKS/R4/caverns /index.htm

Location: About 355 miles SW of Chicago

Description: Windy City Grotto has mapped some 6 miles of the cavern's passages. You need at least four people, suitable equipment, and experience to gain an entry permit (see details online). The cave runs nearly 3 miles at walking-height passage, some of it through a knee-deep stream. Some passages, like Marvin's Misery, are twisting, 3-foot-high crawlways through the muck. You get the range of cave formations, many still growing: stalactites, stalagmites, flowstone, and soda straws, the thin-walled hollow tubes that form as water drips through their centers and deposits rings of calcite around the rim. Inhabitants include cave salamanders, little brown and eastern pipistrel bats, and the federally endangered Illinois cave amphipod, (*Gammerus acherondytes*), a quarter-inch-long crustacean that looks something like a tiny crayfish.

Directions: Take I-55 south for 245 miles to I-255 south. Take I-255 south to IL 3 south. Approximately 4 miles after Waterloo, take the second right (south) onto Kaskaskia Rd. (after the John Deere dealership on the right). Take a left (east) on County KK. Turn right on County G and go about 3 miles. The caverns entrance is on your right.

Show Caves

CAVE OF THE MOUNDS, BLUE MOUNDS, WISCONSIN

(608) 437-3038

www.caveofthemounds.com

Location: About 171 miles NW of Chicago

Description: One-hour tours of the roughly 1,700-foot-long cave, about 20 miles west of Madison are decidedly tame, all upright walking along a paved walkway through lit rooms. What makes this cave unusual is its bright colors, with hues of orange and black thanks to the heavy concentration of iron and manganese. Plus the owners have resisted over-commercializing the cave, which was named a National Natural Landmark in 1988. Though most Chicago cavers don't point their cars north, for more Dairy State caves see the book *Wisconsin Underground* by Doris Green.

Directions: Take I-90 west past Rockford and Janesville. Take US 12/18 west around Madison, exit for US 18/151 west toward Dodgeville. Go about 25 miles on US 18/151, past Mt. Horeb. Cave of the Mounds Rd. is some 6 miles past Mt. Horeb. Turn right (north) on Cave of the Mounds Rd. The cave is roughly 1 mile north of US 18/151.

WYANDOTTE CAVES STATE RECREATION AREA, LEAVENWORTH, INDIANA

(812) 738-2782

www.state.in.us/dnr/forestry/property/wyandtcv.htm

Caving

Location: About 326 miles S of Chicago

Description: Some 25 miles of passages to explore. The 4- or 5-hour Pillar of the Constitution guided spelunking tour has plenty of crawling, climbing, and steep hills; you need a chest of 46 inches or less to squeeze through the aptly named Straits at the end. Highlights: the 145-foot-long elliptical Senate Chamber holds the Pillar itself, an enormous fluted column (the result of a stalactite and stalagmite grown together) of white calcite 25 feet in diameter and 35 feet high. The federally endangered Indiana bat hibernates in the Little and Big Wyandotte Caves from November through March. There's an all-day spelunking tour, but it's mostly just walking. Call ahead for reservations.

Directions: Take I-90/-94 east. Stay on I-90 east into Indiana. Take the I-65/US 12/Dunes Highway/US 20 exit 17 toward Indianapolis. Stay on I-65 south to just north of Louisville. Take the I-64/I-265 exit west. Go west on I-64 about 25 miles. Take exit 105 for IN 135 south. Follow IN 135 south to IN 62 west. Take IN 62 west about 10 miles to the caves.

MARENGO CAVES, MARENGO, INDIANA

(812) 365-2705

www.marengocave.com

Location: About 332 miles S of Chicago

Description: The strenuous 5-hour New Discovery trip traverses undeveloped areas of the cave first uncovered in 1992. Prepare to crawl, haul, squirm, and slosh in the 52° stream. Underground waterfalls abound. Squeeze your way through Blowing Bat Crawl, with the circumference of a big lamp shade. There are also shorter, less muddy trips in the cave's developed sections, along the sodastraw-strewn

Dripstone Trail or speleothem-stuffed Crystal Palace room, complete with cheesy lightshow. Call 2 weeks ahead to reserve a spot on the undeveloped trips.

Directions: Take I-90/-94 east. Stay on I-90 east into Indiana. Take the I-65/US 12/Dunes Highway/US 20 exit 17 toward Indianapolis. Stay on I-65 south to just north of Louisville. Take the I-64/I-265 exit west. Go west on I-64 about 2 miles to exit 118/IN 64 for Georgetown. Follow IN 64 west about 25 miles to the park entrance.

MAMMOTH CAVE NATIONAL PARK, MAMMOTH CAVE, KENTUCKY

(800) 967-2283

www.nps.gov/maca

Location: About 388 miles S of Chicago

Description: With more than 350 miles of surveyed passageways, Mammoth Cave is at least three times longer than any cave known on the planet. Incredibly, geologists estimate that there could be as many as 600 more miles yet to be plotted. The park has been declared a World Heritage Site and International Biosphere Reserve, with some 200 animal species taking up residence—including 42 troglobites adapted exclusively to underground life without light. The cave system shelters three endangered species, the Kentucky cave shrimp, Indiana bat, and gray bat.

Formations galore, including dry formations like gypsum needles and flowers, which curl like white and gold icing from the cave walls. Echo River runs 360 feet below the surface. The wild cave tour runs 6 to 6.5 hours and covers 5.5 miles. Shorter tours are also available along 14 miles of developed cave trails. Call in advance for caving tour reservations. Developed and backcountry camping in the rugged hills sliced by the Green River. Above-ground hiking, paddling, horseback riding, and fishing.

Directions: Follow I-90/-94 east. Stay on I-90 east into Indiana. Take the I-65/US 12/Dunes Highway/US 20 exit 17 toward Indianapolis. Continue on I-65 south past Indianapolis into Kentucky. Take exit 53 at Cave City. Drive about 15 minutes west on KY 70 to the park entrance.

Permits?

IT MAY BE possible to obtain a permit from the city's department of transportation to (legally) visit the Chicago freight tunnel system under the Loop, though it's not yet clear how open the process is to purely recreational visitors. Not surprisingly, it requires a ton of paperwork and decoding of legal jargon. Plus about $50. For details, contact the city's Department of Law at (312) 744-0223. Just don't tell them who sent you.

Where to Connect

Clubs and Organizations

- Windy City Grotto (www.caves.org/grotto/wcg/) is the larger of the two Chicago-area groups. The grotto meets monthly at Aurelio's Pizzeria in Addison (it may return to its former meeting place, at the Field Museum, once construction in the area is finished), maintains a caving library, and puts out *Windy City Speleonews*. The grotto celebrated its 50th anniversary in 2001, making it one of the country's oldest. Regular beginner to advanced trips to southern Illinois, Indiana, Kentucky, and "TAG" territory, a caving hot spot around where Tennessee, Alabama, and Georgia meet (some joint trips with Sub-Urban Chicago Grotto, below). The group is also involved in helping preserve and study bats in local green spaces. For the past several years, Windy City members have helped map caves used by the Maya in Belize.

- Sub-Urban Chicago Grotto (http://hometown.aol.com /GGibula/SUCG.html) is chaired by Gary Gibula, a long-time caver and former president of the Windy City Grotto. The club meets monthly at Connie's Pizza on IL 59 in Aurora and is open to the public. Members receive *Sub-Urban Troglo-News*. Regular beginner to advanced trips throughout the region.

- National Speleological Society (www.caves.org)

- National Caves Association (www.cavern.com)

Book

- Green, Doris. *Wisconsin Underground*: *A Guide to Caves, Mines, and Tunnels in and around the Badger State*. Black Earth, WI: Trails Books, 2000.

THE CITY SOFTENS in a decent snowfall. Sounds seem muffled. Hard angles arc. The saddest, scraggliest tree looks lush, boughs full. Fast-food wrappers, newspapers, cigarette butts, and other urban detritus disappear under a downy blanket.

Sure, people get crazy, hauling out lawn chairs and other obstacles to mark "their" parking spot on public streets (Hate It). But they also get playful, filling otherwise quiet city parks, sticking a tongue out for snowflakes, throwing snowballs, hurling themselves down any bump that passes for a sledding hill. And parka-clad crowds on the verge of giddiness strap on skis to make tracks.

As of this writing, the city was grooming four

lakefront golf courses for cross-country skiing. If you're willing to blaze your own way, you can hit any city park or greenspace with snow on it. Try Lincoln Park, Columbus Park, Washington Park, or Humboldt Park for starters.

Same goes for Cook County Forest Preserve trails, which are ungroomed except for Camp Sagawau, the city's backyard Nordic headquarters. Refer to the "Hiking," "Mountain Biking", and "Biking" chapters to maximize your choices: solid, scenic metro-area picks include Palos and Deer Grove in Cook County, Waterfall Glen in DuPage County, and Des Plaines River Trail in Lake County. Trails at Indian Dunes National Lakeshore, just over an hour train ride from downtown, are open to snowshoeing with a base of 6 inches or more. Glorious.

While local TV newscasters gloat about our increasingly mild winters, city skiers have grown increasingly depressed with the paltry snow offerings. Bob Richards, a local outdoors writer and longtime cross-country ski racer, says 20 years ago there used to be eight or nine ski races in Chicago. Now that's dwindled to just a handful because the white stuff is so much less reliable. The Lakeshore Loppet at Waveland golf course, a onetime city staple that routinely drew hundreds of racers, died out in the mid '80s. But there are a couple solid *Backyard* options here for when the snow gods smile.

And happily, several impeccably groomed options lie just a few hours north of the city; Lapham Peak and McMiller trails in Wisconsin's Kettle Moraine State Forest are gems. The woods help hold the snow long after it's turned to black slush and melted away in the city. Venture farther north to *Meccas* like the legendary American Birkebeiner Ski Trail and your rewards are fresh powder and thick North Woods forest.

"Length" in this chapter refers to total trail miles available, to give you maximum options in places where there isn't just one standout trail (particularly challenging or scenic options are highlighted).

While this chapter focuses on cross-country skiing, it also gives the skinny on other ways to get your snow fix: luge and toboggan runs, ski jumps, ice rinks, and downhill skiing/snowboarding.

Many thanks to Bob Richards for his time and wisdom. And to Phil Van Valkenberg and William Semion for the great information in their *Winter Trails* books. Wax up and have fun.

City Limits

WAVELAND GOLF COURSE AND LAKEFRONT

Location: 3700 N and a few other close-to-downtown options

Length: Variable. Don't expect more than a few miles at each spot, if that. But you've got some 18 miles of virtually uninterrupted lakefront parkland to blaze if you're up for it.

Difficulty: Easy, except when The Hawk (wind) is ripping off the lake in your face

Map: "Chicago's Lakefront" map from Chicago Park District (312-747-2474).

Dogs: Not on groomed trails

Snowmobiles: No

Rentals: See Shops in *Where to Connect* for metro-area rentals. And there was talk of the Park District reviving its lakefront ski rentals (312-742-PLAY, www.chicagoparkdistrict .com).

Heads up: Call the Park District before setting out; policies shift like the wind, and the spots they groom may well change by the time you read this book.

Description: The area around the Waveland clock tower and golf course (formally the Sydney R. Marovitz Golf Course) is one of four spots the city groomed as of this writing, all of them golf courses—or golf-course-like—with wide-open, fairly flat space. Their advantages, however, are clear. You can hop out for a quick ski before or after work or at lunch. Best advice: warm up on the groomed trails, then strike out alongside the Lakefront Trail (see "Running," page 443, and "Biking," page 215) and ski as far as you want. The city usually clears snow from the path itself for cyclists and runners. Anytime there's a decent dump in the city, you'll see skiers blazing trail along the lakefront parks flanking the Big—Very Cold—Blue. Other groomed city spots: Grant Park by Daley Bicentennial Plaza Fieldhouse, 337 E. Randolph St. (closest to downtown); Jackson Park Golf Course at Lake Shore Dr. and Hayes Dr. off 63d St.; Diversey Driving Range in Lincoln Park, 141 W. Diversey Parkway.

Directions: To Waveland, exit Lake Shore Dr. at Irving Park Rd. Go east on Irving Park (it dead-ends at the golf course fence) and follow the park road to the right, past the tennis courts into the parking lot.

To Jackson Park, take Lake Shore Dr. to 63d St./Hayes Dr. exit. Stay west on Hayes to the golf course. There's nearby street parking.

Hit the Ice

THE CITY RUNS nine outdoor ice rinks and offers low-cost Saturday morning lessons at Daley Bicentennial Plaza downtown (337 E. Randolph St., 312-742-7650). The newest addition: a rink at the hugely over-budget Millennium Park downtown (55 N. Michigan Ave., 312-742-PLAY). Rentals available at both downtown rinks.

Neighborhood rinks:

- Warren Park, 6601 N. Western Ave., (312) 742-6600
- Riis Park, 6100 W. Fullerton Ave., (312) 746-5735
- McKinley Park, 2210 W. Pershing Rd., (312) 747-5992
- West Lawn Park, 4233 W. 65th St., (312) 747-8500
- Midway Plaisance, Woodlawn Ave. at 59th St., (312) 747-0233
- Mt. Greenwood Park, 3721 W. 111th St., (312) 747-3690
- Rowan Park, 11546 S. Avenue L. (312) 747-8880

Backyard

CAMP SAGAWAU

Location: About 27 miles SW of Chicago

Length: 4 miles of groomed and tracked trails (loops)

Difficulty: Easy to moderate

Maps: Available on site

Dogs: No

Snowmobiles: No

Rentals: Nordic and skate ski rentals in the old farmhouse. Get there early, rentals stop at 3 P.M.

Heads up: Camp Sagawau is 4 miles west of the Swallow Cliff toboggan slides (see *Scream*, page 413).

Description: Chicago Nordic Central. Impeccably groomed, well-marked, one-way loop trails run through predominant white oak forest and prairie in the Palos and Sag Valley Forest Preserves. Stop by the farmhouse to pick up a free trail pass. Several free clinics, low-cost beginner to advanced lessons in classic and skate skiing from certified instructors. One-hour guided skis with a park naturalist Sunday afternoons. Free intro lessons and short freestyle

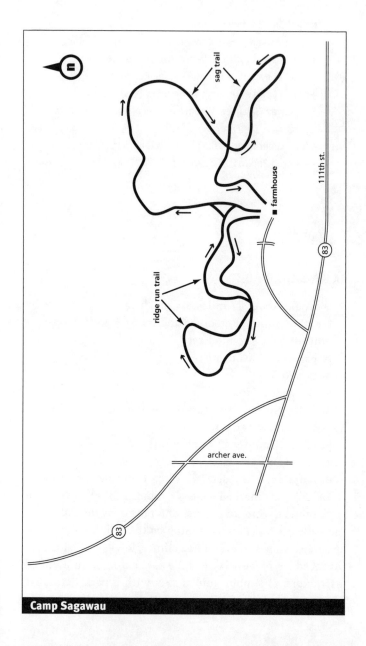

N

sag trail

farmhouse

111th st.

83

ridge run trail

archer ave.

83

Camp Sagawau

sprint during Ski Fest, usually in early January. Call (630) 257-2045 for details.

Route: Newbies should stick to the gentle 4-km Sag Trail. The rolling 2.5-km Ridge Run is for intermediates and up. If you have your own skis, you can pick up any snowy trail (ungroomed) in the 14,000-acre Palos and Sag Valley Forest Preserves (see "Hiking & Backpacking," page 330, and "Mountain Biking," page 271).

Directions: Take I-55 south to Kingery Rd./IL 83. Go south on IL 83 for five stoplights. At the fifth light (111th St.), turn left (east). After about 100 yards turn left into the entrance for Camp Sagawau.

Scream

SCREAMED MYSELF HOARSE the first time I flew down the roughly 100-foot-high, 900-foot-long Swallow Cliff toboggan slides. Nuff said: it's crazy fun. The Cook County Forest Preserve district operates slides in four spots (Swallow Cliff is steepest) from 10 A.M. to 10 P.M. when conditions permit. You can rent the wooden toboggans for $3 an hour; if you've got your own and it passes muster—and fits the track—it's a buck for the day.

Here's where to find the slides:

- Swallow Cliff, IL 83 west of Mannheim Rd./IL 45 in Palos Park, (708) 448-4417
- Jensen Slides, Devon and Milwaukee Aves., near North Branch Trail, in Chicago, (773) 631-7657
- Bemis Woods, Ogden Ave. west of Wolf Rd. in Western Springs, (708) 246-8366
- Deer Grove 5, Quentin Rd. north of Dundee Rd. in Palatine, (847) 381-7868

ARROWHEAD GOLF CLUB AND HERRICK LAKE FOREST PRESERVE

Location: About 27 miles W of Chicago

Length: Usually 5 miles of groomed loop trails, plus about 6.5 miles ungroomed, or lightly groomed, in Herrick Lake Forest Preserve

Difficulty: Easy

Maps: Trail maps from Wheaton Park District (630-653-5800) at the clubhouse.

Dogs: No

Snowmobiles: No

Rentals: On-site ski rentals and lessons available through Wheaton Park District

Heads up: Regular ski and skate ski clinics here. Roughly 3-mile snowshoe trail. No trail fees. For another quality DuPage County spot, head to occasionally groomed Waterfall Glen (see "Mountain Biking," page 276).

Description: I'm usually biased against golf course skiing, but Bob Richards, who organizes the 11K Northern Illinois Nordic race here the second Saturday in January, swears by Arrowhead's merits. Terrain is rolling, not pancake flat, and the one-way loop trails offer up nice twists and turns. Grooming—for diagonal stride or skating—is top notch and draws plenty of training racers. Extend your ski by taking on the largely ungroomed trails in adjacent 767-acre Herrick Lake preserve, through oak woodlands, meadows, wetlands, and prairie.

Directions: Take I-290 west to I-88 west. Exit at Naperville Rd. and follow it north to Butterfield Rd. Turn left (west) on Butterfield and follow for 1.5 miles to the golf course entrance. Ski rentals are in the clubhouse.

Jump

WORD ASSOCIATION. I say ski jumping, you say . . . Fox River Grove? Turns out the Chicago burb nestled in the Fox River valley is home to the nation's oldest continuous Nordic ski jumping club, catching air since 1905 (www.norgeskiclub.com). They've got jumps set up at 5, 10, 20, 40, and 64 meters (that's a 120-foot-high tower).

The Norge Ski Club has 120 or so members, plus about 40 kids who are coached twice a week by people like Scott Smith, a member of the U.S. Ski Team in the 1980s. The club holds two annual tournaments—the third Sunday in January and September—but they jump year-round, landing on plastic made super slick by sprinklers in the heat of summer. If you want a taste of the high life, you can rent the Nordic skis, boots, jump suit, and helmet (providing there's enough equipment to go around) and get lessons at the club. Special events hotline at (847) 639-9718.

Short Hops

ROCK CUT STATE PARK

Location: About 86 miles NW of Chicago

Length: 12–15 groomed miles (loops)

Difficulty: Easy to moderate

Maps: Rough trail map available at the park (815-885-3311). There was talk of marking the unnamed trails by their popular names as referred to in Route, below. Check www.ninordic.org for online trail map. All BSH (Bike, Ski, Hiking) trails open to skiing.

Dogs: Yes

Snowmobiles: Only on designated equestrian/snowmobile trail

Rentals: See Shops in *Where to Connect* for metro-area rentals.

Description: A top Illinois ski site, just outside Rockford. "You really get the sensation of being much farther north than you are," says Bob Richards of Northern Illinois Nordic. The main connecting trail runs atop an unplowed park road. But most trails through the rolling hills of this 3,092-acre park are 8 feet wide, bringing you close to the meadows and hardwood and pine forest. Sightings of deer, wild turkey, owls, and hawks are common here. At dusk, watch for the occasional coyote or fox. Decent hills and turns requiring some skill.

Route: Beginners should head to the fairly level 2.25-mile Vasa Loop (marked BSH) through native prairie in the northeast corner of the park. For hills, head to the West Lake picnic area off the southwest end of Pierce Lake. Or do a roughly 5.5-mile loop around Pierce Lake, starting from Lions Club picnic area, heading north up the park road paralleling I-90 (humping up locally named Tollway Hill), west on the Hart Road trail, south on the ski trail, crossing Willow Creek, and east back to Lions Club through the maples and pines.

Directions: Follow I-90 west for roughly 80 miles to the E. Riverside Blvd. exit. Stay left at the fork at the end of the ramp. Turn left (west) on Riverside. Turn right (north) on Perryville Rd. and then right (west) on Harlem Rd. Use the Harlem Rd. entrance to the park, on the west side of the street.

MORAINE HILLS STATE PARK

Location: About 50 miles NW of Chicago
Length: 9 miles groomed loops
Difficulty: Moderate

Map: Rough trail map available at the park (815-385-1624)

Dogs: Yes

Snowmobiles: No

Rentals: When snow permits, on-site rentals weekends only at McHenry Dam concession (815-385-8272) on the west side of the park. Other options: McHenry Favorite Sport Center (1210 N. Green St. 815-385-1000) in McHenry; Crystal Lake Ski & Bike (corner of Virginia and Pyott Rds., 815-455-5450) in Crystal Lake.

Heads up: About 12 miles to the north, DuPage County's Glacial Park Conservation Area (815-338-6223) has 4–6 miles of lightly groomed, hilly trails. Plus a sledding hill and warming center.

Description: You've got three main connecting loop trails through the 1,690-acre park's lakes, wetlands, wooded hills, and ridges, courtesy of the gravel-rich kames from the last glacier. The one-way color-coded trails are fairly wide with some nice climbs for the Chicago area. Watch for deer, possum, red fox, and coyote in the upland forest of hickory, ash, cherry, hawthorn, dogwood, and oak.

Route: If you've only got time for a short loop, take the quiet, 3-plus-mile Leatherleaf Bog Trail (blue) around the namesake floating mat of sphagnum moss and leatherleaf. For more miles, add the nearly 4-mile Lake Defiance Trail (red) around the 48-acre glacial lake and the 2-mile Fox River Trail (yellow), which runs closest to the ski rental concession at McHenry Dam.

Directions: Take I-90 west to IL 53 north. Stay on IL 53 north until the US 12/Rand Rd. exit. Turn left (west) on Rand Rd. At IL 176/Liberty St. go left (west). Stay on IL 176 until River Rd. Bear right (north) on River Rd. The second park entrance on McHenry Dam Rd. leads to the weekend ski rentals.

LOVE CREEK COUNTY PARK, MICHIGAN

Location: About 95 miles E of Chicago

Length: Roughly 5 miles groomed loop trails, some for skating

Difficulty: Easy to moderate

Maps: Trailboard at trailhead; maps available from Love Creek County Park (616-471-2617, www.berriencounty .org/parks/).

Dogs: No

Snowmobiles: No

Rentals: On-site weekends and for night ski events; weekdays Tuesday–Friday afternoons.

Heads up: Trails lit for night skiing Saturdays until 9:30 P.M. Check the park Web site or call for trail conditions and details. $5 car permit; $2 daily trail fee, $10 annual.

Description: Just outside Berrien Springs, MI, this 150-acre park seems meteorologically disposed to get early lake-effect snow when Chicago is still barren. Reason enough for the quick sojourn. Come for rolling trail through mature beech-maple forest and old fields along the Love Creek Valley.

Route: Pick any of the well-marked, interconnecting loops. The 2.5-mile Red Trail is toughest; 2.5-mile Yellow is groomed for skate and classical; 1.5-mile Green is intermediate; 0.75-mile Orange is beginner.

Directions: Take I-94 east to US 31. Follow US 31 south across the St. Joseph River to Old 31 in Berrien Springs. Shortly after crossing the river, turn left (northeast) on Deans Hill Rd. Take an immediate right onto Pokagon Rd. Follow signs to the park entrance.

KETTLE MORAINE STATE FOREST, SOUTH UNIT, WISCONSIN

Location: About 90 miles N of Chicago

Length: 50-plus groomed miles spread over three trail systems: Scuppernong (11.5 miles), Nordic (22.3 miles), and McMiller (17.3 miles).

Difficulty: Easy to difficult. Beginner options are limited.

Maps and book: Maps available at trailheads, *Winter Trails Wisconsin*.

Dogs: No

Snowmobiles: Only on designated trails, not on ski trails

Rentals: La Grange General Store (US 12 and County H; 262-495-8600) in La Grange rents skis and snowshoes. Quiet Hut (186 W. Main St., 262-473-2950) in Whitewater also rents both.

Heads up: Nordic nirvana within 2 hours drive of the city. Don't miss McMiller trails—classic tough stuff. Classic and skating. Trail conditions at (262) 594-6202. Nonresident vehicle sticker $30 annual, $10 day. Snowshoeing on multiuse trails.

Description: The sheer bounty is enough to delight. But the quality is enough to make a Chicago skier swoon. Serpentine twists and turns punctuated by straightaways through hardwood and pine forest buckled by serious glacial hills. All trails are marked, one-way interconnected loops so you never have to backtrack unless you want to. Scuppernong Ski & Hiking Trail is classic ski only (the other two are classic and skating). Watch for deer. Too much to detail here; below you'll find general loop ratings and highlights. If you're a skilled skier, the McMiller Blue Trail should not be missed. The McMiller trail system was originally designed for ski racers, with long training loops and sweeping uphills and descents. Hit the fireplace at the

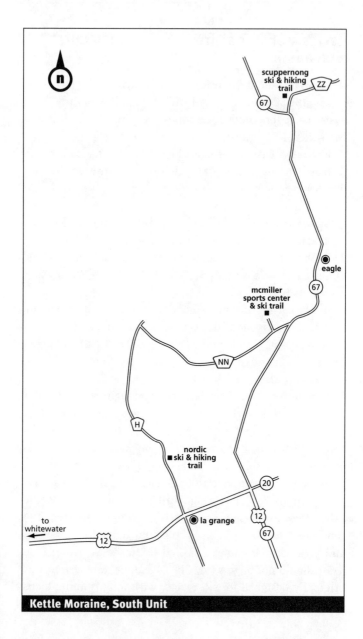

Kettle Moraine, South Unit

McMiller Sports Center warming shelter après ski (weekends only).

Route, Scuppernong Ski & Hiking Trail: Beginners and anyone wanting to avoid a nasty downhill at the end of the trail where the Green and Orange trails meet should stick to the 2.3-mile Red Loop. The 4.2-mile Orange Loop is intermediate, the 0.5-mile Green Loop advanced with a roller coaster at the end. All trails have a backwoods feel.

Nordic Ski & Hiking Trail: The 2.5-mile intermediate Red Loop goes over old farm pastures interrupted by four steep hills; 3.1-mile intermediate Orange Loop is mostly rolling, open trail with great views and some steep sections; 3.2-mile White Loop is a nice, flat, open beginner loop skirting the edge of the woods through scattered pines; 4.3-mile Green Loop, intermediate, cuts through deep forest; 9.2-mile Blue Loop is advanced, especially the back loop.

McMiller ski trails: All loops are intermediate and up: 1.7-mile Red Loop, 2.4-mile Orange Loop, 3.1-mile White Loop, 3.7-mile Green Loop. The 6.4-mile Blue Loop is considered the forest's toughest, starting out an easy rolling glide through the pines, moving into upland hardwood forest with steep, twisting 50- to 70-foot climbs and descents, a brief stint through open prairie, another mile of lung-busting ascents, past an old farm on flats, and then back to 2 miles of ridge hugging and a killer 140-foot climb. The last 0.3 mile let your quaking quads recover on flatlands as you round the back of the shooting range.

Directions: For the Nordic Ski & Hiking Trail, take I-94 west to WI 50 at Kenosha. Go left (west) on WI 50 to US 12, just before Lake Geneva. Follow US 12 north to County H by La Grange General Store. Turn north (right) onto County H. The Nordic Ski & Hiking Trail parking lot is about 1.5 miles on the right.

For McMiller trails, from the intersection of US 12 and WI 67, take WI 67 N until you hit County NN. Turn left (west) on County NN. The parking lot for McMiller Sports Center is about 0.75 mile on the right.

For Scuppernong Ski & Hiking Trail, take WI 67 north through the town of Eagle. At County ZZ, go right (east). The parking lot is on the left.

KETTLE MORAINE STATE FOREST, NORTH UNIT, WISCONSIN

Location: About 150 miles N of Chicago

Length: 17 groomed miles (loops): 9 miles at Greenbush, 8 miles at Zillmer trails

Difficulty: Easy to difficult

Maps and book: Maps available at trailheads, *Winter Trails Wisconsin.*

Dogs: No

Snowmobiles: Only on designated trails; some intersections with ski trails

Rentals: Crossroads Gallery and Crafts (920-533-8866) at the intersection of WI 45 and WI 67 just outside Campbellsport rents skis, Thursday–Saturday only. Parkview General Store off County GGG at Mauthe Lake (262-626-8287, www.parkview-store.com) rents skis and snowshoes.

Heads up: Superlative snowshoeing along an ungroomed 31-mile segment of the Ice Age National Scenic Trail with winter camping possibilities at Adirondack-style shelters along the way (see "Hiking & Backpacking," page 345). Heated log shelter and sledding hill at Greenbush area. Nonresident vehicle sticker $30 annual, $10 day. Trail conditions: Northern Kettle Moraine Ski Club hotline, (920) 467-2099; State Forest office (262) 626-2116; Ice Age Visitor Center (920) 533-8322.

Description: Even if there's no snow in Sheboygan, there's usually enough of the white stuff around Greenbush and its

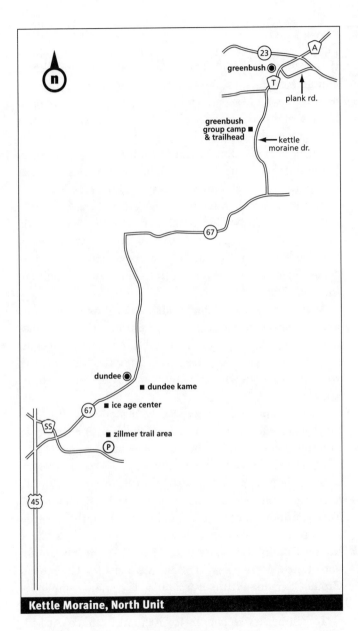

Kettle Moraine, North Unit

excellent trails. "People say there's a microclimate there. I'm not sure if it's myth or reality, but something works there," says ski addict Bob Richards of Northern Illinois Nordic. Rugged, hilly, interconnected loop trails cut through dense red oak and sugar maple forest, jack pine stands, open kettles, and marshland. A local ski club keeps Greenbush trails groomed like a prized show dog for classic and skating, luring hard-core skiers up from the city (there's a donation box at the shelter that helps fund the club's efforts). Zillmer trails are groomed somewhat less zealously and tend to attract more families and novice skiers. But there are definitely enough hills—and a 100-foot drop—on the 5.4-mile Yellow Trail to challenge high-level skiers. Plus views of Dundee Kame, a conical hill plunked down by debris deposited by meltwater running into funnel-shaped holes in the glacial ice.

Route, Greenbush hiking, biking and skiing trails: Four loops: 5.1-mile Purple (advanced); 3.6-mile Green (intermediate); 1.5-mile Red (intermediate); 0.7-mile Pink (beginner/intermediate). Beware: skiers have the right of way with crossing snowmobiles, but not all drivers seem to know it.

Zillmer hiking and skiing trails: Four loops: 5.4-mile Yellow (advanced), 3-mile Red (intermediate), 1.8-mile Green (intermediate), 1.2-mile Blue (beginner/intermediate).

Directions: To Greenbush trails, take I-94 west to Milwaukee. In Milwaukee, take I-43 north to Sheboygan. At Sheboygan, take WI 23 west about 17 miles to County A. Turn south on County A and follow for 0.5 mile to a stop sign in the village of Greenbush. Go straight across Plank Rd. on County T for just under 1 mile. Turn left (south) onto Kettle Moraine Dr. Follow the signs for Greenbush Group Camp for a little over a mile. The group camp lot is on the right.

To Zillmer trails, take I-94 west to Milwaukee. At Milwaukee, take US 45 north. At WI 67 go right (east) to County SS. Turn right (south) on County SS until you hit the trailhead parking on your left.

KETTLE MORAINE STATE FOREST, LAPHAM PEAK UNIT, WISCONSIN

Location: About 114 miles N of Chicago

Length: 17 miles groomed (classic and skate) and ungroomed trails

Difficulty: Easy to difficult. Most options are for intermediate skiers and up; some downhills have signs posted telling novices to remove their skis.

Maps and book: Maps available at trailheads, *Winter Trails Wisconsin*.

Dogs: No

Snowmobiles: No

Rentals: When snow permits, snowshoes and classic and skating skis available on-site Tuesday and Thursday evenings and weekends—any other time head directly to Bicycle Doctor Nordic Ski Shop (105 N. Main St. 262-965-4144) in Dousman.

Heads up: A Must-Ski spot. Night skiing until 10 P.M. Monday–Saturday on 2-mile Meadow Trail. Out-of-state vehicle sticker $10 day, $30 year; $3 day trail pass, $10 year. Trail condition hotline (262) 646-4421; park office (262) 646-3025. Races abound in January/February. Candlelight ski tours. Snowshoe on multiuse and Ice Age trails.

Description: Lapham Peak offers Birkie-level challenge on great groomed trails. Pumped full of Scandanavian and German ancestral blood, Wisconsinites are serious about their skiing, with seemingly every town supporting a Nordic ski club. Families and racers alike flock to Lapham, 25 miles west of Milwaukee, in Delafield, for some of the

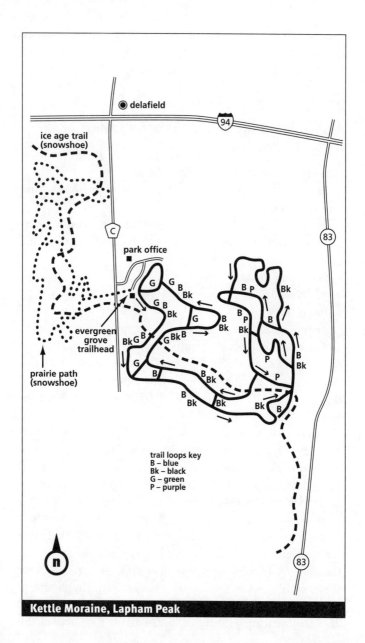

delafield

ice age trail
(snowshoe)

94

83

C

park office

prairie path
(snowshoe)

evergreen
grove
trailhead

G G B
    B Bk
G B
    Bk   G

B P   Bk

B Bk   B P   B
G Bk B   Bk   B
    G   P   Bk
Bk G B   B
    G
    B   B Bk   P
        B Bk   P
    B   Bk Bk Bk   B
    Bk

trail loops key
B – blue
Bk – black
G – green
P – purple

83

n

Kettle Moraine, Lapham Peak

best skiing around. Fast downhills. Two trails, Kettle View and Moraine Ridge, climb to the top of the forest's 1,233-foot ridgetop—southeast Wisconsin's highest peak. Increase A. Lapham, considered the father of the U.S. Weather Bureau, used the peak to receive meteorological data from Pikes Peak in Colorado to predict storms and help avert shipwrecks in Great Lakes ports. Warming shelters at Meadow Trail trailhead and ridgetop in the thick pines.

Route: Four loops. Easy, flat to rolling 2-mile Meadow Trail (green) and 2-mile Kame Terrace Trail (purple). Watch for merging skiers screaming down trails that climb the ridgetop: moderate 5.8-mile Kettle View Trail (blue) and difficult 7-mile Moraine Ridge (black).

Directions: Take I-94 west to exit 285/County C. Go south on County C about 1 mile to the park entrance. Turn left (east) for the park office. Ski rentals are near the red barn in the Evergreen Grove parking area to the right after passing the park office.

Meccas

AMERICAN BIRKEBEINER SKI TRAIL, WISCONSIN

Location: About 400 miles N of Chicago

Length: About 24 miles one way (point-to-point trail)

Difficulty: Difficult. Hills, hills, hills—some steep baddies

Maps and book: Call the Birkie office (715-634-5025) or pick up maps at the Hayward or Cable chambers of commerce or area ski shops. *Winter Trails Wisconsin.*

Dogs: No

Snowmobiles: No

Rentals: Telemark Resort (877-798-4718) in Cable rents

a wide range of skis and snowshoes, plus lessons. In Hayward, New Moon Ski Shop (800-754-8685 or 715-634-8685) rents skis and snowshoes. Both towns are packed with ski shops: check in with the chamber of commerce in Cable (800-533-7454) or Hayward (800-724-2992).

Heads up: Umpteen quality ski options near the Birkie and throughout northwestern Wisconsin, including Telemark Resort trails. See www.norwiski.com for detailed trail descriptions, updated conditions, and links. Birkie trail conditions at (715) 643-5025 ext. 50 or www.birkie.com. Night skiing sections at County OO trailhead in Seeley and Fish Hatchery Park in Hayward. $5 day, $30 annual parking fee for all but North End trailhead, which has a donation box.

Description: Cross-country autobahn. This trail is home to North America's largest cross-country ski marathon (see *Big Bad Birkie* below). It's among the most challenging trails around with unrelenting hills. It's also gorgeous, cutting a slice through Wisconsin's pristine North Woods, crossing only three paved roads along its entire length. The two-way trail runs through Bayfield and Sawyer County Forests but is impeccably maintained and groomed (skating and diagonal stride with one set of tracks on each side) by the American Birkebeiner Ski Foundation. Other than on race day, there's plenty of room to maneuver—it's about 30 feet wide and designed to hold as many as three skiers across.

Route: Ski point-to-point from either end. The toughest hills are in the 4.8-mile stretch from North End trailhead to the elevation marker at the trail's high point, 1,200 feet—a popular shorter ski. It makes for a fun return trip as the uphill-to-downhill ratio turns in your favor. The hills continue after you hit the trail midpoint at County OO in Seeley, but they're more forgiving. Heated shelters at North End trailhead in Cable, County 00 trailhead in Seeley, and Fish Hatchery Park in Hayward at the south trailhead. Hayward has another trailhead at Mosquito Brook Rd.

Directions: Take I-90 west to Madison. From Madison, stay on I-94 north. In Eau Claire, take US 53 north. At Trego, take US 63 northeast into Cable. For the North End trailhead, turn east on County M and follow about 0.2 mile. Watch for the trailhead sign across from the library and natural history museum. Turn right (south) on Randysek Rd. (unsigned) and drive 2 miles to the North End trailhead parking area on the east side of the road.

Big Bad Birkie

N THE NORTH Woods winter of 1973, 35 skiers raced from Hayward to Cable to create their own version of a Norweigian race celebrating the 13th-century Viking warriors—called Birkebeiners for their birch-bark leggings—who saved the country's infant prince from invaders by skiing 55 km to safety.

Today the 51-km American Birkebeiner ski marathon and 23-km Kortelopet (half race) draw more than 6,500 racers from around the world in late February for a 3-day blowout. Not surprisingly, the Norweigan contingent is strong. Some 20,000 spectators come to gawk. And 1,500-plus kids, some as young as 3 years old, stride in the noncompetitive Barnebirkie. There's also a 2.5-km Junior Birkie for 10- to 15-year-olds.

The main event starts at Telemark Resort in Cable; skiers cross the finish line on Hayward's Main St. Hoopla includes ski equipment demos, seminars, citizen and elite sprints, family races, and mass spaghetti feeds. Details from the American Birkebeiner Ski Foundation (715-634-5025, www.birkie.com).

MINOCQUA WINTER PARK AND NORDIC CENTER, WISCONSIN

Location: About 347 miles N of Chicago

Length: 47 groomed miles (skate and traditional loops)

Difficulty: Easy to difficult

Map and book: Trail map available at the day chalet or at (715) 356-3309; *Winter Trails Wisconsin*.

Dogs: No on ski trails; yes on snowshoe trails.

Snowmobiles: No

Rentals: Full-service ski shop on site; rents skate and traditional skis, snowshoes. Certified ski school (715-356-1099).

Heads up: Trails closed Wednesdays. Daily trail pass Monday–Thursday $7, Friday–Sunday $10; season passes available. Open telemark slopes. Groomed snowshoe trails and three specially groomed kids' loops. Snow report/trail conditions at www.skimwp.org.

Description: Tucked in a region blanketed with 3,200 lakes and the Northern Highland American Legion State Forest, Minocqua has 25 intertwining loop trails cutting through white cedar and pines, including some trails reserved just for traditional striding. Lakeland Ski Touring Foundation runs the place; grooming is impeccable. Most trails are rated "more difficult," though there are eight "easiest" trails and five "most difficult." The tough 6.5-km Nutcracker Trail is a classic, wringing maximum challenge from steep glacial ridges, throwing in several killer turns for good measure. Beware this trail in icy conditions unless you're a pro. Bonus: wolves are active in the area.

Directions: Take I-90 west past Madison to I-39/US 51 north. Stay on US 51 north until you hit Minocqua. From Minocqua, go west on WI 70 for about 8 miles. Turn left (south) on Squirrel Lake Rd. and continue about 6 miles. Turn left (east) on Scotchman's Lake Rd. After about 0.5

mile you'll turn right (south) on Minocqua Winter Park Dr. Follow it to the chalet lot.

ACTIVE BACKWOODS RETREATS (ABR) TRAILS, MICHIGAN

Location: About 400 miles N of Chicago

Length: 25 groomed miles (skate and traditional loops)

Difficulty: Easy to difficult

Maps and book: Trail maps available at the warming lodge. *Winter Trails Michigan*.

Dogs: No

Snowmobiles: No

Rentals: Traditional and skate skis, snowshoes on-site

Heads up: Early-season skiing, usually November, though they've gotten lake-effect dumps in October, too. Conditions updated daily at (906) 932-3502, www.michiweb .com/abrski. Daily trail pass $5 (early season $8), 10-punch pass $50, season pass $70. There's a 4-mile snowshoe trail and warming lodge with sauna—aaah.

Description: Serious skiers are on the ABR e-mail list, ready to pile into the car and head north to Ironwood in the fall when owners Dave and Eric Anderson say the magic words ("We're open"). Conditions usually stay good into April; trails are often groomed daily. Biggest climbs and drops, most fairly gradual, run in the 200-foot range. The Upper Peninsula trails cover 400 acres of private land strewn with aspen, hemlock, maple, and Norway pines crisscrossed by streambeds trickling into the Montreal River basin. Some trails follow the river, run over a cedar swamp via boardwalk, or cut through a clutch of 150-year-old white pines passed up by loggers. Popular beginner trails: aptly named Easy Trail or flat Jack Pine Trail. Sunset Trail for intermediates. River Trail for advanced skiers, with Popple Plunge, dropping 150 feet into an aspen grove. Night skiing by headlamp the first and third Tuesday of the month. Moonlight skis once a month.

Directions: Take I-90 west past Madison to I-39/US 51 north. Stay on US 51 north to Ironwood. From US 2 in Ironwood, go south on Lake St. Turn east on Frenchtown Rd. Follow Frenchtown south as it turns into South Range Rd. Follow South Range to the ABR parking lot off West Pioneer Rd.

PORCUPINE MOUNTAINS WILDERNESS STATE PARK, MICHIGAN

Location: About 455 miles north of Chicago

Length: 26 groomed miles (some skate lanes)

Difficulty: Easy to difficult

Maps and books: Porcupine Mountains Ski Area (906-885-5275, www.dnr.state.mi.us) has trail maps. *Porcupine Mountains Wilderness State Park; Winter Trails Michigan.*

Dogs: Yes

Snowmobiles: Snowmobile trails parallel or cross some ski trail sections.

Rentals: The park's Ski Chalet rents and repairs skis and snowshoes.

Heads up: Trekking mecca (see "Hiking & Backpacking," page 351). Supremely solitary backcountry snowshoeing or guided treks on weekends. Nonresident vehicle pass $4 day, $20 annual. Daily trail pass $6 weekday, $8 weekends, includes lift services. No trail fees for snowshoeing. Primitive trailside backcountry cabins with wood stoves fill fast.

Description: Sweeping views of Lake Superior and the closest thing you'll get to mountains in the Midwest. With

60,000-plus acres, this is straight-up U.P. wilderness chock with virgin hardwood-hemlock forest. Average annual snowfall: 175-plus inches. Six connected loop trails radiate from the downhill ski lodge; you get to chairlift up to trail-heads. Most trails have maximum 400-foot elevation change. Ski through active white-tailed deer yards (spots where they congregate to get through the long winters) and along pristine rivers. A classic advanced combo: Nonesuch and River Trail Loops, following an old tram route that leads to an abandoned copper mine and skirting the Union River's bedrock-slicing waterfalls and rapids. Night skiing on the Superior Loop lit by kerosene lanterns Saturday evenings . . . magical.

Directions: Take I-90 west past Madison. Take I-39/US 51 north. Stay on US 51 north to Ironwood. From Ironwood, take US 2 east about 12 miles. At Wakefield, take MI 28 east for 20 miles to Bergland. Turn left (north) on MI 64 at the blinking light. Follow MI 64 north for 18 miles to MI 107 W. Go left (west) on M 107 and follow signs to the ski lodge.

Muskegon Mecca

PLAY OLYMPIAN FOR a day by heading 187 miles northeast of Chicago to Muskegon, MI, home to one of a handful of luge runs in the United States (spandex optional).

Part of the Muskegon Winter Sports Complex at Muskegon State Park, the lower track is 500 feet long and produces speeds of 15 mph; you can hit up to 35 mph on the 720-foot-long upper track, complete with a 79-foot vertical drop. Luge newbies get on-the-spot instruction, plus a helmet, to hit the lower run, but it's possible to graduate to the big one (starting at the 3/4 mark) after a slew of successful practice runs. Three-time luge Olympian Mark Grimmette, who took home silver in Salt Lake City, grew up in Muskegon and helped bring the luge home.

Luge is open Friday–Sunday. The complex also includes lit ice skating and hockey rinks, snowshoeing, and 15 km of groomed cross-country ski trails through white pines. A $40 day-pass gives you access to all facilities. Equipment rentals available on site. Muskegon Winter Sports Complex, (231) 744-9629, www.msports.org.

downhill and snowboarding

SOMETIMES YOU JUST need an adrenaline fix that only downhill skiing and snowboarding can provide. Here is a sampling of some of the better spots within reach of Chicago, offered with a caveat: this is not great downhill ski country. All ski "mountains" definitely belong in quotes. Don't expect glorious talcum-dry powder, long runs, and soaring peaks. That said, the following areas can be good spots to learn—all offer ski and snowboarding lessons—and hone your skills.

Jackie Butzen of Windward Sports says: "You're not going to find much glamorous terrain. But if you can learn to snowboard in the Midwest and you snowboard with what we've got, at any one of these spots, then you can board anywhere in the world. What the Midwest offers that a lot of other places don't is hard-pack ice; you have to learn to hold an edge and that means your skill level can go way up."

- Wilmot Mountain (262-862-2301, www.wilmotmountain .com) in Wilmot, WI, is about 65 miles from Chicago, just over the state line, with eight lifts and six rope-tows. Good beginner spot. Longest run is 2,500 feet; vertical rise 230 feet. Half-pipe is not great, but there is a natural wall going up the side of one of the hills with a few bumps and jumps.

- Alpine Valley (800-227-9395, www.alpinevalleyresort.com) in East Troy, WI, is about 93 miles from Chicago with nine lifts and five rope-tows. Longest run is 3,000 feet; vertical rise 388 feet. Half-pipe and terrain park.

- Cascade Mountain (800-992-2754, www.cascademountain .com) in Portage, WI, is about 175 miles from Chicago with 10 lifts and a snowtubing park. Longest run is 5,280 feet (1 mile); vertical rise 460 feet.

- Devil's Head Resort (800-338-4579, www.devilsheadresort .com) in Merrimac, WI, is about 173 miles from Chicago with 15 lifts. Longest run is 1.25 miles; vertical rise 500 feet. Among the more challenging snowboarding areas; lots of competitions and events with a feature-loaded terrain park and half-pipe.

- Tyrol Basin (608-437-4135, www.tyrolbasin.com) in Mt. Horeb, WI, is about 172 miles from Chicago. Snowboarding is their niche; kind of a teen scene, but they have a decent half-pipe with big-air jumps. Three lifts, two rope-tows, one cable-tow. Longest run is 0.75 mile; vertical rise 300 feet.

- Granite Peak at Rib Mountain State Park (715-845-2846, www.skigranitepeak.com) in Wausau, WI, is about 281 miles from Chicago with five lifts and the tallest mountain in this list. Longest run is 5,280 feet (1 mile); vertical rise 700 feet. Full-length mogul run and expert chutes with 60 to 70-degree grades. Terrain park and half-pipe.

- Boyne Mountain (800-462-6963, www.boynemountain.com) in Boyne Falls, MI, is about 345 miles from Chicago with 12 lifts and 35 km of cross-country ski trails. Longest run is 5,280 feet (1 mile); vertical rise 500 feet. Tubing park, half-pipe, and terrain park.

Where to Connect

Clubs and Organizations

- Chicago Metropolitan Ski Council (www.skicmsc.com) is an umbrella group of some 100 ski clubs across the Midwest. Focus is mostly alpine, but there are some cross-country resources, too.

- Lake Shore Ski Club Chicago (www.lssc.org) organizes cross-country and alpine ski trips around the Midwest; instruction and racing, too. With some 800 members, it's the biggest club around. Club meets first and third Wednesdays of the month at John Barleycorn's Pub in Lincoln Park.

- Northern Illinois Nordic (www.ninordic.org) promotes cross-country skiing in the region. Get on Bob Richards's list-serve to get plugged into everything cross-country ski, from local and regional races to instruction to roller-ski training sessions. E-mail him at bobnanrun@aol.com.

- Joliet Nordic Ski Club (www.jolietnordic.homestead. com/homepage.html) runs group skis, including moonlight skis, at Woodruff Golf Course.

- Nordic Fox Ski Club (www.nordicfox.org) is an active free-heeler club based in Naperville.

- Northwest Nordic Ski Club (630-415-2881, www. nwnordicskiclub.com) in Arlington Heights has been on the scene for a couple decades and runs regional ski trips.

Shops
*For City Limits rentals

- *Viking Ski Shop (3422 W. Fullerton Ave., 773-276-1222) rents and sells skis, snowshoes, and gear; sells snowboards and gear; repair shop.

- *Eastern Mountain Sports (1000 W. North Ave., 312-337-7750, www.ems.com) rents skis; rents and sells snowshoes and gear.

- *Beverly Bike and Ski (9121 S. Western Ave., 773-238-5704) rents and sells skis, snowshoes, and gear; full repair shop.

- Erehwon Mountain Outfitter (1800 N. Clybourn Ave., 312-337-6400, www.erehwonoutdoors.com) sells skis, snowshoes, and gear.

- Uncle Dan's Great Outdoor Store (2440 N. Lincoln Ave., 773-477-1918, www.udans.com) sells snowshoes and gear.

- Moosejaw (1445 W. Webster Pl. at Clybourn Ave., 773-529-1111, www.moosejawonline.com) sells snowshoes and gear.

- Windward Sports (3317 N. Clark St. 773-472-6868) sells snowboards and gear.

- Shred Shop (2121 W. Division St., 773-384-2100, www.shredshop.com) sells snowboards and gear.

- King-Keyser Ski & Racquet Shop (41 S. Washington, Hinsdale, 630-323-4320, www.kingkeyser.com) rents and sells skis and gear; rents snowshoes.

- Wheel Thing (15 S. LaGrange Rd., LaGrange, 708-352-3822, www.bicyclewheelthing.com) rents and sell skis; lessons.

- Village CycleSport (1313 N. Rand Rd., Arlington Heights, 847-398-1650, www.villagecyclesport.com) rents and sells skis and snowshoes.

Events
- Chicago Ski and Snowboard Show (www.chicagoskishow.com) in early November at the Donald E. Stephens Convention Center in Rosemont

- Northern Illinois Nordic 11K at Arrowhead Golf Club in Wheaton (contact Bob Richards at 630-832-1765 or Joe Gollinger at 630-355-6480; www.ninordic.org).

- Joliet Nordic 10K held in late January at Woodruff Golf Course in Joliet (contact Joliet Nordic Ski Club, www.jolietnordic.homestead.com/homepage.html)

- Island Loppet 10K in Blue Island, last Saturday in December, through Blue Island Park District (708-597-6964)

- Crystal Lake Classic 10K at Veterans Acres in February. Call (815) 459-0680 ext. 228 for special events, or the Park District at (815) 459-0680.

- Winter Trails snowshoe festival with guided snowshoe treks, demos, seminars (www.wintertrails.org) in late January at Morton Arboretum in Lisle.

- North American Vasa—12 km, 27 km, and 50 km—in early February in Traverse City, MI (231-938-4400, www.vasa.org)

- White Pine Stampede—10 km, 20 km, 50 km—in early February in Mancelona, MI, north of Traverse City (231-587-8812, www.whitepinestampede.org)

- Noquemanon Ski Marathon in late January (www .noquemanon.com) runs 53 km from Ishpeming in Michigan's U.P. to the shores of Lake Superior in Marquette.

- Badger State Winter Games (608-226-4780, www .sportsinwisconsin.com/bsqwin/), first weekend in February, draws 6,000-plus athletes and includes several cross-country ski races, ski jumping, snowshoeing, downhill skiing, snowboarding, ice hockey, quadrathlon (mountain biking, running, cross-country skiing, and snowshoeing), curling, and figure and speed skating.

- American Birkebeiner ski marathon in February (715-634-5025, www.birkie.com). See page 429.

Books

- DuFresne, Jim. *Porcupine Mountains Wilderness State Park: A Backcountry Guide for Hikers, Campers,*

Backpackers and Winter Visitors. Holt, MI: Thunder Bay Press, 1999.

- Semion, William. *Winter Trails Michigan: The Best Cross-Country Ski & Snowshoe Trails*. Guilford, CT: Globe Pequot Press, 2001.

- Van Valkenberg, Phil. *Winter Trails Wisconsin: The Best Cross-Country Ski & Snowshoe Trails*. Guilford, CT: Globe Pequot Press, 2000.

Links

www.norwiski.com has tons of good info on cross-country skiing in northwest Wisconsin.

www.danenet.wicip.org/madnord, site of the Madison Nordic Ski Club (aka Madnorski), is a great resource for southern Wisconsin spots; detailed trip reports and links.

Silent Sports magazine, www.silentsports.net, maintains a thorough calendar of Midwestern cross-country ski events.

outsidepix.com

YOU CAN RUN most anywhere in the city. Through the plethora of neighborhood parks, biggies like Humboldt Park or Jackson Park, or along the narrow ribbon of Chicago River greenway on the far North Side. Lots of people just walk out their front door and run. Hopefully this chapter will give some inspiration to explore new territory.

It covers just a fraction of what is out there, focusing on a few favorite metro-area trail runs. As always, these are multiuse trails: expect to share space with bikers, in-line skaters (on paved trails), walkers. Happily, all the trails in this chapter allow your dog to be your training partner—but a leash is mandatory. One-way routes here have public-transit options if you care to ditch the car and shuttle plan. See "Biking," page 217, for details on taking a bike aboard.

Many thanks to Brenda Barrera and Eliot Wineberg for their *Chicago Running Guide,* which details loads of metro-area routes and greatly informed this chapter. That's the book to have if you're at all serious about running here.

And you'll be in good company. Chicago is a running city. It's flat and fast. It hosts a world-class marathon and the world's largest triathlon. Especially with the increasingly mild winters of recent years, running is becoming a year-round sport in the city. The lake helps moderate temperatures in the city, making it warmer in winter, cooler in summer.

Thank early-20th-century city architects, who had the wisdom to protect the Lake Michigan shoreline as public land, for giving us the 18-mile Lakefront Trail. It's the crown jewel of Chicago's running scene. It is *the* place to run in the city.

"Even in New York City, you're running in circles in Central Park and there are no mile markers," notes David Patt, CEO of Chicago Area Runners Association, better known as CARA. "We're lucky. We've got a real gem here."

The city has a healthy network of local running clubs, with CARA as the granddaddy. With roughly 8,600 members, it's the third-biggest citywide running organization in the country, behind New York and Atlanta. CARA is the best single source of information on running here, whether you want to hook up on a group training run, find out about clinics, or get a comprehensive calendar of running-related events. The CARA board on the Lakefront Trail at Diversey Parkway and the Inner Drive is a regular meeting spot, with a Sunday 8 A.M. group run that's most active in winter (November–April). Bookmark CARA's Web site, www.cararuns.org. You'll need it.

Bagging
a Peak
of Steel

EACH FEBRUARY A couple thousand runners haul up 1,632 stairs to the 94th floor of the John Hancock Center. That's about 1,000 vertical feet, or just shy of one-fifth mile, up one of the city's man-made mountains. In 2002, the winning time was 10 minutes flat, about 6.4 seconds per floor. Noncompetitive runners can opt to race up 42 floors. Proceeds go toward research, advocacy, and education programs for the American Lung Association of Metropolitan Chicago. Hustle Up the Hancock details at (312) 243-2000, www.lungchicago.org.

City Limits

The 18-mile-long path that stretches along the city's lakefront greenway from Ardmore St. on the North Side to 71st St. on the South Side is urban running ground zero. Plowed of snow (usually) in winter, mobbed like a Bangkok market on sunny summer weekends, the path has half-mile markers so it's easy to track your distance (just be aware that the path often changes with lakefront construction). Some stretches have a cinder path in addition to the two-lane asphalt trail. And there's always the grass—or sand along beach stretches—if your knees can't take the tough stuff. Plenty of water fountains and public bathrooms in the warmer weather. Couldn't be easier to ride your bike to the lake, cruise the path, and pick your run.

Stick to morning runs in summer and you're virtually guaranteed to avoid the crush of humanity that descends on the path as the beach scene heats up. Keep your dog on a tight leash to avoid nasty accidents. And run defensively;

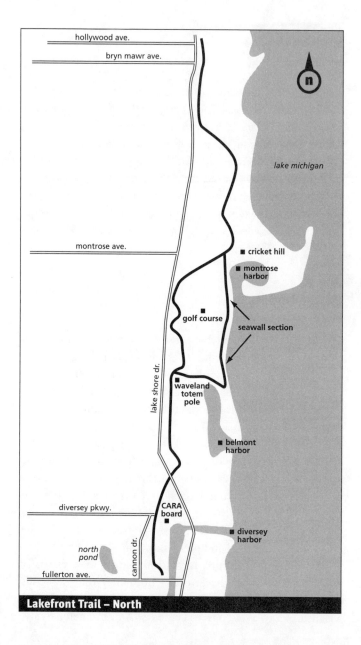

hollywood ave.

bryn mawr ave.

lake michigan

montrose ave.

■ cricket hill

■ montrose harbor

■ golf course

seawall section

lake shore dr.

■ waveland totem pole

■ belmont harbor

diversey pkwy.

■ CARA board

cannon dr.

■ diversey harbor

north pond

fullerton ave.

Lakefront Trail – North

I've seen too many oblivious people on cell phones while biking here. Transit options make it easy to run the segments one way in either direction. Runners often divide the path into three parts: North, Central, and South. Each has its own rewards. Have fun in the fray.

LAKEFRONT TRAIL—NORTH

Location: 5700 N (Hollywood Ave.) to 2800 N (Diversey Parkway)

Length: 4.5 miles one way

Terrain: Asphalt/cinder

Maps and book: Chicago Area Runners Association (312-666-9836, www.cararuns.org) puts out a detailed map; Chicago Park District's free "Chicago's Lakefront" trail map (312-747-2474). *Chicago Running Guide.*

Dogs: Yes

Heads up: Follow Sheridan Rd. north into Evanston and pick up Evanston's lakefront path for more scenic miles (see "Biking," page 215).

Description: Though the zero mile marker starts a half-mile south at Bryn Mawr Ave., the trail begins just north of Hollywood Beach in the shadow of looming lakefront condos. Lots of families and older folks out strolling. A cinder running path runs along much of this section of the multi-use trail, making human traffic jams less of an issue. Plus you get Cricket Hill, a coveted urban mound popular with city runners for hill training (good sledding in winter, too). Great skyline views from Montrose Harbor.

Route: Run south along the cinder path, unless you prefer to share asphalt with bikers and in-line skaters. At Montrose Ave., take a few runs up and down Cricket Hill (by the soccer field). Follow the path east to Montrose Harbor, past the inevitable coterie of fishermen, skirt the harbor's western edge, and run south along the wide limestone path with the seawall and the lake to your left (east) and the golf course to your right (west). Watch for ice in winter. At the end of the golf course by the fenced bird sanctuary, pick up the path west along the parking lot to the wooden totem pole (a popular meeting place). From here to Belmont Ave. the running and multiuse paths join. Pass "Dog Beach" at Belmont Harbor. After the harbor's south end, the running path veers right through the underpass and continues past the driving range to Diversey Harbor. You'll see the CARA board on the path on the south side of Diversey Parkway.

Directions: For Hollywood, by car take Lake Shore Dr. north to the Bryn Mawr exit. Go right (east) into the beach parking lot. Several other beaches south along the trail have parking. By transit, the Red Line L Bryn Mawr stop is closest. Run east to the path.

For Diversey, by car take Lake Shore Dr. to the Fullerton exit. Turn right (north) on Cannon Dr. Turn right (east) into the lot at Diversey Parkway at the harbor's north end. By transit, the Brown Line L Diversey stop is closest, a quick run east to the path.

Running
In
Circles

THE CHICAGO PARK District runs several tracks in neighborhood parks across the city. Below are three of the newer ovals, all 400-meter rubberized surface with four to eight lanes. Lake Shore Park and River Park have lit tracks. As of this writing, the city was discussing adding a track around North Ave. in Lincoln Park.

- Jackson Park, 6401 S. Stony Island Ave., (312) 747-6187
- Lake Shore Park, 808 N. Lake Shore Dr., (312) 742-7891
- River Park, 5100 N. Francisco Ave., (312) 742-7516

LAKEFRONT TRAIL—CENTRAL

Location: 2800 N (Diversey Parkway) to 1200 S (Burnham Harbor)

Length: 5.5 miles one way

Terrain: Asphalt/cinder

Maps and books: See North section, above.

Dogs: Yes

Heads up: Most popular—and crowded—section

Description: I love rounding the bend after the classic North Ave. beach house, painted and shaped like a boat, replete with porthole windows and an "upper deck" café overlooking the Big Blue, passing the old guys with their shirts unbuttoned at the chess pavilion, brows furrowed. Suddenly, the sweep of the city opens in a graceful baylike arc around Oak St. Beach. The Hancock shoots up, all black metal bravado in a strip of vintage brick and stone lakefront high-rises. It never ceases to impress. Run around the Shedd Aquarium on a blustery day and watch the waves crash. Sailboat central.

Route: From the CARA board at the north end of Diversey Harbor, follow the cinder path south. You'll pass the water trough, a glimmering oasis for dripping runners (and the German Shepherd I've seen soaking there). North Pond is across the street (see Option, page 449). Continue past Lincoln Park Zoo; watch for kayakers and rowers in the lagoon. Use the pedestrian/bike bridge to cross over Lake Shore Dr. back to the paved multiuse path around North Ave. Follow the path south. After the chess pavilion you can continue on the multiuse path or, if the crowds are oppressive, drop down to the cement swath along the water. **Stay alert around Oak St. Beach—serious bottlenecks there**. Pass Ohio St. Beach (triathlon swimmers train here), Navy Pier, cross over the Chicago River, pass the Chicago Yacht Club and Monroe Harbor. If the main upper path by

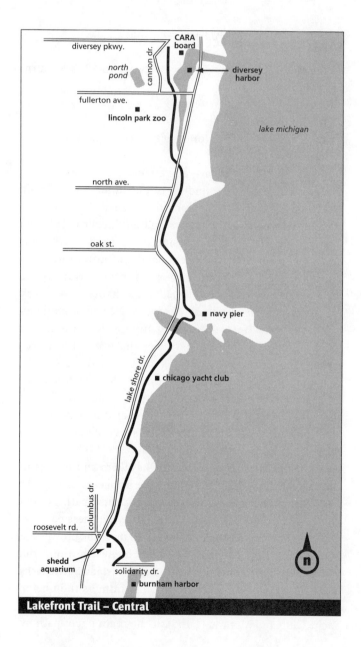

diversey pkwy.

CARA board

cannon dr.

north pond

diversey harbor

fullerton ave.

■ lincoln park zoo

lake michigan

north ave.

oak st.

■ navy pier

lake shore dr.

■ chicago yacht club

columbus dr.

roosevelt rd.

shedd aquarium

solidarity dr.

■ burnham harbor

n

Lakefront Trail – Central

Lake Shore Dr. is crowded, hit the sidewalk by the harbor along the long straightaway to the Museum Campus. Follow the path around Shedd Aquarium and up to Burnham Harbor at the 10-mile marker.

Option: run a 0.8-mile loop around diminutive North Pond, a neighborhood birding spot that perfectly frames the skyline. Excellent namesake restaurant in the refurbished Arts and Crafts–style boat house, too.

Directions: See North section for Diversey Parkway. For Burnham Harbor, by car take Lake Shore Dr. south to the Museum Campus/Roosevelt Rd. exit. Turn right, then left to Columbus Dr. and McFetridge Dr. Metered spots line Solidarity Dr. (come early to nab one).

By transit, take the Red, Green, or Orange Line L to the Roosevelt stop. Run east across Lake Shore Dr. to the path.

LAKEFRONT TRAIL—SOUTH

Location: 1200 S (Burnham Harbor) to 7100 S (South Shore Cultural Center)

Length: 7.5 miles one way

Terrain: Asphalt

Maps and books: See North section, above.

Dogs: Yes

Heads up: Where did the crowds go? Blissfully quiet. Safety-wise, best to run mornings here.

Description: If you're running south, take a minute to turn around and catch only-from-the-South-Side views of downtown. Run past historic beach houses, pine-fringed Promontory Point, Jackson Harbor, and stately Hyde Park and South Shore brownstones and high-rises. Almost uninterrupted lake views. Parts of this trail even roll ever so slightly. The final stretch—it's loud because South Shore Dr. is just feet away—is basically just sidewalk with a line painted down the middle. Stop in the elegant South Shore Cultural Center, a onetime private country club now owned by the Chicago Park District and listed on the National Register of Historic Places. Water and bathrooms there, too.

Route: From the 10-mile marker, head south through Burnham Harbor, past Soldier Field, Meigs Field (the little airport that could, thanks to local politicos), the Museum of Science and Industry, Burnham Park skate park at 31st St., Promontory Point, the refurbished 63d St. beach house, Jackson Harbor (watch for guys hanging off the Harbor Wall; see "Rock Climbing," page 365), and a few golf courses. You'll hit the zero mile marker at 71st St. and the South Shore Cultural Center.

Option: run the 0.4-mile loop around Promontory Point (around 55th St.). Peek in the fairy-castle stone building at the tip. Wish you brought a picnic. Stellar views.

Directions: See Central section for Burnham Harbor. For 71st St./South Shore Cultural Center, by car take Lake Shore Dr. (it turns into South Shore Dr. as you head south) to E. 71st St. Turn left (east) into the South Shore Cultural Center to park.

By transit, the Green Line L E. 63d St. stop is closest to the path's south end. Run east to pick up the trail. Or take the Metra Electric Chicago-University Park line to the South Shore station.

Ultra

OTS OF PEOPLE train hard for months, years, to get strong enough, mentally and physically, to clock a marathon. Then there are those who go beyond. They are, they admit, a small (some may say vaguely masochistic) group of runners driven to do more. They are the ultramarathoners.

Chicago has two ultramarathons, the Chicago Lakefront 50K

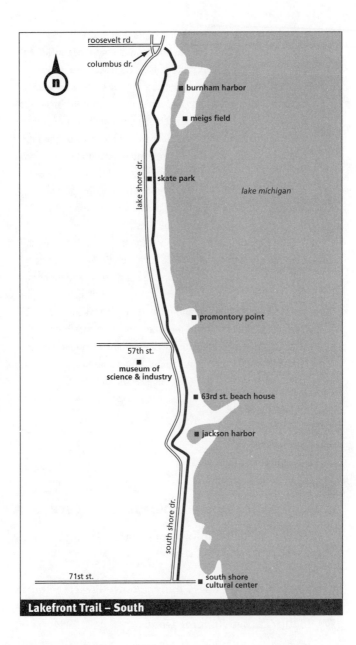

roosevelt rd.

columbus dr.

■ burnham harbor

■ meigs field

lake shore dr.

■ skate park

lake michigan

■ promontory point

57th st.
■
museum of
science & industry

■ 63rd st. beach house

■ jackson harbor

south shore dr.

71st st.

■ south shore
cultural center

Lakefront Trail – South

(31-mile) George Cheung Memorial Race held the first Saturday in April and the Chicago Lakefront 50K and 50-miler in November, usually 3 or 4 weeks after the Chicago Marathon.

Race organizer Stuart Schulman—oh, yeah, he's 63 years old and has 74 marathons and ultras under his belt—says most people are drawn by the pure challenge of pushing the body and mind to their limit. "You have to be able to go out and just beat yourself up all day long. You kind of have to be a glutton for punishment," says Schulman, who ran his first ultramarathon at 50 (he'd been into marathons for a decade or so before). "It's definitely a tough cookie kind of crowd. But you feel higher than a kite when you finish."

The vibe around the ultramarathon is decidedly tighter knit than the Chicago Marathon. It's a fraction of the size, some 140 runners registered for the 2002 spring race, and runners are constantly passing each other since the 50K course covers three 10.3-plus-mile out-and-backs along the lakefront path.

Interested in taking on the 50 miler? "The marathon basically becomes a training run. If you're doing a 50-miler, you probably want a couple marathons under your belt in the 2 or 3 months before the ultra," Schulman says. Details at www.chicagoultra.org.

Backyard

INDIAN BOUNDARY DIVISION FOREST PRESERVE

Location: About 14 miles W of Chicago
Length: 14.5 miles one way
Terrain: Dirt
Maps and book: Cook County Forest Preserve Indian Boundary and Des Plaines Division rough trail maps (708-771-1330). *Chicago Running Guide.*

Running

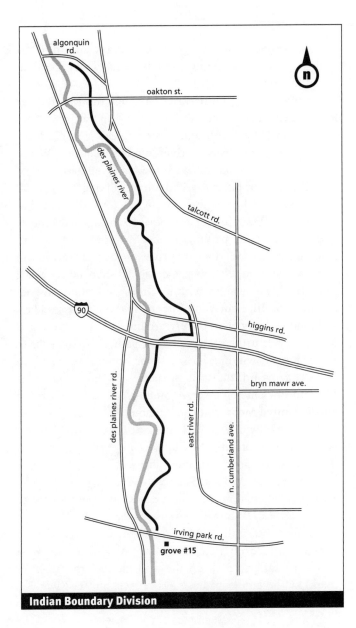

Indian Boundary Division

Dogs: Yes

Heads up: Surprisingly lightly used. A decent rain turns trail to quicksand-like mud. Watch for roots and the occasional fallen tree.

Description: The unmarked trail hugs the Des Plaines River's east bank. You'll be sheltered by a forest of cottonwoods, elms, blue beech, and silver maples—great shade for summer runs, just beware river-loving mosquitos. Watch for great blue herons and waterfowl, as well as the occasional mountain biker (see "Mountain Biking," page 274) and horse. The horses don't seem fazed by the fact that they're in O'Hare's flight path; expect to hear jets overhead.

Route: From the parking lot at Grove 15, head west to pick up dirt trail. Keep the river to your left as you run north and you won't get lost. Occasional spurs heading east from the trail lead to parking areas and main streets. Around 2.5 miles out you'll hit the I-90 underpasses (dark and muddy—easy place to turn around for a 5-mile out and back). Go left using the singletrack path along the edge of the cemetery, winding in a U-shape around it. After you cross Higgins Rd. the trail is easier to follow. You've hit 14.5 miles when you reach Algonquin Rd. and the big sign for the United Methodist campground.

Directions: By car, go west on Irving Park Rd. to N. Cumberland Ave. Soon after N. Cumberland you'll pass several forest preserve groves. Turn left into Grove 15 and park.

By bike, ride Addison St. west to N. Cumberland Ave. Turn right (north) on N. Cumberland Ave. and follow to Irving Park Rd. Follow directions above.

By transit, take the Blue Line L to the Cumberland stop. Run south 0.25 mile to Bryn Mawr Ave., then run west about 0.5 mile to pick up the trail (around the 2.2-mile mark) at the corner of Bryn Mawr Ave. and E. River Rd. From the trail's northern end at Algonquin Rd., the Des

Plaines station on Metra's Union Pacific Northwest Line is about 0.75 mile north and west off Des Plaines River Rd.

NORTH BRANCH TRAIL

Location: Starts within city limits (6400 N/5600 W) and ends N in Glencoe

Length: 20.1 miles one way

Terrain: Paved; some packed dirt, cinder, and crushed limestone sections.

Maps and book: Cook County Forest Preserve's (708-771-1330) "North Branch Bicycle Trail Map" (shows section-by-section mileage) and North Branch and Skokie Division trail maps. *Chicago Running Guide.*

Dogs: Yes

Heads up: Multiple access points make the trail easy to shorten up. Weekends can be crowded.

Description: This winding, at times vaguely rolling, trail follows the North Branch of the Chicago River through prairie, sedge meadows, and forest. Bikers flock here (see "Biking," page 219). Bird while you run. Watch for white tailed deer, kingfishers, and great blue herons around the Skokie Lagoons (see "Bird-Watching," page 311). Your reward for making it to the northern trailhead: cooling down in the sprawling Chicago Botanic Garden. When the weather's fine, grab a drink on the garden deck and soak it all in.

Route: From the southern trailhead at Caldwell Woods head north. Stay right at the path's first fork around the 10-mile mark (the spur heads out to Winnetka Rd.). At Tower Rd. the path splits to loop around the Skokie Lagoons; both directions lead to Dundee Rd. Cross Dundee to enter the Chicago Botanic Garden. Tons of scenic spots to crash and take a breather. The trail ends at the northern tip of the gardens at Lake-Cook Rd.

Option: avoid the pavement and run on roughly 8 miles of packed dirt, cinder, and crushed limestone multiuse trail along the river from about Tower Rd. to Dempster St. Watch for horses.

Directions: By car, take I-94 west to the US 14/Peterson-Caldwell exit (west). Go northwest along Caldwell Ave. about 0.5 mile to Devon Ave. Turn left (west) onto Devon. Park in the Caldwell Woods lot on the right, just east of Milwaukee Ave.

By bike, take the Elston Ave. bike lane north to Devon Ave. (Elston joins Milwaukee around Peterson Ave.). Turn right (east) on Devon Ave. There's a trail entrance on the north side of Devon Ave.

By transit, take the Blue Line L to the Jefferson station. Ride north on Milwaukee Ave. to Devon Ave. Turn right (east) on Devon. Use same trail entrance as above. At the northern trailhead, turn right (east) on Lake-Cook Rd. and follow less than 1 mile to Metra Union Pacific North Line Braeside station on the north side of the street.

ILLINOIS PRAIRIE PATH, MAIN STEM

Location: About 18 miles W of Chicago

Length: 10.5 miles one way

Terrain: Crushed limestone

Map and book: Nonprofit, all-volunteer Illinois Prairie Path (630-752-0120, www.ipp.org) sells a detailed color map for $6. Well-signed trail, trailboards at most major junctions. *Chicago Running Guide.*

Dogs: Yes

Heads up: Easy carfree suburban running. Bonus: by the time you read this, the main stem trail should be extended

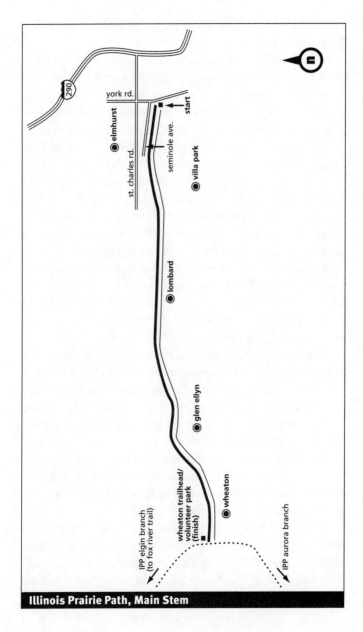

Illinois Prairie Path, Main Stem

across the Des Plaines River east to the Blue Line Forest Park L station.

Description: This is just one leg of the 61-mile trail that runs through three counties in the western burbs. It's not going to transport you deep into the countryside: think suburban pastoral. But it's well tended—and well used—by local runners, with mile markers along its ramrod straight, flat, tree-lined length. Street crossings are of the mellow variety. Some city runners plan their run from one Metra stop to another. It's a fairly simple proposition, since Metra's Union Pacific West Line roughly parallels the main stem with more than a half-dozen stations along its length. The main stem starts at 1st Ave. in Maywood, but as of this writing the first few miles weren't in great shape.

Route: Couldn't be easier. Just follow the main stem path west from Elmhurst into Villa Park, Lombard, Glen Ellyn, and Wheaton. At Wheaton, the IPP branches north and south and eventually meets up with the Fox River Trail (see "Biking," page 232).

Directions: By car, take I-290 west to St. Charles Rd. west. Go west on St. Charles to York Rd. At York Rd. turn left (south) and continue to Seminole Ave. At Seminole—which parallels the path in Elmhurst—turn right (west) and look for a spot. See www.ipp.org for parking areas (mostly free) along the main stem.

By bike, ride west on Washington Blvd. about 12 miles. Turn left (south) at 17th Ave. in Maywood and ride to the IPP main stem trail; it's about 6 miles to the Elmhurst trailhead at York Rd.

By transit, take Metra's Union Pacific West Line to the York 1st Ave. station in Elmhurst. Run south on Cottage Hill Ave. about 0.75 mile to the path. At the north trailhead in Wheaton, the Metra station is right off the path on Liberty Dr.

SWALLOW CLIFF, PALOS AND SAG VALLEY FOREST PRESERVES

Location: About 20 miles SW of Chicago

Length: 6.2-mile loop; many options to extend.

Terrain: Dirt

Map and book: Cook County Forest Preserve's Palos and Sag Valley Divisions rough trail map (708-839-5617 or 708-771-1330). *Chicago Running Guide.*

Dogs: Yes

Heads up: Multiuse trails in the Palos division, north of IL 83, entice with challenging hills but are also *the* metro-area mountain biking mecca, with a staging area at Bullfrog Lake. To explore the area with local experts, hook up with the Palos Roadrunners (708-448-9200, www.heightsgroup.com/running4kicks.htm).

Description: Hills, glorious hills. Thank glacial debris for this rugged, unmarked trail. Gradually climb the bluff that backs the 100-foot-high Swallow Cliff toboggan runs. Some creeks to jump. Take the spur through Cap Sauers, a nature preserve that draws more birders than runners.

Route: From the parking lot, run west toward the woods along the well-trodden trail crossing the bottom of the toboggan runs. The path takes you onto an unmarked counterclockwise loop trail. Follow the wide bridle path along the bottom of the bluff. You'll cross 104th Ave. by the Teasons Woods parking lot (to your right.) After 104th, the path cuts through ravines with several rolling hills. At the junction with another unmarked, wide path heading west, stay left as the path goes downhill to continue the loop. From here the rolling trail winds east. Before crossing back over 104th you'll pass another unmarked trail spur that dead-ends at McCarthy Rd. Cross 104th and pass Horsetail Lake on your right. Stay straight at the next major junction (forest preserve map is especially misleading here); run past the wooden fence. Run through the underpass at 96th Ave. At the first main junction, go left (north) to hit some hills. At the T-junction, go left (west) and cross back under 96th Ave. Follow the trail back to your car.

Directions: By car, take I-55 south to LaGrange Rd./US 45 south. Go south on LaGrange Rd. about 6 miles. After crossing the Calumet-Sag Channel, turn right at the exit for IL 83. Go left (west) on IL 83. Take a quick left (south) into the Swallow Cliff toboggan run parking lot.

WATERFALL GLEN FOREST PRESERVE

Location: About 25 miles SW of Chicago

Length: 9.2-mile loop

Terrain: Crushed limestone, some grass and dirt

Maps and book: Trailboard at the parking lot; DuPage County Forest Preserve map (630-933-7248). *Chicago Running Guide.*

Dogs: Yes

Heads up: Good place to head when dirt trails elsewhere are a mess

Description: So pretty. Rolling trail through pine groves, oak and maple woods, wetlands, savanna, meadows, and prairie chock full of big bluestem, mountain mint, and yellow foxglove. The main 9.2-mile multiuse trail averages 8 feet wide and throws up a couple of bona fide hills as it loops around Argonne National Laboratory (you won't actually see the lab from the loop run). Mowed grass firelanes and footpaths off-limits to bikers (see "Mountain Biking," page 276) are fair game for runners, but most aren't shown on the map and many don't link back with the main trail.

Route: Follow the main loop counterclockwise from the trailhead parking lot (bathrooms and water there). Trail jogs in parts, like about halfway out near the Old Lincoln Park Nursery and power station. There are a handful of street crossings along the trail—be especially careful at Cass Ave. toward the end of the loop.

Directions: Take I-55 south and exit at Cass Ave. south. Continue south on Cass less than 0.25 mile and then turn right (west) onto Northgate Rd. Make another right into the trailhead parking lot.

BUSSE WOODS

Location: About 25 miles NW of Chicago

Length: 7.8-mile loop; out-and-back extensions possible.

Terrain: Paved

Map and book: Cook County Forest Preserve's (708-771-1330) "Busse Woods Bicycle Trail Map," part of the Ned Brown Preserve. *Chicago Running Guide.*

Dogs: Yes

Heads up: Run early in summer to avoid the in-line and bike crowds.

Description: The only place in the metro area where you get to run by an elk herd, usually munching away in the 14-acre enclosure by where you park your car. Sugar maple and basswood dominate the upland forest, swamp white oak and ash in the flats. Spring brings white trillium and wild geranium to the 3,700-acre preserve. Marshes. And 590-acre Busse Lake, a fishing and sail spot (see "Fishing," page 191).

Route: Pick up the clearly marked trail from the north side of the elk pasture. Running the loop counterclockwise, head north through the woods, drop down along Higgins Rd. (right before the intersection of Higgins Rd. and IL 53 you'll come to the fork for the Golf Rd. spur), run south past the North Pool and Busse Lake. The second fork is for

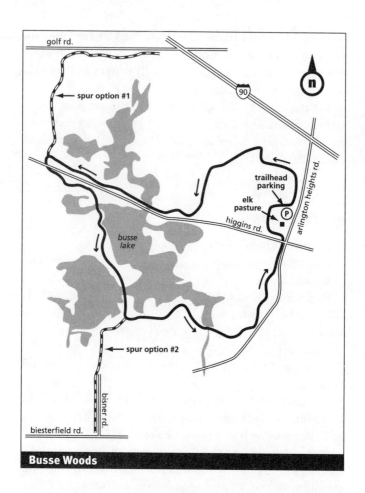

Busse Woods

the Biesterfield Rd. spur. Go east to stay on the main trail, then swing back north, cross the bridge over Higgins Rd., and you're back at the elk.

Options: tack on the 2-mile (one way) north spur through the meadow, past the model airplane flying field to Golf Rd., and the 1.1-mile south spur paralleling Bisner Rd. to Biesterfield Rd.

Directions: Take I-90 west to Arlington Heights Rd. south. Go 0.5 mile to the Ned Brown Forest Preserve entrance on your right (before Higgins Rd.).

Mecca

INDIANA DUNES, INDIANA

Location: About 51 miles SE of Chicago

Length: 4.4-mile loop on Cowles Bog Trail, 3.6-mile loop on West Beach trails

Terrain: Packed dirt, sand, boardwalk/stairs

Maps: Trail maps from Indiana Dunes National Lakeshore in Porter (219-926-7561 ext. 225, www.nps.gov) and Indiana Dunes State Park in Chesterton (219-926-1952, www.state .in.us/)

Dogs: Yes (but not on swimming beaches or on shared horse trails)

Heads up: Virtually every trail makes a good run here. Sand and dunes add challenge. Hit West Beach trails early in summer to avoid dodging beach crowds.

Description: In as long as it takes to drive out to the burbs in fume-sucking traffic, you can hop a train and cross into Indiana for some of the finest trail running around. Bogs. Yellow beech and chokeberry-lined marshes. Fragrant jack pines. Sandy black oak forest. Revelation: a vertical workout on the steep sand dunes that'll have your quads crying and your heart thumping. Finish it off with a bracing dip in Lake Michigan. Your feet will thank you. Try Cowles Bog Trail in winter; the forest stays relatively warm and protected from lake-fed gusts. And you may have it all to yourself. For more trail, try the 2.6-mile Inland Marsh Trail across US 12 from West Beach and 3.7-mile

Bailly Homestead/Chellberg Farm and Little Calumet River Trails south of Cowles Bog off Mineral Springs Rd. Plus the entire state park system . . . see "Hiking & Backpacking," page 333.

Route, Cowles Bog Trail: From the trailhead on the west side of Mineral Springs Rd., follow the well-marked trail through a flat stand of white birch and around the edge of the marsh. You'll pass two spur trails on your left (for shorter loops) as you run deeper into the oak forest and start to scramble up the dune ridge. Run down the dune face to hit a 0.2-mile stretch along the beach. Watch for the trailhead (sometimes half-buried in shifting sands) to head back into the dunes. Eventually you'll pass a wetland and stand of pines. The trail ends at the Greenbelt trailhead. From there, turn left and run north on Mineral Springs Rd. about 0.5 mile back to your car.

West Beach trails: From the parking lot, pick up the Long Lake loop and run counterclockwise. At the T-junction (the shortcut takes you back to where you started), stay right to pick up the east section of the West Beach Trail loop. Turn right at the wooden boardwalk to start the Dune Succession Trail loop—some nice uphills through jack pines and blowouts. Once you hit the beach house you're 0.3 mile from your car.

Directions: By car, take I-94 east to Indiana. For Cowles Bog Trail, exit US 20 northeast. Turn left (north) on Mineral Springs Rd., cross US 12 east, and continue to the trailhead parking on the east side of the road. (The NPS visitors center is a few miles east off US 12.)

For West Beach trails, from I-94 take I-65 north to US 12. Take US 12 east about 4 miles to County Line Rd. Turn left (north) on County Line. Turn right (east) onto West Beach Access Rd. and follow to the parking lot closest to the beachhouse.

By transit, take the South Shore Line train (800-356-

2079, www.nictd.com) from downtown to the Dune Park station. For Cowles Bog Trail, follow signs to Calumet Trail (rough bike trail) paralleling the RR tracks. Walk west along Calumet Trail a little over 1 mile to Mineral Springs Rd. Turn right (north) on Mineral Springs. Pass Greenbelt trailhead on your left. After about 0.5 mile you'll hit the Cowles Bog trailhead on the west side of Mineral Springs Rd. For West Beach trails, get off the train one stop before, at the Ogden Dunes station. Walk west about 1.5 miles to County Line Rd. Turn right (north) onto County Line. Turn right onto West Beach Access Rd. for the trailhead.

▲

exploration

◀ **EXTRA** _____

▼**wild onion and adventure racing**

HE SEPTEMBER WIND kicks up mini sandstorms from the starting line at North Ave. Beach. At 5 P.M., 186 racers take off on foot, backpacks stuffed with maps, band-aids, Gu, and gear. They pick up canoes at Oak St. Beach and portage along the Lakefront Path, dodging bike commuters heading home after work. After Navy Pier, the mass heads for the Lake Shore Dr. Bridge, squeezing single-file through a tight S-curve and capillary-like path under the bridge, barely wide enough to stand with arms outstretched. At Ogden Slip, the racers hand off the canoes to volunteers at the put-in for the Chicago River. One of the first half-dozen or so teams to make it to the water winds up dumping into the choppy green-brown water. I watch them paddle down the Main Stem, bilge-pumping furiously, and think: you poor masochists. You will be wet and miserable for the next 24 hours. . . .

The Wild Onion is a round-the-clock endurance fest exploiting the city wilds with a roughly 100-mile, 24-hour urban adventure of canoeing, kayaking, running/trekking, orienteering, rappelling, cycling, in-line skating, and coasteering, which involves goat-walking on exhausted, trembling quads along the rocky seawall buffering Lake Michigan's shore. Plus a dose of L-riding for good measure. Teams don't see the course coordinates until just a few hours before they line up at the start. The 2000 inaugural race included scaling the city's best man-made mountain (a 103-story climb up the Sears Tower) and navigating a warren of normally off-limits subterranean freight tunnels carved out below the Loop (see "Caving," page 396). To date, race organizers say, there have been no muggings along the all-night course.

In 2001 there were 62 co-ed teams of three, from Eco-Challenge veterans to adventure-race newbies. About half the racers hailed from the metro area. Nine teams finished within the 24-hour cutoff; 27 managed to finish the punishing course at all. A team of Finns took first place with a time of 19 hours, 2 minutes. They were particularly impressed with the city's epic potholes but unimpressed with the directions to the Blue Line L they got from a guy drinking under a bridge.

The number two team, finishing 25 minutes behind the Finns, included elite triathlete Mike Pigg, who says "you're so in the zone in this race. I like the peacefulness around 3 A.M. in Chicago. You get to own the streets for a while. And, yeah, you're in the city, but you're mixing it up with Mother Nature. I like that."

"I don't think people look at the city in the same way ever again after doing this race—I know I don't," says John O'Connor, one of the race's creators and organizers. "You see that their relationship with the city has changed; the city is now their playground."

Details about the Wild Onion, and the Wild Scallion, a shorter version planned for 2002, at (312) 464-3300, www .urbanadventureracing.com. To learn more about the local adventure-racing scene, hook up with a team, or check out group workouts and clinics, contact the Chicago Area Adventure-racing Association (847-675-7488, www.chicagoadventureracing .org).

Where to Connect

Clubs and Organizations

See the CARA website for a lengthy list of affiliated clubs across the metro area.

- CARA, Chicago Area Runners Association (312-666-9836, www.cararuns.org), is the largest citywide running organization. Some 2,000 people went through the group's marathon training program in 2001. A slew of clinics and training programs for all levels. Regular 8 A.M. runs Saturday at Waveland clock tower by the Sydney R. Marovitz Golf Course, about 3600 N and the lake; Sunday at the CARA info board on the Lakefront Trail just south of Diversey Parkway.

- Lincoln Park Pacers Running Club (www.geocities.com /lppacers), around since 1984, has three weekly lakefront runs and regular metro-area trail runs. 200-plus members.

- Frontrunners/Frontwalkers Chicago (312-409-2790, www.frfwchicago.org) is a club for gays, bisexuals, transsexuals, and friends with some 250 members. Saturday 9 A.M. and Tuesday 6:30 P.M. runs and walks from the totem pole off the Lakefront Trail around Addison St.

- Chicago Hash House Harriers (312-409-BEER, www.chicagohash.com). Don't know what hashing is? Hint: nothing to do with Mary Jane.

- Run Big Chicago (www.orik.com/runbig/) is for Clydesdale athletes (men over 170 lbs, women over 135 lbs).

- Chicago Triathlon & Multisport Club (312-944-4113 ext 25, www.chicagotriclub.com)

Shops

- Vertel's (2001 N. Clybourn Ave., 773-248-7400; 24 S. Michigan Ave., 312-683-9600; www.vertels.com) has been part of the Chicago running scene since 1976. Women's running club Wednesday 6 P.M. from the Michigan Ave. store. Women's running clinics first Wednesday of the month at 7 P.M. Regular fun runs from both stores.

- Fleet Feet Sports (210 W. North Ave. at Piper's Alley, 312-587-3338; 4555 N. Lincoln Ave., 773-271-3338; www.fleetfeetchicago.com). Regular fun runs, including women's only, from both stores.

- Universal Sole (3254 N. Lincoln Ave., 773-868-0893, www.universalsole.com) has regular group runs and fitness walks. Team Adidas/Universal Sole Race Team is tops.

- Running Away (1753 N. Damen, 773-395-AWAY, www.runningawaychicago.com) in Bucktown organizes fun runs and early Sunday A.M. trail runs.

Events

With hundreds of metro-area races, there's no way to do justice here. Below are some of the largest, or quirkiest, local races. For a comprehensive listing, see the CARA Web site and race calendars in *Chicago Athlete, Chicago Runner*, and *Windy City Sports*.

- LaSalle Bank Chicago Marathon (312-904-9800, www.chicagomarathon.com) celebrated its 25th anniversary in 2002. Registration capped at 37,500 runners. Held in October; weather can be sunny and 60° or bitter cold. Starts and finishes in Grant Park. Course is flat and fast: as of this writing, the marathon held world records for both men and women (2:05:42, set in 1999 by three-time champion Khalid Khannouchi, and 2:18:47 by Catherine Ndereba).

- Chicago Half Marathon (773-929-6072, www
  .chicagohalfmarathon.com) in early September.

- Mrs. T's Chicago Triathlon (773-404-2372, www
  .caprievents.com) in late August claims the title "world's
  largest" with 6,000 racers.

- LaSalle Bank Shamrock Shuffle (312-904-9814, www
  .shamrockshuffle.com) in March is the country's biggest 8K
  with some 16,000-plus runners.

- Y-Me Race Against Breast Cancer (www.y-me.org/race) on
  Mother's Day in Grant Park draws close to 30,000 5K runners and walkers.

- Chicago Distance Classic (www.chicagodistanceclassic.com)
  in July at the University of Illinois-Chicago campus is one
  of the city's oldest road races and the only 20K in city limits. 5K run and walk, too.

- Proud to Run (312-409-8991, www.frfwchicago.org) is a
  5K/10K run and walk held during Gay Pride weekend late
  June/early July.

- Chicagoland Trail Series for off-road runners. Four trail
  races in 2002, April–November. Contact Universal Sole in
  the city (see Shops, above) or The Runner's Edge (847-853-
  8531, www.tre.com) in Wilmette.

- Elvis Is Alive 5K in August. Humiliating costumes and
  wigs abound. Post-race festivities continue into the night.
  Contact Fleet Feet Sports (see Shops, above).

Book
- Barrera, Brenda, with Eliot Wineberg. *Chicago Running
  Guide: The 40 Best Routes in the Chicago Area.*
  Champaign, IL: Human Kinetics, 2000.

Randy Barnes Photography

Hang Gliding & Skydiving

VETERAN PILOT PETER Birren calls the flat farmland within a couple hours drive of Chicago hang-gliding heaven.

"We regularly get as high here as other spots around the U.S., 5,000 or 6,000 feet up on thermals. There's no vertical real estate, you won't be aiming at a solid piece of mountain granite at 60 mph. The worst thing here is you drag your wing tip in the corn or get behind the treeline and hit turbulence. We've got good schools. And there's wide open air so you can fly forever." Or at least until you hit O'Hare's off-limits airspace.

"For the recreational cross-country pilot, this is God's country," says Rick Bouwmeester, who's been teaching hang gliding at Raven Sky Sports in

471

Whitewater, WI, since he moved from the mountain scene in Vancouver.

True, the thermals here generally are not as strong as out West. And there are no mountains from which to launch flights. But area hang gliders get around that by having an ultralight plane tow them into the air to up to 2,500 feet or so. With aerotowing, you can fly in any wind direction and be towed up to thermals. As long as the sun is shining and it's not too windy, you can fly. (Paragliding isn't so big here—the lighter wing demands pickier conditions which can prove frustrating given the unpredictable winds). Fall and spring tend to produce the best thermals, especially before the crops are up; crops suck up heat rather than deflecting it to produce the vital streams of rising hot air pilots use to gain altitude.

It's easier than ever to learn hang gliding, with two nearby aerotow parks and schools and modern gliders having evolved with Darwinian rigor to weigh in at as little as 48 pounds. For skydiving, the area has several schools where you can take your first tandem flight with an instructor and learn to solo drop, plummeting up to 130 mph toward the patchwork terra firma quilt below.

While we lack peaks to launch from, you can launch from sand dunes piled up along the Lake Michigan shoreline. Mt. Baldy in the Indiana Dunes National Lakeshore is just over an hour drive from downtown. It's vital to check with local experts, like Angelo Mantas, for wisdom and advice before setting out for one of the sites listed later in this chapter. For good general info on the flying sports, check out the U.S. Hang Gliding Association's Web site, www.ushga.org, and the U.S. Parachute Association for Skydiving, www.uspa.org. Fly high.

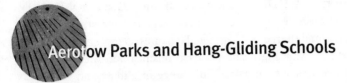

Aerotow Parks and Hang-Gliding Schools

HANG GLIDE CHICAGO

Leland, IL
(815) 495-2212
www.hangglidechicago.com

Location: About 70 miles W of Chicago

Description: Arlan Birkett runs his operation out of the Leland airport hemmed in by pancake-flat, wide-open corn and soybean fields. It was here, on May 24, 2000, that the record for the longest flight east of the Missisippi was set: 213 miles in about 5.5 hours. The pilot landed just 8 miles shy of Ohio.

All instructors are certified and, on average, have been flying for 10-plus years. An intro tandem lesson—where you fly with an instructor—includes about a half-hour worth of ground school (mostly covering safety issues) and runs $125. A beginner tandem package includes three tandem flights and can be done in one morning, weather permitting. There, you get more ground school covering flying technique. It takes about six tandems, on average, to get a beginner rating, or Hang 1.

A full lesson package includes 12 tandem lessons, 6 solos, and 8 hours of ground school. Birkett says about 80% of students are able to earn their novice, or Hang 2, rating before completing the full lesson package. Most students need 20–30 more flights to get enough air time to earn an intermediate, Hang 3, rating. Students can use the school's training equipment for free or, if they're qualified, rent more advanced gliders.

No training hills around to certify foot launching, but Birkett leads a trip at least once every fall for students, novices and above, to learn at Henson's Gap near Chattanooga, TN. Hang Glide Chicago teaches and flies year-round, weather permitting. Full range of gliders and gear; several models to test fly. It's $20 a tow (plus several tow packages) for experienced pilots with their own glider. Pay extra to get towed as high as 10,000 feet.

Directions: Take I-290 west to I-88 west to Sugar Grove exit/IL 56 west. IL 56 west turns into US 30 west. Just beyond Hinckley, take IL 23 south for 11 miles. Turn right (west) onto US 34. The airport is about 2 miles on the right (north) side of road. Tough to miss; there's a DC-3 on the runway.

RAVEN SKY SPORTS, WHITEWATER, WISCONSIN

(262) 473-8800

www.hanggliding.com

Location: About 105 miles N of Chicago

Description: One of the country's oldest and busiest aerotow parks, founded in 1992, is open for business from March to December. Unlike in Leland, the farmland around Whitewater wrinkles and rolls to create nearby beginner hills suited for different wind directions—grassy gentle slopes from 40 to 90 feet high—so you can learn traditional foot launching/landing as well as aerotow skills.

The $225 intro package includes a 6-hour hill class and one tandem aerotow flight (tandem flight only is $145; hill class only is $105). The "100 Flight Plan" includes equipment and all lessons (roughly 15) designed to earn a Hang 2 rating combining hill and aerotow tandem instruction. Paragliding instruction, too.

On a clear day you can see the Chicago skyline. Experienced pilots can get tows to 2,000 feet for $20; add $5 to get to 3,000 feet. Raven Sky sells a wide range of gliders and gear. A hangar holds a menagerie of flying machines—a Superfloater ultralight sailplane, trikes with a three-wheeled carriage—that look like something out of Leonardo Da Vinci's notebooks. Flights of 50 miles are common from Whitewater; owner Brad Kushner says he sees a few 100-milers every summer. The club's distance record is 151 miles. I ran into Jeff Nielsen, one of the first aerotow students here, who holds the local altitude record. One early June he worked the thermals for 7 hours and 45 minutes to hit 10,500 feet from a tow of 1,000 feet. When he finally landed, his jacket was covered in frost.

Directions: Take I-94 west into Wisconsin. Shortly after crossing the border, take WI 50 west for 24 miles. Turn right onto WI 12 west and drive about 30 miles to White-water. Continue through Whitewater and turn right (north) on Tratt St. After 1.5 miles, take a left into Twin Oaks Air-port and Raven Sky Sports.

First Flight

'VE SPENT THE day practicing foot launches and landings on the grassy bunny slopes tucked amid the tidy southeastern Wisconsin farms. Hoist up the 55-pound training glider in the blinding August sun, apply loose grip, start running down the hill, look like something out of the bike scene from *E.T.* when my legs keep pumping in place as I gently lift off and float about 10 feet off the ground thanks to my newfound 34-foot wingspan.

Sure, I've flown in my dreams. I can feel the sensation from those vivid, middle-of-the-night kid dreams, soaring over my old house, skimming the leaves of the giant elms guarding the block, invisible to my friends playing cops and robbers on the street below. But now, it's time for the big time: my first tandem flight via aerotow.

I'm strapped in a bag, stacked above my instructor, Rick Bouwmeester, like a levitating pupa. The motorcycle-like helmet on my head blocks some of the ambient noise of the ultralight engine. The ultralight takes off, we bump and roll along the ground on a wheeled dolly, then lift off. Wind smacks my face. We hit about 2,000 feet, Bouwmeester unclips the tow, and we're flying. Immediately, the glider—and time, for that matter—slows down. All I hear is air and the beep, beep of the altimeter. We corkscrew up a thermal. Bouwmeester reads the wind like a book, pointing out a wind wave undulating over the cornfield below.

We catch another thermal and climb—2,213, 2,230. The wind whips and then goes silent; we just seem to hang, suspended, in the air. I can barely make out two hawks circling in the distance. Earlier, Bouwmeester, who's been hang gliding for 25 years, told me about being attacked by dive-bombing hawks on prior flights. I've got my eye on these two.

I feel a bit like I'm looking through a camera lens at the jigsaw puzzle of cornfields bordered by trees, sunlight glaring off a metal silo. A dark blotch of better-irrigated crops looks vaguely like a bear paw print from the air. Eventually, the thermals peter out. We slowly zigzag down. The tops of trees start to come into focus. At 400 feet or so, the ground rushes up to meet us. Then there's the thud of the wheels landing on the grass. And just like that, we're earthbound once again.

Foot-Launch Ridge-Soaring Sites

Using our Midwestern mountains along the Lake Michigan shoreline as launch sites, pilots feed off the lift that occurs when wind hits the sand dunes and deflects upward. Ridge soaring is something like flying through a tube of air; stray too far from the ridgeline, say more than a couple hundred yards out, and you lose the lift.

Below are a handful of popular ridge-soaring launch sites. None are suitable for beginners. You'll need winds of 20 mph or so to catch a decent ride. And you'll need to show your USHGA rating to get a permit from park authorities (plus make sure you've got your helmet).

Catching the right conditions is a lot trickier than getting an aerotow: wind direction definitely matters. Summer winds are generally too light, but local pilots scan for the random good days to be able to fly in golden summer light, watching the gulls and sailboats play in the lake. In general, conditions are best in fall and spring. The hard core fly in winter when lake-fed thermals are possible, bumping up the potential altitude of a flight.

For details and wisdom on any of these sites, especially the first two, get in touch with Angelo Mantas (Angelo mant@aol.com), a veteran pilot in Skokie who used to teach at Mt. Baldy in Indiana and Tower Hill in Michigan. He's not teaching anymore, but he's always looking for an excuse to get out and fly.

INDIANA DUNES NATIONAL LAKESHORE, PORTER, INDIANA

(219) 926-7561

www.nps.gov

Location: About 60 miles SE of Chicago

Permit: Free from Bailly Ranger Station at 1100 N. Mineral Springs Rd. Contact park officials regarding very specific rules and restrictions on what wind conditions are permitted for pilots, dependent on pilot rating.

Heads up: Landing restricted to launch itself and the beach area in front of the site west to Central Ave.

Description: Launch from about 120 feet above the lake from the west side of Mt. Baldy ridge. The great advantage here: it's top landable (though the landing can be tricky on a straight-in wind). You've got about 13 miles of soarable ridge to the west—stay away from the east, where there's a power plant and the dunes have been knocked flat by development. On average you'll soar some 400–500 feet above the lake, but lake thermals can kick it up to 1,000-plus. Good in a north wind. "On a good day you can fly for hours," Mantas says. "And a nice day at Baldy beats a so-so day of thermaling anytime." Winds have been clocked at 45 mph here.

Directions: Take I-94 east to US 20 east. Jog left (north) on IL 520 to US 12 east. Follow US 12 to the park entrance for Mt. Baldy.

WARREN DUNES STATE PARK, SAWYER, MICHIGAN

(616) 426-4013, (800) 44-PARKS for camping

www.dnr.state.mi.us

Location: About 80 miles NE of Chicago

Permit: $11 daily, $33 annual. Check with park officials for a list of launch and land rules; different spots dependent on pilot rating. Vehicle fee $5 daily, $20 annual for out-of-staters.

Description: Warren Dunes has a long hang-gliding history; early aficionados headed here in the 1970s to learn and train. Good in northwest winds, 20–25 mph. Launch about 80 feet up below the trees on Tower Hill. Once you hit the coastal dunes there are miles of ridge to work. On a good day, you can fly southwest to New Buffalo and back, a 24-mile round-trip with ridgeline all the way, a few gaps to jump. Avoid flying north over the nuclear power plant. Try for a nice, long flight; it's not top landable and you have to haul the glider fully set up through the sand up to the launch. "It's a killer," Mantas says. His friend hit 1,600 feet over the lake here.

Directions: Take I-94 east through Indiana across the Michigan line. Take exit 16 at Bridgman. Go south on Red Arrow Highway 2 miles. Park entrance is on your right.

SLEEPING BEAR DUNES NATIONAL LAKESHORE, EMPIRE, MICHIGAN

(231) 326-5134, (800) 44-PARKS for camping
www.nps.gov

Location: About 320 miles N of Chicago

Permit: Free from visitors center. Hang 2 and under can launch from Pierce Stocking Dr. access, higher ratings can access Pyramid Point and Empire Bluff. Vehicle pass $7 week, $15 year.

Description: Bigger dunes, bigger updraft, higher flight—1,000 feet and over is standard. Three main launching areas: the visitors center in Empire will give you directions to sites when you get your permit (paragliding here, too). If you're Hang 3, you're eligible to fly all three. Logistically, west-facing Sleeping Bear Dune is easiest; you can drive up scenic Pierce Stocking Dr. and walk 100 feet from the overlook parking lot to launch from 450 feet up. It's also the only dune that's top landable, so long as you steer clear of the crowds—with 2 miles of ridge that shouldn't be a problem. Empire Bluff faces northwest and is about a 0.75-mile walk in to the 450-foot-high launch; beach landing. The trickiest spot is Pyramid Point, a narrow slot 370 feet up, facing north, with not a lot of room to bail out. It's about a 0.5-mile hike in straight up. Bill Fifer at Traverse City Hang Gliders says the landing is a killer; it's actually behind the dune. Pilots have gotten high enough here to fly inland and cross country. Expansive views across the milky blue Manitou Passage to North and South Manitou Islands. For area details, including the skinny on a sweet, private camp-and-launch site on a 3-mile-long ridge just south of Frankfort, call Fifer at (231) 922-2844. He also teaches hang gliding, paragliding, and power paragliding (www.serioussports.com/tchanggliders/).

Directions: Take I-94 east to I-196 in Benton Harbor and follow I-196 north into Grand Rapids. At Grand Rapids, take US 131 north around 90 miles to Cadillac and MI 115. Take MI 115 north to MI 22 in Frankfort. Follow MI 22 north through the south part of the national lakeshore into Empire. Turn east on MI 72 to hit the visitors center.

Have Car, Will Fly

IT'S KIND OF like flying a kite from the back of a car or truck, except this is a human being strapped to a glider. The pilot wears a bridle system attached to the car via a 3,000-foot static line of 3/16-inch poly, which in turn connects to the car's back bumper via a hydraulic cylinder and flexible webbing. The driver hits the gas, his eye on a pressure gauge so he can vary the speed of the car to maintain constant tension on the line. Eventually the pressure jumps and the pilot pops up, climbing up to 1,400 feet per minute. When the pilot tops out, the line is released. Free flight commences.

Ultralight towing is more common in these parts, but hard-core pilots like Peter Birren, who heads up the metro-area Reel Hang Glider Pilot Association, like the low cost and portability of static line towing. He says the average release via static tow on a 2-mile road is about 2,200 feet, which rivals the altitude with an ultralight. Auto or truck towing has been around for decades, but Birren says the technique has vastly improved since the early '80s when a Texas physics professor designed a bridle system that targets the center of mass. "It was a total boon for hang gliding in the Midwest flatlands," Birren says.

Happily, beyond the urban edge exists a plethora of good tow sites: long, flat, straight, lightly trafficked roads cutting through treeless farmland largely stripped of power lines, houses, and people. One local favorite is Bong State Recreation Area near Kenosha (its 2.6-mile gravel runway gives away its original intended use as an air force base).

If you're a Hang 3 or better and interested in learning the ins and outs of static towing, get in touch with Birren at Peter@birrendesign.com. Check out the Web site at www.birrendesign.com/rhgpa.home.html. Novices are welcome to hang out and watch.

Skydiving

Beauty in simplicity. Within 15–20 minutes of hopping on a smallish airplane, you're flown to 10,000 to 13,000-plus feet. You jump. You experience almost a minute of pure free fall. You deploy the chute (your first time the instructor will yank the cord or tap you when it's time) and float down to earth within 5 to 7 minutes. Huzzah. Preliminary ground school sessions before a first flight usually run from 20 minutes to an hour. Expect to pay $165 and up for a tandem jump. Many of the outfits below run early spring, weekday, or other specials. All offer beginner-advanced instruction programs. Always call ahead for reservations and details.

CHICAGOLAND SKYDIVING

12637 US 30 West
Hinckley, IL 60520
(815) 286-9200 weekdays, (800) JUMPOUT
www.chicagolandskydiving.com
Location: About 56 miles W of Chicago
Description: About 10 miles west of Aurora, among the closer drop zones to the city. $16 jumps for experienced skydivers Wednesdays and Fridays. The outfit's even got free broadband Internet access so you can work on your laptop while you wait.

Directions: Take I-290 west to I-88 west. Take I-88 west to US 30 west (following signs for Hinckley) for about 15 miles. Chicagoland Skydiving is about 2 miles west of downtown Hinckley; follow signs to the Hinckley airport. The skydiving outfit is at the west end of the airport.

SKYDIVE CHICAGO

3215 East 1969th Rd.
Ottawa, IL 61350
(815) 433-0000, (800) SKYDIVE

www.skydivechicago.com

Location: About 90 miles W of Chicago

Description: Swimming, horseback riding, fishing, and camping facilities. Very popular in summer; call well ahead for reservations. Innovative advanced instruction program.

Directions: Take I-55 south to I-80. Take I-80 west to the first Ottawa exit/IL 71 north. Turn right (north) on IL 71 and go 0.25 mile to Dayton Rd./N. 31st Rd. At Dayton/N. 31st turn left (west) and cross the Fox River. At the first stop sign, at 1961st Rd., turn right. Go straight up the hill at the next stop sign to the entrance.

MILLENNIUM SKYDIVING

3729 S. 0500 East Rd.
Kankakee, IL 60901
(815) 929-9000
www.millenniumskydiving.com

Location: About 62 miles S of Chicago

Description: Night jumps from the Greater Kankakee Airport.

Directions: Take I-94 east to I-57 south to exit 308/IL 50. Head south on IL 50 for 0.5 mile to the Kankakee Airport sign. Turn left (east) and go 0.25 mile to the first left turn (unsigned; it's basically the airport's east boundary road). You're there in 600 yards.

SKYDIVE ILLINOIS

9980 N IL 47
Morris, IL 60450
(815) 941-1149
www.skydive-illinois.com

Location: About 62 miles SW of Chicago

Description: Pick-up service from both Chicago airports and the Amtrak station in Joliet, about 10 miles away. Catch the Amtrak train from Union Station downtown to Joliet (800-872-7245, www.amtrak.com).

Directions: Take I-55 south to I-80 west. Head west on I-80 to IL 47. Turn right (north) on IL 47 and continue a few miles to the Morris Airport. The facility is just south of the airport's main entrance.

SKY KNIGHTS SPORT PARACHUTE CLUB, EAST TROY, WISCONSIN

W1341 County L
East Troy, WI 53120
(262) 642-9494, (800) ET-CHUTE,
www.skydiveskyknights.com

Location: About 93 miles NW of Chicago

Description: About 30 miles southwest of Milwaukee at the East Troy Airport. Offers tandem, static line, and accelerated free-fall jumps.

Directions: Take I-94 west to WI 20 west near Racine. Stay on WI 20 until County L. Go east on County L. You'll hit the club about 1 mile after the airport.

IT'S HARD TO believe that horses were the primary mode of transport in Chicago just a century or so ago, with stables as ubiquitous as Starbucks today. Sadly, there is no longer a place to learn to ride a horse inside city limits; the last surviving city stable stopped running trail rides years back and today only offers lessons and training to top-level dressage students.

For the record, the Chicago Park District says the only place in the city where riders are still allowed to ride (with their own horse) is Washington Park, and that's only with a special permit garnered well in advance. Pretty much the only saddled horses you'll see in the city today are those ridden by Chicago's Finest.

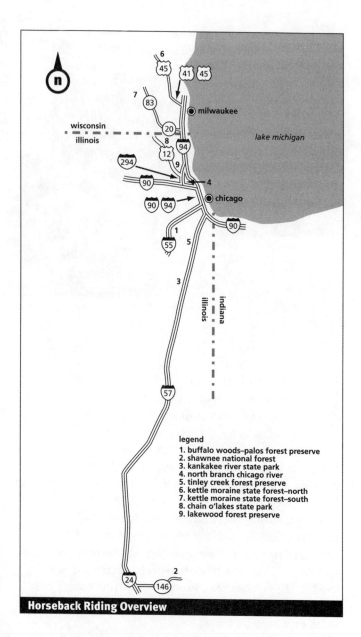

legend
1. buffalo woods–palos forest preserve
2. shawnee national forest
3. kankakee river state park
4. north branch chicago river
5. tinley creek forest preserve
6. kettle moraine state forest–north
7. kettle moraine state forest–south
8. chain o'lakes state park
9. lakewood forest preserve

But the good news is urbanites can still rent a mount and go on a guided ride on metro-area trails surrounding the city: think suburban pastoral, not frontier wilderness. And there are several good suburban options for learning how to ride. To state what will soon become obvious, this chapter assumes you don't own a horse. Therefore, it is limited to a handful of *Backyard* areas with stables that have managed to survive the onslaught of suburban sprawl, spiraling land prices, and bloated liability insurance costs to continue to offer trail rides. There are several quality options farther afield, too. Unless otherwise noted, the stables listed welcome novices. Location and directions below refer to the stables.

So you can still fulfill your inner cowboy (or girl), drifting the blue-green forested hills through Shawnee National Forest or trotting along glacial-scoured land dotted with pothole lakes in Kettle Moraine State Forest.

Now, turn off the "Bonanza" reruns and saddle up.

Backyard

BUFFALO WOODS: PALOS AND SAG VALLEY FOREST PRESERVES

Location: About 18 miles SW of Chicago

Outfitter: Daghem Farms (8214 S. Kean Ave., 708-839-9552) in Willow Springs runs 1-hour guided trail rides covering about 4 miles; year-round, weather permitting.

Description: Rides cover just a small corner of the 14,000-acre Palos preserves, the city's closest facsimile of a backyard wilderness, with sloughs, hills, and mixed woodlands. Canter through mostly flat, forested Buffalo Woods, named for the small herd that used to be fenced off here. In summer, scarlet tanagers flit in the woods; yellow warblers dot the shrubby edges. Ride in fall when the white, black, and red oak flame out.

Directions: Take I-55 south to the LaGrange Rd./US 12/20/45 south exit. Go south to 87th St. Turn left (east) on 87th. Follow 87th to Kean Ave. Turn left (north) on Kean. The stable is on the west side across from the cemetery.

NORTH BRANCH OF THE CHICAGO RIVER

Location: About 16 miles N of Chicago

Outfitter: Freedom Woods (9501 Austin Ave., 847-967-9800) in Morton Grove runs 1-hour to half-day guided trail rides; year-round, weather permitting. Mounts for the disabled through the EquiTherapy Center (847-965-1632), which shares the same facility.

Description: Rides usually walk or trot along the cinder trails threading the woods and meadows along the banks of the meandering North Branch of the Chicago River. What's especially nice is you can go out one-on-one with a guide; if you do have to ride in a group, it's usually no more than five riders, which makes it much easier to scan for the great blue herons, kingfishers, and deer along the river corridor. Recent restoration work has cleared away much of the area's invasive buckthorn to make for woods thick with butterflies and wildflowers in spring and summer. Fleeting glimpses of bikers, runners, and in-line skaters plying the paved North Branch Trail. Popular winter rides when the riverbanks are heaped with fresh snow.

Directions: Take I-94 west to the Dempster St. west exit. From Dempster, turn right (north) on Austin Ave. Austin dead-ends at the stable, north of Church St. Or bike up the North Branch Trail (see "Biking," page 219.)

By transit, take Metra Milwaukee District North Line to the Morton Grove station. Best to call a cab from there to the stable.

TINLEY CREEK FOREST PRESERVE

Location: About 24 miles SW of Chicago

Outfitter: Forest View Farms (16717 S. Lockwood Ave., 708-560-0306) in Tinley Park runs hour-long and multihour guided trail rides, including early-morning trips; year-round, weather permitting. Hay rides and sleigh rides, too.

Description: Cross intimate creeks through the rolling Tinley Moraine. Pass Twin Lakes and Hidden Lake, speckled with great blue herons. Watch for deer and fox through the trees. Spring brings warblers, flycatchers, and wildflower carpets of white trillium in the St. Mihiel Preserve and Yankee Woods. In summer look for ripe blackberries. Scattered fragments of native prairie. Reserve your trail ride ahead of time for a nominal fee to ensure you go out in a small group or one-on-one with a guide. Trainer Kristy Kelly says if you've got an idea for a customized trail ride, float it: "The owner is always up for trying new stuff."

Directions: Take I-94 east to I-57 south. From I-57, exit at 167th St. Continue west on 167th to Lockwood Ave. The stable is on the corner of 167th and Lockwood.

A Dying Breed

 here has been a stable at the corner of N. Orleans and Schiller Sts. since 1872. Noble Horse is the city's last remaining stable, a medieval-style facade tucked between The Cheval Club condos and the Brown Line L tracks in Old Town. In recent years it has managed to survive a fire and mounting pressure from developers. But decades of teaching thousands of city dwellers how to ride a horse (Oprah was a client) have come to an end.

"It was a tough decision, but the cost of doing business in the city, especially with skyrocketing property taxes, just made it impossible to continue," says owner Dan Sampson, a fourth-generation horseman who looks the part in his plaid blanket jacket and dusty boots. The stable continues to teach a small coterie of high-level dressage pupils and has retrofitted its indoor ring to add classical horsemanship performances to its downtown carriage business.

In the 1960s and 1970s the stable owners ran guided trail rides through Lincoln Park. Sampson says he still gets people telling him they remember taking 6-hour rides traversing the linear city park up to Foster Ave. and back. Even into the early '60s, Sampson estimates there were still 10 or so active stables within Chicago proper. By the time he took over Noble Horse in 1984, it was the only one left.

"Of course, there used to be stables on practically every block. The Royalton Tower condos just down the street from us, that was once a stable," Sampson says. "Ours just happened to miss the wrecking ball as the years went by."

He says the city approached him some time ago to talk about the possibility of bringing horseback riding back into the city, but for now it's at a standstill, largely because of liability issues. "We just haven't found a way to make it work. It's a sad state. There really should be something here in the city. We're just severing our history. Practically all the trails we use now were bridle trails; most people don't realize that. Go to Lincoln Park, that's a bridle path, not a jogging path. And I'm saying that as a runner."

Sampson chuckles and ponders whether the trail might offer up better shock absorption with a nice layer of horse dung. Info on horsemanship shows at (312) 266-7878, (877) 424-7500, or www.noblehorsechicago.com.

Short Hops

LAKEWOOD FOREST PRESERVE

Location: About 43 miles NW of Chicago

Outfitter: Happy Trails Stables (26011 N. Rand Rd./US 12, 847-526-0055) in Wauconda runs 1-hour guided trail rides and 2-hour Sunday biscuit-and-gravy breakfast rides; year-round, weather permitting.

Description: With 2,578 acres, Lakewood is Lake County's largest preserve on what was a working farm until the late 1960s. Canter through an open meadow, trot through a mixed oak and walnut forest dotted with ever-green groves, lakes, and marshes. Keep your eyes peeled for coyote around dusk. Blue-winged warblers, ovenbirds, and grasshopper sparrows abound. Home to a 67-acre, poison-sumac-ringed bog harboring more than 100 plant species that is listed on the National Registry of Natural Landmarks.

Directions: Take I-90 west to I-294 north to IL 22/Half Day Rd. Go left (west) on IL 22 to Old McHenry Rd. Go right (northwest) on Old McHenry until it ends at US 12. Turn right (north) on US 12/Rand Rd. and turn into the second driveway on the right.

CHAIN O'LAKES STATE PARK

Location: About 59 miles NW of Chicago

Outfitter: Chain O'Lakes State Park Riding Stable (8916 Wilmot Rd., 815-675-6532) in Spring Grove runs guided trail rides from 40 minutes to 2 hours, mid-April through

October. Hayrides and bonfires for campers on Saturday nights.

Description: Sliced by the Fox River and bordered by three lakes, the 2,793-acre state park is stuffed with powerboats in summer. Happily, the 8 miles of interconnected horse trails are on the park's west end, far from the water-focused fray. Some steep climbs along the dirt trail through a mix of meadow and dense hardwood. The park is home to some of the state's increasingly rare breeding sandhill cranes. Henslow's sparrows sometimes breed in the field by the equestrian Blue Loop trail. Watch for deer and rabbits.

Directions: Take I-90 west to IL 53 north. Follow IL 53 north to Lake-Cook Rd. east. After about 1 mile on Lake-Cook Rd., bear north on Rand Rd./US 12. Follow US 12 north all the way to Wilmot Rd. (US 12 will start to curve west). Turn right (north) on Wilmot and follow to the park entrance on the right; the stable is about 1 mile from the gate.

KANKAKEE RIVER STATE PARK

Location: About 60 miles S of Chicago

Outfitter: Kankakee State Park Riding Stable (6500 N. 5000 W Rd., 815-939-0309) in Bourbonnais runs half-hour to day-long rides; lessons and cookouts, too. Year-round rides, weather permitting.

Description: Stable owner Mary Carol has been guiding riders for 20 years at this long and narrow park. She looks forward to spring, when the air hangs thick with honeysuckle and the white flowers from the Russian ornamental olive trees. Bluebells and violets sprinkle the forest floor, flowering crabapples and greengage plums start to bloom. Starting in late August, the Virginia creeper goes bright red-orange and signals the start of fall color. You won't see much of the Kankakee on the trails; they're about 0.5 mile north tucked in the gently buckling oak and pine woods. Trails are busiest in summer. Private rides for an additional fee; otherwise you may go out with a group of up to 12 in summer, 8 in shoulder seasons. Watch for wild turkey scuttling along the trails.

Directions: Take I-94 east to I-57 south. Follow I-57 south to exit 315/IL 50. Go south on IL 50 to Armour Rd. Turn right (west) on Armour and continue to IL 102. Turn right (north/west) on IL 102 and follow the signs to the stable and park.

KETTLE MORAINE STATE FOREST, SOUTH UNIT, WISCONSIN

Location: About 102 miles N of Chicago

Outfitters: Swinging "W" Ranch (S 75 W36004 Wilton Rd., 262-594-2416) in Eagle, WI, runs 45-minute to half-day guided trail rides, overnight trips, and lessons April through November, more limited offerings December through March. Fantasy Hills Ranch (4978 Town Hall Rd. 262-728-1773, www.fantasyhillsranch.com) in Delavan, WI, has 25-mile, day-long guided trail rides through the state forest, shorter rides through their 70-acre woodlands; moonlight rides and winter sleigh rides.

Description: This narrow, 21,000-acre, glacial-carved corridor is best known for legendary mountain biking (see "Mountain Biking," page 280). Roughly 40 miles of equestrian trails wind north of the John Muir knobbydrome but offer similarly hilly terrain through pine plantations, hardwood forest, and open fields studded with small ponds. You may ride a stretch through a glacial sand plain. Indian summer and fall are splendid times to ride here amid the fiery sumac, away from the throngs and flies. Buttercup-like lavender pasque flowers in spring.

Directions: For Swinging "W" Ranch, take I-94 north to WI 20 west, around Racine. Take WI 20 west to WI 83 north. Take WI 83 north into the town of Mukwonago. Look for County NN by the Pick n' Save. Go left (west) on County NN about 10 miles to the stop sign in Eagle. Go right (north) on WI 67 up the hill. About 1.5 miles past the smiley-face water tower, turn right on Wilton Rd. The ranch is on your left.

For Fantasy Hills Ranch, take I-94 north to WI 50, around Lake Geneva and Kenosha. Go left (west) on WI 50, passing through downtown Lake Geneva. Turn right (north) on WI 67. Continue about 1 mile, then take a left on Town Hall Rd. The stable is at the corner of WI 67 and Town Hall Rd.

KETTLE MORAINE STATE FOREST, NORTH UNIT, WISCONSIN

Location: About 136 miles N of Chicago

Outfitter: Bar-N-Ranch (N1639 County GGG, 262-626-4096 or 262-626-4341 after 6 P.M.; www.bar-ranch.com) in Campbellsport, WI, is one of the few stables to let you rent a horse and ride without a guide (guides are posted along the trail for safety). Mounts from 45 minutes to 1.5 hours, open April to mid-November; longer rides go with guides.

Description: Fewer crowds and more acreage than its southerly cousin, with 39 miles of bridle trail rolling through kettle-pocked, textbook ice age terrain, some of it quite rugged. The stable, opened in 1941, is near Mauthe Lake (swim or fish from the sand beach there). Cross the Ice Age National Scenic Trail (see "Hiking & Backpacking," page 345) on the maple- and sumac-laden Forest Lake Loop trail. Scan for deer, wild turkey, and red fox.

Directions: Take I-94 west to Milwaukee. In Milwaukee, take Fond Du Lac Ave. west to WI 145 to US 45/US 41 north. Continue on US 45 north to Kewaskum. Turn right (east) on WI 28 for about three blocks, then turn left on County S. Stay on County S about 6 miles to County GGG. Take a left on County GGG; the stable is 1 mile down on the right.

Mecca

SHAWNEE NATIONAL FOREST

Location: About 365 miles S of Chicago

Outfitter: Lake Glendale Stables & Outfitters (Lake Glendale Rd. near Lake Glendale Recreation Area, 618-949-3737, www.lakeglendalestables.com) in Golconda runs 1-hour to overnight pack trips, guided and self-guided depending on rider ability.

Description: Wrangler's dream. This is the *other* Illinois, where the land juts skyward into bona fide hills throughout 270,000-acre Shawnee National Forest, crammed with waterfalls, wooded hollows, bluffs, and historic settlements. Far south enough, skimming the Kentucky border, to make spring a much warmer—and earlier—affair than in Chicago. Hikers and equestrians (and the occasional bobcat) share the River to River Trail (see "Hiking & Backpacking," page 353), running 176 miles from Battery Rock on the Ohio to Grand Tower on the Mississippi. Lake Glendale Stables & Outfitters is tucked into the Lake Glendale Recreation Area with some pristine acreage of its own. Overnight trips run to Lusk Creek, a wilderness area where the Perrier creek threads between 100-foot cliffs, nurturing orchids and cacti alike.

Directions: Take I-94 east to I-57 south. Follow I-57 south through the cornfields for about 315 miles. South of Marion, pick up I-24 east (toward Nashville) and follow it to IL 146. Turn left (east) on IL 146 and continue for 15 miles. Go north (left) on IL 145 for roughly 2 miles. Turn right into Lake Glendale Recreation Area (Lake Glendale Rd.). The stable is about 2 miles down on the left.

Where to Connect

Riding Academies

- Glen Grove Equestrian Center (9453 N. Harms Rd., Morton Grove, 847-966-8032)

- Freedom Woods Equestrian Center (9501 Austin Ave., Morton Grove, 847-967-9800)

- EquiTherapy Center (9501 Austin Ave., Morton Grove, 847-965-1632) has mounts specially trained to work with people with disabilities. Accredited by the North American Riding for the Handicapped Association.

- Fitzjoy Farm Riding Academy (12211 S. LaGrange Rd., Palos Park, 708-361-7977)

- Danada Equestrian Center (3 S. 503 Naperville Rd., Wheaton, 630-668-6012), run by the DuPage County Forest Preserve District.

- Daybreak Farm Stables (31668 N. River Rd., Libertyville, 847-367-9585)

- Happy Trails Stables (26011 N. Rand Rd./US 12, Wauconda, 847-526-0055)

- Forest View Farms (16717 S. Lockwood Ave., Tinley Park, 708-560-0306)

Tack Shops

- The Tack Box (5707 Dempster St., 847-470-0064) in Morton Grove is small but well stocked for helmets, boots, pants, and more.

- Libertyville Saddle Shop (2121 Temple Dr., 847-362-0570, www.saddleshop.com) in Libertyville is known throughout the Midwest, with a big online shop to boot (no pun intended).

Resources

- *Illinois Horseback Riding Guide* is a booklet listing horse trails on state lands published by the Illinois Department of Natural Resources; call (217) 782-7498 for a free copy.

- www.stablesdirectory.org has good links to all things equine in the Midwest.

Page numbers in *italics* refer to maps.